Working Minimalism

Current Studies in Linguistics
Samuel Jay Keyser, general editor

Working Minimalism

edited by
Samuel David Epstein
and Norbert Hornstein

The MIT Press
Cambridge, Massachusetts
London, England

Second printing, 2001

© 1999 Massachusetts Institute of Technology

This book was set in Times New Roman by Asco Typesetters, Hong Kong and was printed and bound in the United States.

Library of Congress Cataloging-in-Publication Data

Working minimalism / edited by Samuel David Epstein and Norbert Hornstein.
    p. cm. — (Current studies in linguistics series ; 32)
  Includes bibliographical references and index.
  ISBN 0-262-05058-7 (alk. paper). — ISBN 0-262-55032-6 (pbk. : alk. paper)
  1. Minimalist theory (Linguistics) 2. Grammar, Comparative and general. 3. Linguistics—Research. I. Epstein, Samuel David. II. Hornstein, Norbert. III. Series.
P158.28.W67 1999
410′.1—dc21   99-25106
                                                                    CIP

Contents

Contributors

Željko Bošković
Department of Linguistics
University of Connecticut

Samuel David Epstein
Program in Linguistics
University of Michigan

Robert Freidin
Program in Linguistics
Princeton University

Erich M. Groat
Program in Linguistics
The Graduate School and
University Center
City University of New York

Norbert Hornstein
Department of Linguistics
University of Maryland

Hisatsugu Kitahara
Institute of Cultural and Linguistic
Studies
Keio University

Howard Lasnik
Department of Linguistics
University of Connecticut

Roger Martin
Tsukuba University

Jairo Nunes
Department of Linguistics
Universidade Estadual de
Campinas

Norvin Richards
Kanda University of International
Studies

Juan Uriagereka
Department of Linguistics
University of Maryland

Amy Weinberg
Department of Linguistics/
UMIACS
University of Maryland

Introduction   Samuel David Epstein and
                                      Norbert Hornstein

A Rationale for Minimalism

Minimalism is anchored in the suspicion that at certain times and for certain purposes less can be more.

The qualified tentativeness of our first sentence is entirely deliberate. It is intended to reflect the oft-stated view that minimalism is a research program, not a theory, the distance between minimalist concerns and concrete analyses often being substantial. As with pudding, however, the proof of a program ultimately rests in how good the detailed products that result from taking its strictures seriously look and taste.

The aim of this collection of essays is to illustrate how minimalist concerns can be incarnated in specific proposals subject to the kinds of empirical and theoretical scrutiny found in everyday linguistic research. In other words, these essays are intended to provide models of how to proceed from guiding ideas of minimalism to concrete formal analyses of linguistic phenomena and specific proposals about the structure of the human language faculty. In this introduction, we outline the sorts of minimalist concerns that animate the essays themselves.

The Minimalist Program is many things to many researchers. To us, it grows out of the perceived successes of the principles-and-parameters approach to explaining human grammatical competence.

The central problem for grammatical theory is this: How is it that children are able to acquire grammatical competence despite the impoverished nature of the data serving as input to this process? No one doubts that grammatical competence is influenced by the nature of the primary linguistic data; Parisian children learn French and Cantonese children learn Chinese. However, it is clear that the knowledge attained vastly exceeds the information available in the primary linguistic data, consisting of acoustic disturbances in context. This is, in essence, what Chomsky dubbed "Plato's problem." The greatest virtue of principles-and-parameters accounts is that they provide a viable approach to Plato's problem in the domain of language.

The idea is simple. Children are biologically equipped with a set of principles of grammar, that is, Universal Grammar. These principles have open parameters. Specific grammars arise once the open options are given fixed values, which are determined on the basis of the primary linguistic data. A grammar for a specific language can then be viewed as a vector of these values.

Syntactic research since the mid-1970s can be seen as elaborating this sort of idea and demonstrating its viability. Government-Binding Theory (GB) is the best-known version of a principles-and-parameters theory of Universal Grammar. It has several distinctive features:

- GB is modular; that is, the grammar is divided into various sub-components incorporating well-formedness requirements and organized around distinctive principles, primitives, and rule formats or schemas.
- GB contains a very unconstrained transformational component; that is, the basic movement rule is Move α, which allows any category to move anywhere at any time. Overgeneration is a natural by-product, and the various modules, applied at various levels, filter out all and only the undesired structures.
- GB has four critical levels at which various conditions are applied to filter out illicit structures: D-Structure (DS), S-Structure (SS), Logical Form (LF), and Phonetic Form (PF).
- The central grammatical relation in GB is government. This relation is what lends formal unity to otherwise rather diverse and dedicated subcomponents.

GB has been very successful in illuminating the structure of grammatical competence. As a research program, it has focused on finding a suitable answer to Plato's problem; consequently, its proposals have largely been evaluated by whether they succeed in doing so. This is not to say that other methodological standards have been irrelevant. Simplicity and naturalness have also played a role in evaluating competing proposals. However, in practice, these measures of theory evaluation have been swamped by the requirement of finding principles suitably parameterized to address Plato's problem. To put this point another way, the demands imposed by seeking to simultaneously attain both descriptively adequate grammars and an explanatorily adequate theory have largely overshadowed more standard general benchmarks of theory evaluation such as simplicity, naturalness, and parsimony.

GB's very success, however, dramatically alters the methodological landscape. It has spawned a consensus that principles-and-parameters accounts may well answer Plato's problem in the domain of language. This general and surely tentative consensus allows the other sorts of measures of success to guide minimalist theory construction and (self-)evaluation. In effect, given a principles-and-parameters setting, simplicity, elegance, parsimony, and naturalness move from background to foreground concerns in the construction and evaluation of analyses. To put matters more tendentiously than is warranted: given that principles-and-parameters models "solve" Plato's problem, the paramount research issue becomes which of the conceivable principles-and-parameters models is best, and this issue is (in part) addressed using conventional (not uniquely linguistic) criteria of theory evaluation.

This reorientation, however, prompts a question: how to concretize these heretofore subordinate evaluative notions in the specific research setting that currently obtains. It is here that the Minimalist Program aims to contribute.

Bringing General Methodology to Life

General precepts are all well and good. However, the role of a linguistics research program is to determine how to interpret these extremely general methodological dicta in the more specific setting of syntactic research.

The Minimalist Program deploys two types of economy considerations. The first type we may call measures of *methodological economy*. These are familiar benchmarks such as simplicity and parsimony—that is, standard Ockham's razor sorts of considerations: all things being equal, two primitive relations are worse than one; two levels are better than four; four modules are better than five; more is worse; fewer is better.

The second type we may call measures of *linguistic economy*. These substantive, least effort economy notions generalize themes that have consistently arisen in grammatical research. The idea is that locality conditions and well-formedness conditions reflect the fact that grammars are organized frugally to maximize resources. Short steps preclude long strides (the Shortest Move Condition, the Minimal Link Condition); derivations with fewer rule applications trump those with more (the Shortest

Derivation Condition); movement applies only when it must (Least Effort, Greed); no symbols occur idly in grammatical representations (Full Interpretation); grammatical operations rearrange expressions but do not add novel entities in the course of derivations (the Inclusiveness Condition); it is better to move small units, not large ones, to satisfy a given requirement (movement as feature attraction).

These sorts of considerations promote a specific research strategy: look for the simplest theory whose structure-building operations and representations have a least effort flavor, and determine the empirical consequences to the extent possible. Consistently pursuing this agenda leads in novel—and, in our view, quite revealing and promising—directions.

A Basic Minimalist Model

Chomsky (1995) outlines a model of grammar reflecting minimalist concerns. We review its main features here because it acts as the foil for the chapters that follow.

Chomsky's model has ten key characteristics.

First, it has only two levels, LF and PF. The main argument in favor of eliminating SS and DS is conceptual. A successful theory must capture the fundamental property that grammars pair sound and meaning. If a theory is to posit levels at all (see below), they must be levels that interface with the phonetic and conceptual systems. However, it is not clear that more is conceptually required. Since parsimony counsels against proliferating levels, Chomsky shows that many of the empirical reasons that led to adopting DS and SS can be addressed without postulating any levels other than LF and PF.

Second, recursion is relegated to the transformational component. With the elimination of DS, recursion cannot be a property of the base. However, it is clear that there is no upper bound on sentence length. Therefore, some recursive procedure must obtain. Chomsky revives generalized transformations as the mechanism of grammatical recursion, with iterative rule application partially ordered by the (similarly "resurrected") Strict Cycle Condition.

Third, the grammatical module is embedded in a wider array of cognitive modules. In particular, it interacts with components that interpret sentences both phonetically and conceptually. Thus, grammatical objects must be phonetically and conceptually legible by at least this pair of interfaces. This means that (perhaps not all) the primitives manipulated by the grammatical system, and all members of the interface structures derived, must be composed of expressions that the interfaces can interpret. In the best case, these grammatically produced forms are interpretable in their entirety. The presence of objects not so interpretable causes a derivation to crash. Thus, any grammatical object is licit just in case it can be interpreted fully at the interfaces that meet LF and PF.

Fourth, there are two basic grammatical operations, Merge and Move. As no one can dispute that sentences are composed of words, an operation is conceptually required that can build sentences from words. This operation is Merge. Recall, moreover, that the existence of displacement phenomena is taken as one of the central, perhaps defining, facts about natural languages. Move accommodates these phenomena.

Fifth, Move is a last resort operation. Features that are −Interpretable at one of the interfaces (e.g., Case) must be removed so as to prevent violations of Full Interpretation. Such features are eliminated by being checked in the course of derivations. Move is defined so that any application enables a previously uncheckable feature to get checked. Thus, it is licit only if required to form a fully interpretable phrase marker. Chomsky explores several versions of this principle in his discussion of Greed. He argues for a version in which feature checking must obtain to license every derivational step, settling on a definition akin to one proposed by Lasnik (1995) according to which a move takes place just in case it results in the checking of a feature of either the target or the expression moved.

Sixth, there are different types of features: +Interpretable and −Interpretable (as just noted), strong and weak. Strong features are those that must be checked in overt syntax. Weak features can (and, on minimalist assumptions, must) be checked in the covert component. The strong/weak feature distinction is proposed as part of the elimination of the SS level to accommodate the grammatical differences between languages like English and Chinese with regard to *wh*-movement, and between languages like English and French with regard to verb raising. The variety of features and their various strengths are part of the reanalysis of control, the Extended Projection Principle, existential constructions, and pro-drop phenomena in minimalist terms.

Seventh, moves must be short. This is a substantive economy notion and develops the minimality theme that earlier GB research established (see, e.g., Aoun and Li 1993; Chomsky 1986; Rizzi 1990). Chomsky defines various notions of local domain for movement that incorporate some notion of minimality into the definition of Move—again, a conceptual shift away from principles and filters and toward rules and constraints on rule application. By definition, nonlocal moves are not moves at all. Chomsky considers various ways of conceptualizing this locality condition, settling finally on the notion that movement is actually the result of one feature attracting another. This reconceptualization of Move is also a substantive economy proposal. Feature attraction is taken to be a minimal grammatical relation, and feature movement the minimal type of displacement. This approach is used to define both a metric for the length of a move and cyclic rule applications.

Eighth, features are checked in specifier-head or head-head configurations. The idea is that the relevant locality notions are defined on phrase structure configurations. These provide all the primitive relations that the grammar exploits. In particular, government is removed as being redundant and therefore undesirable. Chomsky considers various ways of executing these ideas. Typically, overt movement targets the specifier of the head containing the feature that attracts it. Covert movement moves the attracted feature alone and need not take the whole category along; thus, covertly moved features are checked in positions adjoined to heads.

Ninth, Chomsky assumes that grammatical operations cannot add features. This principle, the Inclusiveness Condition, leads him to reanalyze X-bar structure in more primitive terms. Bar levels are relational properties of phrases, not primitives of the system. This "bare" theory of phrase structure leads to a revision of Kayne's (1994) Linear Correspondence Axiom, relating a phrase marker's hierarchical structure and its linear ordering. Chomsky adopts a version of this principle but recasts it in terms compatible with his bare phrase structure approach.

Tenth, Chomsky radically distinguishes θ-roles from morphological features like Case. The domains of thematic assignment and morphological checking are disjoint. The former takes place in lexical domains. Moreover, θ-roles are relational. They are not features, hence cannot be "checked," hence cannot license movement. They contrast with morphological features like Case and agreement, which are checked in functional domains and can license movement in the sense that a move is licit only if one of them is checked as a result.

Working Minimalism

The chapters in this volume should be read against the backdrop limned above. The rough picture that emerges is a theory with at most two levels,

PF and LF, that interface with (at least two) not entirely linguistic systems, the articulatory-phonetic and conceptual-intentional systems. These systems impose "legibility" conditions on the outputs of the computational system. Meeting the requirements of Full Interpretation amounts to being in a format that these interfaces can "read." Features that fail this legibility requirement must be eliminated. This is done by moving or merging these features (or the phrases that contain them) to positions where they can be checked. This movement is taken to be optimal in the sense of being regulated by ideals of substantive economy. The moves are short, forced, and as few in number as possible, and they carry the minimum required phrasal/lexical material to discharge the offending features. In Chomsky's terms, the grammar is the optimal realization of interface requirements.

Given this sort of theory, a major (but not unprecedented) research topic is to determine the inventory of features, their distribution, and whether they are or are not Interpretable. Several authors address these questions. Martin argues against Chomsky's appeal to D-features in expressing the Extended Projection Principle, in particular, the requirement that sentences have subjects. He argues that the work that D-features do is largely redundant with the work that Case features do and that this methodologically undesirable redundancy can be eliminated without serious empirical cost. Thus, methodological parsimony suggests that either Case or D-features be eliminated, and the facts suggest that the former are indispensable. This counsels for the elimination of D-features as the basis of the EPP. Martin further provides an interpretive minimalist rationale for Case features consistent with his analysis.

Groat argues (pace Chomsky) that expletives bear Case. He argues that endowing expletives with Case yields an empirically preferable theory of existential constructions and regularizes checking theory by eliminating the option of checking −Interpretable features under Merge. Groat's proposal dovetails with Martin's in further supporting the conclusion that D-features are descriptively redundant and so theoretically unnecessary.

Hornstein argues against the existence of yet another set of features. Specifically, he contends that there is little reason to believe that Q-features exist, hence that there is no process analogous to Quantifier Raising, hence that QR-like operations are theoretically problematic. More interestingly, a minimalist architecture in which the domains of Case checking and θ-assignment are segregated suffices to provide the structure relevant for quantifier scope and binding. Given this, it is better to treat the standard quantifier scope and binding phenomena as piggy-backing on the movements required for checking morphological features such as Case. Hornstein argues that there is empirical support for this methodologically desirable end.

Kitahara also argues against expanding the inventory of features to include the *-feature that Chomsky and Lasnik (1993) proposed to accommodate the well-studied differences between adjunct and argument extractions from islands. Kitahara notes that the *-feature violates both the spirit and the letter of the Inclusiveness Condition. He proposes reanalyzing the relevant data in Case-theoretic terms in the context of an exclusively derivational theory of Universal Grammar.

Features also play a central role in the statement of the Strict Cycle and Shortest Move Conditions (see Chomsky 1995). Freidin provides historical background for the discussion of the cycle and examines Chomsky's arguments for including it in the inventory of principles of Universal Grammar. He argues that the effects of the cycle are better viewed as deriving from the properties of a minimalistically adequate inventory of elementary grammatical operations.

Richards and Bošković both focus on Superiority effects in languages like Bulgarian where all *wh*-elements overtly move to a C-like position in multiple interrogative constructions. These languages pose a challenge to strict cyclic conditions such as the Extension Condition/Featural Cyclicity and its interactions with shortest move requirements. Richards and Bošković provide different mechanisms for accommodating the observed tensions that arise from trying to satisfy both these requirements in an empirically adequate analysis.

Lasnik concentrates on the mechanics of the Move operation. He observes that there is a serious tension among three of Chomsky's views: (a) that traces are needed in A-chains for thematic reasons, (b) that traces are simply copies of moved expressions, and (c) that traces formed by A-movement are invisible for purposes of reconstruction phenomena. He observes that one or another of these assumptions must be dropped and considers the consequences of doing so.

Nunes considers a serious problem for the copy theory of movement: how to accommodate the fact that traces are phonetically silent. He observes that if traces are actually copies, a way must be found to derive their null phonetic status. This characteristic of traces is stipulated in GB. Nunes argues that instead, it can be related to the Linear Correspondence Axiom on the assumption that copies create obstacles to linearization, which, following Chomsky and Kayne, Nunes takes to be a convergence requirement. Nunes further proposes accounting for which copies delete and which surface by appealing to general economy conditions related to how features are checked in the course of a derivation.

Uriagereka also considers linearization processes in a minimalist context. He argues that Chomsky's stipulation that Spell-Out apply but once fails to fully extirpate SS as a level. He proposes that Spell-Out is just another rule, applies as many times as required, and is, (like all rules) subject to economy considerations. He argues that a simplification of the linearization algorithm leads to multiple applications of Spell-Out. It will apply, he argues, whenever the terminals fail to command one another. Spell-Out permits linearization to apply by "flattening" the tree sufficiently so that expressions come to be in the command relations required for his revised Linear Correspondence Axiom to apply. A by-product is that certain island effects are reduced to properties of linearization.

Weinberg shows that Uriagereka's proposal has some attractive parsing implications. She argues that the multiple Spell-Out interpretation of the Linear Correspondence Axiom can be used to account for garden path phenomena. In particular, using Spell-Out, it is possible to deduce both which structures will induce parsing problems and the severity of the problems that arise.

Uriagereka and Kitahara argue that grammars are best interpreted in derivational terms. They both suggest reconsidering the status of levels in Universal Grammar. Epstein provides the background for these suggestions. He argues that the properties of command can be derived if it is viewed as the simple reflection of structure-building rule application (see also Epstein et al. 1998). This suggests that principles of grammar might be deducible from the independently motivated transformational rules and their constrained mode of application. The strongest form of this hypothesis asserts that natural language grammars employ no representational constructs, such as filters, well-formedness conditions on representations, or relations defined upon trees. This makes levels (including LF and PF) unattractive, exposing (addressable) questions regarding the feasibility of their elimination (see esp. Groat 1997).

Conclusion

Programs contrast with analyses in being fecund or sterile rather than true or false. One way of evaluating a research program is to see what sorts of questions it raises, what sorts of ambitions it promotes, and what sorts of analyses it supports. It is our belief that what makes the minimalist enterprise especially exciting is that it brings new and seemingly fundamental questions to the fore. By trying to make do with more parsimonious constructs and thematically more coherent concepts, this form of inquiry often leads to proposals with greater deductive structure and, hence, greater explanatory reach. It also allows old questions to be reexamined in a new light: issues such as the differences between derivational (rule-based) and representational (principle-based) models, the correct statement of locality conditions, the cycle and the naturalness of various rule types, conditions on rules, feature inventories, and the role of the lexicon.

Chomsky (1995, 219) notes that the end result of the Minimalist Program is "a different conception of the mechanisms of language." Just as interesting, we believe, is that it prompts new, important, and overlooked questions, while motivating a reexamination of "old" analyses. We hope that the work gathered here will help advance this innovative and revealing investigation of the human language faculty.

References

Aoun, Joseph, and Yen-hui Audrey Li. 1993. *Syntax of scope*. Cambridge, Mass.: MIT Press.

Chomsky, Noam. 1986. *Knowledge of language: Its nature, origin, and use.* New York: Praeger.

Chomsky, Noam. 1995. Categories and transformations. In *The Minimalist Program*. Cambridge, Mass.: MIT Press.

Chomsky, Noam, and Howard Lasnik. 1993. The theory of principles and parameters. In *Syntax: An international handbook of contemporary research*, eds. Joachim Jacobs, Arnim von Stechow, Wolfgang Sternefeld, and Theo Vennemann. Berlin: Walter de Gruyter. [Reprinted in *The Minimalist Program*, Noam Chomsky. Cambridge, Mass.: MIT Press, 1995.]

Epstein, Samuel D., Erich Groat, Ruriko Kawashima, and Hisatsugu Kitahara. 1998. *A derivational approach to syntactic relations*. Oxford: Oxford University Press.

Groat, Erich. 1997. A derivational program for syntactic theory. Doctoral dissertation, Harvard University, Cambridge, Mass.

Kayne, Richard. 1994. *The antisymmetry of syntax*. Cambridge, Mass.: MIT Press.

Lasnik, Howard. 1995. Last Resort and Attract F. In *Proceedings of the Sixth Annual Meeting of the Formal Linguistics Society of Mid-America*, eds. Leslie Gabriele, Debra Hardison, and Robert Westmoreland. Indiana University Linguistics Club, Bloomington.

Rizzi, Luigi. 1990. *Relativized Minimality*. Cambridge, Mass.: MIT Press.

Chapter 1

Case, the Extended Projection Principle, and Minimalism

Roger Martin

A central question posed within the Minimalist Program (Chomsky 1995) is this: how perfect is the computational component of the human linguistic system (C_{HL})? Perfection, in one sense, means that the structure of C_{HL} is minimally that which is imposed by the structure of external interface systems. Rephrasing the question: is C_{HL} an optimal solution to the conditions imposed by the general architecture of the mind/brain in which it is embedded?[1]

From this point of view, we can classify formal features into three types:[2]

(1) a. Features that can be interpreted by the conceptual-intentional system (C-I)
   b. Features that can be interpreted by the articulatory-perceptual system (A-P)
   c. Features that cannot be interpreted by C-I or A-P

Chomsky refers to features of the type in (1a,b) as +*Interpretable features* and those in (1c) as −*Interpretable features*. Since −Interpretable features are not directly motivated by C-I or A-P, their existence is surprising if C_{HL} is perfect in the above sense.

Still, it is widely assumed that −Interpretable features do exist and furthermore that they must be eliminated in the derivation (either overtly or covertly depending on matters of strength). The latter assumption follows from bare output conditions—more precisely, the principle of Full Interpretation (FI), which states that linguistic levels of representation (LF and PF) consist *solely* of +Interpretable elements. Derivations that do not result in fully interpretable representations crash.

Given FI, the existence of −Interpretable features yields the displacement property of language (itself an apparent departure from perfection) illustrated in (2).

(2) a.   [$_{TP}$ she$_i$ apparently [$_T$ does] not [$_{vP}$ love me anymore]]
     b.   *[$_{TP}$ apparently [$_T$ does] not [$_{vP}$ she love me anymore]]

Chomsky (1995) argues that the derivation underlying (2b) does not converge because some −Interpretable feature fails to be checked (and erased).

However, a significant redundancy reveals itself when the account of (2b) is considered in detail. It turns out that as many as four different −Interpretable features are unchecked in (2b): the Case features of both T and DP, the φ-features of T, and the so-called Extended Projection Principle (EPP) feature of T. This raises the obvious methodological question of whether three distinct *kinds* of −Interpretable features—Case, EPP, and φ—are necessary or whether the redundancy can be narrowed or eliminated.

In this chapter, mostly setting aside φ-features, I examine the overlap between Case and the EPP. In section 1.1, I demonstrate that Case features are irreducible, both for DPs and for heads such as T and *v*. In section 1.2, I argue that the effects of EPP features, on the other hand, mostly follow from independent principles. In particular, I show that a significant portion of the EPP is reducible to Case whereas the residue can be explained by constraints on zero affixation. The elimination of EPP features would significantly narrow the redundancy in (2b) and also address the more fundamental question of why −Interpretable features exist. Still, the conclusion here is tentative, and I point to where I think more work needs to be done in order to show that a reduction is feasible. In section 1.3, I consider the role of Case, suggesting that it is indeed motivated by external demands, although not in a direct way; and I speculate on what might be said about EPP features in these terms if it turns out that they are empirically necessary.

1.1   −Interpretable Case Features

I have stated several reasons to submit −Interpretable features to empirical scrutiny. They are not directly motivated by external conditions; furthermore, there is a significant redundancy between Case and the EPP. However, I show that Case features cannot be eliminated.

1.1.1   Motivating the Case Filter
The Case features of DPs must be distinguished from those of Case-checking heads such as T and *v*. To show that DPs have Case features

that must be checked is not difficult. If they did not, one of the sentences in (3) would be grammatical.

(3) a. *it seems [several students to have been arrested]
    b. *it seems [to have been arrested several students]

(3a) is typically used to establish the existence of a Case Filter. But if there are no EPP features, raising in (3a) may violate Last Resort (discussed more fully in section 1.1.2.1). Hence, we should consider (3b) as well. (3b) can be ruled out if DPs have Case features that must be checked. The same assumption also accounts for the ungrammaticality of the following examples, which would otherwise be mysterious given that nouns and adjectives do not check Case:

(4) a. *[Mary's pictures the girls] won a prize
    b. *Bill is proud Kim

The conclusion that DPs have −Interpretable Case features appears to be unavoidable empirically. Then, there must be ways for these features to be checked given the fact that some derivations converge. I assume that any two features α and β in a checking configuration can enter a checking relation.[3] Checking succeeds only if α and β *match*.[4] Erasure (deletion) of a −Interpretable feature is possible only when checking is successful.[5] Thus, a DP with a Case feature must enter a checking relation with a head containing a matching Case feature at some point in the derivation.

1.1.2 Motivating the Inverse Case Filter

An interesting empirical question now arises: are the matching Case features of T and v also −Interpretable, or do they differ from the Case features of DPs in that they are +Interpretable? Consider the following:

(5) a. *is likely John is clever
    b. *John$_i$ is likely t_i is clever

The ungrammaticality of (5a) could be attributed to the EPP (or more precisely, an unchecked −Interpretable EPP feature). But, as always, we should consider what happens without EPP features. (5a) could still be ruled out on the assumption that the Case feature of T is −Interpretable.

In fact, the ungrammaticality of (5b) suggests this assumption is independently necessary. The crucial difference between (5a) and (5b) is that the EPP is satisfied in the latter. Under a feature-checking analysis of the EPP, it must be possible for a single DP to check multiple EPP features in order to allow successive-cyclic raising.

(6) John$_i$ seems [t_i to be likely [t_i to be clever]]

If nonfinite T has an EPP feature (we will see below that the strongest evidence for the EPP comes from nonfinite clauses), the raised subject in (6) must be capable of checking the EPP feature of each of the embedded clauses as well as that of the matrix.[6] Thus, even if the matrix and embedded Ts in (5b) each have an EPP feature, *John* can check all of them.

Case, on the other hand, appears to be different. There is no reason to think that a single DP can check more than one Case feature.[7] The nominative Case feature of either the embedded or the matrix clause will remain unchecked in (5b), and, if such features are −Interpretable, the derivation will crash.

1.1.2.1   Last Resort: Greed or Enlightened Self-Interest?   Before concluding, on the basis of the ungrammaticality of (5b), that T has a −Interpretable Case feature, we need to consider one other possibility: that the movement violates Last Resort. Two popular definitions of Move/Attract that incorporate Last Resort are stated in (7).

(7)   α can move to (or is attracted by) β only if
      a. some feature of α is checked (and erased) as a result of the operation;
      b. some feature of α or β is checked (and erased) as a result of the operation.

(7a), a weaker version of which was proposed by Chomsky (1993), is referred to as *Greed*; (7b), proposed by Lasnik (1995a) and adopted by Chomsky (1995), is referred to as *Enlightened Self-Interest* (ESI).

Only Greed has any hope of preventing (5b). EPP features alone do not suffice to exclude (5b) since, as we have seen, a single DP can check multiple EPP features. However, one of the applications of Move in (5b) does not satisfy the definition in (7a); it is not "greedy" since it results solely in erasure of some (EPP) feature of T. On the other hand, all applications of Move in (5b) meet the definition in (7b).

Also, as noted in Martin 1992a, Greed alone does not suffice to rule out examples such as (8a,b).

(8)   a. *she$_i$ seems to t_i [that Bill is a fool]
      b. *he$_i$ strikes t_i [that Bill is a fool]

(8a,b) are similar to (5b) in that movement takes place from a Case position to another Case position. The crucial difference is that in (8a,b) there
is a Case mismatch in the original position, as can be seen clearly in (9).

(9) a. *it seems to she that Bill is a fool
    b. *it strikes she that Bill is a fool

Since Case checking is not successful, Greed fails to prevent DP from
legitimately moving to a position where its Case can be checked in (8a,b).

(8a,b) plausibly involve inherent Case. As Chomsky (1995) notes,
depending on the exact properties of inherent Case, these examples may
be excluded for independent reasons. Nonetheless, an identical argument
can be constructed where structural Case is clearly involved. Consider
(10a,b).

(10) a. *I believe [her to seem [*t* is [*t* clever]]]
     b. *I believe it to seem [her is clever]

Chomsky (1995) suggests that Case mismatch *cancels* the derivation. Yet
(5b), (8a,b), and (10a) are uniformly ruled out by the assumption that the
Case features of T and *v* are −Interpretable; hence, we may not need to
stipulate that derivations are canceled because of nonmatching features.

Regardless, there are good reasons to reject Greed altogether. If Greed
is not the correct interpretation of Last Resort, some other way of ruling
out (5b) is needed.[8]

1.1.2.2   Arguments against Greed   One obvious problem with Greed, as
stated in (7a), is that it must be weakened in order to allow successive-
cyclic raising, as in (6). Raising to the specifier of nonfinite T in (6) poses a
problem for Greed since no feature of the moved element is erased as a
result of the operation.

Chomsky (1993) suggests that the intermediate steps of movement in
(6) are ultimately necessary in order for the Case feature of DP to be
checked and that this is compatible with a somewhat weaker version of
Greed. Consequently, Greed must rely on global comparisons, potentially
raising complications of a computational nature (see Chomsky 1995).[9]

Also, it is not clear why the intermediate steps of movement in (6) are
necessary. One possibility is the Minimal Link Condition (MLC). However, Chomsky (1995) subsumes this under the definition in (11).

(11) K attracts F if F is the closest feature that can enter a checking
     relation with (a sublabel of) K.

(11) does not prevent movement of *John* directly to the matrix Case-checking position in one step in (6). The derivation in question does not converge if the embedded T has an unchecked −Interpretable feature. But this is true in (5b) as well; hence, it cannot be convergence alone that is at issue.

Elsewhere (Martin 1993) I provide another argument against Greed. Consider *wh*-questions in English.

(12) a.   I wonder who she saw *t*
      b.   *I wonder she saw who

(12) shows that a *wh*-phrase must overtly move to a [+wh] CP in English. Whereas ESI would be satisfied if movement of the *wh*-phrase results solely in the erasure of a feature of C, Greed requires that (at least) a feature of the *wh*-phrase itself be erased as a result of the operation.

Now consider questions with multiple *wh*-phrases.

(13) I wonder who *t* saw who

Here, only one *wh*-phrase (the closest one by definition) is moved overtly. For well-motivated reasons (such as the absence of island effects and the nonresolution of antecedent-contained deletion), Chomsky (1995) assumes that in-situ *wh*-phrases do not undergo LF movement.[10] If so, the −Interpretable feature of the unmoved *wh*-phrase in (13) will not be checked, incorrectly predicting that the derivation crashes. Thus, whereas ESI is compatible with the hypothesis that there is no LF *wh*-movement, Greed is not.[11]

Also, Lasnik's (1995a,b,c) analysis of expletives requires ESI instead of Greed. Consider (14).

(14) a.   there is/*are someone here
      b.   there *is/are several people here

Chomsky (1986, 1993) captures the agreement facts in (14) by way of covert movement of the postverbal DP (hereafter referred to as the *associate*) to the position of *there*.

Lasnik further argues that the associate has partitive Case, which is checked by *be* (see also Belletti 1988). Consequently, covert raising of the associate to *there* cannot be driven by the need to check Case. Two possible motivations for movement of the associate are (a) *there* lacks φ-features, in which case the −Interpretable φ-features of T still need to be checked (Martin 1992a; Groat 1995; Lasnik 1995b,c), or (b) *there* has an affix feature (Lasnik 1995a; Bošković 1997).

The first possibility violates Greed if the φ-features of DPs are +Interpretable, as suggested by multiple agreement phenomena (Chomsky 1995) as well as by the intuition that they are relevant to interpretation. The second possibility is also incompatible with Greed, as it is inconceivable that DPs (even those with weak determiners) have some morphological feature that is checked by adjoining to *there*.[12] Such a claim would predict that any numeration containing an indefinite but no *there* leads to a crashed derivation—clearly false, as (15) immediately establishes.

(15) someone is here

As Lasnik points out, ESI is compatible with either of these possible motivations for movement of the associate.

We have seen several reasons to think that ESI, not Greed, is the correct way to define Last Resort. But ESI is not capable of explaining the ungrammaticality of (5b) if all that is at stake is an EPP feature. This leads to the conclusion that T and *v* have −Interpretable Case features.[13] Questions about why Case exists and whether its existence is an "imperfection" of human language design remain to be answered (I return to these questions in section 1.3).

1.2 − Interpretable EPP Features

In this section, I discuss EPP features and show that, unlike Case features, they are not empirically well supported. We have seen that, in finite clauses, EPP features are redundant with Case. To test for the EPP, we must look to nonfinite clauses. In fact, one of the strongest potential arguments for the EPP, due to Bošković (1997), is based on nonfinite complements to *BELIEVE*-class verbs. Interestingly, *BELIEVE*-class verbs also seem to provide an argument for Greed. I will argue for an alternative analysis that does not entail the EPP and that allows ESI to be maintained.

1.2.1 EPP Effects in Control and ECM Infinitivals

The classical argument that the EPP exists independently of Case is based on the following type of example:

(16) *it is dangerous PRO to seem that the president is a liar

The only thing that appears to be wrong with (16) is that PRO fails to receive a θ-role (Safir 1985). But why must PRO be present in (16) to begin with? The traditional answer invokes the EPP.[14] However, the null Case analysis of PRO (Chomsky and Lasnik 1993; Martin 1992b, 1996, to appear) makes the EPP superfluous in (16): unless PRO is present to check the null Case feature of nonfinite T, the derivation will crash.

Another argument that is often made for the independence of the EPP comes from so-called exceptional-Case-marking (ECM) constructions.

(17) I believe her$_i$ to have been seen t_i

It is usually assumed that, in (17), *her* has raised only as far as the specifier of nonfinite T by Spell-Out, as illustrated in (18a). But since movement is not Case-driven, assuming that accusative is checked in the higher clause, it must be driven by the need to satisfy the EPP.

(18) a. I believe [$_{TP}$ her$_i$ to have been seen t_i]   (Spell-Out)
     b. I$_j$ [$_{vP}$ her$_i$ t_j believe-v [$_{VP}$ t_V [$_{TP}$ t_i to have been seen t_i]]]   (LF)

However, Bošković (1997), Johnson (1991), Koizumi (1995), Lasnik (1995d), and others argue that object raising is overt in English, in which case the structure of (17) at the point of Spell-Out may instead be along the lines of (19).[15]

(19) [$_{TP}$ I$_k$ believe$_j$-v_l-T [$_{vP}$ her$_i$ t_k t_l [$_{VP}$ t_j [$_{TP}$ to have been seen t_i]]]]

As there is no reason to assume movement to the embedded specifier of nonfinite T in (19), arguments for the EPP based on ECM constructions are considerably weakened.

Nor do examples such as (20) constitute an argument for the EPP.

(20) *I believe to seem that Ana is clever

The Case feature of *believe* must be checked. Further, given the overt raising analysis, this feature is strong, hence must be checked overtly. Thus, (20) is ruled out because of an unchecked strong feature. *Ana* can presumably raise to check an EPP feature, in conformity with ESI, but there is no way to check both the Case feature of the most embedded T and that of the matrix v.

1.2.2 *BELIEVE*-Class Verbs

1.2.2.1 An Apparent Argument for the EPP Bošković (1997) discusses examples similar to (20) that seem to provide a strong argument for the

EPP. Bošković suggests replacing *believe* with *BELIEVE*, identical to *believe* in all respects except that it does not check Case (more precisely, given my assumptions, *BELIEVE* is selected by *v* that does not check Case; I return to this point below). If there are no EPP features, an example otherwise identical to (20) but with *BELIEVE* is predicted to be grammatical.

(21) *I BELIEVE to seem that the president is a liar

The ungrammaticality of (21) tells us either that EPP features exist or that *BELIEVE* does not. Since there is no reason to assume that *BELIEVE* exists, (21) does not provide a strong argument for the EPP.

The real question, however, is whether there are *any* verbs with the properties of *BELIEVE*—in other words, proposition-selecting verbs that do not permit a (proposition-denoting) DP or infinitival as their complement, suggesting that Case is unavailable. On the basis of (22) and (23), Bošković argues that *remark* and *conjecture* are two such verbs in English.[16]

(22) a. John remarked that Ana is clever
     b. *John remarked something
     c. *John remarked Ana to be clever

(23) a. John conjectured that Ana is clever
     b. *John conjectured something
     c. *John conjectured Ana to be clever

The (a) sentences in (22) and (23) show that *remark/conjecture* (semantically) select propositions whereas the (b) and (c) sentences suggest that they lack the ability to check Case. Now we can apply the test:

(24) a. *John remarked to seem Ana is clever
     b. *John conjectured to seem Ana is clever

If no Case features are unchecked in (24), it is not clear why these examples are ungrammatical, aside from the EPP.

Bošković provides several other examples that have the same abstract properties.[17] The assumption that nominals and passives do not have Case features is motivated by the facts in (25).

(25) a. *John's belief [Ana to be clever]
     b. *[Ana to be clever] is believed

Without the EPP, (26a,b) are predicted to be grammatical.

(26) a. *John's belief to seem Ana is clever
     b. *to seem Ana is clever is believed

1.2.2.2 Greed Revisited   (24) and (26) can be ruled out by appealing to
the EPP. But recall that a single DP can check multiple EPP features.
Hence, we must consider raising derivations as well.

(27) a. *John remarked Ana$_i$ to seem t_i is clever
     b. *John conjectured Ana$_i$ to seem t_i is clever

(28) a. *John's belief Ana$_i$ to seem t_i is clever
     b. *Ana$_i$ to seem t_i is clever is believed by John

As noted above, counterparts to (27) with *believe* invariably contain an
unchecked Case feature.

(29) *I believe Bill$_i$ to seem t_i is a liar

An explanation of (29) in terms of Greed is thus redundant with the
assumption that the Case features of T and v must be checked. ESI both
reduces this redundancy and is well motivated empirically. However, a
Case-theoretic analysis is not available for *BELIEVE*-type verbs, passives, and nominals in (27)–(28).

Bošković (1997) concludes that Greed is required in order to rule out
(27)–(28). Assuming Greed, the ungrammaticality of (27)–(28) is straightforward. Movement is not allowed since it results solely in the erasure of a
feature of the target; no feature of *Ana* is checked as a result of the relevant operation. ESI, on the other hand, is silent in these examples.[18]

It appears that (24) and (26) cannot be explained without the EPP.
Furthermore, (27)–(28) seem to require Greed. Below, I will propose an
alternative analysis of these examples that does not lead to the same
conclusions.

1.2.2.3 Propositional Infinitivals and Empty Complementizers   Ormazabal (1995) argues convincingly that both finite and nonfinite propositional
clauses are CPs. Further, following Pesetsky's (1991) analysis, he treats
empty complementizers as affixes. It turns out that these two assumptions
can resolve most of the problems encountered above.

The fact that zero-derived words, such as *belief*, do not allow further
affixation (of certain morphemes) is referred to as *Myers's Generalization*
(Myers 1984). Pesetsky (1991) and Ormazabal (1995) analyze (25a) in

terms of such a constraint. The basic idea is that *believe* cannot support both a zero nominalizer and a zero complementizer. (25b) is also accounted for since there is no c-commanding (or adjacent) head for the zero complementizer to affix to. Setting aside many important details (for these, see Pesetsky 1991; Ormazabal 1995), the point to emphasize is that Pesetsky's and Ormazabal's approach explains the ungrammaticality of (26) and (28) as well.

A possible objection is that an account of (25) in terms of a constraint on affixation is unmotivated since a plausible Case-theoretic analysis exists. Assuming nouns do not check Case, there is no way for the Case feature of *Ana* to be erased in (25a). Something similar can be said for (25b).

However, Ormazabal (1995) provides a very compelling argument that an analysis solely in terms of Case does not suffice. He observes that examples parallel to (25a) are ungrammatical in Spanish, a language where the subject of propositional infinitivals is typically PRO.

(30) a. Hobbes cree   [PRO haber   aterrizado en Marte]
      Hobbes believes   have-INF landed   on Mars
      'Hobbes believes himself to have landed on Mars'
   b. *su creencia (de) [PRO haber   aterrizado en Marte]
      his belief (of)   have-INF landed   on Mars

The ungrammaticality of (30b) is not explained by the inability of nouns to check Case.[19] Also, as Ormazabal shows, a nonpropositional infinitival (IP on his analysis) can be the complement of a noun, as predicted by the zero-affix analysis.

(31) su intención de [PRO aterrizar en Marte]
    his intention of   land-INF on Mars
    'his intention to land on Mars'

Insofar as the zero-affix analysis of nonfinite propositional clauses is independently necessary, (26) does not provide an argument for EPP features, and consequently we do not need to appeal to Greed to block (28). For the moment, Bošković's conclusions based on (24) and (27) remain. However, current ideas about the relationship between accusative Case and external θ-roles imply that there can be no *BELIEVE*-class verbs. I propose that apparent *BELIEVE*-class verbs, such as *remark* and *conjecture*, are zero-derived and that the problematic examples fall under the scope of an explanation like Ormazabal's.

1.2.2.4 The Nonexistence of the *BELIEVE* Class Bošković's arguments for the EPP and Greed are crucially based on the assumption that *BELIEVE*-class verbs exist. However, the existence of transitive verbs that do not check Case is quite mysterious to begin with.[20] *BELIEVE*-class verbs are exceptions to Burzio's Generalization, which states in part: If a verb has an external argument, it checks Case. Bošković sets this potential objection aside, pointing out that Burzio's Generalization itself is unexplained. Counterexamples are perhaps even to be welcomed.

However, Chomsky's (1995) theory of accusative Case and external arguments derives Burzio's Generalization. Chomsky, basically following Hale and Keyser (1993), argues that the configuration for assignment of an external role is created not by a projection of (transitive) V, but by the projection of an empty "causative" verb *v* dominating VP. Furthermore, Chomsky proposes that *v*, not Agr, checks accusative Case. Having an external argument implies having *v*, and having *v* implies having accusative Case. In other words, Burzio's Generalization! And counterexamples to a derived principle should cause one to worry.

I suggest that the mysterious verbs in question involve N-to-V zero derivation. That is, *remark* and *conjecture*, and by hypothesis any other *BELIEVE*-class verbs, are derived from underlying structures involving a zero verb that takes a nominal complement. I assume that the zero verb is a light verb of sorts (i.e., the null counterpart of *make* in *make a remark*, *make a conjecture*, etc.) and that the nominal complement incorporates into it overtly, as shown in (32).

(32)

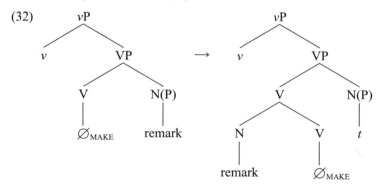

Given this analysis of *remark* and *conjecture*, the ungrammaticality of (24) and (27) follows immediately as an instance of Myers's Generalization.[21] Also, the relative obscurity of this class of verbs (only a few verbs of the *BELIEVE* class have been identified) can be related to the non-productivity of the morphological derivation that underlies them. Equally important, *remark* and *conjecture* no longer constitute counterexamples to a derived Burzio's Generalization, assuming that the incorporated noun ultimately checks the Case of *v* (cf. Baker 1988).

Pesetsky's and Ormazabal's approach makes predictions about the possibility of empty complementizers in finite as well as nonfinite CPs. For example, a finite complement of *believe* can be headed either by an empty complementizer or by *that*, as shown in (33a,b). The nominalization of *believe* in (33c,d) only allows finite complements headed by *that*, since affixation of an empty complementizer to a zero-derived word is blocked by whatever principle derives Myers's Generalization.

(33) a. everyone believed that Zico would soon retire
     b. everyone believed ∅ Zico would soon retire
     c. the belief that Zico would soon retire (was popular)
     d. ?*the belief ∅ Zico would soon retire (was popular)

Given the above analysis, it is predicted not only that *remark* and *conjecture* disallow nonfinite (propositional) complements entirely, since these always have empty complementizers, but also that they only allow finite complements headed by *that*. Consider (34).

(34) a. he remarked/conjectured that Zico would soon retire
     b. ?*he remarked/conjectured ∅ Zico would soon retire

In fact, *BELIEVE*-class verbs differ from *believe* with respect to the possibility of finite complements with empty complementizers exactly as predicted.

Ormazabal's theory of propositional complements, along with an analysis of *BELIEVE*-type verbs that treats them as morphologically complex, eliminates one of the strongest arguments for EPP features and, furthermore, Greed.

1.2.3 Expletives and the EPP

For Chomsky (1995), *there*-type expletives provide another reason to assume EPP features. In (35a), *there* is inserted in the specifier of T solely to check a strong EPP feature. After Spell-Out, the associate raises to T to check Case and agreement, much like what happens overtly in (35b).

(35) a. there is a strange-looking man in the garden
     b. a strange-looking man is *t* in the garden

If EPP-features are to be eliminated, an alternative analysis of (35a) is needed. But if not an EPP feature, what strong feature does *there* check? Three possibilities are (a) Case, (b) φ, (c) Case and φ. Suppose *there* checks Case and the associate raises covertly to check φ-features. As Chomsky observes, we would then expect (36) to be grammatical, where the +Interpretable φ-features of *a strange man* covertly raise from a Case-checked position to check the φ-features of T.

(36) *there seems to a strange man that it is raining

On the other hand, if *there* checks only φ-features, we have to explain why the finite verb agrees with the associate.

(37) a. there is/*are a strange man in the garden
      b. there *is/are two strange men in the garden

If *there* checks Case and φ-features, we face similar problems.

Lasnik's (1995a) theory of expletives avoids these problems and is compatible with the nonexistence of EPP features. Lasnik proposes that *there* checks both Case and φ-features of T. The associate has partitive Case, which is checked by *be* (or perhaps certain other unaccusative verbs). To account for the agreement facts in (37) and the distribution of associates, Lasnik assumes the following properties:

(38) a. *There* is an LF affix.
      b. The associate that hosts *there* at LF must be a DP marked with partitive Case.
      c. An affix and its host must agree for all φ-features.

(38a) provides a driving force for movement of the associate to *there*, assuming affixation satisfies ESI. The assumption that *there* is an LF affix explains why (35a) does not violate the Stray Affix Filter at PF. (38b) blocks examples like (36) whereas (38c) accounts for the agreement facts in (37).[22]

Also, consider the following examples:

(39) a. there$_i$ is expected t_i to be someone here
      b. *there is expected someone$_i$ to be t_i here
      c. we expect someone$_i$ to be t_i here

Chomsky's (1995) account of the impossibility of (39b) crucially relies on the EPP. The relevant point in the derivation is where the VP [$_{VP}$ *be someone here*] is merged with nonfinite T and the partial numeration is {(*expected, 1*), (*is, 1*), (*T, 1*) (*there, 1*)}.

(40) [TP to [VP be [AP someone here]]]

Assuming *to* has a strong EPP feature, the derivation can continue in either of two ways: *someone* raises, or *there* is inserted to satisfy the EPP. That the option of raising *someone* is possible in principle is shown by (39c).

Chomsky argues that Merge is preferred to Move because of economy. If economy conditions are local, we obtain the desired result that direct merger of *there* is the only possibility in (40) (see Chomsky 1995).[23]

This extremely interesting argument, which shows that economy conditions are local and must be thought of derivationally, does not succeed without EPP features. Even so, (39b) can still be ruled out (though not leading to the same conclusions about the nature of economy) since raising of *someone* violates ESI.

1.2.4   EPP Features and the MLC

Chomsky (1995) states the MLC as part of the definition of Move/Attract in (11), repeated here as (41).

(41)   K attracts F if F is the closest feature that can enter a checking relation with (a sublabel of) K.

This explains, for example, the ungrammaticality of (42a).

(42)   a. *Mary seems it was told *t* that Bill is a liar
     b. *it seems was *t* told Mary that Bill is a liar

Given (41), (42a) is not a derivation at all. Although (42b) involves well-defined operations, the derivation crashes since raised *it* cannot check the matrix nominative Case.

The existence of EPP features is often said to be crucial in this account. Consider the derivation at the following point:

(43)   T seems it was told Mary that Bill is a liar

Chomsky assumes that a strong EPP feature in T results in attraction of a D-feature. According to (41), attraction of the D-feature of *Mary* is not possible since the D-feature of *it* is closer.

In a theory without EPP features, the fact that *it* has a D-feature is irrelevant since this feature does not enter into a checking relation. The Case feature of *it* is also irrelevant, having already been erased. However, the +Interpretable φ-features of *it* are both visible and can enter a checking relation with T, thus maintaining the result that (42a) is not a derivation.[24]

An interesting problem exists with Chomsky's account of (42b). Chomsky (1995) assumes that (42b) crashes since the Case features of T and *Mary* are not checked. However, in class lectures (MIT, fall 1995) he points out (attributing the observation to Eduardo Raposo, personal communication) that nothing prevents the formal features (FF) of *Mary* from raising to T and checking Case covertly. The copy created by movement of *it*, even if visible to the computation, no longer has features that enter a checking relation with matrix T; hence, (41) does not block Raposo's derivation.

Chomsky (class lectures) suggests that the Case and φ-features of T must, in effect, be checked simultaneously. In (42b), *it* raises to check the strong EPP feature of T and consequently the φ-features of *it* enter a checking relation with T. Plausibly, as a result the derivation either cancels, since *it* has φ but not Case (i.e., checking φ without Case induces a sort of feature mismatch), or crashes, if it is impossible for the Case feature of T to be checked *after* its φ-features have been checked.

The same can be said in a theory without EPP features. Suppose *it* raises to T to check φ-features. The derivation either cancels or crashes because Case can no longer be checked. If anything, Chomsky's idea follows more naturally if we assume that it is really strong φ-features that are doing the attracting and that Case checking is a reflex of φ-feature checking, as I argue more fully in section 1.3.1.

Also, under Chomsky's proposal, since *it* is attracted to check EPP features, not φ-features or Case per se, a checking relation must be established automatically between *it* and the φ-features of T as a result of the configuration. Otherwise, *it* could ignore φ-features and Case features of T, leaving these for *Mary* to check covertly. Under the alternative approach, the facts again seem to follow more straightforwardly: T attracts *it* to check strong φ-features to begin with, entailing Case checking, which fails.

1.2.5   A Requiem for the EPP?

I have shown that many of the standard arguments for the EPP vanish once plausible and/or independently necessary assumptions are made clear. This suggests that EPP features can and should be eliminated. As tempting as it is to embrace that conclusion, I believe more work needs to be done.

I remain tentative for several reasons. The reduction of the EPP relies heavily on the assumption that objects raise overtly in languages like

English. To show that this is true, despite appearances otherwise, is a major research project (see Koizumi 1995 and Johnson 1991 for serious attempts). Also necessary is the assumption that *there* checks Case and agreement, which further entails that *be* and certain unaccusatives optionally check Case. Again, despite the existence of a vast literature on expletive constructions in many languages, the issues are, in my view, far from settled. Finally, as Anders Holmberg and Norbert Hornstein observe (personal communication), questions concerning Icelandic quirky subjects—where it does not seem that Case/ϕ is driving the movement to [Spec, T]—remain to be addressed. Although I have nothing to say about this largely mysterious phenomenon here, clearly we need to know more about quirky/inherent Case before we can fully dispose of the EPP.

My goal here is not to prove that the EPP can be reduced or eliminated but to show what is at stake in doing so. At the same time, I have suggested an analysis of apparent *BELIEVE*-class verbs, which are often taken to provide the strongest argument for the EPP, that does not rely on EPP features (or Greed).

1.3 Certain Imperfections as Optimal Solutions

Assume, for the sake of discussion, that we indeed live in an ideal world in which the EPP is fiction. Consequently, a good deal of redundancy is eliminated from the theory. This result is most remarkable, however, from the perspective of minimalism. If we think that C_{HL} reduces to conceptual necessity/bare output conditions, −Interpretable features are perplexing objects in such a system. Yet we have seen that some −Interpretable features are empirically necessary.

Maybe C_{HL} is less perfect than we thought. Another possibility, though, is that −Interpretable features actually exist to meet the needs of bare output conditions. In Uriagereka 1997 and Martin 1996, this sort of reasoning is applied to Case.

1.3.1 Case Features

It is generally assumed that domains of L-relatedness play a role at the LF interface (in determining possible binding relations, in crossover phenomena, etc.). Furthermore, the arguments of a predicate must be in the same L-relatedness domain. Exactly how such domains are defined, I leave open, but the simplest hypothesis is that they are no more than sets of sets of features. Then, at least in the many instances where the

$\pm$ _Interpretable_ features of these arguments are nondistinct, C-I cannot tell the multiple arguments of a predicate apart from one another.[25] It is quite plausible that bare output conditions disallow this type of unrecoverable deletion.

Case is arguably the computational system's solution to the problem. Suppose Case exists in the grammar to serve as the necessary label to make sets of +Interpretable features formally distinct.

Technically speaking, when a DP enters a checking relation with the ϕ-features of a head H, if $\phi(DP)$ and $\phi(H)$ match, $\phi(H)$ is erased. Only as a reflex, if H additionally has a Case feature, matching Case (DP) and Case (H) are erased and FF(DP) is given a label. More precisely, suppose FF(DP) = {αCase, IFF}, where α designates a particular value of Case and _IFF_ refers to the +Interpretable formal features. FF(H) = {αCase, ϕ, IFF}, where $\phi \subseteq$ IFF(DP). Then, FF(DP) becomes {R {IFF}}, where R (= α) is the label. FF(H) simply becomes {IFF} after $-$Interpretable ϕ-features are erased.[26]

In sum, without Case (or some similar mechanism), at least some derivations would result in unrecoverable deletion. Thus, bare output conditions demand that the +Interpretable features of arguments in the same domain be formally distinguishable at LF, and it is Case that provides the solution.

What happens in situations where the +_Interpretable_ features of arguments are distinct (such as _I love you_ Instead of _He loves him_)? I do not want to say that Case is not necessary here since it surely is. However, as Uriagereka (1997) suggests, this is not a concern if the mechanisms involved cannot discriminate such situations. In other words, the system is not "smart" enough to work one way when arguments in the same domain are distinguishable by their +Interpretable feature alone and another way when they are not.

1.3.2 EPP Features Revisited

This type of thinking has interesting consequences if it turns out that EPP features are in fact needed. Chomsky has at times speculated that the EPP, insofar as it is real and distinct from Case/ϕ, follows from bare output conditions. Suppose that something like the traditional _theme/ rheme_ distinction is a core part of interpretation by C-I. Further assume that only elements in [Spec, TP] can be distinguished as themes. EPP features themselves do not directly follow from these assumptions but, along the lines of the above speculations regarding Case, having them would be one optimal way to satisfy such a bare output condition.

This "functionalist" approach to the EPP is not unproblematic (Lasnik, to appear). First, although expletives can satisfy the EPP, it is not clear that they are themes.

(44) I believe there to have been someone in the garden

Also, recall examples involving successive-cyclic raising.

(45) someone seems *t* to be likely *t* to have been believed *t* to have been *t* in the garden

Here the EPP is satisfied several times by *someone*. *Someone* is undoubtedly the theme of some clause in (45), but it seems unlikely that it is interpreted as the theme of *every* clause. (46) is simply the sum of these two problems.

(46) there seems *t* to be likely *t* to have been believed *t* to have been someone in the garden

These potentially serious arguments against a functionalist motivation for the EPP do not necessarily carry over to the level of mechanisms. Suppose that a "dumb" computational system cannot tell apart those instances where something attracted to [Spec, TP] is a theme from those where it is not. For the argument to be valid, it suffices that some DPs are themes and that they must move to [Spec, TP] to be so interpreted. The EPP will generalize to include (46)–(48) if the system works in the one simple way it knows how.

1.4 Conclusions

—Interpretable features are problematic conceptually in at least two respects. First, there is overlap in the empirical work done by distinct types of features. Eliminating such redundancy is a general methodological concern of the sciences. Second, insofar as we think that C_{HL} may be perfect or optimal in some serious sense, the existence of features not interpreted by interface systems is surprising.

I considered Case and EPP features in detail. It seems that Case is basically ineliminable for overwhelming empirical reasons. EPP features are less well motivated, many of their effects being deducible from other properties of the grammar. Ideally, we can eliminate EPP features, though the conclusion remains somewhat tentative.

I also suggested a rationalization for the existence of Case (again making certain idealizations). Case features, though not directly motivated by bare output conditions, may be an optimal solution for a system that would otherwise fail to meet certain of these conditions. I then briefly explored the possibility of applying similar reasoning to EPP features, should they turn out to remain.

Still to be answered is the question of how ϕ-features fit into the picture. Unfortunately, to tackle this difficult issue would take me well beyond the fixed limits of this chapter.

Notes

I wish to thank Howard Lasnik and Juan Uriagereka for invaluable help and encouragement at every stage of this research. I am also particularly indebted to Sam Epstein, Anders Holmberg, and Norbert Hornstein for detailed comments on the manuscript. Portions of this material have been presented at the Hizkuntzalaritza-Mintegia Linguistics Seminar of the University of Deusto/University of the Basque Country, the University of Connecticut, and the 4th Numazu Linguistics Seminar.

1. Chomsky calls constraints on language design of this sort *bare output conditions*.

2. In principle, there could be features that are interpretable by *both* C-I and A-P. But, as far as I am aware, none have been proposed.

3. I set aside the question of whether the configuration is best defined in terms of "checking domain," as in Chomsky 1993, or the narrower notion of "extended lexical item," as suggested in Chomsky 1995.

4. We must also define what it means for two features to match. The most straightforward hypothesis is that matching requires *identity*.

5. Two important issues arise. First, is erasure obligatory, where possible, or is it optional? Second, what happens if nonmatching features enter a checking relation? I return to these issues briefly later.

6. This is the empirical basis of Chomsky's assumption that a +Interpretable feature (i.e., one that is never erased) is responsible for checking the EPP feature of T—namely, the categorial feature D.

7. This is not entirely trivial. Consider the example at hand, repeated in (i).

(i) *John$_i$ T$_2$ is likely t_i T$_1$ is clever

The following derivation must be blocked: (a) DP $=$ *John* raises from its θ-position to enter a checking relation with T$_1$; (b) the Case feature of T$_1$ erases; (c) DP further raises to enter a checking relation with T$_2$; (d) both the Case feature of DP and T$_2$ are erased. This derivation will be impossible if erasure of a $-$Interpretable feature is an automatic consequence of a successful checking relation, not an optional operation, and checking relations are symmetric.

8. Another potential argument that Case features are $-$Interpretable comes from the ungrammaticality of (i).

(i) *he remarked it

(i) is assumed to be rejected because the verb *remark* does not check Case. If the Case feature of T is +Interpretable, it never gets erased and can check the (nominative) Case of the object in LF.

9. The following *local* algorithm can subsume Greed for A-movement.

(i) Movement of α to K is possible only if α contains a −Interpretable feature.

Lasnik (1955c) assumes a condition like (i) in addition to ESI for reasons discussed in section 1.2.2.2.

10. In principle, covert *wh*-movement might be possible in a language where the −Interpretable feature of C is weak (however, if objects raise overtly in all languages, a possibility very much worth considering is that −*Interpretable = strong*). In this case, although there is no overt movement, there would be a covert analogue. Japanese may be such a language (with weak C); but see Watanabe 1992 for arguments to the contrary.

11. In Martin 1993, I present this not as an argument against Greed, which was assumed, but as an argument for covert *wh*-movement. However, the argument can easily be turned around: assume there is no covert *wh*-movement and conclude that Greed is false. As Lasnik (1995b,c) further points out, if the −Interpretable feature of a *wh*-phrase were optional, typical Superiority effects could no longer be explained by (11).

(i) *I wonder who who saw *t*

If the object rather than the subject has the −Interpretable feature in question, the closest F that enters a checking relation with C is indeed attracted in (i).

12. Bošković's (1997) analysis is consistent with Greed. He assumes that the driving force of movement is the affixal nature of *there* but argues that instead of the associate raising to *there*, *there* lowers to the associate.

13. If the Case features of T/*v* must be checked, although (ic) is straightforward, an issue arises with respect to (ia,b).

(i) a. I believe that Mary likes Bill
    b. that Mary likes Bill is believed
    c. I believe Mary to like Bill

I assume either that CPs themselves can (optionally) have Case features (see Bošković 1995) or that they are linked to null DPs in argument positions (Stowell 1981).

14. Since English does not have null expletives or pro, and since raising is impossible out of this sort of infinitival, the only element that can satisfy the EPP in (16) is PRO.

15. These authors each make slightly different proposals regarding the position to which the object raises, the overt position of the verb, the location of adverbs, and so on. Also, it should be noted that Bošković (1997) argues that ECM subjects raise to check accusative Case overtly whereas "standard" objects raise post-Spell-Out.

16. Bošković (1994) argues that *remark* is a member of the *BELIEVE* class. Bošković (1997) suggests that one must also control for whether a predicate selects a nonfinite clause (entailing some sort of selection besides s-selection). From the claimed contrast in (i), he concludes that *conjecture* allows a nonfinite clause as its complement whereas *remark* does not.

(i) a. ?Mary was conjectured to like Peter
    b. *Mary was remarked to like Peter

However, I find no contrast between (ia) and (ib); both examples are, at best, marginal.

17. Howard Lasnik (personal communication) suggests still others:

(i) a. I told Mary [that it seems she is intelligent]
    b. *I told Mary [it to seems she is intelligent]
    c. *I told Mary [to seem she is intelligent]

These examples are accounted for by the same analysis I will propose to account for those discussed by Bošković.

18. Lasnik (1995b,c) makes an alternative proposal. He suggests that in addition to ESI, the following principle constrains movement:

(i) Only a DP with an unchecked Case feature is visible for A-movement.

As Lasnik notes, (i) reintroduces a good deal of the redundancy that was eliminated by replacing Greed with ESI. Also, internal to Lasnik's theory of *there* constructions, a further problem arises since the associate in such constructions, which he assumes checks partitive Case with *be*, must somehow be made visible for LF A-movement. For further discussion, see Lasnik (1995b,c).

19. Note that this conclusion is independent of whether PRO has no Case (as in Chomsky 1981) or whether PRO has null Case (as in Chomsky and Lasnik 1993; Martin 1992b, 1996, to appear). If PRO does not have/need Case, whether or not nouns check Case is irrelevant. If PRO has null Case, this presumably can be checked by nonfinite T in both (30a) and (30b).

20. Juan Uriagereka (personal communication) points out that there is a still deeper mystery: namely, the existence of −Interpretable Case features altogether. I return to this question in section 1.3.

21. It should be noted that this account of *remark* and *conjecture* does not explain the intermediate status of (ia,b), as discussed in note 16, predicting instead that they should be completely unacceptable.

(i) a. ??Mary was conjectured to like Peter
    b. ??Mary was remarked to like Peter

However, this seems to be part of a more general problem for the zero-affix theory. Consider the following examples:

(ii) a. *I believe sincerely [∅ Mary to like Peter]
     b. ??Mary is believed sincerely [∅ *t* to like Peter]

Ormazabal (1995) argues that (iia) is illicit because the zero complementizer cannot affix to *believe*. But exactly the same situation should arise with (iib) as well. It is not clear why the passive makes (iib) less deviant than (iia), but whatever accounts for this fact should also explain (i).

22. Lasnik (1995b,c) argues that *there* checks Case but not φ-features, the latter being checked by the associate. (38a–c) are then dispensable, but some other stipulation is needed in place of (38b) to block (36). Also, as I discuss in section 1.2.4, Chomsky (class lectures) argues that Case can only be checked together with φ-features. If correct, that would eliminate this possibility from consideration.

23. Raising of *someone* in (40) will be possible if the partial numeration is {(*we*, *1*), (*v*, *1*), (*T*, *1*), (*expect*, *1*)}, as in the derivation leading to (39c). This is because the derivation preferred by economy, in which *we* is merged with nonfinite T, crashes since *we* fails to receive a θ-role (see Chomsky 1995). In this sense, although economy conditions apply locally, the system still has a global character in that convergence needs to be considered to determine whether a (less economical) derivation is possible.

24. Norbert Hornstein (personal communication) points out a potential hitch in the reasoning. If it is not D-features but φ-features (or Case) that are being attracted, what happens in situations where the features don't match? Consider a derivation at the point shown in (ia).

(i) a. T seem it was told we that Bill is a liar
    b. we T seem it was told *t* that Bill is a liar

The closest set of matching φ-features that enter a checking relation with T are those of FF(*we*). Thus, we should be able to raise FF(*we*), incorrectly generating (ib). The same difficulty arises in ensuring that only the subject, and not an object marked with nominative, raises to T in simple clauses (though here one can argue that accusative could never be checked since the subject is merged in a position not c-commanded by *v*).

A possible solution is to assume that the computational system cannot "see" whether two sets of features match until they are in a checking relation. Perhaps T/*v* in fact attract FF(D), not because T/*v* need a D-feature but because this is where φ-features reside. Whether or not these features match is not discovered until after a checking relation is established.

25. In standard set theory, the set $K = \{\{FF_\alpha\}, \{FF_\beta\}\}$ is identical to the set $K' = \{\{FF_\alpha\}\}$, where $FF_\alpha = FF_\beta$.

26. This analysis explains, among other things, why we find local obviation effects with Case—that is, the fact that two nominative Cases or two accusative Cases never appear in the same minimal domain (e.g., compare *he likes he* with *he thinks he likes him*). This can probably be related to standard Condition B–type obviation effects along the lines suggested by Uriagereka (1997).

A possible criticism of the approach is that it violates a strong interpretation of *inclusiveness*. This depends on exactly what is meant by inclusiveness and how the actual mechanisms of "*R*-marking" work. Note also that the proposal violates inclusiveness no more than the assignment of standard labels internal to the operation Merge.

References

Baker, Mark. 1988. *Incorporation*. Chicago: University of Chicago Press.

Belletti, Adriana. 1988. The Case of unaccusatives. *Linguistic Inquiry* 19, 1–34.

Bošković, Željko. 1994. D-Structure, θ-Criterion, and movement into θ-positions. *Linguistic Analysis* 24, 247–286.

Bošković, Željko. 1995. Case properties of clauses and the Greed Principle. *Studia Linguistica* 49, 32–53.

Bošković, Željko. 1997. *The syntax of nonfinite complementation: An economy approach*. Cambridge, Mass.: MIT Press.

Chomsky, Noam. 1981. *Lectures on government and binding*. Dordrecht: Foris.

Chomsky, Noam. 1986. *Knowledge of language: Its nature, origin, and use*. New York: Praeger.

Chomsky, Noam. 1993. A minimalist program for linguistic theory. In *The view from Building 20: Essays in linguistics in honor of Sylvain Bromberger*, eds. Kenneth Hale and Samuel Jay Keyser, 1–52. Cambridge, Mass.: MIT Press. [Reprinted in *The Minimalist Program*, Noam Chomsky, 167–217. Cambridge, Mass.: MIT Press, 1995.]

Chomsky, Noam. 1995. Categories and transformations. In *The Minimalist Program*, 219–394. Cambridge, Mass.: MIT Press.

Chomsky, Noam, and Howard Lasnik. 1993. The theory of principles and parameters. In *Syntax: An international handbook of contemporary research*, eds. Joachim Jacobs, Arnim von Stechow, Wolfgang Sternefeld, and Theo Vennemann, 506–569. Berlin: Walter de Gruyter. [Reprinted in *The Minimalist Program*, Noam Chomsky, 13–127. Cambridge, Mass.: MIT Press, 1995.]

Groat, Erich. 1995. English expletives: A minimalist approach. *Linguistic Inquiry* 26, 354–365.

Hale, Kenneth, and Samuel Jay Keyser. 1993. On argument structure and the lexical expression of syntactic relations. In *The view from Building 20: Essays in linguistics in honor of Sylvain Bromberger*, eds. Kenneth Hale and Samuel Jay Keyser, 53–109. Cambridge, Mass.: MIT Press.

Johnson, Kyle. 1991. Object positions. *Natural Language & Linguistic Theory* 9, 577–636.

Koizumi, Masatoshi. 1995. Phrase structure in minimalist syntax. Doctoral dissertation, MIT, Cambridge, Mass.

Lasnik, Howard. 1995a. Case and expletives revisited: On Greed and other human failings. *Linguistic Inquiry* 26, 615–633.

Lasnik, Howard. 1995b. Last Resort. In *Minimalism and linguistic theory*, eds. Shosuke Haraguchi and Michio Funaki, 1–32. Tokyo: Hituzi Syobo.

Lasnik, Howard. 1995c. Last Resort and Attract F. In *Proceedings of the Sixth Annual Meeting of the Formal Linguistics Society of Mid-America*, eds. Leslie Gabriele, Debra Hardison, and Robert Westmoreland, 62–81. Indiana University Linguistics Club, Bloomington.

Lasnik, Howard. 1995d. A note on pseudogapping. In *Papers on minimalist syntax*, eds. Rob Pensalfini and Hiroyuki Ura, 143–163. (MIT Working Papers in Linguistics 27.) MITWPL, Department of Linguistics and Philosophy, MIT, Cambridge, Mass.

Lasnik, Howard. To appear. On the locality of movement: Formalist syntax position paper. In *Functionalism and formalism in linguistics, vol. 1*, eds. Michael Darnell, Edith Moravscik, Frederick Newmeyer, Michael Noonan, and Kathleen Wheatley. Amsterdam: John Benjamins.

Martin, Roger. 1992a. Case theory, A-chains, and expletive replacement. Ms., University of Connecticut, Storrs.

Martin, Roger. 1992b. On the distribution and feature content of PRO. Ms., University of Connecticut, Storrs.

Martin, Roger. 1993. On LF *wh*-movement and *wh*-islands. Ms., University of Connecticut, Storrs.

Martin, Roger. 1996. A minimalist theory of PRO and control. Doctoral dissertation, University of Connecticut, Storrs.

Martin, Roger. To appear. Null Case and the distribution of PRO. *Linguistic Inquiry*.

Myers, Scott. 1984. Zero-derivation and inflection. In *Papers from the January 1984 MIT Workshop in Morphology*, eds. Margaret Speas and Richard Sproat, 53–70. (MIT Working Papers in Linguistics 7.) MITWPL, Department of Linguistics and Philosophy, MIT, Cambridge, Mass.

Ormazabal, Javier. 1995. The syntax of complementation: On the connection between syntactic structure and selection. Doctoral dissertation, University of Connecticut, Storrs.

Pesetsky, David. 1991. Zero syntax II: Infinitival complements. Ms., MIT, Cambridge, Mass.

Safir, Kenneth. 1985. *Syntactic chains*. Cambridge: Cambridge University Press.

Stowell, Tim. 1981. The origins of phrase structure. Doctoral dissertation, MIT, Cambridge, Mass.

Uriagereka, Juan. 1997. Formal and substantive elegance in the Minimalist Program: On the emergence of some linguistic forms. In *The role of economy principles in linguistic theory*, eds. Chris Wilder, Hans-Martin Gärtner, and Manfred Bierwisch, 170–204. Berlin: Akademie Verlag.

Watanabe, Akira. 1992. *Wh*-in-situ, subjacency, and chain formation. (MIT Occasional Papers in Linguistics 2.) MITWPL, Department of Linguistics and Philosophy, MIT, Cambridge, Mass.

Chapter 2

Raising the Case of Expletives
Erich M. Groat

In this chapter, I explore the nature of English expletive constructions in the general framework of a minimalist approach to syntactic theory. I address two key questions that have permeated research in this framework: what is the feature content of lexical and functional categories? and what is the role and precise form of economy in computation? Chomsky (1995) explores expletive constructions and uses analyses of them in developing answers to both questions. In particular, he develops an analysis of expletive *there* under which the expletive bears neither Case nor agreement features, and an analysis of derivational economy of a "mixed" global/local nature.

Here, I provide an alternative answer to both questions as far as expletive constructions are concerned. First, I suggest (contra Chomsky 1995) that certain data involving expletive *there* support the hypothesis that the expletive does in fact bear a −Interpretable Case feature that must be checked and deleted (a return to the earlier analyses of, e.g., Chomsky 1991, 1993; Groat 1995; Lasnik 1995). Next, I adopt an analysis of expletives under which they are *raised* from a VP-internal small clause position (Den Dikken 1995; Moro 1997) and show that the stipulation in Chomsky 1995 that the Extended Projection Principle (EPP) allows exceptional checking by merger is unnecessary. Finally, I show that the data motivating Chomsky's "mixed" global/local economy follow naturally from this hypothesis, without recourse to any metric of derivational economy beyond a local conception of Shortest Move.

2.1 Previous Analyses

Chomsky (1991) argues that in sentences like (1), the NP *a man* raises at LF to the specifier of Agr_SP ([Spec, Agr_SP]), adjoining to the expletive *there*.

(1) a. [$_{AgrsP}$ [there] is [$_{VP}$[$_{DP}$ a man] in the room]]   (S-Structure)

b. [$_{AgrsP}$[[$_{DP}$ a man]$_i$ there] is [$_{VP}$ t_i in the room]]   (LF)

Chomsky (1991) assumes that *there* is an "LF affix," meaning that at LF it must have an NP adjoined to it to be interpretable. Thus, the principle of Full Interpretation requires raising of an NP to *there*, in this case the NP *a man*. In (2) (Chomsky's (44a)), *a man* cannot adjoin to *there*, since doing so would presumably result in an Empty Category Principle (ECP) violation.

(2) a. *there seems [$_{CP}$ that [$_{AgrsP}$[a man] is in the room]]   (S-Structure)

b. [[a man]$_i$ there] seems [$_{CP}$ that [$_{AgrsP}$ t_i is in the room]]   (LF)

Since adjunction of *a man* to *there* at LF would result in an ECP violation in (2b), (2a) is ungrammatical. But if the adjunction in (2b) did not occur, *there* would remain unaffixed at LF. Again, for Chomsky (1991), an affix to which nothing has adjoined is uninterpretable. The explanation for the ungrammaticality of (2a), then, relies crucially on the stipulation that *there* is an LF affix.

Later, Chomsky (1993) develops a similar analysis under the assumption that all movement is motivated by the need to check morphological features. In (1a), the NP *a man* must raise at LF in order to check features in [Spec, Agr$_S$P]. The features checked are the noun's φ-features (i.e., person and number, as well as gender or noun class in some languages) and its Case features. φ-features are checked against Agr$_S$ itself (and are referred to as the *N-features of Agr$_S$*). Case features are checked against T (the *N-features of T*), which in English adjoins to Agr$_S$.[1] In moving to [Spec, Agr$_S$P] at LF to check these features, *a man* adjoins to *there*, yielding (1b).

Chomsky (1993) retains the notion that adjunction to *there* is required for it to become an interpretable LF object. It is this interpretive sense in which *there* is considered to be an "LF affix." If *there* remains unaffixed at LF, it is still a legitimate object, and the derivation will converge (assuming all other objects produced by the derivation are legitimate at LF). However, if unaffixed, *there* receives no (coherent) interpretation at LF, so the derivation "converges as semigibberish" (p. 200).

In (2), *a man* already has its Case and φ-features checked in the specifier of the embedded Agr$_S$P and thus will not raise to adjoin to *there*. The result is a convergent derivation that is "semigibberish." The same applies to (3) (Chomsky 1993, (26b)), which the analysis in Chomsky 1991 would not rule out, since raising the object of the preposition should not yield an ECP violation.

(3) *there seems [PP to [DP a strange man]] that it is raining outside

Here, *a strange man* checks its Case and φ-features locally within the prepositional phrase.[2] Thus, there is no need for it to raise to *there* to check features; by the principle of Greed, then, its raising is disallowed, and *there* remains unaffixed at LF. The derivation converges since unaffixed *there* is legitimate, but the LF representation is "semigibberish" since unaffixed *there* is uninterpretable.

The advantage of such an approach is that it avoids invoking the ECP to explain these cases. Because the ECP as a linguistic principle lacks any obvious conceptual naturalness, under minimalist assumptions we eschew stipulating it unless it is clear that we cannot construct an empirically adequate theory without it.

However, as noted in Groat 1995, the stipulation that *there* is a phonologically realized LF affix is problematic. First, *there* is predicted by structure preservation to be a maximal projection, since (a) it occupies a specifier position, and (b) DPs, which are maximal projections, may adjoin to it. But the notion of an XP "affix" is unprecedented. In itself, the hypothesis that such affixes exist is reasonable and interesting; however, making such a claim about *there* introduces a new *class* of morphosyntactic objects: LF phrasal affixes. It seems undesirable to posit a new class of morphosyntactic objects on the basis of one English morpheme, particularly if (as I will argue) it can be avoided.

Most recently, Chomsky (1995) takes a somewhat different approach to expletive constructions. Certain background assumptions differ. First, DPs do not need to check and thereby delete their own agreement features, as these features are +Interpretable. They do, however, bear Case features that must be checked. Second, the T/Agr$_S$ complex no longer exists, since there are by hypothesis no Agr heads under this framework. Instead, T bears both Case and φ-features. Third, the EPP is no longer taken to be a consequence of the obligatory checking of strong Case features. Instead, T universally bears a strong D-feature, checked by any D category (see also Ura 1996).

Fourth, covert movement is restricted to movement of the formal features of heads via adjunction to a functional head whose features they check. No category "larger than" the bundle (FF) of formal features undergoes raising in the LF component. A functional head H "attracts" the formal features of the closest head that H c-commands, where X is "closer to H" than Y is if X c-commands Y.

Fifth, and most importantly, the expletive *there* is hypothesized to bear neither semantic nor Case features. Its only role is to satisfy the EPP: being of category D, it can check the EPP feature (= D-feature) of T. The checking of Case and agreement features in T is postponed until LF in *there*-expletive constructions, at which point feature raising of the formal features of the associate DP to T checks these features.

This approach has the advantage of explaining the contrast in (4).

(4) a. *there seems [$_{CP}$ that a man left]
    b.   it seems [$_{CP}$ that a man left]

If we assume that *it* bears both Case and ϕ-features that can check against T, then (4b) converges; no further checking need apply. If the expletive *there* checked the Case feature but not the ϕ-features of the matrix T, then all that would be left to check at LF in (4a) would be the ϕ-features of T. Now, *a man* in the embedded CP bears +Interpretable ϕ-features, though it has checked and deleted its −Interpretable Case features against the embedded finite T. Thus, LF feature raising could raise the formal features of *a man* to the matrix T and thereby check and delete them. The derivation would converge, and we would incorrectly predict (4a) to be grammatical.

If, on the other hand, the expletive does not check Case features, then we can explain the ungrammaticality of (4a): *a man* has already checked and deleted its −Interpretable Case feature against the embedded finite T, thus has no Case feature to check against the feature of T. The derivation therefore crashes because a −Interpretable Case feature remains in the matrix T at LF.

Thus, we see that the shift made in Chomsky 1995 to the (natural) hypothesis that the ϕ-features of DPs are +Interpretable induces a corresponding shift in the analysis of the feature content of *there*: if *there* bore Case features, then they could check the Case of the matrix T in (4a), while the agreement features of T could be checked at LF by the DP *a man*.

This account similarly explains why (3), repeated here as (5), is ungrammatical.

(5) *there seems [$_{PP}$ to [$_{DP}$ a strange man]] that it is raining outside

Here, the formal features of the DP *a strange man* undergo LF raising to the preposition *to* at LF, checking the Case feature of *to* and of *a strange man* (and possibly the φ-features of *to*, if any). But the Case feature of the matrix T remains unchecked at LF, and the derivation crashes. Furthermore, if the DP were somehow able to check its Case against the matrix T, then the Case feature of *to* would remain unchecked, and the derivation would again crash.

Finally, the proposed approach also explains the impossibility of expletive raising out of finite clauses, as in (6).

(6) *there seems that [t_{there} is a problem]

Although *there* can check the EPP feature of both the matrix and embedded clauses, it checks no (nominative) Case feature. The only category with a Case feature in the phrase marker is the DP *a problem*; if it checks the Case feature of the matrix T at LF, its own (−Interpretable) Case feature is thereby deleted, leaving no way for the (−Interpretable) Case feature of the embedded T to be checked. Similarly, checking of the embedded T's Case features leaves the matrix T unchecked at LF. Either way, a −Interpretable Case feature remains in the representation at LF, and the derivation does not converge, correctly predicting the deviance of (6). Thus, this approach allows us to dispense both with the ECP and with the notion of "LF affix" in such cases.

2.2   Evidence That Expletives Bear Case

I would like to suggest that the hypothesis that expletives lack Case should be reconsidered for both empirical and conceptual reasons. These arguments are not overwhelming, but they should serve to suggest that the alternative analysis is plausible.

First, observe that extraction from the experiencer PP in *seem* constructions is impossible.

(7) *who does it seem to t_{who} that it is raining

In this example, checking of Case features is almost certainly not an issue; there is one argument for each Case-checking head. Rather, some other factor appears to be involved that renders the PP argument of *seems* impervious to extraction of its elements; it is an island of some kind. In light of this, it is reasonable to hypothesize that the ungrammaticality of (5) is due to the island status of the PP.

Second, consider the derivation of (8).

(8) there seems t_{there} to be a problem

First, *there* merges into [Spec, TP] of the embedded nonfinite clause, satisfying the EPP feature of the embedded T. Next, it raises to the matrix [Spec, TP], satisfying the EPP feature of the matrix T. LF raising of the formal features of *a problem* then results in the checking of the −Interpretable Case and agreement features of the matrix T, as desired. But what then rules out (9), in which two expletives are drawn from the lexicon?

(9) *there seems there to be a problem

LF feature raising applies just as in (8), and the EPP features of both the embedded and matrix clauses are satisfied by their respective expletives. The derivation converges, and if *there* is truly semantically vacuous, there should be no difference in interpretation between (8) and (9). Thus, we cannot appeal to an analysis of (9) as "gibberish" (without returning to some notion of "LF affix").

One might describe cases such as (9) as having "too many" expletives in some sense. But if expletives have no Case or semantic features and serve no purpose but to check the EPP feature of T, how can we capture this property? Intuitively, some notion of economy might be invoked: the derivation of (9), though convergent, is in some sense "blocked" by the convergent derivation of (8) that lacks the "extra" expletive. However, unless we are willing to adopt a fully global approach to economy, derivations with differing numerations cannot possibly be comparable. Since the derivations of (9) and (8) are contingent on different numerations (the former with two expletives, and the latter with a single expletive), this approach cannot help us.

Another approach to economy is the "mixed" global/local approach set forth in Chomsky 1993, which I discuss in section 2.4. Under this approach, a derivational step is allowed only if it is the "cheapest" of the set of possible derivational steps. In this sense, the metric is "local," since only the options available at a given choice point in the derivation are compared. However, any option that does not ultimately yield a convergent derivation is excluded from the comparison set. In this sense, the metric is global, since there is no way of knowing whether an operation results in convergence without finishing the particular derivation[3] that follows that operation; thus, given *n* options, (at least) *n* derivations need to be compared. Let us examine this approach with respect to (9) to see whether the correct result obtains.

Consider the point in the derivation of (9) where the first choice point emerges. The structure built so far is as follows:

(10) [$_{TP}$ to [$_{VP}$ be a problem]]

Here, two possibilities exist for checking the EPP feature of the nonfinite T: raising of *a problem* or merger of the expletive into [Spec, TP]. Chomsky (1995) assumes the following economy metric with respect to this choice:

(11) Merge is cheaper than Move.

Let us examine what happens if the apparently cheaper option—merger of *there*—is chosen. If the derivation converges, then the more expensive option—raising of *a problem*—is disallowed, and we need not consider it. We now have the following structure:

(12) [$_{TP}$ there to [$_{VP}$ be a problem]]

The EPP feature of the nonfinite clause has been checked; T has no remaining unchecked and −Interpretable features. We continue the derivation up to the next choice point, shown in (13).

(13) [$_{TP}$ T [$_{VP}$ seems [$_{TP}$ there to [$_{VP}$ be a problem]]]]

The EPP feature of the matrix T must now be checked. There are two operations that can accomplish this: raising of *there*, or merger of the second *there* still in the numeration. Again, let us take the apparently cheaper of the two options, merger; if the derivation converges, then the more expensive option of raising need not be considered. We now have (14).

(14) [$_{TP}$ there T [$_{VP}$ seems [$_{TP}$ there to [$_{VP}$ be a problem]]]]

Now the EPP feature of the matrix clause has also been checked. At this point, the phrase marker may undergo Spell-Out, and since there are no remaining strong features, the derivation yields a legitimate PF representation. Does the derivation yield a legitimate LF representation? Yes: the only remaining features to be checked are the −Interpretable Case and φ-features of the matrix T and the Case feature of *a problem*. Covert feature raising of the formal features of *a problem* to the matrix T accomplishes this, yielding a legitimate LF representation. Since both the PF and LF representations are legitimate, and each step in the derivation was the most economical at that point in the derivation, the derivation converges, incorrectly predicting (9) to be grammatical.

The fact that economy appears unable to capture the deviance of (9) suggests that *there* does check Case and that (9) is ruled out because the embedded *there* has no place to check its −Interpretable Case feature. Thus, there are not "too many" expletives per se, but too many Case features.

A particularly interesting situation arises in sentences such as (15a–c).[4] Recall that the hypothesis that *there* bears no Case feature is motivated by the general impossibility of A-movement (for our purposes, expletive or DP feature raising) out of finite clauses, as in (4) and (6). The sentences in (15a,b) are counterexamples to this generalization.

(15) a.   there looks [$_{CP}$ as if there is a problem with this analysis]
     b.   there look [$_{CP}$ as if there are problems with this analysis]
     c.   *there looks [$_{CP}$ as if there are a problems with this analysis]

In these cases, agreement with the expletive associate is obligatory in *both* finite clauses. This suggests that the formal features (including the φ-features) of the associate adjoin to both the matrix and embedded T, entailing that they may in principle be raised out of a finite clause. But the associate DP could check Case against only one T, since by hypothesis a given DP bears only one Case feature. This again suggests that *there* checks Case: in (15a,b), then, only the φ-features of the matrix and embedded T need be checked by formal feature raising. Since agreement features are +Interpretable features of the associate DP, they do not delete upon checking, and they can check against both Ts.

A question then arises concerning (4a), repeated here as (16).

(16) *there seems [$_{CP}$ that a man left]

Why could the formal features of *a man* not raise covertly to the matrix T and check φ-features, if *there* has already checked the Case features of T? It appears that there is a difference in the nature of the complementizers involved in (15) and (16): *as if* versus *that*. Speculating somewhat, we could perhaps account for the difference by saying that *that*, resembling as it does the demonstrative determiner, bears φ-features that can move to the matrix T; since *that* is closer to the matrix T than *a man*, it would be the only candidate for movement. But if *that* bears insufficient features for checking (lacking, perhaps, number features), then the φ-features of T cannot be fully checked; one might hypothesize that feature mismatch occurs, canceling the derivation (see Chomsky 1995, 309).

The complementizer *as if*, on the other hand, does not bear any obvious relation to a determiner. Let us hypothesize that it is categorially a complementizer, but bears no φ-features whatsoever. It then does not count as a closer potential checker of φ-features for the matrix T, and the features of the associate in (15) are therefore free to cross it.

Regardless, then, of the precise analysis of the difference between extraction possibilities from the embedded clauses in (15) and (16), the data suggest that the contrast results from the differing properties of the complementizers. In any case, to account for the grammaticality of (15a,b), we must assume that *there* does check Case features.

A final bit of evidence that expletives like *there* check Case comes from Spanish constructions found colloquially in Spain and generally in South and Central America. The associate of a null expletive in existential constructions, formed in Spanish with the verb *to have* rather than the copula, may agree with the verb.[5]

(17) a. (pro) había un hombre
         (there) have a   man
         'there is a man'
     b. (pro) habían   dos hombres
         (there) have+PL two men
         'there are two men'

In these cases, the associate may be replaced with an object clitic identical in form to an accusative clitic pronoun.

(18) a. (pro) lo   había
         (there) CL-MASC.SG have
         'there is (one)'
     b. (pro) los   habían
         (there) CL-MASC.PL have+PL
         'there are (some)'

If the null expletive did not check the Case of the matrix T, then we might expect that *haber* has an unaccusative lexical entry that must be chosen in such derivations; the Case feature of T could then be checked by the object. But the fact that an accusative pronoun may be used in place of an indefinite DP suggests that nominative Case is not being checked by the expletive associate. This makes sense under the assumption that *haber* checks accusative Case, or a partitive Case identical in morphological form to the accusative, whereas the null expletive checks the nominative Case of T. Again, it appears that the expletive checks Case.

This leads us to a problem that must be addressed if we assume that expletives check Case features: how does the associate DP check its Case feature, if the Case feature of T is checked by the expletive? Previous analyses of expletive constructions (e.g., Belletti 1988; Lasnik 1992) have hypothesized that nonspecific DPs/NPs may check partitive Case against the verb. Analyzing the licensing of the Case requirements of expletive associates goes beyond the scope of this chapter, but we need not commit ourselves to any particular analysis; it suffices merely to suggest that it is the verb, rather than T, that is responsible for licensing the associate DP in some manner. We have seen that the Case of the associate DP resembles accusative Case in the Spanish examples in (17) and (18), accusative Case being associated with the main verb (or with the "little v" of Chomsky 1995) rather than T. Furthermore, the impossibility in English of expletive-associate constructions in which the associate is a base subject of the clause suggests that the same configuration required for checking accusative Case is required for licensing the associate.

(19) a. *there is a man sleeping
     b. *there is sleeping a man
     c. *there has a man seen a woman

Thus, there is evidence that it is not T that licenses the Case requirements of the expletive associate: T checks the Case of the expletive alone.[6]

Having, I hope, shown that an analysis of expletive-associate constructions in which expletives do bear Case features is plausible, I turn to further consequences of such an analysis.

2.3   Expletive Raising

Once we assume that expletives check Case, an interesting issue arises concerning Chomsky's (1995) analysis of the nature of the EPP. Under this analysis, the EPP is a linguisitic universal, and the EPP feature of T has the property of being able to be checked not only through movement, but also by direct merger with TP. This contrasts with the checking of all other −Interpretable features, which for independent reasons is hypothesized to result only through the operation Attract/Move.[7] The checking of EPP features is by pure stipulation exceptional in this regard. But it turns out that this stipulation is not necessary under an analysis whereby expletives bear Case features.

Under an analysis in which expletives do in fact check Case, their direct merger into [Spec, TP] should not result in checking, since only the EPP feature of T can be checked by direct merger with TP: its Case feature must by hypothesis be checked by movement. Thus, if we are to pursue an analysis in which expletives check the Case features of the TP in whose specifier they reside, we must abandon the possibility that they are merged there directly; rather, they must raise from some position lower in the clause.

Precisely such analyses have been proposed by Moro (1997), Den Dikken (1995), Hoekstra and Mulder (1990), and Zwart (1992), as well as by Burzio (1986) for Italian *ci* constructions. In these analyses, the expletive is base-generated in a small clause with its associate, and it raises out of that clause to matrix subject position ([Spec, TP], for our purposes), as in (20).

(20) there T is [$_{SC}$[a problem] t_{there}] (i.e., *there is a problem*)

Under such analyses, the problem of Case checking by expletives disappears: since the expletive undergoes Move, Case features may be checked.

But it is now unnecessary to claim that the EPP is exceptional in that it can be satisfied by a D category merged directly into [Spec, TP]: if expletives always raise to [Spec, TP] and do not merge there directly, we need not stipulate any special checking mechanism for direct Merge. We thus rid the checking theory of the stipulation that checking of EPP features is exceptional.[8]

In the next section, I examine the consequences of this proposal for the approach to derivational economy alluded to in section 2.2, and I show that the revised hypothesis again simplifies the analysis considerably.

2.4 Raising versus ECM Constructions: An Economy-Independent Account

Chomsky (1995) in fact makes crucial use of the claim that the EPP can be satisfied through direct merger in his account of raising constructions. The relevant examples are given in (21).

(21) a.   there seems [$_{TP}$ t_{there} to be a problem here]
      b. *there seems [$_{TP}$ a problem to be $t_{a\ problem}$ here]

We seek to exclude the derivation in (21b), in which the DP *a problem* raises to [Spec, TP] of the nonfinite clause to satisfy the EPP of that clause, and *there* later merges directly into [Spec, TP] of the matrix clause to satisfy the EPP of the matrix clause. Chomsky analyzes this contrast in the following terms: at the point of the derivation shown in (22), the EPP must be satisfied to ensure cyclicity.

(22) [$_{TP}$ T to be a problem here]

If Merge is a cheaper operation than Move/Attract, then insertion of the expletive *there* is cheaper than movement of *a problem*, excluding the derivation in which *a problem* moves. Thus, *there* must merge, yielding (23).

(23) [$_{TP}$ there T to be a problem here]

There derivation continues, and *there* may raise to the matrix [Spec, TP] to yield (21a), as desired. (21b) is excluded since, given the availability of the expletive, *a problem* will never move to the embedded [Spec, TP].

The argument becomes more complex, however, in the case of exceptional-Case-marking (ECM) constructions. Consider the following sentence:

(24) we believe [$_{TP}$ John to [$_{VP}$ t_{John} be a problem]]

Both (21a) and (24) contain a nonfinite clausal complement of a main-clause verb: a raising construction in (21a), and an ECM construction in (24). Now consider the following point reached in the cyclic derivation of (24):

(25) [$_{TP}$ to [$_{VP}$ John be a problem]]

A problem arises: in this case, we want the DP *John* to move to [Spec, TP] of the nonfinite clause. But a cheaper operation is available: merger of the DP *we*, forming (26).

(26) [$_{TP}$ we to [$_{VP}$ John be a problem]]

We must perform the cheaper operation Merge; thus, *we* is merged into [Spec, TP], satisfying the EPP. Now *we* can move to [Spec, TP] of the higher clause and check its Case there along with the D-feature of the finite matrix T. Furthermore, *John* can undergo LF raising to check Case against *believe*. Thus, the derivation appears to converge, yielding (27).

(27) *we believe [$_{TP}$ t_{we} to [$_{VP}$ John be a problem]]

But note that *we* is not merged into the VP containing *believe* at any point in this derivation and thus receives no θ-role. Under the assumption that θ-Criterion violations yield nonconvergence, (26) does not converge. But if merger of *we* as in (26) is forced over movement of *John*, then the only derivation allowed is the nonconvergent (27), and (24) is underivable.

To solve this problem, Chomsky adopts the mixed local/global approach to economy discussed in section 2.2. Although merger of *we* to [Spec, TP] of the lower clause is cheaper than movement, it does not yield a convergent derivation. Thus, if we restrict the allowable operations at a given choice point (in this case, what should end up in [Spec, TP] of the lower clause) to those choices that yield convergence, merger of *we* in (26) is not an option, since it causes the derivation to crash. The only available operation is movement of *John* to the lower [Spec, TP], correctly yielding (24). At the same time, either merger of *there* or movement of *a problem* in (21) yields a convergent derivation; thus, both options are available, and the cheaper one is chosen: merger of *there*. Thus, (21b) is correctly ruled out, since the cheapest operation that would check the D-feature of the nonfinite T, merger of *there*, was not chosen.

This account is rather complex as well as subtle. Numerous attempts have been made to reduce the problem to one of strictly local economy; see in particular Poole 1995 and Collins 1997, both of which allude to the potential computational complexity of a syntactic system that must examine the full derivation(s) that follow from each choice point in a derivation, and suggest (correctly, I believe) that an optimal theory of economy should include no transderivational computation.

But under the assumption that *there* expletives raise from a low small clause position and that the EPP can be satisfied only through movement, we can explain the data quite simply, without recourse to any economy argument at all.

Recall the sentences to be explained.

(28) a.   there seems to be a problem
     b.   *there seems a problem to be
     c.   we believe John to be a problem
     d.   *we believe to John be a problem

First, let us consider (28a,b) under the assumption that the expletive *there* originates in a small clause with its associate. Both sentences arrive at an intermediate derivational point at which the structure is as follows:

(29) [$_{TP}$ T to be [$_{SC}$ a problem there]]

At this point, either *there* or *a problem* could raise to [Spec, TP] and thereby check the EPP feature, If *a problem* raises, the result is (30).

(30) [$_{TP}$ a problem T to be [$_{SC}$ $t_{a\ problem}$ there]]

But now, building up to the matrix [Spec, TP], we have (31).

(31) [$_{TP}$ T seems [$_{TP}$ a problem T to be [$_{SC}$ $t_{a\ problem}$ there]]]

At this point, the closest checker of the features of T is *a problem*; thus, *there* is prohibited from raising. We then have (32).

(32) [$_{TP}$ a problem T seems [$_{TP}$ $t_{a\ problem}$ T to be [$_{SC}$ $t_{a\ problem}$ there]]]

As (29)–(32) show, (28b) cannot be derived if the expletive is generated in the small clause. We thus correctly predict the ungrammaticality of (28b).

On the other hand, if *there* raises in (29), we obtain (33).

(33) [$_{TP}$ there T to be [$_{SC}$ a problem t_{there}]]

Continuing the derivation, we reach (34).

(34) [$_{TP}$ T seems [$_{TP}$ there T to be [$_{SC}$ a problem t_{there}]]]

Now the closest checker of the matrix T is *there*, and we correctly derive (28a). Note that nothing need be said concerning the relative cheapness of Merge over Move/Attract.

Now let us consider (28c,d). Building up the nonfinite clause, we obtain (35).

(35) [$_{TP}$ T to [John be a problem]]

Given that the features of T cannot be checked by direct merger of any category, the only possibility is for *John* to raise to [Spec, TP], yielding (36).

(36) [$_{TP}$ John T to [t_{John} be a problem]]

No option exists for *we* to merge into the lower [Spec, TP]. It thus merges in [Spec, VP] of the matrix clause,[9] yielding (37).

(37) [$_{VP}$ we believe [$_{TP}$ John T to [t_{John} be a problem]]]

We will then obviously be the closest DP to the matrix T and will move to the matrix [Spec, TP], correctly yielding (28c). Note that (28d) is ungenerable, since only some term c-commanded by the nonfinite T could move to [Spec, TP] to check its EPP feature, and *we* is not one of them.

Could *we* somehow be generated in the lower clause below the nonfinite T, as expletives are under the expletive-raising analysis, and thus raise to

[Spec, TP] and satisfy the EPP there? Apparently not; it could not merge into any specifier position and check a feature, since by hypothesis direct merger into [Spec, XP] does not result in checking. Though simple θ-role assignment would license merger of *we* to a specifier in the nonfinite clause, the θ-Criterion would again be violated if *we* (re-)merged into the higher clause to receive the subject θ-role.[10] Thus, there is no way to "sneak" the DP *we* somewhere in the lower clause into a position from which it could raise to [Spec, TP] and check EPP features there. (28d) is thus underivable.

Thus, we see that the hypothesis that expletives are generated in a small clause with their associates, in conjunction with the simplifying assumption that the EPP features are checked in the same way as any other feature (through movement, or in the present account more strictly derivational sisterhood), yields the correct predictions with respect to the data in (28) without recourse to any economy argument.

2.5 Conclusion

I have reviewed several arguments that the expletive *there* in English, and its null counterpart in Spanish, checks Case features (though not agreement features) in addition to satisfying the EPP. Assuming such an analysis forces us to assume that expletives raise to [Spec, TP] from some lower position in the clause. If this is the case, however, the need to stipulate that the EPP features may be exceptionally checked without movement does not arise. This account is not unprecedented (Moro 1997; Den Dikken 1995), and it allows us to dispense with the sole motivation for the mixed global/local economy analysis of Chomsky 1995.

Notes

An earlier version of this chapter appears as chapter 6 of Groat 1997.

1. I will shortly recast this analysis in terms of the Agr-less theory developed in Chomsky 1995; quite simply, both φ-features and Case features are checked by T.

2. Chomsky (1993) is not specific about the structural nature of this local checking; presumably, there exists an Agr projection dominating the PP, the specifier of which will license Case/φ checking.

3. Or derivations, if other choice points arise in the course of "testing" the option.

4. Some speakers find the sentences in (15a,b) to be less than perfect; there seems to be dialectal variation here, as most speakers I have polled, including myself, find them perfect. All speakers find both (15a) and (15b) considerably better than (15c).

5. For judgments I thank Javier Martin-Gonzales (personal communication).

6. There are of course languages (such as Icelandic and German) that allow transitive expletive constructions as well as expletive constructions with unergative verbs. Given my arguments, it would appear that these languages do have Caseless expletives. Note that nothing in this analysis precludes the existence of Caseless expletives in some languages; my argument then amounts to the stipulation that English (and Spanish) do not have them. However, this may be the greatest drawback of my analysis, since it pushes the problem back a level: why should any language *not* have Caseless expletives? It would be necessary to show that owing to independent morphological properties of such a language, no such expletive could exist, or, if it could, no derivations including Caseless expletives would converge.

7. See Groat 1997 for an analysis of checking that derives this stipulation.

8. Note that we must now assume that expletive *it*, commonly assumed to check EPP, Case, and agreement features, also raises from a lower position. In fact, under Chomsky's (1995) assumptions, this must always have been the case, since *it* has never been hypothesized to check only EPP features.

Another case to consider is pro in pro-drop languages such as Italian.

(i) (pro) sono arrivati due bambini
        have arrived two children
     'two children have arrived'

In these cases, it is not clear that pro checks either Case or agreement features, or for that matter even EPP features. I will not pursue the issue further here.

9. Or [Spec, *v*P], assuming the light verb analysis in Chomsky 1995.

10. In any case, if *we* receives a θ-role in any way other than as subject of *believe* and subsequently does not merge with [$_{VP}$ believe [$_{TP}$ ...]] to receive a subject θ-role, then the subject θ-role of *believe* remains undischarged: again a violation of the θ-Criterion. Whether or not θ-Criterion violations cause derivations to crash is irrelevant here.

References

Belletti, Adriana. 1988. The Case of unaccusatives. *Linguistic Inquiry* 19, 1–34.

Burzio, Luigi. 1986. *Italian syntax: A government-binding approach.* Dordrecht: Reidel.

Chomsky, Noam. 1991. Some notes on economy of derivation and representation. In *Principles and parameters in comparative grammar*, ed. Robert Freidin, 417–454. Cambridge, Mass.: MIT Press. [Reprinted in *The Minimalist Program*, Noam Chomsky, 129–166. Cambridge, Mass.: MIT Press, 1995.]

Chomsky, Noam. 1993. A minimalist program for linguistic theory. In *The view from Building 20: Essays in linguistics in honor of Sylvain Bromberger*, eds. Kenneth Hale and Samuel Jay Keyser, 1–52. Cambridge, Mass.: MIT Press. [Reprinted in *The Minimalist Program*, Noam Chomsky, 167–217. Cambridge, Mass.: MIT Press, 1995.]

Chomsky, Noam. 1995. Categories and transformations. In *The Minimalist Program*, 219–394. Cambridge, Mass.: MIT Press.

Collins, Chris. 1997. *Local economy*. Cambridge, Mass.: MIT Press.

Dikken, Marcel den. 1995. Binding, expletives, and levels. *Linguistic Inquiry* 26, 347–354.

Groat, Erich M. 1995. English expletives: A minimalist approach. *Linguistic Inquiry* 26, 354–364.

Groat, Erich M. 1997. A derivational program for syntactic theory. Doctoral dissertation, Harvard University, Cambridge, Mass.

Hoekstra, Teun, and René Mulder. 1990. Unergatives as copular verbs: Locational and existential predication. *The Linguistic Review* 7, 1–79.

Lasnik, Howard. 1992. Case and expletives: Notes toward a parametric account. *Linguistic Inquiry* 23, 381–405.

Lasnik, Howard. 1995. Case and expletives revisited: On Greed and other human failings. *Linguistic Inquiry* 26, 615–634.

Moro, Andrea. 1997. *The raising of predicates*. Cambridge: Cambridge University Press.

Poole, Geoffrey. 1995. Uninterpretability vs. non-convergence: A case study. Ms., Harvard University, Cambridge, Mass.

Ura, Hiroyuki. 1996. Multiple feature-checking: A theory of grammatical function splitting. Doctoral dissertation, MIT, Cambridge, Mass.

Zwart, C. Jan-Wouter. 1992. Dutch expletives and small clause predicate raising. In *NELS 22*, ed. K. Broderick, 477–491. GLSA, University of Massachusetts, Amherst.

Chapter 3

Minimalism and Quantifier Raising

Norbert Hornstein

My aim in this chapter is to eliminate Quantifier Raising (QR) as a rule of Universal Grammar. In Government-Binding (GB) style theories, QR is the operation that targets quantified NPs (QNPs) in A-positions and moves them to Ā-positions. QNPs contrast with nonquantified expressions (e.g., names) in being uninterpretable unless moved to Ā-positions from which their relative scopes and binding domains are determined (see, e.g., May 1985; Chierchia and McConnell-Ginet 1990). To deny that QR exists is to claim that no rule targeting QNPs as such obtains. Rather, the relative scope and binding properties that QNPs manifest is parasitic on the movements that all NPs undergo to satisfy grammatical demands such as Case requirements and other species of feature checking. This attitude toward QR reflects a more general sentiment concerning interpretation: semantic structure is a by-product of grammatical operations driven by formal concerns. Grammars seek morphological rectitude, not meaning. What meaning there is, is the unintended consequence of this mundane quest.[1]

This global vision motivates the desire to eliminate rules like QR that syntactically target expressions for essentially semantic reasons. This is buttressed by additional theory-internal reasons for dispensing with QR in the Minimalist Program. These largely boil down to the fact that QR and minimalism fit together awkwardly. Consider some illustrations.

First, the Minimalist Program presumes that movement serves to check morphological features. Thus, if QR obtains, its end must be the checking of Q-features. However, in contrast to *wh*-features or focus features or topic features, each of which has overt morphological realization in some language, Q-features are virtually unattested overtly. This suggests that Q-features do not exist and that no movement exists whose concern is to check them.

Second, like wh-, topic, and focus movement, QR yields an Ā-structure. However, QR seems able to append a quantified NP (QNP) to virtually any maximal projection.[2] Thus, it appears that Q-features, if they exist, have no particular position of their own. Rather, they can be sprinkled on any XP to yield the desired abstract movement at LF. Once again, this contrasts with the more familiar features (such as *wh*-features and topic features) that induce Ā-movement to rather specific IP-peripheral positions. One cannot move a *wh*-feature to the front of just any XP or focus an expression by adjoining it to any arbitrary projection.

Third, eliminating QR is a step toward eliminating the antecedent government part of the Empty Category Principle (ECP) from the grammar. Antecedent government does not fit well into minimalism. Its key notions—blocking category, barrier, γ-marking, and so forth—are not easily defined in minimalist terms. Nonetheless, the ECP is critical to theories that employ LF Ā-movement operations. It prevents them from overgenerating. However, if LF Ā-operations like QR (and *wh*-raising) are dispensed with, then the need for antecedent government likewise recedes.[3]

Fourth, if quantifier-scope interactions (QSI) piggyback on the structure of A-chains (i.e., the chains that result from operations that check L-related features), then the clause-boundedness of QSIs in natural languages can be directly accounted for.[4] The general clause-boundedness of quantifier interaction effects reduces to the very local nature of A-movement. In other words, if A-chains define the limits of quantifier scope, then the observed restricted scopal reach of natural language quantifiers follows trivially.

Fifth, the elimination of QR (and other Ā-movements) from LF allows apparent S-Structure conditions like Subjacency and parasitic gap licensing to reposition to LF.[5] For the Minimalist Program, this is a very desirable result. A core tenet is that there are only two grammatical levels—LF and PF—and that only the former has significant phrasal structure. A consequence of this is that all grammatical conditions that GB distributes among D-Structure, S-Structure, LF, and PF must now be largely relocated to LF. LF Ā-movement operations like QR greatly complicate this task. As an illustration, consider parasitic gap (PG) licensing.

Since Chomsky 1982, it has been standardly assumed that PGs must be licensed at S-Structure. This is required in a GB theory to distinguish the acceptable (1a) from the unacceptable (1b).

(1) a.   which book did John read *t* without reviewing *pg*
    b.   *John read every book without reviewing *pg*

The problem (1) poses can be directly traced to the presence of QR, for its application renders the two sentences in (1) structurally analogous at LF.

(2) a.   [which book$_i$ [John read t_i [without reviewing pg_i]]]
    b.   [every book$_i$ [John read t_i [without reviewing pg_i]]]

Thus, if LF Ā-operations exist, then PG licensing cannot be stated neatly at LF. This is a problem for minimalism given the absence of any other suitable level at which to state the condition. However, if QR is eliminated, then there is no difficulty relocating the PG licensing condition to LF. The reason is that there is no more Ā-structure at LF than the overt syntax provides; hence, (1a,b) are no more structurally similar at LF than they are prior to Spell-Out. So, if PG licensing is sensitive to Ā-dependencies (as standardly assumed), then eliminating QR allows one to state this condition at LF without empirical loss—and this is what the Minimalist Program, a theory that eschews S-Structure, requires.

The above points provide part of the motive for what follows: a reanalysis of QSI effects without the benefit of QR. There is one further methodological reason with a minimalist resonance. For the standard instances of QSIs, QR is not required. But if not required, it is not desirable either. The argument below rests on the observation that given the minimalist theory of Case, it is easy to construct an empirically adequate account of quantifier scope exploiting technical machinery already in general use. As I will suggest, the opportunity for exploiting Case chain structure to serve as the basis of QSIs exists in the Minimalist Program for one main reason: the structural configurations for the realization of Case and θ requirements are very different. In GB theories, government unifies all core grammatical relations. Moreover, the domains of Case and θ-assignment are essentially identical in GB. For example, an object is assigned its θ-role in roughly the same position in which it meets its Case requirements.[6] Though the Minimalist Program still retains (more or less) the GB approach to θ-assignment, it construes morphological feature checking in a very different way. It is this difference that the proposal below exploits.

The rest of the chapter is organized as follows. In section 3.1, I outline a way of representing QSIs via the structure of Case chains. In section 3.2, I argue that the theory sketched in section 3.1 has empirical payoffs. In section 3.3, I consider some crosslinguistic QSI data from Japanese, Hungarian, and the Romance languages. In section 3.4, I revisit the details of the proposed analysis in the context of Chomsky's (1995) proposal that Agr projections be eliminated. I consider some ways of implementing the proposal in section 3.1 without exploiting Agr nodes. A necessary feature of both implementations is that "lowering" be permitted. In section 3.5, I consider some influential arguments against lowering rules. In section 3.6, I provide a brief conclusion.

3.1 The Basic Proposal

Assume as background the version of the Minimalist Program set out in Chomsky 1993. The key elements are listed in (3).

(3) a. The VP-internal subject hypothesis: NPs in English begin in VP-internal positions.
    b. NPs in VP-internal positions move to [Spec, Agr] positions to check Case features. In particular, subjects move to [Spec, Agr$_S$] in overt syntax, and objects move to [Spec, Agr$_O$] at LF.
    c. Movement is copying and deletion.
    d. LF is the sole structured grammatical level, and all grammatical conditions hold here.

(3a) has been amply motivated and is no longer controversial (see Kuroda 1988; Koopman and Sportiche 1991). In the Minimalist Program, it reflects the conviction that all θ-roles are assigned within lexical projections.[7] If one further assumes, as Chomsky (1995) does, that all θ-roles are assigned to trivial chains, and that the θ-Criterion is a convergence condition, then all NPs must begin inside lexical shells for derivations to converge. I revisit (3b) in section 3.4. For now, I assume the theory of Case presented in Chomsky 1993. Its distinctive feature is that a D/NP marked with accusative Case is checked in a configuration analogous to one in which a D/NP marked with nominative Case is checked—namely, in a specifier-head configuration with the Case-checking head outside the VP shell. This specifier-head configuration is realized for accusatives in English at LF with the object raising from the VP shell to [Spec, Agr$_O$]. (3c,d) are both standard assumptions. Both are used in accounting for the data in section 3.2.[8]

I make two additional assumptions.

(4) A QNP Q_1 takes scope over a QNP Q_2 iff Q_1 c-commands Q_2.

(5) At the conceptual-intentional (C-I) interface, an A-chain has at most one and at least one member.

(4) is innocuous. It is the commonly assumed algorithm for translating syntactic c-command relations into semantic scope dependencies.[9] (5) is *not* trivial. It generalizes the assumptions concerning deletion in Ā-chains (Chomsky 1993) to all chains.[10] It forces deletion of all copies in an A-chain save one. (5) does not specify which chain members delete. The optimal assumption is that the process is free. it is not important here whether one takes this deletion process to be a fact about the interface interpretation procedure or one about the structure of LF phrase markers themselves. For present purposes, it is immaterial whether all but one member of the LF chain actually delete or whether the members of the chain remain intact until some post-LF interpretive module where only one member of the chain is "chosen" to be interpreted. If the latter is correct, then "deletion" simply amounts to being uninterpreted. If the former is correct, then deletion is an actual grammatical operation and (5) is a convergence requirement. Nothing below chooses between these two interpretations of the deletion process. What is crucial is that some form of deletion exist in A-chains. This is controversial. In section 3.4, I rebut arguments that reconstruction in A-chains is illicit.

(3)–(5) suffice to provide an analysis of QSIs in English. Consider a typical instance. (6) is ambiguous; either the universally quantified object or the indefinite subject is interpreted as taking wide scope.

(6) someone attended every seminar[11]

The LF structure of (6) prior to deletion of copies is (7).[12]

(7) [$_{Agr_S}$ someone [$_{TP}$ T [$_{Agr_O}$ every seminar [$_{VP}$ someone attended every seminar]]]]

Someone raises to [Spec, Agr$_S$] to check its nominative Case in the overt syntax. At LF, *every seminar* moves to [Spec, Agr$_O$] to check accusative Case. Each move leaves a copy of the moved expression behind. Conforming to (5) requires deleting one member of each of the two A-chains. Four possible structures result (deleted expressions are in parentheses).

(8) a. [$_{Agr_S}$ someone [$_{TP}$ T [$_{Agr_O}$ every seminar [$_{VP}$ (someone) [attended (every seminar)]]]]]

b. [$_{\text{Agr}_S}$ someone [$_{\text{TP}}$ T [$_{\text{Agr}_O}$ (every seminar) [$_{\text{VP}}$ (someone) [attended every seminar]]]]]]

c. [$_{\text{Agr}_S}$ (someone) [$_{\text{TP}}$ T [$_{\text{Agr}_O}$ (every seminar) [$_{\text{VP}}$ someone [attended every seminar]]]]]]

d. [$_{\text{Agr}_S}$ (someone) [$_{\text{TP}}$ T [$_{\text{Agr}_O}$ every seminar [$_{\text{VP}}$ someone [attended (every seminar)]]]]]]

Using the interpretive principle (4), we can represent the ambiguity of (6). (8a–c) are LF structures in which *someone* takes scope over *everyone*. In (8d), this QSI is reversed.[13]

The above discussion shows that QSIs in transitive sentences in English can be represented without QR by exploiting the structure of A-chains in a minimalist theory. The assumptions in (3)–(5) are crucial. For example, in the absence of copying and deletion, determinate scope relations among QNPs would not be represented and quantifier-scope depen-dencies would be grammatically underdetermined.[14]

More interestingly, VP-internal subjects are instrumental in allowing objects to take scope over subjects. So too is the assumption that objects check accusative Case outside the VP shell in [Spec, Agr$_O$]. In fact, the VP-internal subject hypothesis and the assumption that accusative Case is checked outside the VP shell in [Spec, Agr$_O$] are actually flip sides of the same minimalist intuition, namely, that the grammar segregates morpho-logical Case and agreement properties from θ-properties. The domain of θ-assignment is the VP shell. Case, in contrast, is checked in a specifier-head relation outside this lexical shell. This separation of functions is a constant refrain within minimalism. It is interesting to observe, therefore, that representing QSIs without QR requires exploiting both halves of this central minimalist dichotomy.[15] The converse is also true. One can inter-pret QR as the technical price a theory that grammatically represent QSIs must pay if it identifies the domains and relations of Case theory and θ-theory.

3.2   Some Empirical Benefits

Having shown how to represent QSIs without the benefit of QR, in this section I provide evidence in favor of this approach. Two features of the analysis are crucial. First, quantifier scope is parasitic on the structure of A-chains. Second, what scope an expression has is a function of which member of its A-chain survives the deletion process.[16]

Consider first different scope interactions manifest in raising and control structures.

(9) a. someone seemed to attend every seminar
    b. someone hoped to attend every seminar

Every seminar can be interpreted as having scope over *someone* in (9a) but not in (9b). This follows from the different structures of the two sentences. At LF, prior to deletion, (9a) has the structure in (10a) typical of a raising construction, whereas (9b) has the structure in (10b) characteristic of control.[17]

(10) a. [someone [T [seem [someone [to [every seminar [someone [attend every seminar]]]]]]]]
     b. [someone [T [someone [hope [PRO [to [every seminar [PRO [attend every seminar]]]]]]]]]

Observe that through judicious deletions it is possible to get a copy of *someone* c-commanded by a copy of *every seminar* in (10a), as in (11).

(11) [(someone) [T [seem [(someone) [to [every seminar [someone [attend (every seminar)]]]]]]]]

At no point do the chains headed by *someone* and *every seminar* interleave in (10b). Hence, for this structure, no amount of deletion can duplicate the effect found in (11).

In sum, if relative scope piggybacks on A-chain structure and reflects relative c-command after deletion, we expect matrix subjects to be able to take scope under embedded-clause objects in raising constructions but not in control structures. This accounts for the contrast in (9).

Consider a second pair of sentences. (12) illustrates that QSIs are sensitive to the Tensed-S Condition. It is possible to interpret *someone* in (12a) as within the scope of *every Republican*. This reading is absent in (12b).

(12) a. someone expected every Republican to win
     b. someone expected that every Republican would win

This contrast follows from previous assumptions. (12a) is an exceptional-Case-marking (ECM) construction. The embedded subject raises to the matrix [Sepc, Agr$_O$] to check its accusative features at LF. The embedded subject in (12b) is marked nominative; its Case is checked in the embedded [Spec, Agr$_S$]. Prior to deletion at LF, the two sentences have the structures in (13).

(13) a. [$_{Arg_S}$ someone [$_{Agr_O}$ every Republican [$_{VP}$ someone [expected [$_{Agr_S}$ every Republican [$_{VP}$ every Republican to win]]]]]]

b. [$_{Agr_S}$ someone [$_{VP}$ someone [expected [$_{Agr_S}$ every Republican would [$_{VP}$ every Republican win]]]]]

Note that the chains headed by *someone* and *every Republican* interleave in (13a) but do not in (13b). Consequently, *every Republican* can c-command (and hence take scope over) *someone* after the relevant deletions, as shown in (14).

(14) [$_{Agr_S}$ (someone) [$_{Agr_O}$ every Republican [$_{VP}$ someone [expected [$_{Agr_S}$ (every Republican) [$_{VP}$ (every Republican) to win]]]]]]

No combination of deletions will allow *every Republican* to c-command *someone* in (13b) and so the analogous interpretation is unavailable for this structure.

The above accounts both rely on Case chains undergirding quantifier scope. For these data, the structure of Case chains alone accounts for the indicated scope contrasts.[18] In GB-style theories, both sorts of data are accounted for in terms of the ECP (see, e.g., Aoun and Hornstein 1985). As the ECP is an unwelcome condition in the Minimalist program, a side benefit of this approach is that it can handle these contrasts without invoking it.

Let us turn next to a different set of interactions, ones that highlight the effect of assumption (5). The Minimalist Program assumes (see (3d)) that there is only a single level at which grammatical conditions can apply: LF. I now review some data that rely on the combination of (3d) and (5). Consider the interaction of relative quantifier scope and binding.

Higginbotham (1980) observes that (15a) is ambiguous, with either the subject or the object taking widest scope. (15b) is similarly ambiguous so long as the pronoun is not interpreted as bound by *someone*. However, on the bound reading, the sentence can only be interpreted with the indefinite subject outside the scope of the *every* phrase.

(15) a. someone played every piece of music you knew

b. someone$_i$ played every piece of music he$_i$ knew

The requirement that *someone* take wide scope in (15b) follows from the assumptions made above. The LF structure of the sentence prior to deletion is (16a). To be interpreted as bound, the pronoun must be c-commanded by its antecedent at LF (for the standard discussion of this, see Higginbotham 1980). However, this forces *someone* to c-command the *every* phrase. Given (4), this in turn leads to an LF structure in which *someone* takes scope over the *every* phrase, as in (16b,c).

(16) a. [$_{Agr_S}$ someone [$_T$[$_{Agr_O}$[every piece of music he knew] [$_{VP}$ someone [$_{VP}$ played every piece of music he knew]]]]]]

   b. [$_{Agr_S}$ someone$_i$ [$_T$[$_{Agr_O}$[every piece of music he$_i$ knew] [$_{VP}$ (someone) [$_{VP}$ played (every piece of music he knew)]]]]]]

   c. [$_{Agr_S}$ (someone$_i$) [$_T$[$_{Agr_O}$[(every piece of music he$_i$ knew)] [$_{VP}$ someone [$_{VP}$ played every piece of music he knew]]]]]]

Given the minimalist assumptions in Chomsky 1995, these data cannot be similarly handled in a theory that represents QSIs via QR. The problem is as follows. Chomsky argues that Ā-chains minimize the restrictor in Ā-position at LF. In effect, this forces QR to move bare Qs. But if just bare Qs move, then (17) is a legitimate LF structure where the pronoun can be bound by the variable t_j while *some* is c-commanded by *every*.[19]

(17) [$_{IP}$ every$_i$ [$_{IP}$ some$_j$ [$_{IP}$ t_j [$_{VP}$[t_j one] played [t_j piece of music he knew]]]]]]

There are further cases of interactions between quantifier scope and binding. A classic one is discussed by Aoun (1982). He observes that in a raising structure—(18a)—*someone* can be interpreted as within the scope of the embedded *every* phrase. However, if the raised subject binds a matrix pronoun or anaphor, this reading disappears and *someone* must be interpreted as having wider scope than the *every* phrase—(18b,c).

(18) a. someone seemed (to Bill) to be reviewing every report
   b. someone$_i$ seemed to his$_i$ boss to be reviewing every report
   c. someone$_i$ seemed to himself$_i$ to be reviewing every report

The LF structures of (18b,c) are shown in (19).

(19) a. [someone$_i$ seemed to his$_i$ boss [(someone) to be [every report [(someone) reviewing (every report)]]]]]

   b. [someone$_i$ seemed to himself$_i$ [(someone) to be [every report [(someone) reviewing (every report)]]]]]

If *someone* is to bind the matrix pronoun/anaphor in (19), the embedded copy must delete. This makes it impossible for the *every* phrase to c-command *someone*. Consequently, *someone* must be interpreted as outside the scope of the *every* phrase.

Similar effects occur in simple clauses with adjuncts. (20a,b) are ambiguous, with either the *every* phrase or *someone* taking wide scope. (20c,d), with *someone* binding into the adjunct, are no longer ambiguous. *Someone* must take wide scope.

(20) a. someone serenaded every woman
 b. someone reviewed every brief
 c. someone$_i$ serenaded every woman before he$_i$ left the party
 d. I got someone to review every brief without leaving the office

We can account for these interactions between scope and binding just as we did above if we assume that adjuncts are adjoined to VP or higher.[20] If *someone* is to bind into the adjunct, the copy inside the VP shell must delete, as this copy does not c-command the adjunct. The copy in [Spec, Agr$_S$] thus determines the scope of *someone*. However, the *every* phrase cannot take scope over this position, as no *every* copy c-commands it. (21a,b) are the relevant LF structures.

(21) a. [$_{Agr_S}$ someone$_i$ [$_T$ every woman [$_{VP}$[$_{VP}$ (someone) serenaded (every woman)] [before he$_i$ left the party]]]]
 b. [$_{Agr_S}$ someone$_i$ [$_T$ to [$_{Agr_O}$ every brief [$_{VP}$[$_{VP}$ (someone) review (every brief)] [without PRO$_i$ leaving the office]]]]]

This reasoning further implies that if the object (rather than the subject) binds into the adjunct, then scope ambiguities will persist. This seems to be correct, as (22a) can be read with *someone* either in the scope of the *every* phrase or outside it. This is because (22a) has two well-formed LF structures. In (22b), the extant *every* phrase c-commands the undeleted *someone*. In (22c), the opposite c-command relations obtain.

(22) a. someone questioned every suspect$_i$ before he$_i$ was released
 b. [$_{Agr_S}$ (someone) [$_{Agr_O}$ every suspect$_i$ [$_{VP}$[$_{VP}$ someone questioned (every suspect$_i$) [before he$_i$ left]]]]]
 c. [$_{Agr_S}$ someone [$_{Agr_O}$ every suspect$_i$ [$_{VP}$[$_{VP}$ (someone) questioned (every suspect$_i$) [before he$_i$ left]]]]]

This theory has another consequence. I have argued that subjects that bind into adjuncts must take wide scope because VP-internal subjects fail to c-command adjuncts. This implies that if a subject binds into a complement rather than an adjunct, it should be able to take scope inside the object since the VP-internal subject position c-commands the complement position. Hence, the copy in [Spec, Agr$_S$] can delete and binding will remain licit. This is illustrated in (23). Here, *someone* can be interpreted within the scope of the *every* phrase with the indicated binding. The relevant LF structures are provided in (24).

(23) a. someone$_i$ asked every attendant if he$_i$ could park near the gate
   b. John got someone/at least one patron$_i$ to tell every critic that he$_i$ hated the play

(24) a. [$_{Agrs}$ (someone) [$_{Agr_O}$ every attendant [$_{VP}$ someone$_i$ asked (every attendant) if he$_i$ could park near the gate]]]
   b. John got [$_{Agrs}$ (someone/at least one patron) to [$_{Agr_O}$ every critic [$_{VP}$ someone/at least one patron$_i$ tell (every critic) that he$_i$ hated the play]]]

The interaction between scope and binding illustrated here cannot be easily duplicated in a grammar that delivers quantifier scope via QR yet retains the standard binding theory. The problem arises because in such a theory, relative quantifier scope is sensitive to the $\bar{A}$-positions of $\bar{A}$-chains whereas binding is sensitive to the A-positions of these chains. For example, a quantified object can take scope over a subject by QRing over it while the subject remains outside the VP shell in some [Spec, IP] from which it can bind into the adjunct. So, for example, with QR in the LF arsenal, (25) is a perfectly fine LF representation of (20c). Here, the object takes scope over the subject, and the subject binds into the adjunct.

(25) [every woman$_i$ [someone$_j$ [$_{Agrs}$ t_j [$_{Agr_O}$ t_i [$_{VP}$[t_j [$_{VP}$ t_j serenaded t_i] before he$_i$ left the party]]]]]]

In sum, a QR-based theory fails to capture dependencies between relative quantifier scope and binding. The reason is that the grammatical expression of quantifier scope—the QRed expression—is different from the object relevant for Case and binding effects in such a theory. The former is a matter of $\bar{A}$-chain structure whereas the latter is the province of A-chain configuration. The present proposal identifies scope markers and anaphoric anchors. The c-command domain of the same grammatical element determines both its binding properties and relative scope. We thus expect one to potentially restrict the other.[21]

3.3 Some Crosslinguistic Considerations

Thus far, I have argued that English QSIs can be accounted for without LF $\bar{A}$-movement. The structure of A-chains suffices. The $\bar{A}$-operation I have considered has been QR, and the A-chains at issue are those driven by Case theory. However, the logic of the proposal is more general than this. Japanese scrambling constructions manifest a version of the same logic.[22]

Saito (1992) demonstrates that clause-internal scrambling (CIS) and long-distance scrambling (LDS) are quite different operations. CIS is an instance of A-movement, LDS an instance of Ā-movement. A-movement is distinguished from Ā-movement in two ways. A-movement rescinds weak crossover (WCO) effects and licenses anaphoric binding. English raising constructions illustrate this.

(26) a. no one$_i$ seems to his$_i$ mother [t_i to be ugly]
   b. the men$_i$ seem to each other$_i$ [t_i to be ugly]

The matrix subjects in (26) are able to licitly bind the indicated pronoun/ reciprocal. The fact that this is possible indicates that the trace in the embedded clause is the residue of A-movement. When the trace is the residue of Ā-movement, neither binding is permitted.

(27) a. *who$_i$ does it seem to his$_i$ mother [t_i is ugly]
   b. *which men$_i$ does it seem to each other$_i$ [t_i are ugly]

In Japanese, CIS functions like raising whereas LDS resembles *wh*-movement. (28) indicates that CIS obviates WCO effects. (29) shows that it licenses reciprocal binding.

(28) a. ?*[Masao-wa [Hanako-ga   pro$_i$ yomu mae-ni] dono hon$_i$-o
         Masao-TOP Hanako-NOM   read   before   which book-ACC
         yondal] no
         read   Q
         'Masao read which book before Hanako read'
   b.   dono hon$_i$-o   [Masao-wa [Hanako-ga e_i yomu mae-ni]
         which book-ACC Masao-TOP Hanako-NOM   read   before
         [t_i yonda]] no
            read   Q
         'which book did Masao read before Hanako read it'

(29) a. ?*[Masao-ga [[otagai$_i$-no   sensei]-ni [karera$_i$-o
         Masao-NOM   each other-GEN teacher to   they-ACC
         syookaisita]]] (koto)
         introduced   (fact)
         'Masao introduced them to each other's teachers'
   b.   [karera$_i$-o [Masao-ga   [[otagai$_i$-no   sensei]-ni [t_i
         they-ACC Masao-NOM   each other-GEN teacher to
         syookaisita]]]] (koto)
         introduced   (fact)
         'them, Masao introduced to each other's teachers'

In contrast, LDS induces WCO effects and fails to license reciprocal binding, as in (30a) and (30b), respectively.

(30) a. *dono ronbun$_i$-ni-mo [sore$_i$-no tyosya]-ga [John-ga t_i
every paper-DAT it-GEN author-NOM John-NOM
manzokusita to] omotteiru (koto)
was satisfied COMP thinks (fact)
'*every paper$_i$, its$_i$ author thinks that John was satisfied with'

b. *[karera$_i$-o [Masao-ga [otagai$_i$-no sensei]-ni [$_{CP}$[$_{IP}$
them-ACC Masao-NOM each other-GEN teacher to
Hanako-ga t_i hihansita] to] itaa]] (koto)
Hanako-NOM criticized COMP said (fact)
'*them$_i$, Masao said to each other's teachers that Hanako criticized t_i'

What happens with respect to relative quantifier scope? As is well known, without scrambling, relative quantifier scope in Japanese reflects S-Structure c-command relations.[23] Interestingly, CIS induces ambiguities. LDS, in contrast, does not. (31a) is unambiguous. The nominative subject *dareka-ga* must be interpreted as having wide scope. In (31b), however, the accusative *dareka-o* has been clause-internally scrambled, and now either the subject can take scope over the object or conversely. In other words, CIS, a species of A-movement by the standard diagnostic tests, fosters novel QSIs.

(31) a. dareka-ga daremo-o semeta
someone-NOM everyone-ACC blamed
'someone blamed everyone'

b. [dareka-o [daremo-ga [t_i semeta]]]

What of LDS? It is inert. Overt LDS to an Ā-position does not permit the scrambled expression to take wide scope. In (32), *daremo-ni* cannot take scope over the matrix *dareka-ga* despite having been overtly moved there. ((32) is from Bošković and Takahashi 1998.)

(32) daremo$_i$-ni dareka-ga [Mary-ga t_i atta to] omotteiru (koto)
everyone-DAT someone-NOM Mary-NOM met that thinks (fact)
'everyone, someone thinks that Mary met'
= for some person x, x thinks that Mary met every y
≠ for every person y, some person thinks that Mary met y

Saito (1992) provides independent evidence from the scrambling of *wh*-morphemes that LDS in Japanese is semantically inert. He observes that *wh*-elements scrambled outside the domain of their related Q-morphemes are nonetheless licensed at LF, as in (33).

(33) dono hon$_i$-o   [Masao-ga [$_{CP}$[$_{IP}$ Hanako-ga t_i tosoyokan-kara
      which book-ACC Masao-NOM   Hanako-NOM   library-from
      karidasita] ka] siritagatteiru] (koto)
      checked out Q   wants-to-know (fact)
      '*which book, Masao wants to know Hanako checked out from the library'

Saito assumes that lowering is both possible and required at LF. That this is possible follows if indeed the position to which LDS moves a scrambled expression is semantically inert. Were it not, lowering the *wh*-morpheme at LF would violate Full Interpretation.

For our purposes, the interesting fact is that this form of overt Ā-movement seems incapable of altering quantifier-scope patterns whereas A-movement can. This supports the view that QSIs are sensitive to A-movement rather than LF Ā-movement.

This said, things cannot be quite so simple. There are well-known cases of languages in which *overt* Ā-movement does appear to determine the relative scope of quantified expressions. One of the best-studied cases is Hungarian. In Hungarian, D/NPs, whether quantificational or not, are typically moved from IP to various presentential positions. This movement fixes the relative scopes of the QNPs (see É. Kiss 1991 and Szabolesi 1995; examples are from the latter). (34) illustrates this.

(34) a. sok   ember mindenkit felhívott
          many men   everyone   phoned
          = many men > everyone
      b. mindenkit sok ember felhívott
          = everyone > many men

It appears, however, that in the absence of this movement, Hungarian overt structure does *not* disambiguate quantifier scope. Szabolcsi (1995) provides examples of postverbal QNPs that have not been Ā-moved. She indicates that these QNPs enjoy the same scope ambiguities attested in English. In short, for these cases, S-Structure fails to determine relative scope.

(35) egy keddi   napon harapott meg   hatnál több kutya
      a   Tuesday day-on bit-PFX   more than six   dogs bit
      minden fiút
      every boy
      'it was on Tuesday that more than six dogs bit every boy'
      = more than six dogs > every boy
      = every boy > more than six dogs

How are we to interpret these Hungarian facts? First, it seems that relative quantifier scope can piggyback on Ā-chains. This is consistent with the larger picture outlined in the introductory paragraphs, the central idea being that there are no rules *specifically* for fixing quantifier scope. There is no rule of grammar whose concern it is to ensure that quantified expressions reside in scope positions. This, however, does not prohibit quantifier scope from piggybacking on the structure of Ā-operations required for other reasons, as in Hungarian.

Szabolcsi (1995) makes a very interesting proposal in this regard. She argues that pre-IP positions in Hungarian make rather specific informational demands on the expressions that inhabit them. In contrast to positions occupied by expressions in Japanese LDSs, these positions are semantically active. As evidence for this, Szabolcsi argues that the QNPs in presentential position in Hungarian are not actually interpreted as (generalized) quantifiers, in contrast to the interpretation of such expressions in postverbal positions in Hungarian or quite generally in English. Rather, the pre-IP positions in Hungarian have more specific interpretive requirements associated with them. The structure of the clause, she proposes, is (36).[24]

(36) [Topic* [Quantifier* [Focus [Negation [Verb [NP*]]]]]]

Nominal elements in the first three positions, Szabolcsi insists, are not interpreted simply as quantifiers. This is not surprising for elements in Topic and Focus positions, whose informational contributions to interpretation have been well studied. However, Szabolcsi argues that even QNPs in the "Quantifier" slot are not interpreted as generalized quantifiers but rather "provide subjects of predication" in more or less complex ways. Only some kinds of D/NPs can do as much. Those that cannot are barred from this position just as certain D/NPs are barred from being Foci or Topics because they cannot fulfill the informational requirements these positions demand.

If Szabolcsi is correct, then it is possible to combine the English and Japanese facts with the Hungarian ones as follows. Deletion of copies is free, but the resulting LF structure must be interpretable. If pre-IP positions make interpretive demands, then the deletion process must leave a copy in these positions. But because only one copy can survive to the C-I interface, this will freeze the relative scopes of expressions that move there. This is what happens in Hungarian, if Szabolcsi is correct. If, however, the landing sites of movement are not associated with any specific informational tasks, as for example in Case positions or LDS positions, then the general properties of the grammar have free play and we end up with the English and Japanese data reviewed above.

One further point is worth mentioning in the context of the Minimalist Program. The considerations in the introductory paragraphs strongly suggest that if $\bar{\text{A}}$-movement obtains in a grammar, it should be overt. What is minimalistically awkward is covert $\bar{\text{A}}$-movement. This is consistent with the data above.

The overall picture that emerges concerning QSIs is the following. Relative quantifier scope is computed from structures required for independent grammatical reasons. There are no quantifier scope rules per se in the grammar. Rather, quantifier scope is determined by deleting copies that movement induces, leaving but one at the C-I interface. Which copy survives determines what sort of binding can occur, what the relative scopes of the expressions can be, and what informational structure the sentence can bear. The interaction of all of these factors should be the norm.

The empirical virtue of this picture is that it provides a way of dealing with the crosslinguistic variety QSIs manifest. Consider one last example. The Romance languages appear to allow certain kinds of QSIs but not others. For example, it is apparently difficult for a subject to take scope under an object in Spanish. It is considerably easier for an indirect object to take scope over a direct object, however. Thus, *todos dios* can take scope over *alguien* in (37a) but it cannot take scope over *un libro* in (37b).[25]

(37) a. alguien   vio a todos dios
        someone saw   everyone
     b. Juan dio   un libro a todos dios
        Juan gave a   book to everyone

Why this contrast? Recent work by Barbosa (1994) is suggestive. She argues that Romance subjects are in fact topics.[26] If this is correct, then we would expect subject positions in Romance to pattern like those in Hungarian; namely, we would expect their overt positions to be their scope positions. In other words, as in Hungarian, copies of elements in [Spec, Topic] would have to be retained in order to meet Full Interpretation. This, in turn, requires deleting all other copies. As a result, the scope position of subjects in Romance is, in effect, frozen in the Topic slot. Nonsubjects, however, are not topics and so their scope interactions should pattern like those found in English. The data in (37) are consistent with this.[27]

3.4   Doing without Agr Positions

The above analysis of QSIs makes critical use of Agr projections. Chomsky (1995) has subjected these projections to a minimalist critique, concluding that they are superfluous and so should be eliminated from Universal Grammar. This raises the technical issue of whether the above analysis can be duplicated using this sparser phrase structure.

Before I argue that it can be, one methodological point is worth making. The Minimalist Program is just that: a *program*. It outlines a worthy goal: to see how close we can get to a theory guided by concerns of simplicity and conceptual necessity. Assume for a moment that its strictures prove to be too austere in some domain and that some of its ideals clash with what we take to be an empirically well supported theory. What are our methodological options? There are at least two. We could decide that the analysis should be set aside and that we should stick to our minimalist principles. Or we could decide to retain the analysis and retreat from the minimalist assumptions that clash with it. Neither alternative is in and of itself preferred. Minimalism is not a theory but a set of guidelines for constructing grammatical theories. These guidelines gain their interest from being both conceptually elegant and empirically adequate. Pretty principles with short empirical reach do nobody any good. Consequently, being minimalistically suspect does not imply that Agrs should be dispensed with. It simply argues that an analysis that can do equally well without them is better off. As it happens, the above analysis can do without them.

Let's return to the analysis itself. The key element is that quantifier scope is grammatically a free rider. It exploits the structures made available by other processes. In English, this other process is Case checking. Chains formed by checking Case interact with a deletion process constrained to yield single-membered chains to provide D/NPs with their scopes. Agrs are implicated to the degree that Case is checked in the specifiers of Agr projections. To see what a theory without Agrs looks like, we must consider how Case is checked when Agrs are eliminated.

Chomsky proposes the following technology. Lexical elements are bundles of features. Among these are "formal features" (FFs) that include categorial, Case, and number features among others. All nominal expressions receive Case features, as previously. However, at LF, feature bundles rather than categories move to accommodate checking requirements.[28] An illustration will clarify matters.

Accusative Case is checked at LF by raising the FFs of the object and adjoining them to those of the verb. The verbal FFs have risen to T to check V (erbal)-features such as tense and agreement. (38) displays the relevant LF structure. Call the formal features of a constituent A $FF(A)$. The element from which the FF(A) moves is A. I assume, following Chomsky, that the FFs adjoin to the elements that check the relevant features. Hence, FF(V) raises to T to check nominative Case and FF (Obj) raises to V to check accusative Case. I similarly assume that (FF(V), V), (FF (Obj), Obj), and (Subj, Subj) are the relevant chains formed by these operations.

(38)

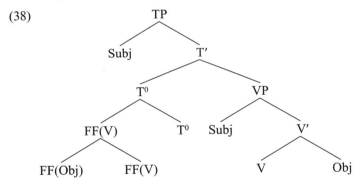

Given structures like (38), it is possible to mirror the account in section 3.1 on the following assumptions:

(39) a. FF (X) and X have the same quantificational force.
       b. FF (V) raises to T at LF and FF (Obj) raises to V at LF, leaving copies of the moved FFs behind.
       c. Any chain member can delete and all but one must.
       d. In (38), Subj in [Spec, TP] c-commands FF (Obj), and FF (Obj) adjoined to FF (V) c-commands Subj in [Spec, VP].

(39a) allows the scope of an expression to be represented by its FFs. Chomsky (1995, 273ff.) notes that FFs are potential binders. This increases their powers to include quantificational force. This in turn allows FF adjunction to fully mimic the effects of category raising to Agr. (39b) states that features are checked at LF by raising FFs. This is essentially Chomsky's main proposal for LF operations, which is assumed here. It is a necessary part of his elimination of Agr projections.[29] (39c) restates the key deletion mechanism of the analysis in section 3.1. In particular, the free deletion process permits "lowering" at LF, and this is responsible for getting subjects in the scope of objects. (39d) amounts to adopting the definition of c-command in (40) and the assumption that if a node B excludes a node C, then B does not dominate C. Hence, in (38), T' dominates FF (Obj) but neither FF (V) nor T^0 does. (40) differs from more standard definitions (e.g., Aoun and Sportiche 1983) in that all projections, not just maximal ones, count.

(40) A c-commands B iff every node that dominates A dominates B.

With this translation manual, an Agr-less analysis accounts for the data reviewed above.[30] The reason is that it expresses the same general sentiments as the prior version. In particular, it divorces the domains of Case and θ requirements, and it gives enough structure to feature-checking chains to support the attested scope interactions.[31] The verb (or its features) checks FF (Obj) after raising out of the VP shell to T^0. Thus, accusative Case is checked within the TP and θ-endowed within the VP.

A key feature of the revised approach is the definition of c-command. (39d)/(40) aim to achieve a particular end: objects can take scope over subjects only if subjects "lower" to [Spec, VP] at LF, that is, only if the copy of the subject chain deletes and the copy in [Spec, VP] is retained. This is crucial, for it permits this technology to account for the correlation between scope and binding reviewed in section 3.2. As an illustration, consider (20c) once again.

(20) c. someone$_i$ serenaded every woman before he$_i$ left the party

Someone cannot take scope under *every woman* in (20c). Given FF movement, (20c) has the LF structure (41) prior to deletion.

(41) [$_{TP}$ someone [[FF (every) + FF (serenade)] + Past] [$_{VP}$[$_{VP}$ someone serenaded every woman] before he . . .]]

(39c) requires deletion of all but one member of every chain. If *someone* in

[Spec, TP] is deleted and FF (*every*) is retained, the result is an LF structure in which the object takes scope over the subject. However, here *someone* cannot bind the pronoun, as it fails to c-command it. To bind the pronoun, we must retain the copy in [Spec, TP]. But in this position, *someone* must take scope over the *every* phrase, as it c-commands all copies of the *every* chain.

Consider what happens if we replace (39d)/(40) with a definition of c-command that permits FF (*every*) adjoined to FF (V) to take scope over the subject in [Spec, TP]. A version of Aoun and Sportiche's (1983) definition will do, as it ignores intermediate projections in calculating c-command. If adopted, this definition both allows the object to take scope over the subject and allows the subject to bind into the adjunct. (42) licenses both aspects of this interpretation (curly brackets indicate deletion), as FF (*every*) c-commands *someone* in [Spec, TP] and *someone* in [Spec, TP] c-commands *he*.

(42) [$_{TP}$ someone [[FF (every) + FF (serenade)] + Past] [$_{VP}$[$_{VP}$ {someone}
      serenaded {every woman}] before he . . .]]

As this reading is unavailable for (20c), we must assume that the correct definition of c-command is the one given in (39)/(40).[32]

This conclusion has an interesting theoretical consequence. Chomsky (1995, 377), following Reinhart (1995), proposes integrating QR into the Minimalist Program as a last resort principle. He assumes that a Q can adjoin to either T^0 or V.[33] It does so if T or V has an LF affix feature able to host such FF(Q). This feature is licensed iff it leads to an interpretation not otherwise available.[34] Note that the structure that results from such proposed raising is entirely identical to (42). However, if the structure in (42) is correct, this configuration fails to allow the object to take scope over the subject. Thus, this way of integrating QR into the Minimalist Program is empirically inadequate. To my knowledge, there is no other concrete proposal for consistently integrating QR into the Minimalist Program.

The discussion in this section points to two conclusions. First, it is possible to cover the ground reviewed in section 3.2 in an Agr-less grammar. However, doing this requires exploiting "lowering" rules in the grammar, namely, some version of (5)/(39c). This device is essential.[35] Second, once such lowering exists, other QR-like devices are both unnecessary and empirically awkward. In the next section, I rebut some empirical arguments purporting to show that lowering does not exist.

3.5 Arguments against Lowering

The key technical innovation of the present analysis is to allow the equivalent of "lowering" or "reconstruction" in A-chains. This is achieved through the combination of two other processes. Movement leaves behind copies—(3c)/(39b)—and all but one copy in a chain must delete—(5)/(39c). The fact that deletion is unconstrained allows for reconstruction effects when higher copies are deleted and lower ones retained. I have proposed that interpretive considerations might prevent the deletion of certain copies; for example, [Spec, Topic] might have to be filled at LF for interpretive reasons at the C-I interface.[36] However, there is no grammatical restriction on what can or must delete and, as a result, there is no principled prohibition against "lowering" operations. However, empirical arguments have been raised against allowing reconstruction in A-chains. it is the purpose of this section to defuse them.

Chomsky and Lasnik (1993) argue against A-lowering rules based on the following data:

(43) a. everyone didn't leave
      b. everyone seems not to have left

They argue that *everyone* in (43a) can be interpreted as being in the scope of matrix negation. In contrast, *everyone* in (43b) cannot be interpreted as being in the scope of the embedded negation. If lowering/reconstruction were available, however, we would expect the latter to support this interpretation, as after lowering the relation between the reconstructed *everyone* and the embedded *not* is analogous to the one between the matrix *everyone* and the matrix *not* in (43a). In effect, we would expect (44) to be a possible LF structure.

(44) [(everyone) seems [everyone not to [have [(everyone) left]]]]

This argument has an empirical flaw. Consider (45).

(45) a. John would prefer for everyone not to leave
      b. John wants very much for everyone not to leave

These sentences do not support interpretations in which *not* takes scope over *everyone*. It appears that a nonreduced *neg* in an embedded clause does not take scope over an adjacent *everyone*. Thus, even if lowering were permitted in (43b), we would not expect the interpretation that Chomsky and Lasnik observe to be absent.[37]

Chomsky (1994, n. 27) provides two further arguments. He observes that (46) can only be understood as a Principle B violation.

(46) John$_i$ expected [him$_i$ to seem to me [t to be intelligent]]

However, were reconstruction possible, the violation should be obviated, with *him* appearing in the position of *t* c-commanded by *me*. The relevant LF structure is (47).

(47) John expected [(him) to seem to me [him to be [(him) intelligent]]]

There are two responses to this argument. First, it is empirically suspect. Chomsky does not state which version of the binding theory he has in mind, but he seems to be assuming that *me* in (47) can function like an intervening subject to block Principle B. This assumption is unsupported. Were it true, we would expect that *him* could be coindexed with *John* in (48), since *Mary* c-commands it (as indicated by the Principle C violation in (49)). However, it is marginal (at best) for *John* to antecede *him* in (48). But if so, then the fact that the same holds in (47) is what we expect.

(48) John expected it to be preferred by Mary for him to be intelligent

(49) *John expected it to be preferred by her$_i$ that Mary$_i$ to be intelligent

There is a second reply to this argument, even assuming that the data are unequivocal. There are resources within the Minimalist Program for dealing with Chomsky's observations if we adopt two assumptions about the interpretation of LF structures at the C-I interface.

(50) a. A definite argument must be outside the lexical shell at LF.
     b. Intermediate chain links are invisible at the C-I interface.

(50a) is a version of the mapping hypothesis advocated by Diesing (1992), building on work by Heim (1982) and Kratzer (1989). It prevents definites from receiving an interpretation at the C-I interface if they reside within the VP shell.[38]

Chomsky (1995, 300ff.) proposes (50b) and provides both theory-internal and empirical motivation for it. The proposal gains naturalness if one thinks of chains on analogy with X′ projections. Both are constructed objects within the Minimalist Program. Both have "tops," "bottoms," and "middles." In both cases, the "middles" are invisible at the C-I interface. If X-bar structure is functionally interpreted, then it is very natural to think of chain structure in this way as well. In effect, then, the head of a chain is analogous to XP and the tail is similar to X^0. This makes intermediate links similar to X's. In the Minimalist Program, X's are invisible at the C-I interface (Chomsky 1995). By parity of reasoning, intermediate chain positions should be invisible as well. (50b) makes this assumption explicit.

Let's now return to the LF structure of (46) prior to deletion.

(47) John expected [$_{IP}$ him to seem to me [$_{IP'}$ him to be [$_{AP}$ him intelligent]]]

Him moves twice, resulting in a three-member chain. (50b) renders the second copy in [Spec, IP'] invisible at the C-I interface. (50a) requires the lowest copy to delete, as it is definite. This leaves only the head of the chain as a viable candidate for interpretation at the C-I interface. However, this copy cannot be anteceded by *John* without violating Principle B. In short, (50) directly accounts for Chomsky's observation.

It similarly handles Chomsky's other case. Chomsky observes that the PRO in (51) has the "quasi-agentive status commonly conferred on the 'surface subject' position" (1994, 436, n. 27).

(51) PRO to appear [*t* to be [*t* intelligent]] is harder than one might think

The PRO originates inside the lexical shell of *intelligent*, whence it receives its θ-role. It then raises twice. On the assumption that arbitrary PRO is definite and that intermediate links are invisible, the only place that PRO can appear and receive an interpretation at the interface is the head position of the A-chain, as Chomsky suggests.

It is reasonable to treat arbitrary PRO as definite. Its meaning is roughly equivalent to that of the impersonal pronoun *one*. (52) is a close paraphrase of (51).

(52) for one to appear to be intelligent is harder than one might think

Note that neither *one* nor PRO can appear in *there* constructions, which follows if both are definite.

(53) a.   one might be indicted for this
      b.   *there might be one indicted for this
      c.   *John expects there to be PRO indicted for this

In sum, given that arbitrary PRO and pronouns are definites and assuming (50), we can fully account for the examples noted by Chomsky and still allow reconstruction in A-chains.

Consider one further set of arguments against reconstruction in A-chains.[39] If reconstruction is free, what prevents the binding of anaphors in overt subject position?[40]

(54) a. *himself likes John
　　 b. *each other like the men

In other words, what prevents an LF structure like (55) after lowering?[41]

(55) [$_{IP}$ (himself) [$_{Agr_O}$ John [$_{VP}$ himself likes (John)]]]

In (55), the anaphor is c-commanded by an appropriate antecedent and so should be acceptable.

It is evident that unacceptability follows since anaphors are definites. As a result, (50a) requires that the copy inside the VP shell delete. This leaves (56) as the only interpretable LF structure of (54). In (56), the anaphor c-commands its antecedent.

(56) [$_{IP}$ himself [$_{Agr_O}$ John [$_{VP}$ (himself) likes (John)]]]

If (54) is embedded in a raising construction, similar unacceptability results.

(57) *himself seems to Bill to be intelligent

(57) has the LF structure (58) in which licit binding of the anaphor is impossible.

(58) [himself seems to Bill [(himself) to be [(himself) intelligent]]]

The most deeply embedded copy is deleted by (50a). The copy in the embedded subject position is invisible by (50b). Thus, the only copy that is licit at the C-I interface is the one in matrix subject position. This copy, however, c-commands its antecedent.

Note that licit binding results if the strictures in (50) are respected. For example, if an indefinite NP containing an anaphor is raised, binding is acceptable.

(59) pictures of himself seem to Bill to be beautiful

(60) [(pictures of himself) seem to Bill [(pictures of himself) to be [pictures of himself beautiful]]]

(60) is a possible licit LF structure. The matrix copy of the chain is deleted and the embedded subject is invisible by (50b). The deepest member of the chain inside the lexical shell is retained. This is licit, as the NP is indefinite and so adheres to (50a).[42]

In this section, I have considered various arguments against reconstruction in A-chains and have shown them to be either empirically suspect or accommodatable while still permitting A-chain reconstruction. I conclude, therefore, that A-chain reconstruction is a licit process.

3.6   Conclusion

I argued in the introductory paragraphs that the Minimalist program does not easily embrace LF Ā-movement rules like QR and that A-movement has certain charms given minimalist assumptions. Further, I argued that the quantifier-scope effects that motivated QR in GB theories can be handled with the sorts of A-movements that the Minimalist Program makes central if we assume that reconstruction in A-chains is possible. In my view, there is an additional strong conceptual reason—mentioned briefly above but important to stress here—for thinking that this treatment of QSIs is right for a minimalist theory. A key feature of the Minimalist Program is that it divorces the domains of θ-role assignment and feature checking (and in this regard contrasts with GB-style theories). The former takes place inside the lexical shell. Objects typically receive roles in complement positions; external arguments typically receive them in a specifier-head configuration. Features, in contrast, are generally checked outside the lexical shell in specifier-head configurations or adjunction to X^0s, depending on which vintage minimalist theory one consults. This division of grammatical labor suffices to get an account like that in section 3.1 off the ground. Without it, QSIs can be integrated into the grammar only by means of operations like QR. The fact that the present account critically exploits such deep-seated minimalist assumptions speaks to its naturalness given minimalist concerns. Combined with its theoretical virtues (mooted in the introduction) and its empirical advantages (displayed in sections 3.2–3.4), the viability of an A-chain approach to QSIs makes any resort to QR-like operations an unwanted encumbrance to a minimalist theory.

Notes

Some of the material in this chapter is further elaborated in Hornstein 1995. A somewhat similar approach to quantifier-scope interactions is proposed in Kitahara 1996. Research on this chapter was supported by NSF grant SBR 9601559.

1. For a contrasting vision of how grammars integrate quantifiers, see Beghelli 1993.

2. This assumption holds in most of the theories of QR in the GB literature. See, for example, May 1985 and Aoun and Li 1993. These two influential works allow (and empirically require) QPs to adjoin to any XP.

3. It is also necessary to eliminate the other Ā-movement operations at LF, such as *wh*-raising. See Hornstein 1995 for some suggestions. For alternatives, see Reinhart 1995, Tsai 1994.

4. The clause-boundedness of QR has been widely observed (see Aoun and Hornstein 1985; Chomsky 1975; Chierchia 1995; Cooper 1983; May 1977).

5. This point was brought to my attention by Alan Munn.

6. I emphasize "roughly," for not all Case positions are thematic.

7. Chomsky, adverting to Hale and Keyser 1993, suggests that this in turn follows from an interpretation of θ-roles as essentially relational.

8. Uriagereka (this volume) argues that the Minimalist Program does not require that LF and PF be levels. The analysis presented below survives using his alternative assumptions.

9. (4) is not a principle of grammar. Rather, it is a correspondence rule relating grammatical structure to semantic interpretation. It observes that there is a correlation between semantic scope and syntactic c-command and states what the relation is. Why this relation obtains is an interesting question. A natural answer is that semantic interpretation rules exploit syntactic structure (e.g., interpretation is bottom up using LF trees). Why c-command is the relevant notion is addressed by Epstein (this volume) and Uriagereka (this volume).

10. This means that it rejects the view that "reconstruction" can be reduced to some yet-to-be-specified property of operator-variable structures as Chomsky suggests.

11. There have been persistent claims that the reading in which the object takes scope over the subject is in some ways marked (see Chomsky 1995; Pica and Snyder 1995; Reinhart 1995). Even if this is so, which I believe is unclear at best, it is quite easy to force the "marked" readings. Thus, on the favored reading of (i), each poem is recited by a different girl; that is, the object takes scope over the subject.

(i) a different girl recited every poem

The substantive points argued for in this section can be made using *a different N* in place of the simple indefinite.

12. I abstract away from possible V-movement at LF. See section 3.4 for discussion.

13. Juan Uriagereka has pointed out to me that the fact that the subject is interpreted as taking scope over the object in three out of four of the grammatical LF structures could be the source of the reported preference for interpreting the subject as having wide scope.

14. Several theories of QSI have this character (see, e.g., May 1985; Aoun and Li 1993). This said, a grammatical theory is more empirically exposed, and thus more interesting, to the degree that it structurally disambiguates interpretation. Of course, this demand might have other untoward consequences. However, methodologically, it is the one to start with.

15. QNPs inside PPs also enter into QSIs in English. The approach outlined above can be extended to accommodate these cases as well. For details, see Hornstein 1995, 175–177.

16. It is not chains that have scope but members of chains. This contrasts with approaches in terms of "chain" scope (see Aoun and Li 1993; Barss 1986).

17. This assumes that control is not reduced to movement as proposed in Hornstein 1999a. If control is reduced in this way, further assumptions are required to cover these facts (for details, see Hornstein, 1999b). Interestingly, it appears that not all control structures block QR. In effect, many seem to pattern like raising structures, though others do not. For the nonce, I assume that the standard description (due to Burzio (1986)) is correct: control contrasts with raising in blocking QR.

18. This is an important point. The structure of Case (A-) chains is motivated quite independently of the theory of quantifier scope. The fact that it suffices to handle an interesting range of QSIs as well puts a considerable methodological burden on those who wish to augment the theory of grammar by including QR, a rule whose sole purpose is to integrate quantificational data into linguistic theory.

19. We can interpret this LF structure as follows. Assume propositions are interpreted post-LF in tripartite fashion (in the style of Heim 1982); that is, the proposition is divided into quantifiers, restrictors, and nuclei. This puts the quantifiers out on the left, followed by the restrictors and then the nuclear scope. This gives an LF structure like (17) the interpretation (i).

(i) every x, some y [[(musician y) & (x piece of music y knew)] → y played x]

20. This is contra Larson 1988. It is consistent with the assumptions in Chomsky 1995.

21. GB theories that determine scope at S-Structure similarly predict interactions between scope and binding. The problem with these theories is that they are incapable of accommodating the basic quantifier scope facts unaided. In effect, QR-like rules are introduced. See Williams 1986, Hornstein and Weinberg 1990 for discussion. More recent proposals in Reinhart 1995 suffer from similar failings; see section 3.4.

22. I assume in what follows that scrambling is indeed movement to the scrambled position. See Saito 1992 for discussion. However, there is another option (explored in Bošković and Takahashi 1998), in which the "scrambled" expression is lowered at LF. Bošković and Takahashi's analysis is compatible with the proposal in section 3.1, so I consider the implications of the more standard treatment here.

23. See Aoun and Li 1993 for the most elaborate discussion of this. For a reanalysis of their results in a framework similar to the one outlined in section 3.2, see Hornstein 1995, chap. 8.

24. The "*" indicates that several of these expressions can occur here. Szabolcsi notes that (36) is inspired by work by Beghelli (1993).

25. These judgments are somewhat idealized. There appears to be quite a bit of idiolectal variation here.

26. This was first suggested by Jaeggli (1982).

27. Barbosa distinguishes French from the other Romance languages. Recently, Manzini and Savoia (1998) have argued that French subjects are also Topics.

28. It does not matter here why this is so and what reasons Chomsky provides in favor of this assumption. Nor does it matter for current purposes whether or not Chomsky is correct that a theory that moves features is preferable to one that moves categories. I here adopt Chomsky's assumptions to see whether they can support an empirically adequate account of QSIs.

29. In fact, Chomsky (1995, 270ff.) goes further. If only feature bundles move at LF, then, he argues, the only permissible operation is adjunction. If so, movement to [Spec, Agr] is impossible.

30. As the data in section 3.3 all involve overt movement, the analysis mooted there remains the same given the revised assumptions in (39).

31. Note that this requires FF(D) to check Case, not FF(N). The reason is that it is Ds, not Ns, that have quantificational force. If scope piggybacks on Case chains, it must be D-features that check Case.

32. One is tempted to go further. Epstein (this volume) argues that c-command is not a grammatical primitive. Instead, it reflects the derivational history of the string. If so, then [spec, TP] must asymmetrically c-command T^0, as it is adjoined to T', which dominates T^0. If we assume that the overt relations are preserved at LF, then elements that adjoin to T^0 or adjoin to elements adjoined to T^0 must remain asymmetrically c-commanded by [Spec, TP]. In effect, what covert movement does is allow elements that move at LF to receive c-command domains by participating in the derivational history of the overt elements they have adjoined to and become parts of. Chomsky has suggested (MIT class lectures, 1995) that feature bundles actually become integrated into the feature matrix of the head to which they adjoin. If this is so, they cannot have scope greater than that of the head of which they are a part. Combined with Epstein's account, this would restrict the c-command domain of FFs moving at LF to the heads that they combine with, as the definition in (39)/(40) states.

33. Chomsky actually proposes that it adjoins to T or v, the verbal element that licenses external arguments. Presumably, FF (v) can host the Q-feature as well.

34. This is also problematic. As stated, it should permit unbounded QR. For example, it should be possible for the *every* phrase to take scope over the matrix subject if the matrix T or V has this affix feature.

(i) someone said that Bill talked to everyone about Mary QR should also freely violate the ECP, contrary to fact.

35. The specific version of the Agr-less approach developed here relies on raising V-features at LF. However, if Vs are not in TP at LF (see Lasnik 1999; Hornstein 1995, chap. 5), then there seems little hope of covering the data reviewed here. It seems necessary to raise D/NP expressions out of the VP shell if QSIs are to be accounted for. This can be done by exploiting Agr projections, adjoining to raised Vs, or overtly raising objects prior to Spell-Out. If lowering is involved in QSIs, as argued above, there are no other plausible alternatives.

36. It is unclear at this point whether this implies that the derivation converges but receives a "gibberish" interpretation or that it fails to converge because it receives no adequate interpretation. As the former is conceptually the better option, I assume it until there is evidence that the stronger version is required.

37. A variant of this argument is provided by Lasnik and Saito (1992). See Hornstein 1995, 244, n. 54, for discussion.

38. There is no reason for treating the mapping hypothesis as a convergence condition. I assume here that LF structures that fail to respect it result in gibberish.

39. These were brought to my attention by Joseph Aoun and Howard Lasnik.

40. The case mismatch in (54a) is irrelevant to the main point, as a similar problem arises with (i).

(i) *I expect for himself to like John

41. I represent this using Agr$_O$ as it is easier to visualize. The same structure can be recreated in an Agr-less structure.

42. In Hornstein 1995, chap. 8, I discuss effects of (50a) in the context of WCO constructions. The anaphoric cases are highly problematic for that analysis. These problems are resolved if (50b) is assumed.

References

Aoun, Joseph. 1982. On the logical nature of the binding principles: Quantifier Lowering, double raisings of "there" and the notion empty element. In *Proceedings of NELS 12*, eds. James Pustejovsky and Peter Sells. GLSA, University of Massachusetts, Amherst.

Aoun, Joseph, and Norbert Hornstein. 1985. Quantifier types. *Linguistic Inquiry* 16, 623–636.

Aoun, Joseph, and Yen-hui Audrey Li. 1993. *Syntax of scope*. Cambridge, Mass.: MIT Press.

Aoun, Joseph, and Dominique Sportiche. 1983. On the formal theory of government. *The Linguistic Review* 2, 211–236.

Barbosa, Pilar. 1994. A new look at the null subject parameter. Paper presented at CONSOLE III, University of Venice.

Barss, Andrew. 1986. Chains and anaphoric dependence. Doctoral dissertation, MIT, Cambridge, Mass.

Beghelli, Filippo. 1993. A minimalist approach to quantifier scope. In *NELS 23*, vol. 1, ed. Amy J. Schater. GLSA, University of Massachusetts, Amherst.

Bošković, Željko, and Daiko Takahashi. 1998. Scrambling and Last Resort. *Linguistic Inquiry* 29, 347–366.

Burzio, Luigi. 1986. *Italian syntax*. Dordrecht: Reidel.

Chierchia, Gennaro. 1995. *Dynamics of meaning*. Chicago: University of Chicago Press.

Chierchia, Gennaro, and Sally McConnell-Ginet. 1990. *Meaning and grammar.* Cambridge, Mass.: MIT Press.

Chomsky, Noam. 1975. Questions of form and interpretation. In *Essays on form and interpretation.* Amsterdam: Elsevier, 1977.

Chomsky, Noam. 1982. *Some concepts and consequences of the theory of government and binding.* Cambridge, Mass.: MIT Press.

Chomsky, Noam. 1993. A minimalist program for linguistic theory. In *The View from Building 20: Essays in linguistics in honor of Sylvain Bromberger,* eds. Kenneth Hale and Samuel Jay Keyser. Cambridge, Mass.: MIT Press. [Reprinted in *The Minimalist Program,* Noam Chomsky. Cambridge, Mass.: MIT Press, 1995.]

Chomsky, Noam. 1994. Bare phrase structure. (MIT Occasional Papers in Linguistics 5.) MITWPL, Department of Linguistics and Philosophy, MIT, Cambridge, Mass. [Published in *Evolution and revolution in linguistic theory: Essays in honor of Carlos Otero,* eds. Héctor Campos and Paula Kempchinsky. Washington, D.C.: Georgetown University Press, 1995, and *Government and Binding Theory and the Minimalist Program,* ed. Gert Webelhuth. Oxford: Blackwell, 1995.]

Chomsky, Noam. 1995. Categories and transformations. In *The Minimalist Program,* 219–394. Cambridge, Mass.: MIT Press.

Chomsky, Noam, and Howard Lasnik. 1993. The theory of principles and parameters. In *Syntax: An international handbook of contemporary research,* eds. Joachim Jacobs, Arnim von Stechow, Wolfgang Sternefeld, and Theo Vennemann. Berlin: Walter de Gruyter. [Reprinted in *The Minimalist Program,* Noam Chomsky. Cambridge, Mass.: MIT Press, 1995.]

Cooper, Robin. 1983. *Quantification and syntactic theory.* Dordrecht: Reidel.

Diesing, Molly. 1992. *Indefinites.* Cambridge, Mass.: MIT Press.

Hale, Kenneth, and Samuel Jay Keyser. 1993. On argument structure and the lexical expression of syntactic relations. In *The view from Building 20: Essays in linguistics in honor of Sylvain Bromberger,* eds. Kenneth Hale and Samuel Jay Keyser. Cambridge, Mass.: MIT Press.

Heim, Irene. 1982. The semantics of definite and indefinite noun phrases. Doctoral dissertation, University of Massachusetts, Amherst.

Higginbotham, James. 1980. Pronouns as bound variables. *Linguistic Inquiry* 11, 679–708.

Hornstein, Norbert. 1995. *Logical Form.* Oxford: Blackwell.

Hornstein, Norbert. 1999a. On control. *Linguistic Inquiry* 30, 69–96.

Hornstein, Norbert. 1999b. Movement and chains. *Syntax.*

Hornstein, Norbert, and Amy Weinberg. 1990. The necessity of LF. *The Linguistic Review* 7, 129–167.

Jaeggli, Osvaldo. 1982. *Topics in Romance syntax.* Dordrecht: Foris.

É. Kiss, Katalin. 1991. Logical structure in linguistic structure. In *Logical structure and linguistic structure*, eds. C.-T. James Huang and Robert May. Dordrecht: Kluwer.

Kitahara, Hisatsugu. 1996. Raising quantifiers and Quantifier Raising. In *Minimal ideas*, eds. Werner Abraham, Samuel David Epstein, Höskuldur Thráinsson, and C. Jan-Wouter Zwart. Philadelphia: John Benjamins.

Koopman, Hilda, and Dominique Sportiche. 1991. The position of subjects. *Lingua* 85, 211–258.

Kratzer, Angelika. 1989. Stage and individual level predicates. In *Papers on quantification*. (NSF Grant Report.) Department of Linguistics, University of Massachusetts, Amherst.

Kuroda, S.-Y. 1988. Whether we agree or not. *Lingvisticæ Investigationes* 12, 1–47.

Larson, Richard. 1988. On the double object construction. *Linguistic Inquiry* 19, 335–391.

Lasnik, Howard. 1999. *Minimalist analysis*. Oxford: Blackwell.

Lasnik, Howard, and Mamoru Saito. 1992. *Move α*. Cambridge, Mass.: MIT Press.

Manzini, Maria Rita, and Leonardo M. Savoia. 1998. Parameters of subject inflection in Italian dialects. Ms.

May, Robert. 1977. The grammar of quantification. Doctoral dissertation, MIT, Cambridge, Mass.

May, Robert. 1985. *Logical Form*. Cambridge, Mass.: MIT Press.

Pica, Pierre, and William Snyder. 1995. Weak crossover, scope, and agreement in a minimalist framework. In *Proceedings of the 13th West Coast Conference on Formal Linguistics*, eds. Raul Aranovich, William Byrne, Susanne Preuss, and Martha Senturia. Stanford, Calif.: CSLI Publications. [Distributed by Cambridge University Press.]

Reinhart, Tanya. 1995. *Interface strategies*. Research Institute for Language and Speech, University of Utrecht.

Saito, Mamoru. 1992. Long-distance scrambling in Japanese. *Journal of East Asian Linguistics* 1, 69–118.

Szabolcsi, Anna. 1995. Strategies for scope taking. In *Working papers in the theory of grammar 2.1*. Research Institute for Linguistics, Hungarian Academy of Sciences, Budapest.

Tsai, Wei-tien Dylan. 1994. On economizing the theory of A-bar dependencies. Doctoral dissertation, MIT, Cambridge, Mass.

Williams, Edwin. 1986. A reassignment of the functions of LF. *Linguistic Inquiry* 17, 265–299.

Chapter 4

Eliminating * as a Feature (of Traces)

Hisatsugu Kitahara

From a minimalist perspective, a "perfect language" should meet the Inclusiveness Condition (Chomsky 1995, 228).[1]

(1) No new objects are added in the computation apart from rearrangement of lexical properties.

Recent developments such as the replacement of indexing by the interpretive version of binding theory (Chomsky and Lasnik 1993) and the reduction of (inherent) bar levels to relational properties (Chomsky 1994) meet this condition. As an extension of this (arguably natural) minimalist condition, in this chapter I propose a derivational analysis of movement asymmetries that eliminates *-features (assigned by Chomsky and Lasnik's (1993) *-marking apparatus, a descendant of Lasnik and Saito's (1984, 1992) γ-marking apparatus). The chapter is organized as follows. In section 4.1, I review the central aspects of Chomsky and Lasnik's (1993) *-marking analysis of movement asymmetries. In section 4.2, I propose an alternative analysis that dispenses with *-features. In section 4.3, I examine the timing of feature movement, which is crucial to the proposed analysis. In section 4.4, I extend the proposed analysis to a potential problem. In section 4.5, I discuss a derivational aspect of the proposed analysis.

4.1 *-Features

As is well known, *wh*-island violations involving adjuncts are more severe than *wh*-island violations involving arguments.[2]

(2) ??what do you wonder [CP whether John fixed *t*]

(3) *how do you wonder [CP whether John fixed the car *t*]

In the derivation of (2), the raising of *what* induces a *wh*-island violation and yields marginal deviance. In the derivation of (3), the raising of *how* similarly induces a *wh*-island violation but yields severe deviance. Chomsky and Lasnik (1993) argue that this asymmetry reduces to the difference between the two relevant chains resulting at LF. Following Lasnik and Saito (1984, 1992), they propose that traces created by *wh*-island extraction are uniformly marked * upon their creation (i.e., *-creation is a property of certain movements), and a *-marked trace t^* is taken to be an offending trace at LF (i.e., the appearance of t^* in the LF representation gives rise to severe deviance). Let us examine the central aspects of this *-marking analysis of (2) and (3).

First, consider the following structures assigned to (2) and (3), respectively:

(4) [$_{CP}$ what do you wonder [$_{CP}$ whether John [t^* [$_{VP}$ fixed t]]]]

(5) [$_{CP}$ how do you wonder [$_{CP}$ whether John [t^* [$_{VP}$ fixed the car t]]]]

In each derivation, the long-distance *wh*-movement adjoins the lowest *wh*-category to the embedded verbal projection and then moves it to the specifier of the matrix C. The second half of this successive-cyclic *wh*-movement crosses the *wh*-island, thereby forming a *-marked intermediate trace.[3] Chomsky and Lasnik propose that the creation of such a *-marked trace yields marginal deviance (a Subjacency effect), as stated in (6).

(6) An expression is marginally deviant if its derivation forms a *-marked trace t^*.

The marginal deviance of (2) follows from (6).

Now consider the greater degree of deviance exhibited by (3). To capture this increased deviance, Chomsky and Lasnik incorporate Uniformity Condition into their analysis.[4]

(7) A chain CH is a legitimate LF object only if CH is uniform with respect to P, where P is a property determined at a position of CH.

Given (7), CH = (*what*, t^*, t) (formed by the derivation of (2)) is taken to be nonuniform because its head is in an Ā-position but its tail is in an A-position. By contrast, CH = (*how*, t^*, t) (formed by the derivation of (3)) is taken to be uniform because it consists only of Ā-positions. Appealing to this positional (uniformity-based) distinction, Chomsky and Lasnik propose the following general condition—a special case of the principle of derivational economy (Epstein 1992):

(8) Syntactic operations in general are possible only to form a legitimate LF object.

Given (7) and (8), they argue that deletion is permissible in the nonuniform CH = (*what*, t^*, t) because it is not yet a legitimate LF object (and deletion would make it legitimate), but deletion is impermissible in the uniform CH = (*how*, t^*, t) because it is already a legitimate LF object.[5] In their analysis, therefore, the derivation of (2) deletes an offending trace of CH = (*what*, t^*, t) (yielding (9)), but the derivation of (3) leaves CH = (*how*, t^*, t) unaffected (yielding (10)).

(9) [$_{CP}$ what do you wonder [$_{CP}$ whether John [$_{VP}$ fixed t]]]

(10) [$_{CP}$ how do you wonder [$_{CP}$ whether John [t^* [$_{VP}$ fixed the car t]]]]

Given that the *-marked trace t^* survives only in the derivation of (3) (thereby appearing in (10)), Chomsky and Lasnik propose that the appearance of t^* in the LF representation gives rise to severe deviance (an Empty Category Principle (ECP) effect), stated as (11).

(11) An expression is severely deviant if its derivation fails to delete a *-marked trace t^* (thereby allowing t^* to appear in the LF representation).

The severe deviance of (3) follows from (11).

To summarize, *wh*-island extraction forms a *-marked trace in the derivations of (2) and (3). Such a *-marked trace deletes in the derivation of (2), but not in the derivation of (3). Consequently, (2) exhibits marginal deviance due to the creation of t^*, but (3) exhibits severe deviance due to the creation of t^* and the appearance of t^* in the LF representation. The *-marking analysis thus captures the marginal deviance of (2) and the severe deviance of (3).

As stated above, the *-marking analysis crucially rests on the assumption that a *-feature, which is not a lexical feature—since it appears nowhere in the lexicon—is a feature unique to traces and enters into a derivation as the output of certain movements. It is this assumption that contradicts the Inclusiveness Condition.

4.2 MLC-Violating Applications of Attract

Given that the *-marking analysis violates the Inclusiveness Condition, in this section I propose an alternative analysis (which dispenses with *-features) under the attraction theory of movement (Chomsky 1995).

Chomsky (1995, 297) interprets the movement of α to a position in the checking domain of K as K attracting α instead of as α moving to K.[6] Under this attraction view of movement, he proposes that K attracts α if (a) K c-commands α (Chomsky 1995, 253) and (b) α can enter into a checking relation with K (Chomsky 1995, 280; Lasnik 1995).[7] Given this definition of Attract, let us formulate the shortest movement property as a constraint on the application of Attract: the Minimal Link Condition (MLC).[8]

(12) K cannot attract α if there is β, β closer to K than α, such that K attracts β.

The notion of closeness is understood in terms of c-command (Chomsky 1995, 358).[9]

(13) β is closer to K than α is if β c-commands α.

Given these assumptions, let us return to the contrast between (2) and (3). First, consider (2) (yielding marginal deviance), repeated here.

(2) ??what do you wonder [$_{CP}$ whether John fixed t]

Here, instead of invoking a *-marking apparatus, I propose that the marginal deviance of (2) results directly from employing an application of Attract that raises *what* over *whether*. Given that *whether* (occupying the specifier of the embedded C) c-commands *what* (occupying the complement of the embedded V), *whether* is closer to the matrix C than *what* is. Now suppose that the *wh*-feature of *whether* is +Interpretable; hence, it is accessible throughout the derivation, whether checked or not (Chomsky 1995). Then, a violation of the MLC results when Attract raises *what* over *whether*. This analysis replaces (6) by (14).

(14) An expression is marginally deviant if its derivation employs an MLC-violating application of Attract.

The marginal deviance of (2) follows from (14). Notice that with "constraints on transformations" such as (12), there is no need to mark anything in the course of a derivation.

Now consider (3) (yielding severe deviance), repeated here.

(3) *how do you wonder [$_{CP}$ whether John fixed the car t]

The derivation of (3) similarly employs an application of Attract that raises *how* over *whether* (thereby violating the MLC). But, unlike the derivation of (2), it exhibits severe deviance. The task facing the current approach is to explain this contrast without introducing any new features (such as *-features) into a derivation. Here, instead of the positional (uniformity-based) distinction between the two chains (which determines whether subsequent operations (deletions) can apply to them), I appeal to the following already existing Case-theoretic distinction between *what* and *how*:[10]

(15) *What* bears a Case feature, but *how* does not.

Given (15), I adopt the following general (and independently motivated) condition on feature deletion (Chomsky 1995, 280):[11]

(16) −Interpretable features such as Case features must be deleted for convergence.

The notion of convergence is defined as follows (Chomsky 1995, 220):

(17) A derivation D with a pair (π, λ) converges if π and λ consist only of legitimate objects at PF and at LF, respectively.

Given (16) and (17), it follows that *what* cannot be a legitimate LF object unless its Case feature undergoes deletion. Now suppose that the overt *wh*-movement (to the specifier of the matrix C) precedes an operation deleting the Case feature of *what*.[12] Then, the two instances of *wh*-movement (affecting *what* and *how*, respectively) can be characterized as follows: the *wh*-movement affecting *what* (bearing a Case feature) does not form a legitimate LF object, whereas the *wh*-movement affecting *how* (bearing no Case feature) does form a legitimate LF object.[13] Given this characterization, I propose that the severe deviance of (3) results directly from the employment of an MLC-violating application of Attract that forms a legitimate LF object as its output. This analysis replaces (11) by (18).

(18) An expression is severely deviant if its derivation employs an MLC-violating application of Attract that forms a legitimate LF object as its output.

The severe deviance of (3) follows from (18). Here again, there is no need to mark anything in the course of a derivation.[14]

As shown above, the proposed analysis (incorporating (14) and (18)) captures the marginal deviance of (2) and the severe deviance of (3), and does so with no reference to noninclusive annotations (such as *-features). Note that the analysis appeals to neither the Uniformity Condition nor the positional distinction to determine the legitimacy of LF objects. Also, it dispenses with intermediate traces (including *-marked ones). Consequently, it allows each instance of movement to be one-step movement directly to a checking position.[15]

4.3   Feature Movement

The proposed analysis of the marginal deviance of (2) crucially rests on the assumption that the overt *wh*-movement (to the specifier of the matrix C) precedes a later operation deleting the Case feature of *what*, which is understood to be an instance of feature movement. In this section, I examine the relative ordering of the *wh*-movement and such feature movement.

Chomsky (1995, 262) advances the theory of movement with a new proposal that replaces Attract α by the operation Attract F (F a feature). However, Attract F raises more than F, suggesting that raising of the larger unit containing F is required by the interface conditions. Chomsky proposes that Attract raises F along with just enough material to ensure convergence. To satisfy the articulatory-perceptual (A-P) interface conditions, Attract raises the smallest category containing F (that allows PF convergence). Informally speaking, isolated features and other scattered parts of words are taken to be unpronounceable. If the A-P interface conditions are irrelevant, Attract raises a minimal unit containing F (that allows LF convergence), which is understood to be a collection of formal features FF(F) of F.[16] Adopting these assumptions, I propose the following algorithm:

(19) Attract raising FF(F) from α renders the remaining part of α
        unpronounceable.

Given (19), a violation of Full Interpretation (FI) at PF results when Attract raises FF(F) from α, such that α is a category that needs to be pronounced.[17]

Now recall (2) (yielding marginal deviance), repeated here, and consider how (19) interacts with the derivation of (2).

(2) ??what do you wonder [CP whether John fixed *t*]

Consider the following structure, constructed in the derivation of (2):

(20) [John fixed what]

Suppose that the next step is to check a Case feature of *what* against the verb. There are two possibilities: Attract raises either *what* or FF(*what*).

But notice, the first option, raising *what* (to a position in the checking domain of the verb, from which *what* c-commands *John*), blocks the subsequent subject raising of *John*.[18] Also notice, given (19), the second option, raising FF(*what*), renders *what* (which needs to be pronounced) unpronounceable, thereby inducing a violation of FI at PF. Thus, neither option counts as a step toward convergence; hence, the derivation of (2) proceeds without checking the Case feature of *what*.[19] At some later stage in the derivation, the following structure is constructed:

(21) [what do you wonder whether John fixed *t*]

At this stage, there are two possible ways to check the Case feature of *what* against the verb: Attract raises either the entire trace of *what* or FF(*t*). Here, the subject raising of *John* has already taken place, and the trace of *what* (which bears no PF features) does not enter into the determination of PF legitimacy. Thus, either option appears to be a step toward convergence. But recall that Attract raises F along with just enough material to ensure convergence; hence, feature movement is preferred to category movement, when possible. Thus, Attract raises FF(*t*) to a position in the checking domain of the verb—an instance of feature movement.[20]

As shown above, in the derivation of (2), the overt *wh*-movement (to the specifier of the matrix C) precedes the feature movement deleting the Case feature of *what*, and the ordering of the two operations follows from the analysis of feature movement (incorporating (19)).[21]

4.4   Feature Strength

The following contrast poses a potential problem for the analysis of feature movement just proposed:[22]

(22) *what do you wonder [$_{CP}$ whether [$_{TP}$ *t′* was fixed *t*]]

(23) ??what do you wonder [$_{CP}$ whether Mary thinks [$_{CP}$ [$_{TP}$ *t′* was fixed *t*]]]

In each derivation, a violation of the MLC results when Attract raises *what* over *whether*. The current analysis could capture this contrast if the MLC-violating application of Attract (raising *what* over *whether*) forms a legitimate LF object in the derivation of (22), but not in the derivation of (23). This follows if the deletion of the Case feature of *what* precedes the overt *wh*-movement (to the specifier of the matrix C) in the derivation of (22), but not in the derivation of (23). In this section, I argue that this is in fact the case, providing an account of the above contrast, which requires an elaboration of feature strength.

Chomsky (1995, 234) takes the following to be a descriptive property of feature strength:

(24) Suppose that the derivation D has formed Σ containing α with a strong feature F. Then, D is canceled if α is in a category not headed by α.

Given (24), he argues that the Extended Projection Principle (EPP) reduces to a strong D-feature of T (which is a categorial feature divorced from a Case feature of T). Consider the following structure, in which TP immediately dominates the head T (bearing a strong D-feature) and its complement VP:

(25) [$_{TP}$ T VP]

Suppose, as a next step, that Merge concatenates TP with the head C, forming (26).

(26) [$_{CP}$ C [$_{TP}$ T VP]]

In (26), T with a strong D-feature is dominated by CP, a category not headed by T. Given (24), this derivation (violating the EPP) cancels at this point and never converges. Thus, the deletion of a strong D-feature of T (via the creation of the specifier of T) necessarily precedes the concatenation of TP and C.

Now return to the derivations of (22) and (23). Consider the following structure common to both derivations:

(27) [$_{TP}$ T was fixed what]

Given (24), the next step is to check the strong D-feature of T. There are two possibilities: Attract raises either *what* or FF(*what*). The first option, raising *what*, induces deletion of features including the strong D-feature of T and the Case feature of *what*. The second option, raising FF(*what*), does the same work, but it also renders *what* (which needs to be pronounced) unpronounceable, thereby inducing a violation of FI at PF. Thus, the first option is selected, and Attract raises *what* to a position in the checking domain of T, forming (28).

(28) [$_{TP}$ what [$_{T'}$ T was fixed *t*]]

In (28), the features including the strong D-feature of T and the Case feature of *what* undergo deletion. Consequently, later in the derivation, the *wh*-movement affects *what* (bearing no Case feature) and forms a legitimate LF object. Thus, (24) predicts that each derivation should yield severe deviance—an incorrect result.

Given that (24) is too strong, let us replace it with (29), which interprets feature strength as a defining property of Spell-Out (Kitahara 1997).[23]

(29) Spell-Out applies to Σ only if Σ is free from a strong feature F.

Let us assume that Σ is free from a strong feature F if neither Σ nor its associated numeration contains a category with F.[24] Then, given (29), Spell-Out is applicable to Σ only after F undergoes deletion. This interpretation of feature strength no longer blocks the overt *wh*-movement (to the specifier of the matrix C) from preceding the deletion of a strong D-feature of T. Notice that, after the *wh*-movement but before the application of Spell-Out, Attract can raise FF(t) (t, the direct object trace of *what*) to a position in the checking domain of the most deeply embedded T. Consequently, the features including the strong D-feature of the most deeply embedded T and the Case feature of *what* undergo deletion (before the application of Spell-Out). Recall that this feature movement does not interfere with the determination of PF legitimacy because the trace of *what* bears no PF features. Suppose that each derivation proceeds with this order (with the overt *wh*-movement preceding the deletion of the Case feature of *what*). Then, the *wh*-movement (violating the MLC) affects *what* (bearing a Case feature) and does not form a legitimate LF object. Thus, (29) predicts that each derivation should yield marginal deviance—again, an incorrect result.

Given that (29) is too weak, I suggest a further elaboration of feature strength (supplementary to (29)). Consider (22) and (23), repeated here.

(22) *what do you wonder [$_{CP}$ whether [$_{TP}$ t' was fixed t]]

(23) ??what do you wonder [$_{CP}$ whether Mary thinks [$_{CP}$ [$_{TP}$ t' was fixed t]]]

A (minimal) difference between (22) and (23) is that the former induces an MLC violation involving the subject of the clause headed by C bearing a strong *wh*-feature (a variant of Determiner), whereas the latter induces an MLC violation involving the subject of the clause headed by C bearing no strong *wh*-feature. Taking this difference to be crucial, I propose the following condition (Kitahara 1997):

(30) α and β cannot be concatenated if some sublabel of α and some sublabel of β are both strong.

The construct "sublabel" is defined as follows (Chomsky 1995, 268):

(31) A sublabel of K is a feature of the zero-level projection of the head
H(K) of K (including those features adjoined to H(K)).

Given (30) and (31), the deletion of the strong D-feature of T necessarily precedes the concatenation of TP and C when C bears a strong *wh*-feature. Now return to the derivations of (22) and (23).

In the derivation of (22), the deletion of the strong D-feature of the embedded T must preceded the concatenation of the embedded TP and the embedded C that bears a strong *wh*-feature. This entails that the deletion of the Case feature of *what* must precede the overt *wh*-movement (to the specifier of the matrix C). Consequently, later in the derivation, the *wh*-movement affects *what* (bearing no Case feature) and forms a legitimate LF object. Thus, the derivation of (22) yields severe deviance. By contrast, in the derivation of (23), the deletion of the strong D-feature of the most deeply embedded T need not precede the concatenation of the most deeply embedded TP and the most deeply embedded C that bears no strong *wh*-feature. Suppose that deletion of the strong D-feature of the most deeply embedded T occurs after the overt *wh*-movement (to the specifier of the matrix C) but before the application of Spell-Out. That is, Attract overtly raises FF(t) (left by the *wh*-movement) to a position in the checking domain of the most deeply embedded T—an instance of overt feature movement. Then, the *wh*-movement affects *what* (bearing a Case feature) and does not form a legitimate LF object. Thus, the derivation of (23) yields marginal deviance.

As shown above, under the proposed analysis of feature strength (incorporating (29) and (30)), the contrast between (22) and (23) receives an explanation.[25]

4.5 A Remaining Question

As demonstrated in the preceding sections, the observed contrasts (exhibited by (2)–(3) and (22)–(23)) follow from the current assumptions (none of which appeals to *-features). One remaining question that I address in this section is stated in (32).

(32) Why does an MLC-violating application of Attract yield a greater degree of deviance when it forms a legitimate LF object as its output?

Suppose that only the rule applications forming legitimate LF objects directly instruct the LF system by requiring it to interpret such newly formed LF objects. I take "directly" to mean "derivationally." That is, such rule applications instruct the LF system as the derivation proceeds— a derivational model of syntax (Epstein 1994, this volume; Epstein et al. 1998). Then, informally speaking, increased deviance can be characterized as follows:

(33) Increased deviance is the result of a derivational instruction (provided by the output of an MLC-violating application of Attract) to the LF system.

Given (33), let us briefly review the relevant aspects of the derivations of (2), (3), (22), and (23).

First, consider the two applications of Attract affecting *what* in the derivations of (2) and (23), namely, *wh*-movement (violating the MLC) and feature movement (deleting a Case feature of *what*). In each of these derivations, the *wh*-movement does not make *what* a legitimate LF object because *what* still bears a Case feature. Consequently, it does not allow the LF system to interpret *what* at this point in the derivation. Instead, the subsequent feature movement makes *what* a legitimate LF object because it deletes the Case feature of *what*. Consequently, it requires the LF system to interpret *what* at this later stage. In each derivation, therefore, it is the feature movement (a violation-free application of Attract) that instructs the LF system to interpret *what*.[26]

Now consider the applications of Attract affecting *how* and (passive-subject) *what* in the derivations of (3) and (22), respectively. In each of these derivations, the *wh*-movement (violating the MLC) applies to the *wh*-category bearing no −Interpretable features, thereby making it a legitimate LF object at this point in the derivation. In each derivation, therefore, it is the *wh*-movement (to the specifier of the matrix C) (an MLC-violating application of Attract) that instructs the LF system to interpret the *wh*-category.

Although further research is necessary to attain a more comprehensive understanding of the derivational model of syntax, in which certain rule applications derivationally instruct the LF system, the proposed analysis of movement asymmetries (developed here) has demonstrated that *-features are eliminable by assigning a derivational approach greater prominence.

Notes

I would like to thank Jun Abe, Noam Chomsky, Norbert Hornstein, Yasuhiko Kato, Ruriko Kawashima, Masatoshi Koizumi, Howard Lasnik, Masayuki Oishi, Christopher D. Tancredi, Takashi Toyoshima, Masanobu Ueda, and especially Samuel D. Epstein for valuable comments. All remaining errors are, of course, my own. An earlier version of part of this chapter appeared in *Reports of the Keio Institute of Cultural and Linguistic Studies* 29, 65–78, 1997. The research reported here was supported in part by the Ministry of Education, Science, Sports and Culture (Grant-in-Aid for Encouragement for Young Scientists #10710235) and the Keio University Special Grant-in-Aid Innovative Collaborative Research Project (1997–98).

1. Chomsky (1995, 228) assumes that (1) holds (virtually) of the computation deriving LF representations (but not the computation deriving PF representations).

2. Argument versus adjunct asymmetries such as the one exhibited by (2) and (3) have long occupied the center of syntactic investigation (see, e.g., Aoun 1985; Chomsky 1981, 1986; Cinque 1990; Epstein 1987, 1991, 1992; Huang 1982; Kayne 1984; Lasnik and Saito 1984, 1992; Manzini 1992; Rizzi 1990). For recent discussion of these (and other related) asymmetries, see Hornstein 1995 and the references cited there.

3. In the Minimalist Program, each instance of movement is triggered by the necessity of feature checking (Chomsky 1993, 1994, 1995), and it is arguably one-step movement directly to a position in which feature checking takes place (Abe 1993; Kitahara 1994, 1997). After briefly reviewing Chomsky and Lasnik's (1993) *-marking analysis, which allows successive-cyclic movement, I will propose an alternative analysis that makes no use of non-feature-driven movement to intermediate landing sites. Under this alternative analysis, successive-cyclic movement, if it exists, should be analyzed as separate feature-driven movements (not as a single one-step movement).

4. For detailed discussion of the Uniformity Condition, see, among others, Browning 1987, Chomsky and Lasnik 1993, Fukui 1993, Oishi 1993.

5. Chomsky and Lasnik (1993) assume that operator-variable constructions $CH = (\alpha, \beta)$ are legitimate LF objects if α is in an $\bar{A}$-position and β heads a legitimate (uniform) chain.

6. For detailed discussion of the checking configuration, see Chomsky 1995, 299.

7. The notion of c-command is defined as follows (Chomsky 1986; Reinhart 1976):

(i) K c-commands α iff every category dominating K dominates α, $K \neq \alpha$, and neither dominates the other.

For proposals concerning the deduction of the empirically desirable aspects of (i), see Epstein 1994, this volume, and Epstein et al. 1998.

8. Chomsky (1995, 297–311) proposes that the shortest movement property—the MLC—is a defining property of Attract. But then, by definition, there would be

no MLC-violating movement. Here, I take the MLC to be a constraint on the application of Attract (not a defining property of Attract), and I examine certain MLC-violating movements.

9. Closeness has been interpreted in terms of c-command and equidistance (see, e.g., Chomsky 1993, 1994, 1995; Holmberg 1986; Jonas 1995, 1996; Jonas and Bobaljik 1993; Thráinsson 1993). Here, equidistance is ignored as it is irrelevant to the discussion.

10. Elsewhere (Kitahara 1994, 1997), appealing to (15), I propose a chain formation analysis of movement asymmetries, which dispenses with a *-marking apparatus but necessitates a condition on chain formation. In sections 4.3 and 4.4 of this chapter, I advance the current analysis by reinterpreting the central aspects of the chain formation analysis presented there.

11. Chomsky (1995, 280) distinguishes between deletion and erasure. Here, I ignore the difference between the two operations, as it does not affect any of my proposals.

12. In section 4.3, I examine the ordering of *wh*-movement and an operation deleting the Case feature of *what*.

13. I assume that PF features (which are relevant only to PF) do not enter into the determination of LF legitimacy.

14. The proposed analysis similarly captures the following contrast (Rizzi 1990):

(i)   *how many pounds do you wonder [$_{CP}$ whether John weighted t]

(ii) ??what do you wonder [$_{CP}$ whether John weighted t]

This contrast follows if the argument *what* bears a Case feature, but the quasi argument *how many pounds* does not. This assumption is supported by the following contrast:

(iii) *150 pounds was/were weighted t by John

(iv)   the potatoes were weighted t by John

The contrast between (iii) and (iv) follows if the argument *the potatoes* bears a Case feature, but the quasi argument *150 pounds* does not. Given such a Case-theoretic distinction between arguments and quasi arguments, the severe deviance of (i) follows from (18) and the marginal deviance of (ii) follows from (14).

The proposed analysis further captures the marginal deviance of the following cases:

(v)   ??where do you wonder [$_{CP}$ whether John fixed the car t]

(vi) ??when do you wonder [$_{CP}$ whether John fixed the car t]

The marginal deviance of (v) and (vi) follows if *where* and *when* each bear a Case feature. This assumption is supported by the following two facts: (a) *where* and *when* can appear as a complement of a preposition (e.g., *from where*, *since when*), and (b) *there* and *then* can be analyzed as pronominal forms of *where* and *when*. On the basis of (a) and (b), Huang (1982) proposes that *where* and *when* are categories that can appear as a complement of a phonetically null preposition. Given that such a null preposition, just like other prepositions, bears a Case feature, its complement (e.g., *where, when*) also bears a Case feature. Thus, the marginal deviance of (v) and (vi) follows from (14).

15. Samuel D. Epstein (personal communication) has pointed out to me that the proposed analysis raises a kind of ordering paradox. Under standard assumptions, movement never forms an LF object unless it is the final operation in the derivation, but all the relevant applications of Attract (discussed above) occur in the middle of the derivations. I will come back to this problem in section 4.5.

16. See Chomsky 1995, 265, and Kitahara 1997 for relevant discussion of such a minimization of pied-piped material. Also see Lasnik 1999 and Ochi 1997 for recent discussion of the issues related to pied-piping and feature strength.

17. (19) may follow if (a) feature movement is feature stripping (with no copying process) and (b) the computation deriving PF representations operates on α only if the integrity of (feature components of) α holds (i.e., no feature is stripped away from α).

18. For detailed discussion of this blocking effect in languages with no overt verb movement (such as English), see Chomsky 1995, Kitahara 1997, and the references cited in note 9.

19. Note that the current analysis "postpones" the checking of the Case feature of *what* without appealing to Procrastinate (Chomsky 1993, 30).

20. Chomsky (1995, 303) assumes that "formal features of trace are deleted (hence erased) if they are not necessary for the formation of legitimate LF objects that satisfy FI." Also, he (1995, 381, n. 12) assumes that "the features of a chain are considered a unit: if one is affected by an operation, all are." Given these assumptions, in the derivation of (2), the Case feature of *what* (which must be deleted for convergence) remains in the trace of *what*, and a later operation (affecting the trace of *what*) deletes it.

21. Suppose that Procrastinate is eliminated. Then, in principle, feature movement can be overt or convert. In section 4.4, I explore the possibility of overt feature movement.

22. For pre-minimalist discussion of the contrast between (22) and (23), see Chomsky and Lasnik 1993, Lasnik and Saito 1984, 1992.

23. Spell-Out splits a derivation into two parts: one forming π (a PF representation) and the other forming λ (an LF representation). Given the structure Σ already constructed, Spell-Out applies to Σ and strips away from it those elements relevant only to π. For further discussion, see Chomsky 1995, 229.

24. Chomsky (1995, 225) assumes a numeration to be "a set of pairs (LI, i) where LI is an item of the lexicon and i is its index, understood to be the number of times that LI is selected."

25. The following case appears to be problematic for the proposed analysis:

(i) ??who do you think [$_\alpha$ pictures of t_{wh}] were stolen t_α

Chomsky (1995, 328) states that "[(i)] is a Condition on Extraction Domain

(CED) violation in Huang's (1982) sense if passive precedes *wh*-movement, but it is derivable with no violation (incorrectly) if the operations apply in countercyclic order, with passive following *wh*-movement." It is true that (30) does not force the strict-cyclic subject raising of α in the derivation of (i), but as Kawashima and Kitahara (1996) and Groat (1995) have independently pointed out, this effect of strict cyclicity is deducible from the Linear Correspondence Axiom (Kayne 1994), interpreted in terms of the derivational definition of c-command (Epstein 1994, this volume). Thus, in principle, countercyclic movements are permitted but strictly limited to certain feature movements. For further discussion of derivational analyses of (i), see Epstein et al. 1998. See also Collins 1994, 1995, 1997 and Kitahara 1994, 1995, 1997 for relevant discussion of economy-based analyses of (i).

26. Note that, under this derivational view, *wh*-movement may still interact with the determination of scope. For relevant discussion, see Epstein et al. 1998.

References

Abe, Jun. 1993. Binding conditions and scrambling without A/Ā distinction. Doctoral dissertation, University of Connecticut, Storrs.

Aoun, Joseph. 1985. *A grammar of anaphora*. Cambridge, Mass.: MIT Press.

Browning, M. A. 1987. Null operator constructions. Doctoral dissertation, MIT, Cambridge, Mass.

Chomsky, Noam. 1981. *Lectures on government and binding*. Dordrecht: Foris.

Chomsky, Noam. 1986. *Barriers*. Cambridge, Mass.: MIT Press.

Chomsky, Noam. 1993. A minimalist program for linguistic theory. In *The view from Building 20: Essays in linguistics in honor of Sylvain Bromberger*, eds. Kenneth Hale and Samuel Jay Keyser, 1–52. Cambridge, Mass.: MIT Press. [Reprinted in *The Minimalist Program*, Noam Chomsky, 167–217. Cambridge, Mass.: MIT Press, 1995.]

Chomsky, Noam. 1994. Bare phrase structure. (MIT Occasional Papers in Linguistics 5.) MITWPL, Department of Linguistics and Philosophy, MIT, Cambridge, Mass. [Published in *Evolution and revolution in linguistic theory: Essays in honor of Carlos Otero*, eds. Héctor Campos and Paula Kempchinsky, 51–109. Washington, D.C.: Georgetown University Press, 1995, and *Government and Binding Theory and the Minimalist Program*, ed. Gert Webelhuth, 383–439. Oxford: Blackwell, 1995.]

Chomsky, Noam. 1995. Categories and transformations. In *The Minimalist Program*, 219–394. Cambridge, Mass.: MIT Press.

Chomsky, Noam, and Howard Lasnik. 1993. The theory of principles and parameters. In *Syntax: An international handbook of contemporary research*, eds. Joachim Jacobs, Arnim von Stechow, Wolfgang Sternefeld, and Theo Vennemann, 506–569. Berlin: Walter de Gruyter. [Reprinted in *The Minimalist Program*, Noam Chomsky, 13–127. Cambridge, Mass.: MIT Press, 1995.]

Cinque, Guglielmo. 1990. *Types of Ā-dependencies*. Cambridge, Mass.: MIT Press.

Collins, Chris. 1994. Economy of derivation and the Generalized Proper Binding Condition. *Linguistic Inquiry* 25, 45–61.

Collins, Chris. 1995. Toward a theory of optimal derivations. In *Papers on minimalist syntax*, eds. Rob Pensalfini and Hiroyuki Ura, 65–103. (MIT Working Papers in Linguistics 27.) MITWPL, Department of Linguistics and Philosophy, MIT, Cambridge, Mass.

Collins, Chris. 1997. *Local economy*. Cambridge, Mass.: MIT Press.

Epstein, Samuel D. 1987. Empty categories and their antecedents. Doctoral dissertation, University of Connecticut, Storrs.

Epstein, Samuel D. 1991. *Traces and their antecedents*. New York: Oxford University Press.

Epstein, Samuel D. 1992. Derivational constraints on Ā-chain formation. *Linguistic Inquiry* 23, 135–159.

Epstein, Samuel D. 1994. The derivation of syntactic relations. Ms., Harvard University, Cambridge, Mass. [Paper presented at Harvard University Linguistics Department Forum in Synchronic Linguistic Theory, December 1994.]

Epstein, Samuel D., Erich M. Groat, Ruriko Kawashima, and Hisatsugu Kitahara. 1998. *A derivational approach to syntactic relations*. New York: Oxford University Press.

Fukui, Naoki. 1993. A note on improper movement. *The Linguistic Review* 10, 111–126.

Groat, Erich. 1995. On the redundancy of syntactic representations. Ms., Harvard University, Cambridge, Mass. [Paper presented at the 18th GLOW Colloquium.]

Holmberg, Anders. 1986. Word order and syntactic features in the Scandinavian languages and English. Doctoral dissertation, University of Stockholm.

Hornstein, Norbert. 1995. *Logical Form: From GB to minimalism*. Oxford: Blackwell.

Huang, C.-T. James. 1982. Logical relations in Chinese and the theory of grammar. Doctoral dissertation, MIT, Cambridge, Mass.

Jonas, Dianne. 1995. Clause structure and verb syntax in Scandinavian and English. Doctoral dissertation, Harvard University, Cambridge, Mass.

Jonas, Dianne. 1996. Clause structure, expletives and verb movement. In *Minimal ideas: Syntactic studies in the minimalist framework*, eds. Werner Abraham, Samuel D. Epstein, Höskuldur Thráinsson, and C. Jan-Wouter Zwart, 167–188. Amsterdam: John Benjamins.

Jonas, Dianne, and Jonathan David Bobaljik. 1993. Specs for subjects: The role of TP in Icelandic. In *Papers on Case and agreement I*, eds. Jonathan D. Bobaljik and Colin Phillips, 59–98. (MIT Working Papers in Linguistics 18.) MITWPL, Department of Linguistics and Philosophy, MIT, Cambridge, Mass.

Kawashima, Ruriko, and Hisatsugu Kitahara. 1996. Strict cyclicity, linear ordering, and derivational c-command. In *Proceedings of the Fourteenth West Coast Conference on Formal Linguistics*, eds. José Camacho, Lina Choueiri, and Maki Watanabe, 255–269. Stanford, Calif.: CSLI Publications. [Distributed by Cambridge University Press.]

Kayne, Richard. 1984. *Connectedness and binary branching*. Dordrecht: Foris.

Kayne, Richard. 1994. *The antisymmetry of syntax*. Cambridge, Mass.: MIT Press.

Kitahara, Hisatsugu. 1994. Target α: A unified theory of movement and structure-building. Doctoral dissertation, Harvard University, Cambridge, Mass.

Kitahara, Hisatsugu. 1995. Target α: Deducing strict cyclicity from derivational economy. *Linguistic Inquiry* 26, 47–77.

Kitahara, Hisatsugu. 1997. *Elementary operations and optimal derivations*. Cambridge, Mass.: MIT Press.

Lasnik, Howard. 1995. Last Resort. In *Minimalism and linguistic theory*, eds. Shosuke Haraguchi and Michio Funaki, 1–32. Tokyo: Hituzi Syobo.

Lasnik, Howard. 1999. On feature strength: Three minimalist approaches to overt movement. *Linguistic Inquiry* 30, 197–217.

Lasnik, Howard, and Mamoru Saito. 1984. On the nature of proper government. *Linguistic Inquiry* 15, 235–289.

Lasnik, Howard, and Mamoru Saito. 1992. *Move α: Conditions on its application and output*. Cambridge, Mass.: MIT Press.

Manzini, Maria Rita. 1992. *Locality: A theory and some of its empirical consequences*. Cambridge, Mass.: MIT Press.

Ochi, Masao. 1997. Move or Attract?: Attract F and the pied-piping chain. Ms., University of Connecticut, Storrs. [Paper presented at Open Linguistics Forum, University of Ottawa.]

Oishi, Masayuki. 1993. LF legitimacy and chain formation. Ms., Tohoku Gakuin University, Sendai, Japan.

Reinhart, Tanya. 1976. The syntactic domain of anaphora. Doctoral dissertation, MIT, Cambridge, Mass.

Rizzi, Luigi. 1990. *Relativized Minimality*. Cambridge, Mass.: MIT Press.

Thráinsson, Höskuldur. 1993. On the structure of infinitival complements. In *Harvard working papers in linguistics 3*, eds. Höskuldur Thráinsson, Samuel David Epstein, and Susumu Kuno, 181–213. Department of Linguistics, Harvard University, Cambridge, Mass.

Chapter 5

Cyclicity and Minimalism   Robert Freidin

For well over three decades, some notion of the cyclic nature of transformations, and of derivations more generally, has guided theorizing about the nature of the language faculty. In this chapter, I evaluate current discussions of cyclicity in terms of previously identified empirical and conceptual motivations for a syntactic cycle. In section 5.1, I give a brief history of the cycle in generative grammar, showing in particular that the original motivation for a cycle is no longer valid under current basic assumptions. In section 5.2, I discuss the current status of the syntactic cycle under various proposals within the Minimalist Program. I demonstrate how all of the empirical motivation cited for stipulating a cyclic principle falls under other independently motivated principles and analyses, so that stipulating a cyclic principle is redundant with respect to other parts of grammar (cf. Freidin 1978). In section 5.3, I evaluate recent proposals for deriving the empirical effects of a generalized cyclic principle from other principles of grammar. I subject these proposals to a minimalist critique, showing that they are based on nonminimal assumptions. Instead, I propose that the empirical effects of a generalized cyclic principle can be derived from a theory of elementary transformational operations that is optimal from a minimalist perspective.

5.1 The Cycle in Generative Grammar: A Brief History

The transformational cycle was first proposed around 1964 as a way to eliminate generalized transformations from the theory while accounting in a natural way for some empirical observations about the general operation of transformations.

Within the earliest formulations of transformational grammar, phrase structure rules were assumed to be nonrecursive. Recursion in phrase structure was handled instead by generalized transformations, which applied to two or more phrase markers, either embedding one inside another or conjoining them. In addition to these generalized transformations, there were singulary transformations, which operated on a single phrase marker (P-marker). As a result, a derivation was represented by a transformation marker (T-marker), indicating how the system of transformations applied.

Consider the example discussed in Chomsky's 1964 lectures at the Linguistic Society of America Summer Institute (Chomsky 1966). Sentence (1) would be derived from three base P-markers underlying the (kernel) sentences (2), the derivation being represented by the T-marker (3), where B1, B2, and B3 represent each of the base P-markers.

(1) I expected the man who quit work to be fired

(2) a. I expected it
    b. someone fired the man
    c. the man quit work

(3)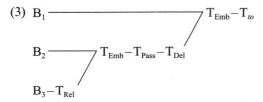

$$B_1 \underline{\hspace{5cm}} \diagup T_{Emb} - T_{to}$$
$$B_2 \underline{\hspace{2cm}} \diagup T_{Emb} - T_{Pass} - T_{Del}$$
$$B_3 - T_{Rel}$$

The T-marker (3) shows that the three base P-markers in (2) are processed as follows. First, (2c) ($= B_3$) undergoes the transformation that turns it into a relative clause. Next, that derived P-marker is embedded in the P-marker for (2b) ($= B_2$), after which the passive transformation converts the expanded P-marker into a passive construction (*the man who quit work was fired by someone*) and a deletion transformation removes the phrase *by someone*. Finally, the resulting P-marker is embedded into the P-marker underlying (2a) ($= B_1$) and the embedded sentential structure is converted into an infinitival.

Putting aside the antiquated nature of the particulars of this analysis, the incorporation of T-markers in the theory of grammar created several complications. One concerned the then-evolving semantic theory for generative grammar first proposed by Katz and Fodor (1963). Katz and Fodor had to propose two types of projection rule, whose purpose was to construct readings for constituents. Type I projection rules operated on underlying P-markers to construct a reading. Type II projection rules were proposed to account for the effects of generalized transformations that applied to pairs of P-markers. Katz and Postal (1964) demonstrated that the contribution of generalized transformations could be limited to the amalgamation of readings of the P-markers joined together by the operation. Thus, the only function of type II rules was to assign the reading of the embedded structure (a base P-marker) to the P-marker into which it was embedded.

Another complication concerning generalized transformations involved restrictions on the organization of T-markers as discussed by Fillmore (1963). As interpreted by Chomsky (1966), Fillmore's observations were essentially that (a) generalized transformations need not be ordered (in contrast to singulary transformations), (b) there are no cases where a matrix P-marker must be operated on by a singulary transformation before a constituent P-marker is embedded in it by a generalized transformation (though there are cases where a singulary transformation must apply to the matrix P-marker after the constituent P-marker has been embedded), and (c) the embedding operation should be viewed as a substitution operation that inserts a sentential P-marker in place of a "dummy symbol" Δ (equivalent to a categorially unspecified position). As Chomsky noted, the earlier theory of T-markers allowed for more complex orderings between singulary and generalized transformations. He concluded, "It is therefore quite natural to generalize from these empirical observations, and to propose as a general condition on T-markers that they must always meet Fillmore's conditions," as illustrated in (3) (1966, 62). However, as Chomsky also noted, this condition as formulated "appears to be quite ad hoc" (p. 62).

Chomsky's solution was to eliminate generalized transformations in favor of allowing recursion in phrase structure rules so that they could construct generalized P-markers directly. To account for the kind of ordering restrictions Fillmore observed, Chomsky introduced the transformational cycle as a general principle of rule application.[1] The linear sequence of singulary transformations applies to the most deeply embedded sentential structure in the generalized P-marker. Then, as Chomsky outlines the process, "Having completed the application of the rules to each such structure, reapply the sequence to the 'next-higher' structure dominated by S in the generalized phrase-marker" (1966, 63). This continues until the root S has been so processed.

Chomsky gave the argument for the cycle as follows:

The advantages of this modification are obvious. It provides a more highly structured theory which is weaker in expressive power; in other words, it excludes in principle certain kinds of derivational pattern that were permitted by the earlier version of transformational theory, but never actually found. Since the primary goal of linguistic theory is to account for specific properties of particular languages in terms of hypotheses about language structure in general, any such strengthening of the constraints on a general theory is an important advance. Furthermore, there is good internal motivation for enriching the structure (and hence decreasing the expressive power) of transformational theory in this way, namely, in that this modification permits us to eliminate the notion of "generalized transformation" (and with it, the notion "T-marker") from the theory of syntax. Hence the theory is conceptually simpler. Finally, the theory of the semantic component can be simplified in that type two projection rules are no longer necessary at all. (1966, 65)

As stated, the argument rests on a mixture of empirical and conceptual/methodological issues. The reduction in expressive power is motivated by the empirical fact that certain derivational patterns are not found in natural languages. The elimination of generalized transformations and T-markers, as well as of type II projection rules in the semantic component, simplifies the theory conceptually. The general methodological goal of accounting for the specific properties of individual languages via general principles of language also favors postulating the cycle.

At this stage in the development of the theory of transformational grammar, the cycle was used as an argument for eliminating generalized transformations. Yet the current theory of bare phrase structure has reintroduced generalized transformation into the theory of grammar, at the same time relying on a version of the cyclic principle. Since this does not lead to any obvious problem, it should be clear that there is no conceptual incompatibility between the cycle and generalized transformations. Actually, generalized transformations became superfluous with the introduction of recursion in phrase structure rules. Without phrase structure rules, generalized transformations are again necessary to embed one piece of phrase structure within another.

Following the enunciation of the cyclic principle, a new empirical argument for the cycle was introduced. The general form of the argument involved identifying a pair of transformations α and β such that the derivation of some sentence of a language required the applications $\alpha > \beta > \alpha$, where α had to apply before β in a particular sentential domain and then α had to apply after β in a higher sentential domain. Such arguments tried to establish that the application of β depended on the prior application of α and the second application of α depended on the prior application of β.[2] Such arguments turned out to be quite fragile, primarily because they were based on particular formulations of transformational rules. Change the formulation of the rule and the argument collapsed. For example, Ross's (1976) important analysis of the cyclic nature of pronominalization depended on the existence of a transformational operation (called pronominalization) that converts a referential expression into a coreferential pronoun. The argument vanishes under current analyses where pronouns are inserted in a derivation directly from the lexicon and later interpreted. Several other specific empirical arguments were based on the existence of a *There*-Insertion transformation and of a Raising transformation that included the extraposition of the infinitival predicate—rules that play no role in the current principles-and-parameters framework. However, even where these rules were assumed, this form of empirical argument for the cycle turned out to be defeasible. Kimball (1972) demonstrated that transformations could apply in a strict linear fashion: transformation T_1 applies iteratively to increasingly larger domains and then another transformation T_2 applies to the derived P-marker in the same fashion, so that the strict linear ordering $T_1 > T_2$ holds globally. Kimball showed how such linear derivations generated the same structures that cyclic derivations produced. (See Freidin 1976 for further discussion of the empirical motivation for the cycle based on rule-ordering arguments.)

The formulation of the cycle in Chomsky 1965 and 1966 left open the possibility that a singulary transformation could still apply to a cyclic subdomain of the current cycle, in violation of the spirit though not the letter of the cyclic principle. Thus, the application of a rule to a matrix sentential domain would create a context for the application of a rule to a constituent sentential domain. Chomsky (1973) proposed a sharper formulation of the cyclic principle that eliminated this loophole. This reformulation, called the *Strict Cycle Condition* (henceforth SCC), is given in (4).

(4) *Strict Cycle Condition*
    No rule can apply to a domain dominated by a cyclic node *A* in such a way as to affect solely a proper subdomain of *A* dominated by a node *B* which is also a cyclic node. (1973, 243)

Chomsky (1973) mentioned one example relevant to the SCC, given in (5) (= his (57) and (58)), but did not go into the details of the analysis.

(5) a. *what did he wonder where John put
    b. COMP he wondered [s COMP John put what where]

Given an underlying structure (5b), if *where* moves into the embedded COMP position, then movement of *what* into the matrix COMP is blocked by other principles—notably the Subjacency Condition, which prohibits movements that extract an element out of more than one bounding node at a time. The derivation of (5a) violating the SCC is given in (6).

(6) a. COMP he wondered [s[COMP what] John put *t* where]
    b. [COMP what] he wondered [s[COMP *t*] John put *t* where]
    c. [COMP what] he wondered [s[COMP where] John put *t* *t*]

In (6a–b), *what* moves successive-cyclically to each COMP position. Then, in (6c), the movement of *where* to the empty embedded COMP violates the SCC.[3] This derivation is somewhat different from the kind that the original formulation of the cycle was designed to prohibit—that is, derivations where a rule could apply solely to the matrix domain prior to the embedding of the constituent domain in a way that would facilitate the application of a rule applying solely to the constituent domain. In this instance, the rule applying to the matrix domain involves a term in the constituent domain. Nonetheless, examples like (5a) constitute the empirical content of the SCC.

In Freidin 1978, I identified other cases that are ruled out by the SCC, including cases of NP-movement, and showed that, given trace theory, the empirical effects of the SCC can be subsumed under other independently motivated principles—specifically, parts of the θ-Criterion, what eventually became the Case Filter, and the Subjacency Condition construed, crucially, as a condition on representations. Given that the SCC appears to be totally redundant with respect to other necessary parts of the theory, it was argued that the SCC is superfluous and can be dropped as an axiom of Universal Grammar (UG). The elimination of the SCC suggested that the facts of derivation may be epiphenomenal and that what was actually important were the representations generated by the rules of grammar. Thus, in the case of (5a) it didn't matter whether the derivation of the sentence violated just the SCC or Subjacency (or both together on one derivation) because the output gave the same representation, which violated Subjacency construed as a condition on representations. In short, it didn't matter whether derivations conformed to the SCC or not because any deviant sentence whose derivation violated it would be excluded by independently motivated conditions.

5.2 The Current Status of the Syntactic Cycle

With the advent of the Minimalist Program, syntactic theory has undergone several fundamental changes that radically affect the former analyses of the cycle, including the empirical content of the principle. In this section, I review how the relevant changes affect the earlier analyses.

Consider the derivation of (5a) under minimalist assumptions. Since there are no phrase structure rules or X-bar schemas, the phrase structure of the example is built up from the interaction of the concatenation operation (Merge) with the lexicon (perhaps via a numeration). Given that the relevant portion of the derivation concerns only the movement of the *wh*-phrases, I will ignore the movement and feature checking of the subjects and objects. One stage of (5a)'s derivation will be (7).

(7) +Q [John put what where]

The Q-feature is strong in English because it induces overt *wh*-movement. Therefore, under current analyses, the feature must be checked as soon as it is introduced into the derivation; otherwise, the derivation will cancel. More precisely, if the Q-feature is a feature of a complementizer C, then the derivation cancels unless it is checked within CP, a projection of C.[4] Therefore, one of the *wh*-phrases in (7) must raise to check the Q-feature to prevent the derivation from canceling. Since this movement takes place prior to Spell-Out, the whole *wh*-phrase must move to [Spec, CP], giving (8).

(8) [$_{CP}$ what +Q [John put what where]]

Notice that the movement of *what* does not produce an empty category. Rather, the trace of the moved phrase is just a copy of the phrase. The derivation continues to build on (8) by adding lexical material until it reaches the external complementizer.

(9) +Q [he wondered [$_{CP}$ what +Q [John put what where]]]

At this point, in order to get the derivation to violate the SCC, the Q-feature of *what*, assuming it is +Interpretable and therefore cannot delete, should be available to raise to check the Q-feature in the matrix C. That this is ever possible seems unlikely. Generally, when a *wh*-phrase checks a strong Q-feature, it cannot move on. Thus, (10) is never possible even when the derivation involves movement of *what* through the sentential complement CP.

(10) *what did he wonder Bill bought

However, even if it were possible to raise *what* to the matrix [Spec, CP], the copy of *what* in the complement CP would block the movement of *where* (via substitution) to the internal CP. Furthermore, Last Resort would also block the movement of *where* since the Q-feature in the complement CP has already been checked and therefore there would be no motivation for moving *where* at all. This also holds for the possible adjunction of *where* to the complement CP.

There is of course another derivation of (5a), which violates the SCC but would not be blocked by Last Resort. Consider the derivation that has reached the stage given in (11).

(11) +Q [he wondered [$_{CP}$ +Q [John put what where]]]

Assume for the moment that the unchecked strong Q-feature in the complement CP has not caused the derivation to cancel, as it would under the analysis in Chomsky 1995. The derivation that violates the SCC involves movement of *what* directly to the matrix CP, followed by the movement of *where* to the complement CP. In this derivation, each movement checks a strong feature and therefore satisfies Last Resort. Whether the interclausal movement to the matrix CP can occur before the intraclausal movement to the complement CP depends on how the movement operation is construed. If the operation is Move, then the closest landing site is the complement CP and therefore the interclausal movement violates the Minimal Link Condition (MLC; see Chomsky 1995, 296, (82)). But if the operation is Attract, then the interclausal movement should be allowed because there is no closer *wh*-phrase to attract. The intraclausal movement is allowed under either interpretation of the movement operation. Now if we reverse the order of the two movements, the results are different. If *where* moves to the complement CP first, then the movement of *what* to the matrix CP will violate the MLC even on the interpretation of the movement operation as Attract since *where* in the complement CP is closer to the attractor Q-feature in the matrix CP than *what* in complement object position.

We have discovered here that under current analytical assumptions concerning the construction of phrase structure and the interpretation of movement as a feature-checking operation, the empirical motivation for the SCC as an independent principle is limited to a very particular interpretation of the theory. Thus, there is a derivation of (5a) that violates the SCC but would be tolerated by the current theory only if the movement operation is construed as Attract and not Move and, crucially, an unchecked strong feature does *not* cancel a derivation. Otherwise, the empirical effects of the SCC appear to be handled by an independently motivated principle (Last Resort) plus the definition of feature strength and therefore provide no motivation for postulating the SCC as an axiom of the theory.

Before we consider cyclicity in the literature on minimalism, it is worth asking whether the original motivation for the cycle reappears, given that generalized transformations are again responsible for generating generalized P-markers. The answer appears to be negative because the procedure for constructing phrase structure does not allow for embedding operations of the sort that existed in the earlier theory. Embedding is not brought about by a substitution operation that replaces a dummy node Δ with a sentential construct. Rather, the sentential complement becomes embedded in a VP by concatenating with a verb that constitutes the head of the phrase created. Therefore, there is no way that the matrix domain is constructed separately from the complement domain so that the matrix domain could undergo some transformational operation prior to the embedding of the complement domain.[5] Therefore, the general procedure for constructing phrase structure itself precludes the possibility that the original formulation of the cycle was meant to prohibit.

Chomsky (1993) proposes a constraint on substitution operations that gives in effect a version of the strict cycle. Recall that the 1993 proposal includes two substitution operations: a binary operation GT (generalized transformation), which maps two P-markers onto a single generalized P-marker, and a singular operation Move α, which maps one P-marker onto another. Both operations work in the same fashion. Each operation targets a P-marker K, adds $\varnothing$ ("a designated empty position"), and substitutes α for $\varnothing$. For Move α, α is a P-marker contained within the target K. The new version of the strict cycle requires that "substitution operations always extend their target" (p. 23).

(12) *Extension Condition*

For substitution, $\varnothing$ must be *external* to the targeted P-marker K.

(12) prevents the substitution operation (as opposed to the adjunction operation, which creates two-part categories) from doing any kind of embedding with respect to the P-marker it operates on.

Chomsky offers two empirical arguments for this condition. First, without (12) "we would lose the effects of those cases of the ECP [Empty Category Principle] that fall under Relativized Minimality" (p. 23). Chomsky cites examples relating to superraising, the Head Movement Constraint, and *wh*-islands.

Consider the superraising example cited in (13) (= Chomsky's (19a)).

(13) [$_{I'}$ seems [$_{IP}$ is certain [John to be here]]]

Chomsky is assuming here that (13) could be a stage in a legitimate derivation, whereas under the analysis in Chomsky 1995 this derivation would presumably cancel because the strong D-feature of the complement I of *seems* has not been checked within its maximal projection (see below for further discussion). The derivation that violates the Extension Condition involves the insertion of *it* into the embedded IP after *John* has moved to the matrix [Spec, IP], extending the targeted embedded projection of I but not the whole P-marker, yielding (14).

(14) *[$_{IP}$ John [$_{I'}$ seems [$_{IP}$ it is certain [$_{IP}$ John to be here]]]]

The strength of the argument for a cyclic principle based on Relativized Minimality violations like superraising depends on three points: (a) that such constructions could actually be generated in this way, (b) that this derivation is not prohibited by any other principle or analysis that is more general, and (c) that there are no other possible derivations of these constructions that are not ruled out by the Extension Condition. In the latter case, we might wonder whether some generalization is being missed.

Regarding (a), it is not obvious that a [Spec, IP] position in the complement of *seems* can be created after that IP has been embedded in the matrix VP by concatenating with the matrix verb. For one thing, such an operation raises nontrivial questions about derived constituent structure (see section 5.3 for further discussion). Nonetheless, there is a derivation of the appropriate sort that will not run into such problems: namely, moving *John* successive-cyclically first to the [Spec, IP] of the complement of *seems* and then to the matrix [Spec, IP], then substituting *it* for the intermediate trace of *John*. Under the copy theory of movement operations, we might be inclined to disallow the substitution of *it* on the grounds that *it* is distinct from *John* and therefore the operation would violate the nondistinctness conditions on substitutions (cf. Chomsky 1965). The effect of the nondistinctness condition is to prohibit the deletion of information from a derivation. In this way, it is really just another way to express the recoverability condition on deletions. Suppose we recognize this redundancy between the two conditions and eliminate nondistinctness in favor of recoverability, which has a broader coverage. Now, does the deletion of a trace violate recoverability? Presumably, it does not in the case of PF since trace deletion there is general requirement (see Nunes 1995). In the case of LF, the trace of the foot of a chain may be necessary for interpretation, but apparently the intermediate traces of the chain in question are not and thus presumably could be deleted without violating recoverability. If so, then substitution of *it* for *John* should be allowed.

This suggests that the copy theory of movement does not block trace erasure via substitution. The analysis carries over to all the examples considered in Freidin 1978—for instance, (5)–(6). Interestingly, both (5a) and the superraising case (14) contain chains that violate Subjacency. However, if there is no level of S-Structure, as assumed in current work, then Subjacency interpreted as a condition on representations would have to apply at LF. Nonetheless, we probably do not want to rely on such an analysis because the notion of bounding category is essentially unmotivated under minimalist assumptions and therefore suspect.

Fortunately, there is another, more fundamental way to eliminate these derivations without recourse to suspect notions like bounding category or appeals to a cyclic principle. Let us suppose that there are no substitution operations in UG. That is, we assume that the elementary operations of UG are limited to concatenation (adjunction) and deletion. In earlier theories, the substitution operation was required for lexical insertion and therefore it was reasonable to assume that it was generally available for movement operations as well. Now that lexical items are inserted into a derivation by the concatenation operation, there is no reason to assume the existence of movement by substitution.

If this analysis is on the right track, then it is at least questionable whether there is a countercyclic derivation of the superraising construction (14). Furthermore, the proposed analysis automatically addresses point (b) above—namely, whether the countercyclic derivation is prohibited by some other principle or more general analysis. Putting aside the fact that the derivation violates Subjacency construed as a condition on chain representations at LF, it is prohibited by the elimination of substitution as an elementary transformational operation of UG. The only remaining question is whether concatenation can apply to a subphrase of a P-marker. See section 5.3 for discussion of why this may be generally prohibited.

Let us turn now to point (c), concerning other possible derivations of these constructions that do not violate the Extension Condition. Given the separation of feature-moving operations and category-moving operations, it may be possible to derive the superraising violations without violating either the Extension Condition or the strong feature analysis. Consider, for example, the following derivation. First, the D-feature of *John* in (13) raises to check the strong D-feature of *is*. Next, *it* is merged with the resulting P-marker, checking the agreement and Case features of *is* and the Case of *it*. Notice that the insertion of *it* here does not violate the Extension Condition, nor does it involve leaving an unchecked strong feature, which would automatically cancel the derivation. At this point, the D-feature of *John* can raise to the matrix I, checking another strong D-feature. Suppose then that the nominal phrase *John* merges with the matrix projection of I, thereby generating the violation of superraising that we are attempting to avoid by invoking cyclicity in some form, but without violating cyclicity.

This derivation raises several questions. One crucial question concerns whether or not feature movement involves only the movement of a single feature or, as assumed in Chomsky 1995,[6] the set of formal features of a lexical item—FF(LI). If the former, then the cyclic merger of *it* could be involved in checking the agreement and Case features of *is*, as proposed. If the latter *and* if the pied-piped FFs enter into a checking relation with I, then the Case feature of *it* would not be checked, causing the derivation to crash at both LF and PF. Under this analysis, the superraising construction violates Full Interpretation, not some formulation of the SCC. Suppose, however, that even under the interpretation that Move F automatically involves the pied-piping of FF(LI), it is possible that feature checking of Case and agreement features involves the specifier-head relation. This ought to be possible because that is exactly how all the features of I will be checked in a simple expletive construction (e.g., (15)).

(15) it is likely that John will be here on time

That is, *it* will merge with *is likely that John will be here on time*, creating a specifier-head relation with *is* and checking not only its −Interpretable Case and agreement features, but also its strong D-feature. So even on the pied-piping analysis of feature movement, it may not be necessary for the "free rider" features, those that have been carried along, to enter into feature-checking relations when the feature that carries them does.

Another question that arises concerns the movement of *John* rather than *it* to the matrix [Spec, IP]. If it were a simple question of movement of categories, then movement of the nominal *John* over the nominal *it* would violate the MLC. However, under the Move F analysis, the situation is not so straightforward. Given that minimally only a feature (along with other associated FF(LI)) will move to check the strong D-feature of the matrix I, it is possible that the moved D-feature of *John* will move again, rather than the features of *it* in the complement [Spec, IP]. Notice that the two positions are equidistant, because they are both in the checking domain of I (as discussed above), and therefore cannot be distinguished so that the MLC will prefer one movement option over the other.[7]

The final step in the derivation of (14) involves the movement of the nominal category *John* to the matrix [Spec, IP]. If category movement is motivated solely for the purpose of convergence at PF but not for feature checking, then *John* moves directly from the IP complement of *certain*, presumably attracted by its FFs that merged with *seem*. This movement violates the MLC only if *it* can be attracted to the matrix [Spec, IP] instead of *John*. But if all the FFs of *it* have been checked in the complement of *seems*, then there is no reason to move *it* at all. If this is correct, then the derivation of the superraising case converges.

The convergent derivation of the superraising construction involves at least one highly suspect property: namely, that the features of a finite verb (or I) can be checked by the features of different nominal expressions. This could be avoided if feature checking is obligatory. Thus, the Case feature of *John* will be checked by *is* and therefore could not be raised to the matrix clause to check the Case feature of *seems*. This would follow from the economy condition on fewest steps. Checking the D-feature of I by raising the FFs of a nominal expression and then checking the Case and φ-features by merger of an expletive counts as two steps whereas checking all these features using only the raising operation counts as one step. This interpretation would ensure that the expletive winds up in the matrix [Spec, IP] since this is the only position in which its Case feature will be checked.[8]

Under this analysis, (14) could result only if the expletive checks all the relevant features of *is*. Then the movement of *John* from the complement of *certain* directly to the matrix clause would be blocked by the MLC if

Move F applies to the D-feature or the φ-features of the nominal. However, if Move F applies to the Case feature, then the MLC would not block the movement because the Case feature of *it*, having been checked, is no longer accessible. Thus, (14) could still converge, even if the two-step feature-checking option discussed above is blocked. Alternatively, the MLC could be strengthened so that the FFs that get carried along and enter into a checking relation are also considered in the determination of minimal links. Then, even when the Case feature chain does not violate the MLC, the D- and φ-feature chains will.

If the superraising construction (14) does actually converge, then we might expect that some principle of economy will prefer the derivation of (16) to that of (14).

(16) [$_{IP}$ it [$_{I'}$ seems [$_{IP}$ John is certain [$_{IP}$ John to be here]]]]

Thus, at the point in the derivation shown in (17) where there is a choice between moving the features of *John* and merging *it*, Move F is preferred to Merge.

(17) [$_{I'}$ is certain [$_{IP}$ John to be here]]

If this generalizes to all derivations, then singulary transformations will be preferred to generalized transformations. Presumably, the computational system for human language (C_{HL}) tries to make maximal use of what is already in a P-marker before incorporating additional material (but cf. Chomsky 1995, 347).

Like the superraising case we have considered in such detail, the Head Movement Constraint (HMC) case is assumed to involve the insertion of a lexical item within a P-marker. An HMC violation can be generated from (18) if *fix* is moved to C and then *can* is inserted in VP or IP.

(18) [$_{C'}$ C [$_{I'}$ John [$_{VP}$ fix the car]]]

The Extension Condition blocks the insertion of the modal. Such potential derivations are dubious on quite general grounds. C normally attracts only the finite form of the verb. If so, then there will be no reason for a nonfinite verb form to move to C and hence no way to generate HMC violations. If this line of reasoning is viable, then perhaps the entire range of HMC problems is just the result of an overly general and imprecise analysis.

Unlike the superraising and HMC cases, the *wh*-island case does not involve an instance of lexical insertion that is supposed to violate the

Extension Condition. One derivation from (19) violates the Extension Condition straightforwardly.

(19) [$_{C'}$ C [$_{IP}$ John wondered [$_{C'}$ C [$_{IP}$ Mary fixed what how]]]]

If Move α targets the matrix C', creating $\varnothing$ external to C' and substituting *how* for $\varnothing$, then (12) prevents Move α from targeting the complement C' and moving *what* to the complement [Spec, CP].[9] This derivation is also ruled out because of the unchecked strong Q-feature in the complement CP at the point that *how* is moved to matrix CP. So far, there is no strong empirical argument for the Extension Condition based on these examples.

There is of course a derivation of the *wh*-island violation (20) from (19) that violates neither the Extension Condition nor the strong feature cancellation analysis: namely, *what* moves to the complement [Spec, CP] and then *how* moves to the matrix [Spec, CP].

(20) [$_{CP}$ how did [$_{IP}$ John wonder [$_{CP}$ what C [$_{IP}$ Mary fixed what how]]]]

The second movement constitutes a clear violation of the MLC if the Q-feature of *what* in the [Spec, CP] of the complement could be attracted to check the Q-feature of the matrix C.[10]

Given these analyses, no Relativized Minimality violation provides strong evidence for a cyclic principle.

Another empirical argument for the Extension Condition that does not involve Relativized Minimality violations concerns raising to complement position. Chomsky (1993) notes that given the Extension Condition, a structure like [$_{X'}$ X YP] cannot be mapped onto [$_{X'}$ X YP ZP] where ZP is raised from YP or inserted by GT. The strength of this argument depends on two closely linked assumptions: (a) that this consequence is unique to the Extension Condition and (b) that substitution operations will construct these structures that the Extension Condition is needed to prohibit. The second assumption, on which the first relies, seems far from obvious. It presupposes a substitution operation so unstructured that it can insert a designated empty position virtually anywhere in a P-marker. Furthermore, the operation that could map [$_{X'}$ X YP] onto [$_{X'}$ X YP ZP] would be both structure-building and structure-destroying in a way that substitution operations are not supposed to be. So it seems doubtful that this kind of mapping would arise naturally.

Chomsky (1995, 328) cites another case related to overt cyclicity involving the interaction of NP- and *wh*-movements (also A- and Ā-movements).

(21) *who was [$_\alpha$ a picture of t_{wh}] t_{was} taken t_α by Bill

The *wh*-movement violates the Condition on Extraction Domain (CED), but can be derived without violating that condition if *wh*-movement to [Spec, CP] precedes NP-movement into [Spec, IP] countercyclically. Chomsky states that the countercyclic derivation is prohibited by the current analysis of feature strength. The strong feature of I unchecked by NP-movement will cause the derivation to cancel before *wh*-movement can apply. He also suggests two other ways to exclude the countercyclic derivation of (21). But before we examine those, it is worth taking a closer look at the strong feature analysis.

For (21), too, the separation of category movement from feature movement has the potential for undermining the strong feature cancellation analysis. Thus, it might be possible for the strong D-feature of I to be checked via feature movement and still move *who* from the VP position. This would entail that it is possible to create the [Spec, IP] position after the phrasal projection of I has been embedded in CP as the complement of C. The overt movement of the NP is not forced by the strong feature cancellation analysis unless we assume that the strong feature of I is checked as a result of that movement, contrary to the Move F analysis. Therefore, the countercyclic derivation of (21) appears to argue for retaining the Extension Condition.

The problem with the Extension Condition is that it should prohibit feature movement generally since such operations (including overt head movement) do not extend the targeted P-marker as required.[11]

Chomsky (1995) suggests two other ways of preventing the countercyclic derivation of (21). One involves some notion of economy. Although the NP-movement in both derivations is the same, the *wh*-movement in the countercyclic derivation is longer and therefore might be excluded by comparing length of steps in derivations. As Chomsky notes, this is not appealing because it requires "a 'global' notion of economy of the sort we have sought to avoid" (P. 328). This would require that both derivations converge even though the construction is clearly deviant; therefore, the admissible (by hypothesis) cyclic derivation would have to be blocked in some other way. Another alternative Chomsky considers is the provision that "α can be attracted to K only if it contains no trace" (p. 365, (200)), which he proposes as a strengthening of the proviso that only the head of a chain may be attracted. This rules out the NP-movement in the countercyclic derivation rather than the *wh*-movement.[12] Under this analysis, we lose the generalization expressed by the CED that extractions out of subject phrases in finite clauses are generally prohibited whether the subject phrase is created by movement or merger.

So far, we have been discussing how to eliminate the countercyclic derivation of (21). However, since (21) is deviant, all derivations must be eliminated—either the derivation is prohibited or the representations derived violate some output condition at PF or LF. Although Chomsky mentions the CED in reference to the cyclic derivation, we cannot appeal specifically to this condition because its formulation involves the notion "government," which has been excluded from discussion within the Minimalist Program on the grounds that it is illegitimate. Therefore, the cyclic derivation of (21) must be excluded in some other way.

To this end, let us take a closer look at the cyclic derivation under the copy theory of movement, which involves the three steps illustrated in (22).

(22) a. [$_\beta$ a picture of who] was taken [$_\alpha$ a picture of who]
      b. was [$_\beta$ a picture of who] was taken [$_\alpha$ a picture of who]
      c. who was [$_\beta$ a picture of who] was taken [$_\alpha$ a picture of who]

In (22a,b), α is a trace of its copy β. However, in (22c), β now contains a trace of *who* whereas α does not. Suppose that this renders α distinct from β so that α cannot function as the trace of β. The derivation would crash at LF because the nominal *a picture of* could not be assigned a θ-role. In other words, (21) constitutes a θ-Criterion violation—specifically, Functional Relatedness (Freidin 1978), now subsumed under FI. Note that if the cyclic derivation crashes, then we cannot resort to economy to rule out the countercyclic derivation.

Returning now to the countercyclic derivation of (21), we have a number of options for excluding it. Under the copy theory of traces, the relevant steps of the derivation proceed as in (23).

(23) a. was [$_{IP}$ was taken [$_\alpha$ a picture of who]]
      b. who was [$_{IP}$ was taken [$_\alpha$ a picture of who]]
      c. who was [$_{IP}$[$_\beta$ a picture of who] was taken [$_\alpha$ a picture of who]]

In (23b,c), *who* in α is the trace of *who* in the matrix [Spec, CP]. In (23c), *who* in β, which is presumably a copy of α. is also a trace of *who* in [Spec, CP]. By construction, β binds α and *who* in [Spec, CP] binds *who* in α. What is not clear is the relation between *who* in [Spec, CP] and *who* in β. If we suppose that *who* in [Spec, CP] binds *who* in β, then we might object to the chain (who, who_β, who_α) on the grounds that the link between who_β and who_α is ill formed because who_β does not bind who_α. Alternatively, if we impose the derivational definition of c-command (Epstein, this volume), then who in [Spec, CP] will not c-command β, hence who in β. Since by construction who in β is a trace, β contains an unbound trace in violation of the Proper Binding Condition.

Under the copy theory of movement, there may be yet another explanation for the deviance of (21) regarding trace deletion. Consider the standard assumption that nontrivial chains must reduce at PF to trivial chains; that is, all traces must be erased because nontrivial chains are illegitimate objects at PF, violating FI. The general case involves a chain whose linear order reproduces the linear order of the copies in the P-marker and in which each adjacent pair of copies is in an asymmetric c-command relation such that the head of the chain asymmetrically c-commands the trace adjacent to it, that trace asymmetrically c-commands the trace adjacent to it, and so on to the foot of the chain. Such chains generally reduce to trivial chains at PF.

Before we discuss how this situation does not obtain in the derivations (22) and (23), we need to consider whether a copied element is necessarily always a trace of its copy. In this regard, consider (24).

(24) [$_{NP}$ books about language] seem [$_{IP}$[$_{NP}$ books about language] to be selling well]

Presumably, there is only one chain to consider, the chain involving the NP *books about language* and its trace in [Spec, IP]. That is, there is no chain between *books* in the matrix IP and the copy in the complement IP, and similarly for *about* and *language*. From this perspective, what is odd about a derivation like (22) is that a copied element *who* is not a trace when the phrase containing it is moved, but then becomes a trace when it alone is moved later. One way to deal with this is, as suggested above, to treat the phrase containing the nontrace copy as distinct from the phrase containing the trace copy. Presumably, this will block the required θ-role assignment. Furthermore, α and β would not form a chain and hence there would be no reason to delete α at PF.

Alternatively, we might resolve the issue as follows. Suppose that once a head-trace relation is established between two copies in a derivation, all copies must be considered as part of the chain. Thus, in both (22) and (23), the chain (25) is what must undergo chain reduction via trace deletion.

(25) (who, who$_\beta$, who$_\alpha$)

However, (25) does not conform to the standard case because *who*$_\beta$ does not asymmetrically c-command *who*$_\alpha$ (cf. Takahashi 1994). The counter-cyclic derivation adds another failure of asymmetric c-command between the first two elements of the chain on the derivational c-command analysis. The first is of course sufficient to block trace deletion in both derivations. As a result, both derivations crash at PF because they both contain ille-gitimate nontrivial chains, in violation of FI. If this is a viable analysis, then it should be preferable to one that requires an additional stipulation, like the Extension Condition, to impose cyclic derivations.

So far, we have yet to identify a strong empirical argument for the strict cycle based on the Extension Condition.[13] The empirical motivation for the Extension Condition based on Relativized Minimality violations seems to dissolve when we probe the details of the analysis. Chomsky (1995) reassesses these cases, noting that they involve two situations: (a) countercyclic operations and (b) skipping an already filled position. As we have seen with the superraising and *wh*-island cases, the MLC alone blocks countercyclic operations. Chomsky claims that the countercyclic insertion of heads does not arise (viz., HMC violations) because heads are inserted only by pure merger, which satisfies the Extension Condition.[14] The other situation, involving skipped positions, is generally blocked by the MLC. This leads Chomsky to conclude that there may be no need to impose the Extension Condition on overt category movement.

5.3 Generalized Cyclicity

Although it seems that all the empirical consequences of SCC violations identified so far can be handled by other mechanisms that have been proposed, the question remains whether derivations do in fact adhere to cyclic operations as a result of general constraints on the computational system. In the earliest account that attempted to derive the empirical effects of the SCC from principles of UG (Freidin 1978), these effects are a fortuitous consequence of the combined effects of several principles of UG. In the more recent analyses discussed above, countercyclic deriva-tions are blocked by various stipulations—for example, that substitutions must create positions external to the targeted P-marker (the Extension Condition) or that an unchecked strong feature in a maximal projection cancels a derivation. These seem like retreats from earlier deductive accounts because they are based on a descriptive statement rather than on general principles that have some conceptual plausibility. The analysis based on FI and the MLC is an attempt to reconstruct a more deductive account under minimalist assumptions.

In this section, I review some more recent attempts, also based on minimalist assumptions, to deduce strict cyclicity from more fundamental principles of grammar. I begin with a brief discussion of the nature and role of transformation under a theory of bare phrase structure and end with a somewhat different perspective on cyclicity that follows naturally from the fundamental concepts of that theory.

For concreteness, let us assume the following version of the bare phrase structure theory. Phrase structure is constructed by classical adjunction, a structure-building operation that concatenates two categories and projects the label of one of them. This operation can apply to two items in a numeration (or perhaps directly in the lexicon), or to a lexical item and a P-marker that has been constructed as part of the derivation, or to two such P-markers. All three possibilities can generate a specifier-head configuration, whereas perhaps only the first two can generate a head-complement configuration. When the elements adjoined are not from the same P-marker, the operation acts as a generalized transformation. In contrast, the adjunction elementary can apply to two elements of a single P-marker, in which case the operation acts as a singulary transformation. Even though the adjunction elementary is involved in lexical insertion, phrase structure generation, and movement (both overt and covert), the conditions on its application differ depending on whether it operates as a generalized or singulary transformation. In the former case, adjunction operates on categories; in the latter, it is presumably restricted to the adjunction of a feature to a category. In standard practice, the former case is called Merge and the latter, Move (or Attract/Move). In addition, there must be some further operation that accounts for the pied-piping of a phrasal category in the case of overt category movement.

From this perspective, the issue of cyclicity concerns the application of the adjunction elementary to a nonroot category during a derivation, since presumably this application could have occurred at the point in the derivation where the adjunction site was the root node. Thus, adjunction to a nonroot, either by Merge or by Move, constitutes a countercyclic application. In other words, every category in a P-marker marks a cyclic domain in some sense, not just those categories that form domains for movement rules as in earlier analyses.

Kitahara (1997) attempts to account for generalized cyclicity in terms of a new analysis of the operations Move and Merge. He claims that there is a distinction to be made between the cyclic and countercyclic (noncyclic in his terminology) operations of Move and Merge. Cyclic Move, for example, consists of a single elementary operation: concatenate α and Σ, forming Σ'. It should be obvious that this is just classical adjunction. This operation maps (26a) onto (26b).

(26) a.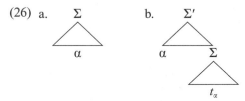

In contrast, countercyclic Move is more complicated. The targets of the operation, α and K, are contained in Σ, so concatenation of α and K forms $L = \{\gamma, \{\alpha, K\}\}$. The insertion of L into the P-marker now requires an extra operation, which Kitahara calls "replacement" mapping (27a) onto (27b).

(27) a.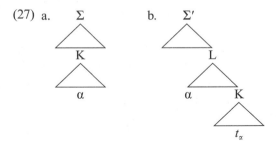

Thus, countercyclic Move on this analysis requires two elementary operations instead of one. Kitahara applies the same analysis to Merge. The preference for cyclic operations over countercyclic operations results from a general economy condition that prefers shorter derivations.

(28) *Shortest Derivation Condition*
   Minimize the number of elementary operations necessary for convergence. (Kitahara 1997, 32)

Under this analysis, cyclicity of rule application follows from general economy considerations.[15]

Even though Kitahara's analysis is more general and therefore may seem more appealing than one based on feature strength, the claim that there is an elementary operation of replacement seems problematic. For one thing, it seems doubtful that this elementary operation plays a role in legitimate derivations. If it does not, then there is no motivation for claiming that it exists at all. Its sole purpose would be to act as an extra operation so the economy analysis succeeds. We could just as easily say that the function postulated for this operation is illegitimate, thereby eliminating the need to appeal to economy—the line of inquiry I will pursue below. Kitahara claims that the erasure operation is an instance of replacement in which a feature F is "replaced" by the empty element $\varnothing$. However, there is no clear reason why this replacement is required if by erasure F becomes inaccessible to any further operation of C_{HL}.[16] The minimal solution should be simply to eliminate the feature.

Yet even if we grant that there could be an elementary operation of replacement that is responsible for erasure of features, it alone could not account for the work Kitahara attributes to it in the case of countercyclic Move. In erasure, the replacement operation has the effect of simply substituting a feature for the empty element. In Move, as shown in (27), replacement results in the deletion of Σ and the projection of Σ' from L as well as the substitution of L for K.[17] The deletion of Σ here cannot be the result of replacement so some other elementary operation would have to be involved.

Under earlier theories of elementary operations (see Freidin 1992), there were a maximum of three such operations, substitution, adjunction, and deletion, each of which performed one of the three basic operations on structure: structure preservation, structure creation, and structure destruction, respectively. Although a structure-preserving operation has been dropped in recent analyses, the other two kinds of operation are surely conceptually necessary. On minimalist assumptions, we would expect that elementary operations perform only these basic and simple structural tasks. From this perspective, Kitahara's replacement operation, when it applies countercyclically, performs several truly elementary operations, including the structure-destroying erasure of Σ and the structure-building replacement of K with L.[18] Hence, it is clear that the operation of replacement as characterized for countercyclic movement operations in Kitahara 1997 is simply not an elementary operation; therefore, it seems unlikely that it would be part of C_{HL}.

Kawashima and Kitahara (1996), Collins (1995, 1997), and Epstein et al. (1998) make proposals to block countercyclic derivations generally as violations of Kayne's (1994) Linear Correspondence Axiom (LCA), a

general constraint on linear ordering in P-markers. Rather than discuss
the different proposals here, I will restrict my comments to the analysis
presented in Collins 1997.

Collins claims that countercyclic operations generally yield structures
that violate the LCA. Consider, for example, his discussion of countercyclic Merge. He assumes that given a set of syntactic objects Σ (i.e., a
numeration) containing three elements (SOs), a countercyclic derivation
like (29) can occur.

(29) a. $\Sigma = \{\alpha, \beta, \gamma\}$
     b. Merge(α, β)
        $\Sigma = \{\gamma, \{\alpha, \beta\}\}$
     c. Merge(γ, α)
        $\Sigma = \{\{\gamma, \alpha\}, \{\alpha, \beta\}\}$

The step (29c), which is allowed by Collins's definition of Merge (which I
will not discuss here), creates a structure in which the two distinct nonterminals dominating β and γ are not in a c-command relation; hence,
neither asymmetrically c-commands the other, in violation of the LCA.
Collins gives (30) as an illustration of the structure generated by (29).

(30)

β α γ

As a concrete example, Collins gives a derivation for the countercyclic
insertion of a subject into [Spec, VP] after VP has been merged with T.
The relevant steps are given in (31).

(31) a. $\Sigma = \{\text{John}, \{T, \{\text{saw, me}\}\}\}$
     b. Merge(John, {saw, me}) = {John, {saw, me}}
        $\Sigma = \{\{T, \{\text{saw, me}\}\}, \{\text{John}, \{\text{saw, me}\}\}\}$

In this case, *John* and *T* are the terminals that fail to be ordered with
respect to each other. Collins notes that this analysis for countercyclic
merger applies as well to countercyclic movement.

Though intriguing, the LCA analysis of countercyclic Merge seems
seriously flawed. First, note that Collins's treatment of Merge would not
be allowed under Chomsky's characterization.

Clearly, then, C_{HL} must include a second procedure that combines syntactic
objects already formed. A derivation converges only if this operation has applied
often enough to leave us with just a single object, also exhausting the initial nu-

meration. The simplest such operation takes a pair of syntactic objects (SO_i, SO_j) and replaces then by a new combined syntactic object SO_{ij}. Call this operation *Merge*. (1995, 226)

Under Chomsky's formulation, Merge creates a new syntactic object, which surely must be treated as a single object by subsequent legitimate applications of Merge. Presumably by "replacing" the pair of syntactic objects with a new single object, Merge loses the ability to access the parts that have been replaced.[19] Furthermore, there is a crucial difference between the unordered set of elements in the initial numeration and the set of elements created by Merge—namely, the latter constitute ordered sets (assuming of course that Merge gives a linear order to the objects it concatenates).[20] So instead of (31a) as input to Merge, we have (32).

(32) $\Sigma = \{$John, $\langle T, \langle$saw, me$\rangle\rangle\}$

Under Chomsky's characterization of Merge, (32) contains two syntactic objects (*John* and the ordered set $\langle T, \langle saw, me \rangle\rangle$), not three (*John, T, $\langle saw, me \rangle$*) or four (*John, T, saw, me*).[21]

Turning now to countercyclic Move, it may be that some version of the LCA will prohibit the operation from applying in legitimate derivations —presumably, such derivations will crash at PF because they contain elements that cannot be assigned a linear order.

The analysis based on the LCA assumes that countercyclic operations are in some sense possible, though they have consequences that are later filtered out. Alternatively, the bad consequences of a countercyclic operation might be immediate, as I will suggest in what follows. What I would like to propose is that the issue of countercyclic movement crucially concerns the question of derived constituent structure, which is central to transformational analysis.

Recall that from the beginning of modern generative grammar (e.g., Chomsky 1955/1975), transformations are defined as operations that apply to analyzed strings. As Chomsky notes (1955/1975, 320), "We must provide a *derived* constituent structure of transforms, for one thing, so that transformations can be compounded." Thus, if we cannot specify the derived constituent structure for a transform, then it cannot serve as the input to another transformation. In earlier theories, a significant amount of information about derived constituent structure came from phrase structure rules. For example, Emonds's structure-preserving hypothesis (see Emonds 1970, 1976) proposed that the derived constituent structure from the application of structure-preserving rules was determined by the phrase structure rules of the base (cf. Chomsky's (1955/1975) discussion of the derived structure of the passive *by* phrase). However, with the demise of phrase structure rules and the advent of bare phrase structure theory, we no longer have phrase structure rules or schemas to provide derived constituent structures. Under the bare phrase structure theory, the transformational operations that create constituent structure also specify derived constituent structure.

On minimalist assumptions, we might expect that the processes that create constituent structure are the only ones that provide derived constituent structure. In other words, there are no separate processes for determining derived constituent structures.

From this perspective, consider the problem of assigning derived constituent structure to an operation that moves a phrase to concatenate with a nonroot category. For concreteness, suppose that the object of a passive predicate is moved to form [Spec, IP] after the IP has been merged with a complementizer as in (33).

(33) [CP that [IP was elected [NP Adam]]]

Notice that in (33), the target of the operation is IP, the maximal projection of I and the complement of *that*. When the NP *Adam* concatenates with IP, IP must project a category so that the NP will now by construction c-command the IP. The syntactic relations between the moved phrase and its target are no different from those that would have arisen if the target had been the root category at the point where the movement applied. However, it is not clear that the moved constituent or the newly projected IP bear any relation to the complementizer that c-commands the target IP. To see how this works, consider the structure derived from the cyclic movement of the object to [Spec, IP].

(34) [CP that [IP[NP Adam] [I* was elected [NP Adam]]]]

In (33), CP immediately dominates the IP *was elected Adam*, whereas in (34), CP immediately dominates the IP *Adam was elected Adam*. To construct (34) from the countercyclic derivation, the syntactic relation between the complementizer *that* and the moved NP *Adam* would have to be redefined; and, as a result, the relation between *that* and the IP *was elected* would also have to be redefined. These redefinitions would require some additional grammatical mechanism. Therefore, unless such a mechanism can be motivated on independent grounds, there is no reason to assume it is available.[22]

Given that there is no redefinition mechanism, what happens when we attempt to move a phrase to concatenate with a nonroot category? One possibility is that when the concatenation occurs, the nonroot category projects to create a three-dimensional P-marker, which can then be ruled out by the LCA. However, if there is little motivation for three-dimensional P-markers in the first place, then we want to avoid postulating such entities. However, if P-markers are only two-dimensional, there is no way for a category to project once it has become a constituent of another category. If the concatenation via movement cannot be carried out because the target cannot project in the normal way, then it seems reasonable to assume that such operations are not possible.

This analysis raises questions about the status of head movement and feature movement to heads more generally, as well as the status of covert movement. With respect to covert movement, there are two primary cases to consider: Quantifier Raising (QR) and object movement (e.g., in English). There are proposals for the analysis of quantifiers that eliminate QR (see Kitahara 1996; Hornstein 1995). If object movement is actually overt in English, as argued by Lasnik (1995) and others, then perhaps there is no covert movement of categories at all. Turning to head movement, notice that this operation causes a problem only if we insist that the output is a string consisting of the moved head followed by the functional head it is adjoined to. The adjunction analysis appears to be redundant given that the head itself enters the derivation with whatever features the functional head represents (e.g., tense or agreement). Given that there is no need for such redundant constructions, a less problematic way to effect head movement would be to substitute the lexical head for the functional head. Thus, there may be a limited role for substitution in grammar after all. The substitution analysis for head movement would eliminate the problem posed by the absence of redefinition mechanisms.[23]

If this analysis is on the right track, then the reason neither countercyclic Merge nor countercyclic Move can apply is that the elementary operation itself does not permit this. On minimalist assumptions, this should be the optimal explanation. It makes no appeal to external factors like economy, constraints on linear ordering, or other UG principles. Certain kinds of derivations are excluded simply on the grounds that the elementary operations of C_{HL} are so constructed that they cannot occur.

Notes

A version of this chapter was presented at the Fourth Seoul International Conference on Linguistics (August 1997). I would like to thank Dong-Whee Yang and the other participants for their comments. I would also like to thank Sam Epstein and Norbert Hornstein for useful comments on an earlier draft, and Howard Lasnik for helpful discussion of some of the issues discussed herein.

1. It is worth noting here that Chomsky (1966) does not actually refer to his solution as "the cycle" or mention "the cyclic application of rules." The first mention of the notion "transformational cycle" occurs in Chomsky 1965, 29, in reference to the application of phonological rules. On page 134, Chomsky proposes that "the rules of the base ... apply cyclically, preserving their linear order," to generate generalized P-markers. Two paragraphs later, Chomsky proposes that the linear sequence of singular transformations apply cyclically to generalized P-markers.

2. Note that such arguments never appear in Chomsky's discussion of the cycle, nor are they referred to as evidence for the cycle.

3. This analysis assumes that the trace of the moved *wh*-phrase *what* can be replaced by the *wh*-phrase *where*. As will be discussed below, such analyses may not be possible under current assumptions about the nature of traces. For detailed discussion, see Freidin 1978.

4. According to Chomsky (1995, 233), a strong feature is simply "one that a derivation 'cannot tolerate'" and therefore causes a derivation to cancel unless it is checked when it is introduced. This principle of cancellation requires that the strong Q-feature not be attached to the *wh*-phrase. If it were, any derivation containing a *wh*-phrase with a strong Q-feature would cancel.

5. Note, however, that the analysis in Chomsky 1993 explicitly assumes that the generalized transformation is a substitution operation and that P-markers corresponding to those of Chomsky 1955/1975 could be constructed. Thus, the original problem can arise for which the cycle was proposed as a solution. Given that such analyses are not possible under a theory of bare phrase structure, I will not discuss Chomsky's (1993) analysis further here.

6. See page 265, where Chomsky claims that "there are strong empirical reasons for assuming that Move F automatically carries along FF(LI)" (though he cites none).

7. This equidistance opens up the possibility that the FFs of *it* rather than *John* will raise to check the features of *seem*. In fact, this would be forced if the Case feature of *John* was checked by *is*, leaving the Case feature of *it* unchecked unless it moves to the matrix clause. Note that this creates the rather odd situation where the Case feature of a phonetically realized nominal expression is checked even though the nominal itself remains in a "Caseless position." In other words, this feature-checking analysis of Case allows us to dissociate Case from the phonetically realized nominal that bears it, whereas under the old Case Filter analysis it was the phonetically realized nominal expression itself that was subject first and foremost to the Case Filter.

If the FFs of *it* do move, then we might expect that *it* itself would also raise to the matrix clause, rather than *John*, because the FFs of *it* were raised to check the features of *seem*. Yet it appears that the FFs of *it* and *John* are identical (i.e., the φ-features and the Case feature), so perhaps there is no way to distinguish which set of features goes with which nominal category once they have been moved. If θ-roles belong to the set of FFs (see Lasnik 1995; Bošković and Takahashi 1998), then there is a way to distinguish the two sets of FFs. This would avoid the situation of having the features of one expression move for checking and the category of another expression move to satisfy convergence at PF.

8. There is still the possibility that the expletive will be merged in the complement of *seems* and raised into the matrix clause. This would presumably block the movement of *John* to [Spec, IP] of the complement of *seems*. Strangely, then, even though the Case feature of *John* has been checked, *John* remains in a Caseless position. This could be avoided if at least the Case feature is checked only in a specifier-head relation—a return to the more traditional analysis. The problem with this approach is that it runs afoul of the just-mentioned economy condition on fewest steps. Furthermore, it appears to undermine the analysis of feature movement as adjunction to a head. If some features must be checked via the specifier-head relation, then why not all features (e.g., φ-features and D-features)? Alternatively, we could block the merger of the expletive in the complement of *seems* on the grounds that it does not enter into any checking and/or θ-relation in that IP.

9. The trouble with this analysis is that in focusing on the derivational history, we are forced to provide two quite different explanations for why *wh*-island violations are prohibited, depending on which movement occurs first. Alternatively, from a representational perspective, there is only one problem no matter how the derivation proceeds: namely, the long-distance trace binding violates the MLC. However, this analysis crucially depends on the MLC's *not* being part of the definition of the movement operation and also on there being at least one internal output condition, hence not a bare output condition.

10. It seems as if we are forced to this conclusion even though it is generally not possible for a *wh*-phrase to check more than one Q-feature in C (see (10)), which suggests that the Q-feature is more like a Case feature on a nominal than a D-feature. Otherwise, there is no obvious way to block the derivation. Notice that unlike the superraising case, where there is an admissible convergent derivation (16), the *wh*-island case yields only deviant results.

11. On the basis of this consideration, Chomsky (MIT class lectures, fall 1995) has rejected the Extension Condition as the right formulation of the cyclic principle.

12. Chomsky suggests that this restriction "may be too strong even within the core computational system" (p. 365), but says no more about it. Notice that there are other, more general problems with this proposal. First, it is essentially a complicated stipulation, which should be avoided unless it has some as yet undisclosed broad empirical effects that only it can achieve. Second, it is not clear how it applies if feature and category movement are separated. Presumably, categories

do not move to check features, so it is not clear how a category (whether it contains a trace or not) will be attracted to K in the first place.

13. In a note, Chomsky (1993, 46, n. 26) remarks,

Depending on other assumptions, some violations might be blocked by various "conspiracies." Let us assume, nevertheless, that overt substitution operations satisfy the extension (strict cycle) condition generally, largely on grounds of conceptual simplicity.

If the analyses of the various empirical problems that appear to bear on the issue of cyclicity are on the right track, then imposing a cyclicity condition on derivations like the Extension Condition cannot be defended "on grounds of conceptual simplicity" because it requires a stipulation that is unnecessary. All the empirical examples cited as evidence for cyclicity can be handled by independently motivated conditions that can be argued to be intrinsic parts of C_{HL}.

14. In Chomsky 1995, 248, this is virtually stipulated on the grounds that merger with nonroot categories would constitute a complication with potentially serious consequences that would require strong motivation. In the absence of such motivation, Chomsky assumes that "Merge always applies in the simplest possible form: at the root." As we will see, this may follow from the nature of elementary operations and therefore need not be stipulated.

15. This is basically the same sort of analysis that appears in Kitahara 1995. The earlier analysis is not valid under bare phrase structure theory, whereas this one is not obviously incompatible.

16. Kitahara (1997, 34) claims that $\varnothing$ is "an actual symbol of mental representation with no feature," but does not explain how it serves any particular function. On minimalist grounds, it would be preferable to avoid postulating such apparently functionless elements. It is also not obvious that $\varnothing$ will not cause a problem for FI at one interface or both.

17. Note that the projection of Σ' cannot be attributed to the concatenation of α and K, which projects L.

18. Not only Σ is lost, but also the fact that K was an immediate constituent of Σ.

19. If this is correct, it excludes proposals that head movement may be accomplished by first concatenating a head that has been embedded in a P-marker with a functional head via merger outside the P-marker and then reintroducing the complex via merger with the P-marker (i.e., sideward movement (Nunes 1995) or interarboreal movement (Bobaljik and Brown 1997)).

20. The LCA depends on this assumption as well. Since it seems to be a fairly standard assumption for phrase structure analysis under the bare phrase structure theory, I will not comment further.

21. Even if we put all this aside, there is another consideration that may render Collins's analysis untenable. Notice that the countercyclically merged subject *John* will have to raise to check the EPP feature of *T*. When it does, *John* and *T* will no longer be in violation of the LCA. Since the offending trace will not show up at PF, the countercyclic derivation will not be prohibited by the LCA. Hence, the strict cycle does not follow from the LCA as Collins claims.

22. It is worth noting that Watanabe (1995) proposes the concept of redefinition, formulated as (i), as the conceptual basis of cyclicity.

(i) *Avoid Redefinition*
Avoid redefinition as much as possible.

He considers various interpretations of (i)—for example, as a global economy condition and as a simplicity measure for generalized transformations. Note that this analysis assumes the existence of redefinition procedures for transforms. The claim I make here is somewhat sharper: there are no redefinition procedures and therefore it follows that countercyclic operations will yield uninterpretable structures.

23. Still to be dealt with is the feature movement analysis of feature checking. Notice that there is even less motivation for the adjunction of features to a head than for the adjunction of a lexical head to a functional head, since the effects of such adjunction are invisible at PF— and at LF, too, for all intents and purposes. As noted above, the case of expletive insertion suggests that the Case and φ-features of I must be checkable from [Spec, IP]—unless we assume that the FFs of the expletive in [Spec, IP] move down to the head I for the purposes of checking. This would of course require some kind of redefinition mechanism. Alternatively, checking as adjunction of FFs to a head will have to be reanalyzed as something along the lines of specifier-head agreement, as in previous analyses, or a more direct relation between the features moved and the features of the target head, perhaps establishing a chain between the two sets of features.

References

Bobaljik, Jonathan, and Samuel Brown. 1997. Interarboreal operations: Head movement and the extension requirement. *Linguistic Inquiry* 28, 345–356.

Bošković, Željko, and Daiko Takahashi. 1998. Scrambling and Last Resort. *Linguistic Inquiry* 29, 347–366.

Chomsky, Noam. 1955/1975. *The logical structure of linguistic theory*. Chicago: University of Chicago Press.

Chomsky, Noam. 1965. *Aspects of the theory of syntax*. Cambridge, Mass.: MIT Press.

Chomsky, Noam. 1966. *Topics in the theory of generative grammar*. The Hague: Mouton.

Chomsky, Noam. 1973. Conditions on transformations. In *A festschrift for Morris Halle*, eds. Stephen R. Anderson and Paul Kiparsky, 232–286. New York: Holt, Rinehart and Winston.

Chomsky, Noam. 1993. A minimalist program for linguistic theory. In *The view from Building 20: Essays in linguistics in honor of Sylvain Bromberger*, eds. Kenneth Hale and Samuel Jay Keyser, 1–52. Cambridge, Mass.: MIT Press. [Reprinted in *The Minimalist Program*, Noam Chomsky 167–217. Cambridge, Mass.: MIT Press, 1995.]

Chomsky, Noam. 1995. Categories and transformations. In: *The Minimalist Program*, 219–394. Cambridge, Mass.: MIT Press.

Collins, Chris. 1995. Toward a theory of optimal derivations. In *Papers on minimalist syntax*, eds. Rob Pensalfini and Hiroyuki Ura, 65–103. (MIT Working Papers in Linguistics 27.) MITWPL, Department of Linguistics and Philosophy, MIT, Cambridge, Mass.

Collins, Chris. 1997. *Local economy*. Cambridge, Mass.: MIT Press.

Emonds, Joseph. 1970. Root and structure preserving transformations. Doctoral dissertation, MIT, Cambridge, Mass.

Emonds, Joseph. 1976. *A transformational approach to English syntax*. New York: Academic Press.

Epstein, Samuel David, Erich Groat, Ruriko Kawashima, and Hisatsugu Kitahara. 1998. *A derivational approach to syntactic relations*. New York: Oxford University Press.

Fillmore, Charles. 1963. The position of embedding transformations in a grammar. *Word* 19, 208–231.

Freidin, Robert. 1976. The syntactic cycle: Proposals and alternatives. Indiana University Linguistics Club, Bloomington.

Freidin, Robert. 1978. Cyclicity and the theory of grammar. *Linguistic Inquiry* 9, 519–549.

Freidin, Robert. 1992. *Foundations of generative syntax*. Cambridge, Mass.: MIT Press.

Hornstein, Norbert. 1995. *Logical Form: From GB to minimalism*. Oxford: Blackwell.

Katz, Jerrold, and Jerry Fodor. 1963. The structure of a semantic theory. *Language* 39, 170–210.

Katz, Jerrold, and Paul Postal. 1964. *An integrated theory of linguistic descriptions*. Cambridge, Mass.: MIT Press.

Kawashima, Ruriko, and Hisatsugu Kitahara. 1996. Strict cyclicity, linear ordering, and derivational c-command. In *Proceedings of the Fourteenth West Coast Conference on Formal Linguistics*, eds. José Camacho, Lina Choueiri, and Maki Watanabe, 255–269. Stanford, Calif.: CSLI Publications. [Distributed by Cambridge University Press.]

Kayne, Richard. 1994. *The antisymmetry of syntax*. Cambridge, Mass.: MIT Press.

Kimball, John P. 1972. Cyclic and linear grammars. In *Syntax and semantics I*, ed. John P. Kimball, 63–80. New York: Seminar Press.

Kitahara, Hisatsugu. 1995. Target α: Deducing strict cyclicity from derivational economy. *Linguistic Inquiry* 26, 47–77.

Kitahara, Hisatsugu. 1996. Raising quantifiers without Quantifier Raising. In *Minimal ideas: Syntactic studies in the minimalist framework*, eds. Werner Abraham, Samuel David Epstein, Höskuldur Thráinsson, and C. Jan-Wouter Zwart, 189–198. Amsterdam: John Benjamins.

Kitahara, Hisatsugu. 1997. *Elementary operations and optimal derivations.* Cambridge, Mass.: MIT Press.

Lasnik, Howard. 1995. A note on pseudogapping. In *Papers on minimalist syntax*, eds. Rob Pensalfini and Hiroyuki Ura, 143–163. (MIT Working Papers in Linguistics 27.) MITWPL, Department of Linguistics and Philosophy, MIT, Cambridge, Mass.

Nunes, Jairo. 1995. The copy theory of movement and linearization of chains in the Minimalist Program. Doctoral dissertation, University of Maryland, College Park.

Ross, John Robert. 1976. On the cyclic nature of English pronominalization. In *To honor Roman Jakobson*, 1669–1682. The Hague: Mouton.

Takahashi, Daiko. 1994. Minimality of movement. Doctoral dissertation, University of Connecticut, Storrs.

Watanabe, Akira. 1995. The conceptual basis of cyclicity. In *Papers on minimalist syntax*, eds. Rob Pensalfini and Hiroyuki Ura, 269–291. (MIT Working Papers in Linguistics 27.) MITWPL, Department of Linguistics and Philosophy, MIT, Cambridge, Mass.

Chapter 6

Featural Cyclicity and the Ordering of Multiple Specifiers

Norvin Richards

Chomsky (1995) suggests that we derive cyclicity by assuming something like the following principle, which I will refer to as *Featural Cyclicity*:

(1) A strong feature must be checked as soon as possible after being introduced into the derivation.

This principle essentially claims that the unit of the cycle is the maximal projection; once a strong feature has been introduced, no operations that do not check strong features (e.g., merger of another head that has its own features to be checked) can take place until the strong feature is checked. Together with the assumptions that (a) Merge always expands the tree and (b) overt movement can take place only in response to a strong feature, this principle derives cyclicity in a pleasingly minimalist way. Consider the derivations in (2)–(3).

(2) a.

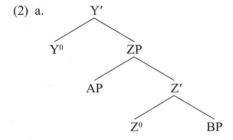

b.

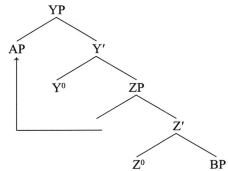

c.

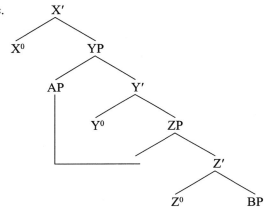

d.

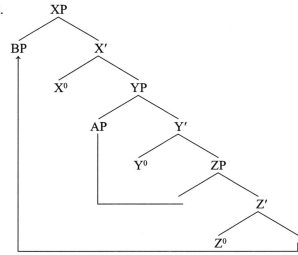

(3) a.

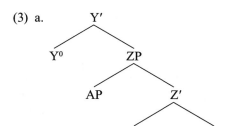

b.

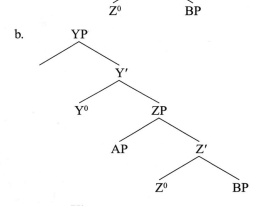

c.

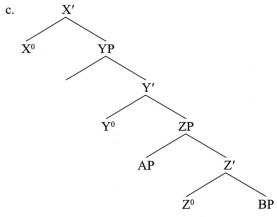

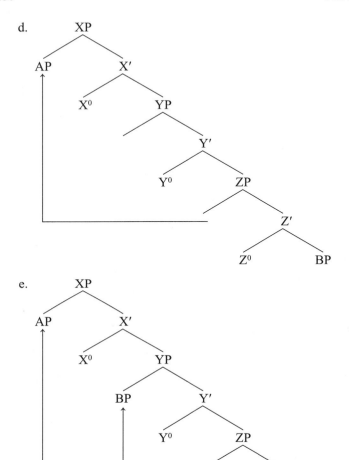

(2) and (3) both involve a ZP with specifier AP and complement BP, to which are added the heads Y^0 and X^0, both of which bear a strong feature that might in principle attract either AP or BP. (2) is the well-formed, Cyclicity-obeying derivation; in (3), by contrast, Cyclicity is disobeyed, as BP moves to [Spec, YP] after XP has already been projected (in step (3e)). The principle in (1) correctly distinguishes between the two derivations. In the well-formed derivation in (2), the strong features introduced in the

heads Y^0 and X^0 are checked in the steps immediately after the features are introduced, as (1) requires. In (3), on the other hand, the strong feature introduced in Y^0 in step (3a) is not checked until step (3e). Featural Cyclicity thus correctly rules out the derivation. As Kitahara (1994, 1997) observes, Cyclicity, along with Shortest Move, yields the effects of Pesetsky's (1982) Path Containment Condition; intersecting paths are forced to nest, rather than cross, as we have seen.

This way of deriving cyclicity avoids problems raised by head movement for Chomsky's (1993) definition of cyclicity. Chomsky (1993) suggests that all operations must necessarily expand the tree. This requirement successfully distinguishes between the derivations in (2) and (3), but it is always violated by head movement, which apparently never expands the tree.[1] The definition of cyclicity in terms of strong features, on the other hand, can be satisfied by head movement, as long as the head movement is checking a strong feature.

The two versions of cyclicity might also make different predictions in cases of movement to multiple specifiers of a single head. Suppose a head is generated with two strong features and attracts two XPs, as in (4).

(4) a.

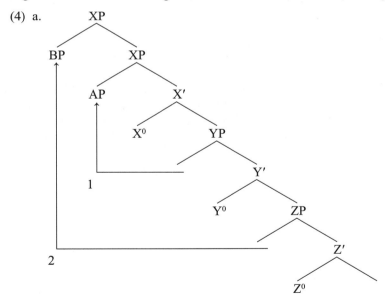

b.

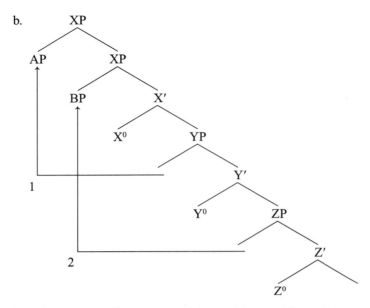

In (4a), the two specifiers are treated just like specifiers of two separate heads; the landing site of the first movement is lower than the landing site of the second. In (4b), on the other hand, the two paths cross, and the second movement lands closer to the head than the first.

Chomsky's (1995) version of cyclicity does not distinguish between the two derivations. As long as both XPs are moving to check a strong feature, either derivation ought in principle to be possible.[2] In fact, depending on what version of Shortest Move we assume, we might expect the derivation in (4b) to be preferred over that in (4a). Consider the derivation in (4b) again, step by step.

(5) a.

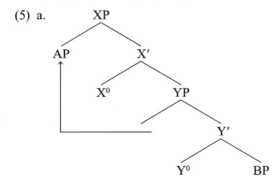

b.
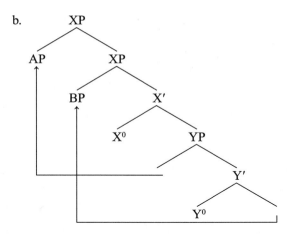

In (5a), AP moves into a specifier of XP. In (5b), BP moves—but where does it move to? Does it go to a specifier outside the one occupied by AP, or to a specifier inside the one occupied by AP? Featural Cyclicity, as we have seen, allows both options. Shortest Move might draw a distinction between these operations, however; if the specifier inside the one containing AP is closer, in the relevant sense, to the base position of BP than the one outside AP is, then Shortest Move will require movement to "tuck in" to the lower specifier, as shows in (5a).

Consider, on the other hand, the predictions of Chomsky's (1993) derivation of cyclicity from a requirement that every operation expand the tree. Depending on the definition of "expanding the tree" being assumed, we might expect this version of cyclicity to rule out the derivation in (4b); the second move here does not expand the tree. Alternatively, we might appeal to a notion of equidistance of multiple specifiers and define "expansion" in such a way that movement to a specifier that is equidistant with the highest specifier in the tree "expands the tree" in the relevant sense. Such a version of cyclicity would allow both derivations in (4), as does Featural Cyclicity. However, once multiple specifiers are defined as equidistant for purposes of expanding the tree, it would presumably be impossible to invoke Shortest Move to force the derivation in (4b), as we did in the above discussion of Featural Cyclicity; equidistant specifiers, by definition, should be equally favored as landing sites by Shortest Move. Thus, a version of cyclicity that forces every operation to expand the tree either allows only nested paths to multiple specifiers, as in (4a), or allows paths to multiple specifiers to freely either nest or cross, depending on how "expansion" is defined.

A feature-based notion of cyclicity, then, along with a certain conception of Shortest Move, predicts that multiple specifiers of a single head will be treated very differently from specifiers of multiple heads. Paths to multiple specifiers ought to cross, rather than nest, thus maintaining the base c-command relation (and, in principle, the base order) among XPs that move to them. This prediction is crucially not shared by Chomsky's (1993) version of cyclicity, which forces all operations to expand the tree; depending on the definition of "expand the tree," movements to multiple specifiers either will have to nest or will yield freely ordered specifiers, but should not be forced to cross. I will argue that paths to multiple specifiers of a single head do indeed cross, all other things being equal; the version of cyclicity to be preferred is the featural one.

6.1   Multiple *Wh*-Movement

Let us consider the case of multiple *wh*-movement, one case in which movement to multiple specifiers is arguably involved. In some languages, multiple *wh*-movement is subject to a restriction on the order of movement; the highest *wh*-word must be moved first.

(6) a.   who *t* bought what
    b.   ??what did who buy *t*

This is plausibly viewed as an effect of Shortest Attract; the C^0 that attracts the *wh*-words prefers to attract *who* rather than *what*, since *who* moves a shorter distance. Movement of *what* then follows anyway; but on the assumption that the grammar cannot look ahead in the derivation, this is irrelevant to the choice of which *wh*-word to move first.

In certain other languages, Superiority phenomena seem to take on a rather different form. Standard assumptions seem to make precisely the wrong predictions for *wh*-movement in some multiple overt *wh*-movement languages. Rudin (1988) shows that such languages can be divided into two groups: those that impose no ordering on multiple fronted *wh*-words (Serbo-Croatian, Polish) and those that do (Bulgarian, Romanian). For those languages that do impose such an ordering, the order essentially preserves the base c-command order.

(7) *Bulgarian* (Rudin 1988, 472–473)
   a. koj kogo vižda
      who whom sees
      'who sees whom'
   b. *kogo koj vižda
      whom who sees

If we wish to maintain the idea that movement always expands the tree, creating a specifier higher than all the existing structure, we must apparently conclude here that the lower of the two *wh*-words (*kogo* 'whom' in (7a)) must move first. Another possibility, of course, would be to say that the order of *wh*-movements in this case is just as in English: *koj* 'who' moves first, followed by movement of *kogo* 'what' to a lower specifier. On this account, the paths of these multiply-fronted *wh*-words must obligatorily cross, rater than nest.

Thus far, the generalization appears to be that Superiority effects arise when *wh*-words move on different levels (as in English) and that movement paths obligatorily cross when multiple *wh*-words move on the same level (as in Bulgarian). In fact, there is further evidence for this generalization from Japanese, in which both patterns can be observed.

Takahashi (1993) notes that Japanese long-distance scrambling of *wh*-words exhibits a Superiority effect; scrambling of a *wh*-word over another *wh*-word is impossible.

(8) *Japanese* (Takahashi 1993, 664)
   a. John-ga [Bill-ga dare-ni [Mary-ga nani-o   tabeta to]
      John-NOM Bill-NOM who-DAT Mary-NOM what-ACC ate   that
      itta to] omotteiru no
      said that thinks   Q
      'who does John think that Bill told that Mary ate what'
   b. **dare-ni** John-ga [Bill-ga *t* [Mary-ga nani-o tabeta to] itta to]
      omotteiru no
   c. ***nani-o** John-ga [Bill-ga dare-ni [Mary-ga *t* tabeta to] itta to]
      omotteiru no

This is what the proposed generalization leads us to expect; here, a single *wh*-word is being attracted in the overt syntax, so it must obey Superiority, just as in English. In multiple long-distance scrambling of *wh*-words, on the other hand, the paths must apparently cross, just as expected.

(9) *Japanese* (Takako Aikawa, personal communication)

    a. John-ga [Tanaka-sensee-ga   dare-ni nani-o   yomaseta
        John-NOM Tanaka-teacher-NOM who-DAT what-ACC read-CAUS
        to] itta no
        that said Q
        'who did John say Professor Tanaka made read what'

    b. dare$_i$-ni nani$_j$-o   John-ga   [Tanaka-sensee-ga $t_i t_j$
        who-DAT what-ACC John-NOM Tanaka-teacher-NOM
        yomaseta to] itta no
        read-CAUS that said Q

    c. *nani$_j$-o   dare$_i$-ni John-ga   [Tanaka-sensee-ga $t_i t_j$
        what-ACC who-DAT John-NOM Tanaka-teacher-NOM
        yomaseta to] itta no
        read-CAUS that said Q

The availability of both the English pattern and the Bulgarian pattern in a single language seems to indicate that these patterns are indeed properties of particular constructions, rather than of languages; it is not simply that Bulgarian is a "path-crossing" language whereas English is a "Superiority" language.

We have seen, then, that in all the cases in which the ordering of multiple *wh*-movements to a single landing site can be observed, the paths must apparently cross. In cases in which a single *wh*-movement to a single landing site takes place, the highest available *wh*-word must move. As observed above, this is precisely what a featural theory of cyclicity, together with a certain definition of Shortest Move, predicts. Given these assumptions, we expect the highest *wh*-word to move first, followed by "tucking in" of the next highest *wh*-word to a specifier below the landing site of the first movement. Such a derivation does seem to give the correct word order.

In fact, there is also evidence that the derivation proceeds in the order predicted, with the higher *wh*-word moving first, just as in English. Such evidence will necessarily have to involve a phenomenon that is sensitive to the order of syntactic operations. The data in (10) seem to exemplify such a phenomenon.

(10) *Bulgarian* (Roumyana Izvorski, Ani Petkova, Roumyana Slabakova, personal communications)

    a. *koja kniga$_i$ otreče senatorât [mâlvata če
       which book denied the-senator the-rumor that
       pravitelstvoto iska da zabrani t_i]
       the-government wanted to ban
       'which book did the senator deny the rumor that the government wanted to ban'

    b. ?koj senator koja kniga$_i$ otreče [mâlvata če
       which senator which book denied the-rumor that
       pravitelstvoto iska da zabrani t_i]
       the-government wanted to ban
       'which senator denied the rumor that the government wanted to ban which book'

(10) shows that a Complex NP Constraint violation in Bulgarian can be redeemed by moving another *wh*-phrase into another specifier of the same C^0. In earlier work (Richards 1997, 1998), I suggested that this fact should be dealt with by the same theory that accounts for the well-known contrast between (11a) and (11b).

(11) a. *what do you wonder whether John bought *t*
      b. who wonders whether John bought what

The generalization, in both English and Bulgarian, seems to be that a *wh*-movement can disobey Subjacency if a Subjacency-obeying movement to the same position has already occurred. In Richards 1997, 1998, I claim that this kind of interaction between dependencies, in which a well-formed dependency "redeems" another dependency that would be ill formed in isolation, is pervasive in the grammar, and I attempt to construct a general theory of such interactions. I develop a principle called the *Principle of Minimal Compliance*, which effectively permits the computational system to "ignore" those portions of a syntactic structure that have already been determined to be participating in a well-formed dependency.

    Note that this phenomenon is apparently sensitive to the order of operations; the Subjacency-obeying movement must precede the Subjacency-violating movement, as (12) shows.

(12) a. who$_i$ t_i persuaded [the man who bought which car$_j$] to sell the hubcaps

b. *which$_i$ car did John persuade [the man who bought t_i] to sell
   which hubcaps

(12a) is another case of a well-formed movement (here, movement of *who*)
licensing a later ill-formed movement (here, movement of *which car* out of
the relative clause to the matrix [Spec, CP]). (12b) is another attempt to
license an ill-formed movement with a well-formed movement, but in this
case, the well-formed movement is that of *which hubcaps*, which follows
the ill-formed movement of *which car*.[3] Apparently, then, the licensing
movement must precede the movement it licenses. In English, of course,
this means that the licensing movement will be overt and the licensed
movement covert, since only the first *wh*-movement to a given position is
overt in English. However, the Bulgarian facts, which parallel the English
facts but involve only overt movements, suggest that the overt/covert
distinction has nothing to do with this phenomenon.

We have seen, then, that Subjacency amelioration can serve as a diagnostic for the order of movements; if one movement is to license another,
the Subjacency-obeying movement must occur first. Consider the Bulgarian facts again.

(13) *Bulgarian* (Roumyana Izvorski, Ani Petkova, Roumyana Slabakova,
     personal communications)
   a. *koja   kniga$_i$ otreče senatorât [mâlvata   če
      which book denied the-senator the-rumor that
      pravitelstvoto iska   da zabrani t_i]
      the-government wanted to ban
      'which book did the senator deny the rumor that the
      government wanted to ban'
   b. ?koj   senator koja kniga$_i$ otreče [mâlvata   če
      which senator which book denied the-rumor that
      pravitelstvoto iska   da zabrani t_i]
      the-government wanted to ban
      'which senator denied the rumor that the government wanted to
      ban which book'

In the well-formed (13b), the Subjacency-obeying *wh*-phrase *koj senator*
'which senator' linearly precedes the Subjacency-violating *wh*-phrase *koja
kniga* 'which book'. If the chain of reasoning outlined above is correct,
this means that *koj senator* must have moved to [Spec, CP] first, followed
by movement of *koja kniga* to a lower [Spec, CP]. This is precisely what
Featural Cyclicity, along with Shortest Move; predicts.

In fact, there is independent evidence from both Japanese and Bulgarian that in those languages, as in English, Subjacency-obeying movements must precede Subjacency-disobeying movements in the derivation. Consider the Subjacency violations in (14) and (15).

(14) *Bulgarian* (Roumyana Izvorski, personal communication)
    *kakvo$_j$ kazva tozi služitel na [žurnalistite,   kojto razsledvat
    what   tells   this official to the-journalists who investigate
    [mâlvata, če   pravitelstvoto   iska   da zabrani t_j]],
    the-rumor that the-government wants to ban
    če komunistite   sa   zabludili redaktorite im
    that the-Communists AUX deceived the-editors their
    'what does this official tell journalists who are investigating the rumor that the government wants to ban that the Communists have deceived their editors'

(15) *Japanese* (Takako Aikawa, Shigeru Miyagawa, personal communications)
    *John-ga [Bill-ga [Mary-ga nani-o   katta   ka dooka]
    John-NOM Bill-NOM Mary-NOM what-ACC bought whether
    sitteita to] itta no
    knows that said Q
    'what did John say that Bill knows whether Mary bought'

In Bulgarian, an example like (14) can be improved by overt extraction of the matrix subject.

(16) *Bulgarian* (Roumyana Izvorski, personal communication)
    ??koj$_i$ kakvo$_j$ kazva t_i na [žurnalistite,   kojto razsledvat
    who what   tells   to the-journalists who investigate
    [mâlvata, če   pravitelstvoto   iska   da zabrani t_j]],
    the-rumor that the-government wants to ban
    če komunistite   sa   zabludili redaktorite im
    that the-Communists AUX deceived the-editors their
    'who tells journalists who are investigating the rumor that the government wants to ban what that the Communists have deceived their editors'

Here, the landing site of the well-formed extraction precedes the landing site of the ill-formed extraction; by hypothesis, this indicates that well-formed extraction has preceded ill-formed extraction in the derivation.

The opposite order of operations, on the other hand, yields an ill-formed sentence.

(17) *Bulgarian* (Roumyana Izvorski, personal communication)
   *kakvo$_j$ kogo$_k$ kazva tozi služitel na [žurnalistite,   kojto
   what   who   tells   this official to the-journalists who
   razsledvat [mâlvata,   če   pravitelstvoto   iska   da zabrani t_j]],
   investigate the-rumor that the-government wants to ban
   če   komunistite   sa   zabludili t_k
   that the-Communists AUX deceived
   'what does this official tell journalists who are investigating the
   rumor that the government wants to ban that the Communists have
   deceived who'

Here, ill-formed movement of *kakvo* 'what' is followed by well-formed movement of *kogo* 'who' from the object position of an embedded clause that is the complement of the matrix verb, and the result, as expected, is ill formed.

Because the extraction sites in (17) are not in a c-command relation with respect to each other, Superiority places no requirements on the order in which they move to the matrix [Spec, CP]. Moving the *wh*-words in the opposite order improves the sentence.[4]

(18) *Bulgarian* (Roumyana Izvorski, personal communication)
   ??kogo$_k$ kakvo$_j$ kazva tozi služitel na [žurnalistite,   kojto
   who   what   tells   this official to the-journalists who
   razsledvat [mâlvata,   če   pravitelstvoto   iska   da zabrani t_j]],
   investigate the-rumor that the-government wants to ban
   če   komunistite   sa   zabludili t_k
   that the-Communists AUX deceived
   'who does this official tell journalists who are investigating the
   rumor that the government wants to ban what that the
   Communists have deceived'

This is again as expected; *kogo* 'who' is the *wh*-word that is not being extracted out of an island, so if it arrives in the matrix [Spec, CP] first, the sentence should improve.

Turning to Japanese, it is clear that addition of a *wh*-word c-commanding the island from which ill-formed extraction takes place improves an example like (15), repeated here as (19).

(19) *Japanese* (Takako Aikawa, Shigeru Miyagawa, personal communications)
*John-ga [Bill-ga [Mary-ga nani-o katta ka dooka]
John-NOM Bill-NOM Mary-NOM what-ACC bought whether
sitteita to] itta no
knows that said Q
'what did John say that Bill knows whether Mary bought'

(20) ?John-ga dare-ni [Bill-ga [Mary-ga nani-o katta
John-NOM who-DAT Bill-NOM Mary-NOM what-ACC bought
ka dooka] sitteita to] itta no
whether knows that said Q
'who did John tell that Bill knows whether Mary bought what'

This is as expected; in (20), *dare-ni* 'who' is the highest available *wh*-word and will therefore be attracted first, licensing later extraction of *nani-o* 'what' out of the *wh*-island.

Speakers differ on the well-formedness of sentences in which the additional *wh*-word is outside the island but does not c-command it.

(21) *Japanese* (Takako Aikawa, Shigeru Miyagawa, personal communications)
%John-ga [Bill-ga [Mary-ga nani-o katta ka dooka]
John-NOM Bill-NOM Mary-NOM what-ACC bought whether
sitteita to] dare-ni itta no
knows that who-DAT said Q
'who did John tell that Bill knows whether Mary bought what'

For some speakers, (21) is better than (19) but worse than (20); for others, (20) and (21) are equally good. I assume that the ambiguous status of examples like (21) has something to do with the availability of distinct derivations for such examples, corresponding to the Bulgarian examples (17) and (18). Because the *wh*-words in (21) are not in a c-command relation with respect to each other, they can in principle be attracted to the matrix C^0 at LF in either order. Only the order in which the Subjacency-obeying movement precedes the Subjacency-disobeying movement will make the sentence better than (19). In (20), by contrast, Shortest Attract forces a derivation in which the well-formed movement precedes the ill-formed movement. The degraded status of (21) for some speakers might reflect a need to "search" for a well-formed derivation in this case.

Thus, it would appear that in Japanese and Bulgarian, as in English, Subjacency-amelioration effects hold only when the well-formed movement precedes the ill-formed movement.[5] The distribution of these effects can therefore be used as evidence for the derivational claim made by this theory; in cases of movement to multiple specifiers, movement to a higher specifier precedes movement to a lower specifier in the derivation.

6.2   Multiple A-Specifiers

We have now seen that the predictions of a theory incorporating Featural Cyclicity and a certain notion of Shortest Move seem to be borne out in cases of multiple *wh*-movement; we can successfully explain ordering restrictions on *wh*-movement in a variety of languages using fairly simple assumptions. Given such simple assumptions, however, we expect to find this pattern arising quite generally in all cases involving movement to multiple specifiers of a single head. Is it possible to find evidence for this theory from the domain of A-movement, for example?

(22) shows that Japanese local scrambling, which might in principle be thought to involve movement to multiple A-specifiers, does not appear to exhibit any Superiority effects. Two arguments can be scrambled over the subject in either order.

(22) *Japanese*
     a. Taroo-ga gakusei-ni hutari hon-o   ageta
        Taroo-NOM student-DAT two   book-ACC gave
        'Taroo gave books to two students'
     b. Gakusei-ni hutari hon-o   Taroo-ga ageta
        student-DAT two   book-ACC Taroo-NOM gave
     c. hon-o   gakusei-ni hutari Taroo-ga ageta
        book-ACC student-DAT two   Taroo-NOM gave

Of course, there may be any of a number of confounding factors preventing us from observing the effects of Superiority here; there may, for example, be more than one attracting head involved. Developing a complete theory of scrambling is well beyond the scope of this chapter. In the next section, I will simply try to show that Superiority effects do indeed hold in a certain subset of A-scrambling cases, which suggests that the general account of Superiority developed above may be on the right track. It is well known that local scrambling interacts with such semantic properties as definiteness, specificity, and quantifier scope. I will try to show that when these effects are controlled for, local scrambling does obey Superiority, as defined here. In section 6.2.1, I will show that local scrambling that has no semantic effects obeys Superiority. In section 6.2.2, I will present evidence suggesting that local scrambling that violates Superiority does in fact involve multiple attractors.

6.2.1   Idiom Chunks

One phenomenon to consider is the scrambling of idiom chunks. Idiom chunks are presumably nonreferential and therefore impervious to any effects scrambling might have on discourse properties. If it is these effects that are responsible for the apparent failure of A-scrambling to conform to Superiority, then we might expect to get a clearer picture by looking at the scrambling of idiom chunks. Miyagawa (1994) notes that scrambling of idiom chunks in Japanese is confined to short-distance scrambling, as in (23a); long-distance scrambling, as in (23b), is impossible.

(23) *Japanese* (Miyagawa 1994, 20–21)
  a.   kosi-o   John-ga   *t* orosita
       hip-ACC John-NOM   lowered
       'John sat down'
  b. ?*kosi-o   Mary-ga   [John-ga   *t* orosita to]   itta
       hip-ACC Mary-NOM John-NOM   lowered that said
       'Mary said that John sat down'

Idiom chunks, then, may apparently only be A-scrambled; there are certain attractors that are capable of attracting ordinary NPs but not idiom chunks. We might hope to find that in fact, there is only a single attractor in each clause that is capable of attracting idiom chunks. It is interesting to note, in this connection, that multiple idiom chunks do indeed appear to obey Superiority in their short-distance scrambling. If scrambling affects only one idiom chunk, it must raise the higher of the two.

(24) *Japanese* (Shigeru Miyagawa, Kazuko Yatsushiro, personal communications)
  a.   Taroo-ga   hi-ni   abura-o sosoida
       Taroo-NOM fire-DAT oil-ACC   poured
       'Taroo made things worse'
  b.   hi-ni   Taroo-ga   *t* abura-o sosoida
       fire-DAT Taroo-NOM   oil-ACC   poured
  c. *abura-o Taroo-ga   hi-ni   *t* sosoida
       oil-ACC   Taroo-NOM fire-DAT   poured

Both idiom chunks may also be scrambled, but the two paths must cross.

(25) *Japanese* (Shigeru Miyagawa, Kazuko Yatsushiro, personal
    communications)
    a.   hi$_i$-ni   abura$_j$-o Taroo-ga $t_i t_j$ sosoida
           fire-DAT oil-ACC Taroo-NOM   poured
           'Taroo made things worse'
    b.   *abura$_j$-o hi$_i$-ni   Taroo-ga $t_i t_j$ sosoida
           oil-ACC fire-DAT Taroo-NOM   poured

In terms of the theory developed here, we may understand these data as
indicating that there is only a single attractor in each Japanese clause that
is capable of attracting idiom chunks; this can be linked to the fact that
idiom chunks, unlike ordinary NPs, cannot be long-distance-scrambled.
For the account to succeed, we must assume that this attractor is incapable of attracting the subject of the clause. If attraction of the subject were
possible, it would be forced by Shortest Attract, and scrambling of idiom
chunks past the subject would be impossible. In fact, Saito (1985) has
argued on independent grounds that subjects cannot be scrambled in
Japanese.

"Superiority," then, does not affect only $\bar{\text{A}}$-movement. Furthermore, as
we saw with A-movement, multiple A-movements to a single attractor
must apparently cross and not nest, just as the account developed here
predicts.

6.2.2 Scrambling Generally

I have just presented a case of semantically vacuous local scrambling that
apparently must obey Superiority. In this section, I will argue further that
scrambling with crossing paths is (or can be) the result of multiple
attraction by a single attractor, whereas scrambling with nesting paths
must involve multiple attractors.

The argument is based on a kind of relativization in Japanese that violates islands, discussed by (among others) Kuno (1973), Hasegawa (1984),
and Ochi (1996).

(26) *Japanese* (Ochi 1996)
     [[e_i e_j kiteiru] huku$_j$-ga   yogoreteiru] kodomo$_i$
           wear   clothes-NOM dirty   child
         'the child$_i$ that the clothes$_j$ that t_i is wearing t_j are dirty'

Here, relativization of the operator associated with *kodomo* 'child' seems
to take place from inside a relative clause modifying *huku* 'clothes', in

violation of the *Wh*-Island Constraint and the Condition on Extraction Domain. As Hasegawa (1984) notes, such relativization, is strongly constrained, at least for some speakers. Hasegawa observes that the relative clause out of which relativization takes place (which I will call, for purposes of exposition, the *contained* relative clause) must modify the subject of the relative clause by which it is contained. Thus, (26) contrasts with (27).

(27) *Japanese* (Ochi 1996)
   *[[Mary-ga   [e_i e_j kiteiru] huku$_j$-o   tukutta] kodomo$_i$
   Mary-NOM   wear   clothes-ACC made   child
   'the child$_i$ that Mary made the clothes$_j$ that t_i is wearing t_j'

In fact, the conditions on the positioning of the contained relative clause are somewhat freer than this. In particular, this kind of relativization can be affected by scrambling, as well as by constructions that have been argued to involve multiple specifiers. Thus, there is a contrast between (28a) and (28b), as well as between (29a) and (29b).

(28) *Japanese* (Takako Aikawa, Shigeru Miyagawa, personal communications)
   a. *[Taroo-ga   [e_i e_j kaita] hon$_j$-o   katta] sakka$_i$
      Taroo-NOM   wrote book-ACC bought author
      'the author$_i$ that Taroo bought the book$_j$ that t_i wrote t_j'
   b. ?[Taroo-ga   [e_i e_j kaita] hon$_j$-ga   suki na sakka$_i$
      Taroo-NOM   wrote book-NOM likes   author
      'the author$_i$ that Taroo likes the book$_j$ that t_i wrote t_j'

(29) *Japanese* (Takako Aikawa, Shigeru Miyagawa, personal communications)
   a. *[Taroo-ga   [e_i e_j kaita] hon$_j$-o   katta] sakka$_i$
      Taroo-NOM   wrote book-ACC bought author
      'the author$_i$ that Taroo bought the book$_j$ that t_i wrote t_j'
   b. ?[[e_i e_j kaita] hon$_j$-o   Taroo-ga   katta] sakka$_i$
               wrote book-ACC Taroo-NOM bought author
      'the author$_i$ that the book$_j$ that t_i wrote t_j, Taroo bought'

As (28) shows, the contained relative clause can modify the object of a double-*ga* predicate; such predicates have been analyzed (see Ura 1996) as having the multiple *ga*-marked elements in multiple specifiers of a single head. Furthermore, (29) shows that scrambling can affect the acceptability of contained relative clauses; a contained relative clause can modify a direct object that has been scrambled to the front of its clause.

Though I will not try here to develop a full theory of the nature of this kind of relativization, the contrast in (28) suggests that contained relative clauses can be used as a test for structure. If a noninitial argument is capable of hosting a contained relative clause, we may conclude that it and the preceding argument(s) are in multiple specifiers, as in (28b), rather than in separate maximal projections, as in (28a).

Having established this, let us turn to the distribution of contained relatives in double object constructions. On the theory proposed here, scrambling of both double objects that preserves the base c-command relation between the scrambled arguments may involve scrambling to multiple specifiers of a single head. Scrambling that alters the base c-command relation, on the other hand, must necessarily involve movement to distinct maximal projections. The prediction, then, is that scrambling that preserves the base order will allow contained relative clauses to modify either object, since the objects, like the *ga*-marked nominals in (28b), are in multiple specifiers of a single head. Scrambling that alters the base order, on the other hand, will allow a contained relative clause only on the first object, since the two objects must be in specifiers of different heads, like the subject and object in (28a).

In order to test this prediction, we must first determine the base order of double object constructions in Japanese, which is not a straightforward task. Miyagawa (1997) argues convincingly that both IO-DO (indirect object–direct object) and DO-IO word orders can be base-generated in Japanese. His claim is that the distinct base-generated orders correspond to different structural realizations of the indirect object; in the IO-DO order, he says, the IO is a dative-marked NP, whereas in the DO-IO order, it is a PP. One argument for this conclusion is provided by the distribution of floated numeral quantifiers, which, as he argues in Miyagawa 1989, can modify NPs but not PPs. These quantifiers can appear on the IO in the IO-DO order, but not in the DO-IO order.[6]

(30) *Japanese* (Miyagawa 1989)
    a. Mary-ga   tomodati-ni hutari CD-o   okutta
        Mary-NOM friend-DAT two   CD-ACC sent
        'Mary sent two friends a CD'
    b. *Mary-ga   CD-o   tomodati-ni hutari okutta
        Mary-NOM CD-ACC friend-DAT two   sent

Now we are in a position to test the predictions of the theory being developed here. We have seen that a floated numeral quantifier on the dative argument signals an IO-DO base order. Thus, in cases in which the double objects are scrambled to the left of the subject and the dative argument is marked by a floated numeral quantifier, we expect to find that a contained relative clause can modify the second object only when the base IO-DO order is maintained. If the order is DO-IO, then scrambling must have involved specifiers of distinct attractors, and a contained relative clause on the second object should no longer be possible.

The sentences in (31), then, form a minimal pair.[7]

(31) *Japanese* (Takako Aikawa, Shigeru Miyagawa, personal
     communications)
   a. ?[seijika-ni   hutari [t_i t_j kyoonen osieta] Tanaka-san-no
       politician-DAT two   last-year taught Tanaka-HON-GEN
       kodomo$_j$-o Hanako-ga   syookaisita] sensee$_i$
       child-ACC   Hanako-NOM introduced   teacher
       'the teacher$_i$ that Hanako introduced the children$_j$ of Mr.
       Tanaka that t_i taught t_j last year to two politicians'
   b. *[seijika-o   [t_i t_j kyoonen osieta] Tanaka-san-no
       politician-ACC   last-year taught Tanaka-HON-GEN
       kodomo$_j$-ni hutari Hanako-ga   syookaisita] sensee$_i$
       child-DAT   two   Hanako-NOM introduced   teacher
       'the teacher$_i$ that Hanako introduced the politician to two of the
       children$_j$ of Mr. Tanaka that t_i taught t_j last year'

In both cases, the contained relative clause modifies the second NP in the relative clause. In the first case, however, the base order of the scrambled double objects is preserved, and the word order is therefore compatible with movement to multiple specifiers of a single attractor; relativization into the second nominal is therefore possible. In the second case, the base order of the scrambled elements is not preserved, and scrambling must, on this account, involve movement to specifiers of distinct maximal projections. The contrast between (31a) and (31b) thus follows from this theory, given a theory of locality that distinguishes between multiple specifiers of a single head and specifiers of distinct heads. It is worth noting that the ill-formed example (31b) improves considerably if the numeral quantifier *hutari* 'two' is dropped.

(32) *Japanese* (Takako Aikawa, Shigeru Miyagawa, personal
     communications)
     ?[seijika-o   [t_i t_j kyoonen osieta] Tanaka-san-no   kodomo$_j$-ni
      politician-ACC   last-year taught Tanaka-HON-GEN child-DAT
      Hanako-ga   syookaisita] sensee$_i$
      Hanako-NOM introduced   teacher
     'the teacher$_i$ that Hanako introduced the politician to the children$_j$
     of Mr. Tanaka that t_i taught t_j last year'

This is consistent with Miyagawa's (1997) approach to local scrambling in
Japanese. Recall that floated numeral quantifiers crucially force a base
IO-DO order, since this, by hypothesis, is the order in which IO is an NP,
and floated numeral quantifiers can only modify NPs. In (32), however,
there is no floated numeral quantifier; thus, a base DO-IO order is possible in this case. In other words, the scrambled objects can reflect the base
order, and relativization out of the second object should be possible,
which appears to be the case.[8]

   In this section, we have seen that scrambling that does not preserve the
base order must involve multiple attractors. The most straightforward
theory about scrambling, then, can apparently be maintained; scrambling
is subject to the general conditions on movement discussed here. The
apparent violations of Superiority found in scrambling are a result of the
availability of multiple attractors. Speakers apparently may posit exactly
as many attractors as are necessary to account for the word order of a
particular sentence.

6.3   Other Applications

In the preceding sections, we have seen evidence that nested paths are a
result of multiple attraction by multiple attractors, whereas crossing paths
are a result of multiple attraction by a single attractor. To the extent that
this generalization is accurate, we are entitled to suspect the work of a
single attractor in cases where paths must obligatorily cross. In this section, I
will briefly discuss other cases of this type. Space requirements prevent me
from arguing at any length that these phenomena do indeed involve movement to multiple specifiers; see Richards 1997 for further discussion.

6.3.1   Object Shift
One case in which crossing paths are standardly invoked is the movement
of arguments from their base positions to their Case-checking positions.

Such movement has traditionally been thought to involve obligatorily crossing movement to the specifiers of three distinct heads.[9]

(33) $[_{Agr_SP}$ $[_{Agr_{IO}P}$ $[_{Agr_OP}$ $[_{VP}$ S   IO   DO]]]]

This assumption is taken to account, for instance, for the data in (34).

(34) *Icelandic* (Collins and Thráinsson 1993, 143, 149, 154)
   a.   ég lána **ekki** Maríu bækurnar
        I lend not Maria books
        'I do not lend Maria the books'
   b.   ég lána Maríu **ekki** bækurnar
   c.   ég lána Maríu bækurnar **ekki**
   d.   *ég lána bækurnar **ekki** Maríu
   e.   *ég lána bækurnar Maríu **ekki**

Examples such as these are typically thought to involve shifting the NPs in question over the relevant adverbs. Crucially, in these cases no reordering of the arguments with respect to other arguments is possible; (35), for instance, is ungrammatical, indicating that the paths of the indirect and direct objects cannot nest.

(35) *Icelandic* (Collins and Thráinsson 1993, 145)
     *ég lána bækurnar Maríu **ekki**
     I lend books   Maria not

Given the approach developed here, we might take the obligatory crossing of the paths in this case to indicate that only a single attractor is at work. That is, we might alter (33) to (36).

(36) $[_{Agr_VP}$ $[_{VP}$ S   IO   DO]]

We might assume, then, that argument shift is always triggered by a single AgrP head, which obligatorily triggers overt raising of some nonnull set of arguments (that is, at least the subject, and possibly some of the other arguments), the Case features of which are checked by Agr. There are a number of other assumptions that are consistent with these data. For instance, I have represented the head responsible for Case checking as having no other function. Another possibility would be to say that this head also plays some other role. For example, it might be the head that assigns a θ-role to the subject; we would then need to assume that the subject can have its Case checked in situ. Note that as long as Merge is preferred to Move (see Chomsky 1995), the subject will have to be merged before the other arguments are moved to [Spec, Agr$_V$P]; thus, we still predict that the paths of IO and DO to [Spec, Agr$_V$P] will obligatorily cross and will be forced by Shortest Move to land under the specifier occupied by the subject, even if the subject is base-generated in [Spec, Agr$_V$P].[10]

6.3.2 [Spec, NegP]

Another case in which obligatorily crossing paths have been reported in the literature is the phenomenon of "negative fronting." Izvorski (1995) reports, for instance, that negative elements in Bulgarian undergo a kind of movement that is subject to the same ordering restrictions as *wh*-movement (and see Haegeman 1995 for discussion of similar facts in West Flemish).

(37) *Bulgarian* (Izvorski 1995, 66)
    a. nikoj   na nikogo ništo   ne beše kazal
          nobody to nobody nothing not AUX said
          'no one had said anything to anyone'
    b. *ništo   na nikogo nikoj   ne beše kazal
          nothing to nobody nobody not AUX said

(38) *Bulgarian* (Izvorski 1995, 66)
    a. koj na kogo kakvo beše kazal
          who to whom what AUX said
          'who said what to whom'
    b. *kakvo na kogo koj beše kazal
          what to whom who AUX said

Thus, negative fronting, like object shift, should be analyzed in this theory as involving movement to multiple specifiers of a single head.

6.3.3 Cliticization

Another case in which multiple movements appear to obligatorily cross is that of cliticization in many languages.

(39) *Serbo-Croatian* (Franks 1997, 1998)

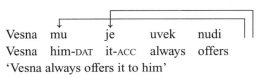

    Vesna mu   je   uvek   nudi
    Vesna him-DAT it-ACC always offers
    'Vesna always offers it to him'

(40) *Tagalog*

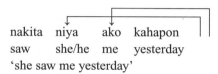

nakita   niya   ako   kahapon
saw   she/he   me   yesterday
'she saw me yesterday'

In the theory developed here, this would indicate that such clitics are all syntactically moving to check their features against a single head. Evidence that something like this may in fact give the correct structure for the clitic cluster is presented by Stjepanović (1998), who notes the following ellipsis possibilities for the clitic cluster in Serbo-Croatian:

(41) *Serbo-Croatian* (Stjepanović 1998)
    Øna mu   ga   je   dala,...
    she him-DAT it-ACC AUX-3SG gave
    'she gave it to him ...'
    a. ...a   i   ja **sam   mu   ga**   [dala]
          and also I AUX-1SG him-DAT it-ACC gave
          '... and I gave it to him as well'
    b. ...a i ja **sam mu** [ga dala]
    c. ...a i ja **sam** [mu ga dala]
    d. *...a i ja **sam** [mu] **ga** [dala]

On the assumption that ellipsis targets constituents, these ellipsis data argue that the structure of the clitic cluster is as shown in (42).

(42)

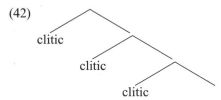

This, of course, is the structure predicted by the approach developed above. Many interesting questions now arise, which I am not in a position to address here. Are the clitics in (39)–(41) in multiple specifiers? What happens in cases in which clitics attach to a head with specifiers? In part, this will depend on the content of the notion "specifier," an issue that is not crucial to the theory developed here. In a bare theory of phrase structure, we presumably expect the syntactic position of moved elements to follow from independent principles of syntax. We would not be surprised to find, for instance, that clitics are forced for morphosyntactic reasons to "tuck in" to positions below the specifiers in which fully phrasal categories check features. The only requirement of the theory developed here would be that the landing site of each movement be as low as possible.

This approach to clitic ordering also leads to the expectation that the order of clitics in a language will always reflect the hierarchical relations between the base positions of the cliticized elements. It should generally be true, for instance, that in a language in which IOs c-command DOs, dative clitics will precede accusative clitics, whereas in a language in which DOs c-command IOs, the reverse will be true.

6.4 Shortest (Move)

I began by suggesting that the strict ordering of multiple specifiers might be due to Shortest Move. The basic idea was that in cases of movement to multiple specifiers of a single head, Featural Cyclicity makes no distinction between crossing and nesting paths; both involve multiple checking of a strong feature. On a certain version of Shortest Move, it should prefer movement to a lower specifier over movement to a higher specifier. That is, we should be able to employ a version of Shortest Move to choose (43b) over (43a), which is the correct result.

(43) a.

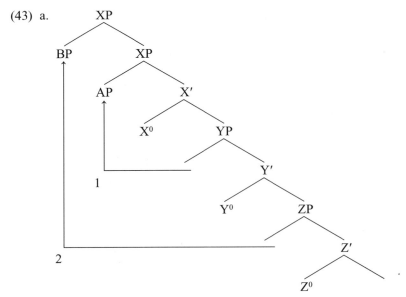

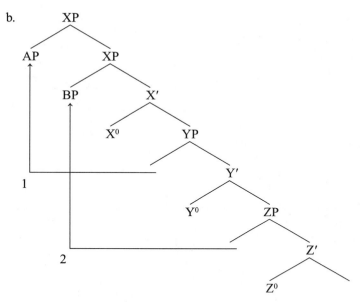

To get this result, we will need a version of Shortest Move that differs from the one now commonly assumed. Shortest Move will have to be sensitive both to potential movable elements and to potential landing sites. That is, (44) will have to be a violation of Shortest Move whether X is a movable element that could have moved to A or a possible landing site for the kind of movement involved in movement from B to A (see Murasugi 1992 for a theory of Shortest Move of this kind, and Ochi 1997 for a similar proposal).

(44) A   X   B

Let us define a version of Shortest Move with this property. Consider the operation Attract, illustrated in (45).

(45) a. $K\ [_\alpha\ F]$
     b. $[_{\alpha'}\ F']\ K\ [_\alpha\ F]$

The attractor K attracts the feature F, causing the creation of a copy of F and the minimal element α containing F that allows convergence; at a minimum, α is the formal features of F, but it may also be forced by well-formedness conditions imposed by the PF and LF interfaces to be some constituent containing the formal features of F. In the case of overt *wh*-movement, for instance, α might be an entire NP, although the feature F is simply the *wh*-feature; the NP is "pied-piped" for reasons having to do with requirements on well-formed PF objects. The copy α' of α then merges with K, entering K's checking domain.

Attract, then, may be stated as in (4b).

(46) *Attract*

An attractor K attracts a feature F, creating a copy α' of an element α containing F and merging α' with K. The relations between α', K, and F must all obey Shortest.

Shortest is defined in (47).

(47) *Shortest*

A pair P of elements $\{\alpha, \beta\}$ obeys Shortest iff there is no well-formed pair P' that can be created by substituting γ for either α or β, and the set of nodes c-commanded by one element of P' and dominating the other is smaller than the set of nodes c-commanded by one element of P and dominating the other.

Shortest will crucially constrain the relations between K and F, and between α' and F. The effect of Shortest on the relation between K and F will be to force the attractor to attract the nearest available mover. Its effect on the relation between α' and F will be to force movement to choose the closest available landing site; in the case of movement to multiple specifiers, for instance, the landing site will have to be the closest available specifier, as desired. Furthermore, Shortest's effect on the relation between α' and F will prevent movement of F past an attractor that could attract F, since the intervening attractor could have an element γ in its specifier that would enter into a well-formed dependency with F. As Attract is defined in (46), it also requires the relation between α' and K to obey Shortest. This is purely for the sake of simplicity; this requirement plays no role in the theory. Requiring this relation to obey Shortest will have no effect other than to force every movement to multiple specifiers to choose the closest available specifier, a result already derived by the effects of Shortest on the relation between α' and F.

In principle, we might split the constraint Shortest into two parts, referring to the effect of Shortest on the relation between K and F as *Shortest Attract*, and to the effect of Shortest on the relation between α' and F as *Shortest Move*. As the theory has been developed here, these are simply labels for the effects of Shortest on different types of elements; the constraints Shortest Move and Shortest Attract are not formally distinct.

Another conclusion this theory forces is that the specifiers in (43) are not "equidistant," at least not from the perspective of elements that are moving into them. The lower specifier will have to be closer to a moving element than a higher specifier would be.

6.5   Conclusion

I have tried to show that Chomsky's (1995) notion of Featural Cyclicity is to be preferred over earlier versions of cyclicity. A theory assuming Featural Cyclicity predicts—correctly, I have argued—that multiple movements will cross rather than nesting just in case their destinations are multiple specifiers of a single head. I have claimed that this is true for both A- and Ā-movement, which allows us to derive these facts from a straightforward theory based on Featural Cyclicity and Shortest Move.

Notes

A number of people deserve heartfelt thanks for their help. The theory developed here was independently developed in Mulders 1996, to appear, and I would like to thank Iris Mulders for much insightful discussion of the relevant issues. David Pesetsky was also enormously helpful and encouraging in the development of the theory. For assistance with specific languages, I would like to thank Ani Petkova, Roumyana Slabakova, and especially Roumyana Izvorski for their help with Bulgarian, and Takako Aikawa, Shigeru Miyagawa, and Kazuko Yatsushiro for their discussion of the Japanese facts. Thanks, too, to Elena Anagnostopoulou, Noam Chomsky, Sam Epstein, Danny Fox, Lyn Frazier, John Frampton, Steven Franks, Kleanthes Grohmann, Norbert Hornstein, Roumyana Izvorski, Kyle Johnson, Kiyomi Kusumoto, Winnie Lechner, Martha McGinnis, Shigeru Miyagawa, Gereon Müller, Uli Sauerland, Junko Shimoyama, Peggy Speas, Peter Svenonius, Pius Tamanji; audiences at WCCFL 16, SCIL 7, the Penn Linguistics Colloquium, CUNY, and Potsdam; and the participants of my fall 1997 syntax seminar at the University of Massachusetts, Amherst, for their helpful comments and suggestions. Responsibility for remaining problems is mine alone.

1. See Bobaljik and Brown 1997 for another approach to circumventing this problem.

2. The case of movement to multiple specifiers raises another potential question about this version of cyclicity. Assuming that the two movements are not simultaneous, how can a derivation in which two strong features are introduced at the same time satisfy Featural Cyclicity at all? Whichever feature is checked first, the other feature must presumably "wait" for the first feature-checking operation to take place before it can itself be checked. One can imagine a number of solutions, which I will not try to discuss here. One approach would be to understand the requirement that strong features be checked "immediately" as meaning that they must be checked "as soon as possible"—in particular, before any operations that do not check strong features are performed. Another approach, following

Chomsky 1995, 234ff., would be to state the condition on strong features as one that cancels the derivation if at any point a strong feature is present on a head that is not the head of the structure in which it is contained.

3. Here I assume, as is standard, that covert movements follow overt movements in the derivation.

4. Judgments are apparently subtle here, but my informant says that (16) is better than (18) (Roumyana Izvorski, personal communication). I have no account to offer for this fact.

5. There is one interesting deviation from this pattern, which I discuss in Richards 1997; in both Japanese and Bulgarian, extraction from an island may be improved by a *subsequent* well-formed *wh*-movement, just in case the offending island c-commands the extraction site of the well-formed movement (see Richards 1997 for arguments that the relevant movement is indeed subsequent in Japanese).

(i) *Bulgarian* (Roumyana Izvorski, personal communication)

?kakvo$_j$ kogo$_k$ kazva tozi služitel na [žurnalistite,   kojto razsledvat t_j],
what   who   tells this official to the-journalists who investigate

če komunistite   sa zabludili t_k
that the-Communists AUX deceived

'what does this official tell journalists who are investigating that the Communists have deceived who'

(ii) *Japanese* (adapted from Watanabe 1992, 270–271)

John-wa [Mary-ga nani-o   katta ka dooka] dare-ni tazuneta no
John-TOP Mary-NOM what-ACC bought whether who-DAT asked   Q

'who did John ask whether Mary bought what'

I discuss this pattern further in Richards 1997, where I link this form of multiple-*wh* interaction with the very similar conditions on parasitic gaps in languages like English. The effect has been controlled for in the examples in the text by embedding the offending island further, so that it fails to c-command the "redeeming' extraction site.

6. (30b) can be improved by focusing the accusative argument.

7. In (31), the possessor *Tanaka-san-no* on the NP out of which relativization takes place guards against the possibility that the relativized element is actually a possessor of the NP, rather than a position inside the contained relative clause.

8. The difference between (31b) and (32) is apparently not based simply on length; replacing the numeral quantifier in (31b) with another word leads to a similar improvement.

(i) *Japanese* (Shigeru Miyagawa, personal communication)

?[seijika-o   [t_i t_j kyoonen osieta] Tanaka-san-no   kodomo$_j$-ni kesa
politician-ACC   last-year taught Tanaka-HON-GEN child-DAT   yesterday

Hanako-ga   syookaisita] sensee$_i$
Hanako-NOM introduced   teacher

'the teacher$_i$ that Hanako yesterday introduced the politician to the children$_j$ of Mr. Tanaka that t_i taught t_j last year'

(i) is just as long as (31b), but is like (32) in lacking a numeral quantifier modifying the dative argument, and is just as good as (32). The most straightforward parsing account of these facts therefore does not appear to be correct.

9. Here I abstract away from questions about the base position of the subject; this is assumed by Koizumi (1993) and Collins and Thráinsson (1993), for instance, to be base-generated below Agr$_{IO}$P but above Agr$_O$P.

10. See Mulders 1996, to appear, for an analysis of transitive expletive constructions that involves movement to multiple specifiers of which one is filled by Merge.

References

Bobaljik, Jonathan David, and Samuel Brown. 1997. Interarboreal operations: Head movement and the extension requirement. *Linguistic Inquiry* 28, 345–356.

Chomsky, Noam. 1993. A minimalist program for linguistic theory. In *The view from Building 20: Essays in linguistics in honor of Sylvain Bromberger*, eds. Kenneth Hale and Samuel Jay Keyser, 1–52. Cambridge, Mass.: MIT Press. [Reprinted in *The Minimalist Program*, Noam Chomsky, 167–217. Cambridge, Mass.: MIT Press, 1995.]

Chomsky, Noam. 1995. *The Minimalist Program*. Cambridge, Mass.: MIT Press.

Collins, Chris, and Höskuldur Thráinsson. 1993. Object shift in double object constructions and the theory of Case. In *Papers on Case and agreement II*, ed. Colin Phillips, 131–174. (MIT Working Papers in Linguistics 19.) MITWPL, Department of Linguistics and Philosophy, MIT, Cambridge, Mass.

Franks, Steven. 1997. South Slavic clitic placement is *still* syntactic. Paper presented at Penn Linguistics Colloquium, University of Pennsylvania, Philadelphia.

Franks, Steven. 1998. Clitics in Slavic. Paper presented at Workshop on Comparative Slavic Morphosyntax, Indiana University, Bloomington.

Haegeman, Liliane. 1995. *The syntax of negation*. Cambridge: Cambridge University Press.

Hasegawa, Nobuko. 1984. On the so-called "zero pronouns" in Japanese. *The Linguistic Review* 4, 289–341.

Izvorski, Roumyana. 1995. On WH-movement and focus-movement in Bulgarian. *Proceedings of CONSOLE 2*.

Kitahara, Hisatsugu. 1994. Target-α: A unified theory of movement and structure-building. Doctoral dissertation, Harvard University, Cambridge, Mass.

Kitahara, Hisatsugu. 1997. *Elementary operations and optimal derivations*. Cambridge, Mass.: MIT Press.

Koizumi, Masatoshi. 1993. Object agreement and the split VP hypothesis. In *Papers on Case and agreement I*, eds. Colin Phillips and Jonathan Bobaljik, 99–148. (MIT Working Papers in Linguistics 18.) MITWPL, Department of Linguistics and Philosophy, MIT, Cambridge, Mass.

Kuno, Susumu. 1973. *The structure of the Japanese language*. Cambridge, Mass.: MIT Press.

Miyagawa, Shigeru. 1989. *Syntax and semantics 22: Structure and Case marking in Japanese*. San Diego, Calif.: Academic Press.

Miyagawa, Shigeru. 1994. Nonconfigurationality within a configurational structure. Ms., MIT, Cambridge, Mass.

Miyagawa, Shigeru. 1997. Against optional scrambling. *Linguistic Inquiry* 28, 1–26.

Mulders, Iris. 1996. Multiple checking and mirrored specifiers: The structure of CP. Ms., Utrecht University.

Mulders, Iris. To appear. Mirrored specifiers. In *Linguistics in the Netherlands 1997*.

Murasugi, Kumiko. 1992. Crossing and nested paths: NP movement in accusative and ergative languages. Doctoral dissertation, MIT, Cambridge, Mass.

Ochi, Masao. 1996. On the nature of relativization in Japanese. Paper presented at CONSOLE 5, University College London.

Ochi, Masao. 1997. Move or attract? Paper presented at WCCFL 16.

Pesetsky, David. 1982. Paths and categories. Doctoral dissertation, MIT, Cambridge, Mass.

Richards, Norvin. 1997. What moves where when in which language? Doctoral dissertation, MIT, Cambridge, Mass.

Richards, Norvin. 1998. The Principle of Minimal Compliance. *Linguistic Inquiry* 29, 599–629.

Rudin, Catherine. 1988. On multiple questions and multiple *wh*-fronting. *Natural Language & Linguistic Theory* 6, 445–501.

Saito, Mamoru. 1985. Some asymmetries in Japanese and their theoretical implications. Doctoral dissertation, MIT, Cambridge, Mass.

Stjepanović, Sandra. 1998. On the placement of Serbo-Croatian clitics: Evidence from clitic climbing and VP ellipsis. In *Annual Workshop on Formal Approaches to Slavic Linguistics: The Connecticut meeting, 1997*, eds. Željko Bošković, Steven Franks, and William Snyder. Ann Arbor, Mich.: Michigan Slavic Publications.

Takahashi, Daiko. 1993. Movement of *wh*-phrases in Japanese. *Natural Language & Linguistic Theory* 11, 655–678.

Ura, Hiroyuki. 1996. Multiple feature-checking: A theory of grammatical function splitting. Doctoral dissertation, MIT, Cambridge, Mass.

Watanabe, Akira. 1992. Subjacency and S-Structure movement of *wh*-in-situ. *Journal of East Asian Linguistics* 1, 255–291.

Chapter 7

On Multiple Feature Checking: Multiple *Wh*-Fronting and Multiple Head Movement

Željko Bošković

My goal in this chapter is to examine the phenomenon of multiple movement to the same position, in particular, the driving force behind such movement. I will do this through case studies of two phenomena: multiple *wh*-fronting and multiple head movement of verbal elements. In section 7.1, I discuss multiple *wh*-fronting, focusing on the order in which multiple movement of *wh*-phrases to the same position proceeds (i.e., on Superiority effects with such movement). The data are drawn from Serbo-Croatian and Bulgarian. In section 7.2, I discuss multiple head movement—specifically, partial V-movement derivations for Dutch V-clustering constructions and VP-ellipsis in Serbo-Croatian double participle constructions.

7.1 Multiple *Wh*-Fronting

Rudin (1988) argues that despite their superficial similarity, Bulgarian and Serbo-Croatian multiple *wh*-fronting constructions such as (1a) and (1b), respectively, have very different structures.

(1) a. koj kakvo vižda
     who what sees
     'who sees what'
   b. ko šta vidi
     who what sees
     'who sees what'

Rudin argues that in Bulgarian, all fronted *wh*-phrases are located in the interrogative [Spec, CP]. She argues further that in Serbo-Croatian, only the first *wh*-phrase is located in [Spec, CP]. Other fronted *wh*-phrases are located below the interrogative CP projection. They are thus fronted for reasons independent of the +*wh*-feature. I will refer to fronting of *wh*-phrases that is not motivated by checking the strong +*wh*-feature of C as *non*-wh-*fronting*.

In Bošković 1997a,c, 1998c, I show that there is even a deeper difference between Bulgarian and Serbo-Croatian multiple *wh*-fronting constructions. In particular, I show that in Serbo-Croatian constructions such as (1b), no *wh*-phrase has to move to [Spec, CP] overtly. That is, the first *wh*-phrase in (1b) may also undergo non-*wh*-fronting. Since most of the arguments to this effect presented in those works are rather involved, I will repeat only one of them here. The argument concerns the interpretation of multiple questions.

It is well known that a pair-list answer is obligatory in English questions such as (2).[1]

(2) who bought what

(2) cannot be felicitously asked in the following situation: John is in a store and in the distance sees somebody buying a piece of clothing, but does not see who it is and does not see exactly what the person is buying. He goes to the sales clerk and asks (2).

Interestingly, questions such as (2) are not crosslinguistically banned from having single-pair answers (for relevant discussion, see Bošković 1998b). Thus, the Japanese and Chinese counterparts of (2) can have either single-pair or pair-list answers.[2] That is, in addition to being used in situations appropriate for pair-list answers, (3) can be used in the situation described above. (I illustrate the relevant points with respect to Japanese. Chinese patterns with Japanese in the relevant respect.)

(3) dare-ga   nani-o   katta   no
    who-NOM what-ACC bought Q
    'who bought what'

Nonsubject questions such as (4) can also have single-pair answers.

(4) John-wa dare-ni   nani-o   ageta no
    John-TOP who-DAT what-ACC gave   Q
    'who did John give what'

One obvious difference between English and Japanese/Chinese is that the former is a language with overt movement of *wh*-phrases to [Spec, CP], whereas the latter are *wh*-in-situ languages; that is, interrogative [Spec, CP]s are filled in overt syntax by a *wh*-phrase in English, but not in Japanese and Chinese.[3] It is possible that syntactic movement of a *wh*-phrase to [Spec, CP] for some reason forces the pair-list interpretation. French confirms this conjecture.

French can employ either the in-situ or the *wh*-movement strategy in questions.[4] Significantly, single-pair answers are possible in French, but only with in-situ questions. Thus, the in-situ multiple question in (5a) can have a single-pair answer. This answer is degraded with (5b), involving overt *wh*-movement.[5]

(5) a. il a   donné quoi à qui
       he has given what to whom
       'what did he give to whom'
    b. qu'a-t-il donné à qui

The contrast between (5a) and (5b) strongly indicates that the single-pair answer is possible only when no *wh*-phrase moves to [Spec, CP] overtly.

Turning now to the interpretation of multiple questions in South Slavic, notice that, as expected, Bulgarian, a multiple *wh*-fronting language in which interrogative [Spec, CP]s are obligatorily filled by a *wh*-phrase overtly, patterns with English in that (6) requires a pair-list answer.

(6) koj kakvo e kupil
    who what is bought
    'who bought what'

Significantly, Serbo-Croatian patterns with languages in which *wh*-phrases do not have to move to [Spec, CP] overtly in the relevant respect. Thus, Serbo-Croatian (7) can have either a pair-list or a single-pair answer.[6]

(7) ko je šta   kupio
    who is what bought
    'who bought what'

This indicates that Serbo-Croatian questions are well formed even when no *wh*-phrase moves to the interrogative [Spec, CP] overtly. For more evidence to this effect, see Bošković 1997a,c, 1998c.

Apparently, fronting of Serbo-Croatian *wh*-phrases is not necessarily driven by the checking of the strong +*wh*-feature of C. Notice also that all *wh*-phrases must be fronted in Serbo-Croatian questions, which confirms that the fronting is not driven by the checking of this feature.[7]

(8) a.   ko   šta   kupuje
         who what buys
         'who buys what'
     b. ?*ko kupuje šta

In fact, as noted in Bošković 1997c, Serbo-Croatian *wh*-phrases generally cannot remain in situ even on the echo question reading. The unacceptability of (9) on this reading confirms that the obligatoriness of fronting Serbo-Croatian *wh*-phrases is independent of the +*wh*-feature.

(9) ?*Jovan kupuje šta
     Jovan buys   what

What is the driving force of this obligatory non-*wh*-fronting of *wh*-phrases in Serbo-Croatian? Stjepanović (1998a) argues convincingly that it is focus. She shows that contrastively focused non-*wh*-phrases must move overtly in Serbo-Croatian. (*Jovana* in (10) is contrastively focused.)

(10) JOVANA$_i$ su istukli t_i
     Jovan   are beaten
     'Jovan, they beat'

She furthermore argues that Serbo-Croatian *wh*-phrases are inherently focused and therefore must undergo focus movement (see Stjepanović 1998a for empirical evidence for this claim based on the distribution of sentential adverbs). This is not surprising given that a similar phenomenon is attested in a number of other languages, for example, Aghem, Basque, Hungarian, Somali, and Quechua (see, e.g., Horvath 1986; Rochemont 1986; E. Kiss 1995). In fact, Horvath (1986) argues that if a language has a special position for contrastively focused phrases, *wh*-phrases will move to that position. This seems plausible, given the similarity in the interpretation of *wh*-phrases and contrastively focused phrases. In contrast to simple new information focus, with contrastive focus the set over which the focus operates is closed. As Stjepanović notes, a similar situation is found with *wh*-phrases, whose value is drawn from an inferable and therefore closed set of items, delimited by the question itself.

7.1.1 Multiple *Wh*-Fronting and Superiority
An interesting property of non-*wh*-fronting—or, more precisely, focus fronting—of *wh*-phrases in Serbo-Croatian is that it does not exhibit any

Superiority effects. Consider the following multiple *wh*-fronting constructions from Bulgarian (11) and Serbo-Croatian (12).

(11) a. koj kogo e vidjal
         who whom is seen
         'who saw whom'
     b. *kogo koj e vidjal
     c. koj kak udari Ivan
         who how hit   Ivan
         'who hit Ivan how'
     d. *kak koj udari Ivan

(12) a. ko   je koga   vidio
         who is whom seen
     b. koga je ko vidio
     c. ko   kako udara Ivana
         who kow hits   Ivan
     d. kako ko udara Ivana

These data indicate that fronted *wh*-phrases in short-distance matrix
questions in Bulgarian are subject to strict ordering constraints, which is
not the case in Serbo-Croatian. The order of fronted *wh*-phrases in Bulgarian appears to follow from the Superiority Condition. Chomsky's
(1973) original formulation of the condition, which accounts for the contrast between (14a) and (14b) (*who* is superior to *what*), is given in (13).

(13) No rule can involve X, Y in the structure . . . X . . . [. . . Z . . .
     WYV . . .] where the rule applies ambiguously to Z and Y, and Z
     is superior to Y. The category A is superior to the category B if
     every major category dominating A dominates B as well but not
     conversely.

(14) a. who$_i$ did John tell t_i that he should buy what
     b. ?*what$_i$ did John tell who that he should buy t_i

We shall see in section 7.1.2 that multiple *wh*-fronting constructions provide support for the economy account of Superiority (Chomsky, MIT
class lectures, 1989—also see, e.g., Bošković 1997b, in press a; Cheng
1997; Kitahara 1993; Oka 1993), under which the effects of the Superiority Condition follow from the requirement that the +*wh*-feature of C be
checked in the most economical way, that is, through the shortest movement possible.[8] The underlying assumption here is that movement to

[Spec, CP] obligatorily triggers specifier-head agreement with C, which in turn results in the checking of the +*wh*-feature of C. Rudin (1988) argues that adjunction to [Spec, CP] in Bulgarian proceeds to the right; in other words, the *wh*-phrase that is first in the linear order is the one that moves first to [Spec, CP]. Given rightward adjunction to [Spec, CP], (11a–d) indicate that the nominative *koj* must move to [Spec, CP] before accusative and VP adjunct *wh*-phrases, checking the +*wh*-feature of C in the most economical way (i.e., through the shortest movement possible). (11b) and (11d), where the accusative and the adjunct *wh*-phrase move first, checking the strong +*wh*-feature of C, are then ruled out because the +*wh*-feature of C is not checked through the shortest movement possible.

A slightly different account is available under Koizumi's (1994) proposal that instead of multiple adjunction to [Spec, CP], Bulgarian multiple *wh*-fronting constructions involve multiple specifiers of C. Under this analysis, Superiority still forces the highest *wh*-phrase in (11) (*koj*) to move to [Spec, CP] first. Richards (1997) suggests that when the second *wh*-phrase undergoes *wh*-movement, Shortest Move forces it to move to the lower specifier. This way, the *wh*-phrase crosses fewer nodes than it would if it were to move to the higher specifier.

We have seen that strict ordering of fronted *wh*-phrases in Bulgarian provides evidence that *wh*-movement in Bulgarian is sensitive to Superiority. Turning now to Serbo-Croatian, recall that Serbo-Croatian constructions such as (12) do not have to involve *wh*-movement at all; that is, the *wh*-phrases in such constructions move overtly independently of the +*wh*-feature. Free ordering of fronted *wh*-phrases in such constructions then appears to indicate that non-*wh*-fronting (more precisely, focus movement of *wh*-phrases) is not sensitive to the Superiority Condition.[9] The correctness of the descriptive generalization reached with respect to Serbo-Croatian—that this movement is not subject to Superiority—is confirmed by certain data from Bulgarian, noted in Bošković 1997b.

As noted above, Rudin (1988) shows that all *wh*-phrases in Bulgarian must be located in [Spec, CP] overtly. We have also seen that, like English, Bulgarian exhibits Superiority effects in all types of questions. To account for this, I assume that, as in English, in Bulgarian the interrogative C has a strong +*wh*-feature and its specifier must always be filled in overt syntax. However, checking the strong +*wh*-feature of C cannot be the only motivation for movement to [Spec, CP] in Bulgarian. If this were the case, it would suffice to move only one *wh*-phrase to [Spec, CP], as in English. However, in Bulgarian all *wh*-phrases must be fronted.

(15) a. *koj e vidjal kogo
who is seen whom
'who saw whom'
b. koj kogo e vidjal
c. *koj udari Ivan kak
who hit Ivan how
'who hit Ivan how'
d. koj kak udari Ivan

Bulgarian apparently also has obligatory non-*wh*-fronting of *wh*-phrases. Following Stjepanović's (1998a) proposal for Serbo-Croatian, in Bošković (in press a) I suggest that Bulgarian non-*wh*-fronting is also an instance of focus movement.[10] Under this analysis, one *wh*-phrase in Bulgarian multiple questions moves to check the strong +*wh*-feature of C (i.e., it undergoes *wh*-movement). Movement of other *wh*-phrases is an instance of pure focus movement (i.e., it is motivated only by focusing). Observe now that, if *wh*-movement, which affects only one *wh*-phrase, is subject to the Superiority Condition, and focus movement, which affects all *wh*-phrases, is not, the Superiority Condition should affect only one *wh*-phrase. More precisely, the highest *wh*-phrase should move first (satisfying Superiority with *wh*-movement)[11] and then the order of movement should not matter (given that focus movement is not subject to Superiority). As noted in Bošković 1997b, in press a, this is exactly what happens in Bulgarian. ((16) and (18) indicate that *kogo* is higher than *kak* and *kakvo* prior to *wh*-movement.)[12]

(16) a. kogo kak e tselunal Ivan
whom how is kissed Ivan
'how did Ivan kiss whom'
b. ?*kak kogo e tselunal Ivan

(17) a. koj kogo kak e tselunal
who whom how is kissed
'who kissed whom how'
b. koj kak kogo e tselunal

(18) a. kogo kakvo e pital Ivan
whom what is asked Ivan
'whom did Ivan ask what'
b. ?*kakvo kogo e pital Ivan

(19) a. koj kogo kakvo e pital
       who whom what is asked
       'who asked whom what'
     b. koj kakvo kogo e pital

We have seen so far that *wh*-movement is, and focus movement is not, subject to Superiority. The question now is whether we can deduce the exceptional behavior of the latter movement with respect to Superiority (i.e., economy of derivation) from deeper principles. In the next section, I will explore possible answers to this question.

7.1.2 Why Is Focus Movement of *Wh*-Phrases Insensitive to Superiority?

One way of accounting for the lack of Superiority effects with focus movement is to push this movement into the PF component and assume that the relevant principles of economy of derivation do not apply there. In Bošković 1997c, 1998c, I show that at least in certain cases, phonological information has an effect on the focusing of *wh*-phrases. This indicates that PF plays at least some role in the phenomenon. The question is, however, whether the phenomenon can be pushed into the phonology in its entirety. I will not attempt to answer this question here. I merely note two potential difficulties for the all-around PF movement analysis of focus fronting. Focus movement obviously has semantic import, which can be difficult, though perhaps not impossible, to account for if the movement is pushed into PF and if the traditional model of the grammar, where the derivation splits into PF and LF, is adopted. Notice also that most other instances of PF movement argued for in the literature are very local, involving linearly adjacent words.[13] This is not the case with focus movement, which can take place across clausal boundaries. These are not necessarily insurmountable problems. The PF movement analysis certainly merits more serious consideration than I have given in here. I turn now to an analysis that considers focus movement a syntactic operation.[14]

In Bošković, in press a, I present a principled economy explanation for the different behavior of focus movement and *wh*-movement with respect to Superiority. I argue that focus movement and *wh*-movement differ with respect to where the formal inadequacy driving the movement lies. It is standardly assumed that with *wh*-movement, the inadequacy driving the movement (i.e., the relevant strong feature) lies in the target. This is why it suffices to front only one of the *wh*-phrases in (20) overtly. *What* checks the strong +*wh*-feature of C so that there is no need for other *wh*-phrases to undergo *wh*-movement.[15]

(20) what did John give to whom when

Turning now to focus movement, the very fact that every *wh*-phrase must undergo focus movement indicates that the inadequacy driving the movement (i.e., the strong feature) resides in the *wh*-phrases, not in the target of the movement. If the relevant strong feature were to reside in the target, it would suffice to front only one of the *wh*-phrases in Serbo-Croatian multiple questions such as (21).[16]

(21) a.   ko šta gdje kupuje
          who what where buys
          'who buys what where'
     b. *ko kupuje šta gdje
     c. *ko šta kupuje gdje
     d. *ko gdje kupuje šta

Focus movement thus differs from *wh*-movement with respect to where the strong feature driving the movement resides. With focus movement, the strong feature resides in the elements undergoing movement, and with *wh*-movement in the target. In Bošković, in press a, I argue that this difference is responsible for the different behavior of focus movement and *wh*-movement with respect to Superiority.[17] Consider the following abstract configurations for *wh*-movement and focus movement. (In the following discussion, I assume the economy account of Superiority, which deduces Superiority effects from the requirement that each feature be checked in the most economical way, that is, through the shortest movement possible. See section 7.1.1)

(22) Wh-*movement*
     F   *wh*-phrase$_1$ *wh*-phrase$_2$ *wh*-phrase$_3$ [18]
     +wh   +wh   +wh   +wh
     strong weak   weak   weak

(23) *Focus movement*
     F   *wh*-phrase$_1$ *wh*-phrase$_2$ *wh*-phrase$_3$
     +focus +focus   +focus   +focus
     weak   strong   strong   strong

The functional head F has a strong feature in (22). The feature has to be checked through the shortest movement possible. Hence, *wh*-phrase$_1$ will have to move to F. If *wh*-phrase$_2$ or *wh*-phrase$_3$ moves to check the strong feature of F, a Superiority violation results under the economy account of Superiority.

In (23), the strong feature resides in *wh*-phrases. Again, the relevant feature must be checked through the shortest movement possible, which is movement to F. The order in which the *wh*-phrases check their strong focus feature against F (i.e., the order of movement to the FP projection) is irrelevant. For example, the derivation in which *wh*-phrase$_1$ checks its focus feature before *wh*-phrase$_2$ and the derivation in which *wh*-phrase$_2$ checks its focus feature before *wh*-phrase$_1$ are equally economical. The same nodes are crossed to check the strong focus feature of the *wh*-phrases. (I assume that only maximal projections count here.) Hence, no Superiority violation results, regardless of the order in which the *wh*-phrases move.

Under the economy account of Superiority, we thus correctly predict that Superiority effects will arise in the constructions in question when the strong feature driving the movement belongs to the target (when the relevant operation is Attract), but not when it belongs to the elements undergoing movement (when the relevant operation is Move). On the other hand, under Chomsky's (1973) original formulation of the Superiority Condition, given in (13), as well as most other accounts of Superiority (see, e.g., Cheng and Demirdache 1990; Lasnik and Saito 1992; Pesetsky 1982), the facts under consideration remain unaccounted for. Under the most natural application of these accounts to multiple *wh*-fronting constructions, we would expect to get Superiority effects with both *wh*-movement and focus movement.[19] The problem with these accounts is that it is simply not possible to make the information concerning where the formal inadequacy driving the movement lies, which determines whether a question will exhibit a Superiority effect, relevant to Superiority in a principled way. We thus have here empirical evidence for the economy account of Superiority.

Before leaving the Move/Attract account, let me clarify how it applies to Bulgarian. In Bulgarian constructions such as (16)–(19) and (ia,b) in note 12, the *wh*-phrases have a strong focus feature and C has a strong +*wh*-feature. None of the features can be checked before the interrogative C is introduced into the structure. Once C is introduced, all the features can be checked. The question is in which order they will be checked. As far as the strong features of the *wh*-phrases are concerned, the order does not matter. For example, whether the strong focus feature of *koj* in (17) is checked first or last, the same number of maximal projections will be crossed to check it. This is not true of the strong feature of C, which has to be checked by the highest *wh*-phrase—namely, *koj*. Since *wh*-phrases do not care in which order they move, and since C does care about the order (*koj* must move first), a way to make everybody happy is to move *koj* first and then move the remaining *wh*-phrases in any order.[20]

The account presented in Bošković, in press a, is based on the assumption that strength can reside in elements undergoing movement, not just in the target. We have seen empirical evidence for this assumption from multiple *wh*-fronting constructions. Notice, however, that it would be conceptually more appealing if the formal inadequacy triggering movement were to always reside in the target. Then, it would be possible to overcome the inadequacy as soon as it enters the structure. This is generally not possible with formal inadequacies residing in moving elements. There, it is necessary to wait until the checker enters the structure, which increases computational burden. I will show now that the relevant facts concerning multiple *wh*-fronting can be rather straightforwardly restated without positing strength in moving elements, given a particular view of multiple feature checking. Furthermore, the above account of the exceptional behavior of focus movement with respect to Superiority can be maintained in its essentials.

In his discussion of Icelandic multiple subject constructions, Chomsky (1995) proposes that one and the same head can attract a particular feature F more than once. We can think of multiple attraction by the same head as follows: (a) there are elements that possess a formal inadequacy that is overcome by attracting 1 feature F, (b) there are elements that possess a formal inadequacy that is overcome by attracting 2 features F, (c) there are elements that possess a formal inadequacy that is overcome by attracting 3 features F, and so on. In this system, it seems natural to have elements that possess a formal inadequacy that is overcome by attracting all features F.[21]

The attractor for *wh*-movement in languages like English ([+wh] C) is an Attract-1F head. When there is more than one potential attractee, Attract-1F elements will always attract the highest potential attractee (i.e., the attractee that is closest to them), given that every requirement must be satisfied in the most economical way. Hence, we find Superiority effects with Attract-1F heads. Suppose now that the focus attractor is an Attract-all-F element. The focus attractor would then have to attract all focus-feature-bearing elements. It is clear that we would not expect any

Superiority effects with Attract-all-F elements. For example, the Attract-all-F property of the focus head in the abstract configuration in (23) is clearly satisfied in the same way from the point of view of economy regardless of the order in which the *wh*-phrases move to the focus head. Regardless of whether the *wh*-phrases move in the 1-2-3, 1-3-2, 2-1-3, 2-3-1, 3-1-2, or 3-2-1 order, the same number of nodes will be crossed to satisfy the Attract-all-focused-elements inadequacy of the relevant head. Hence, by economy, all orders should be possible. We thus account for the lack of Superiority effects with focus movement.[22]

The Attract-all-F account maintains the essentials of the above analysis of the different behavior of focus movement and *wh*-movement with respect to Superiority without positing formal inadequacies driving movement in moving elements (we are dealing here with a pure Attract system), which appears appealing conceptually. The different behavior of focus movement and *wh*-movement with respect to Superiority follows from focus movement's having the Attract-all-F property, and *wh*-movement's having the Attract-1F property.[23]

7.2 Multiple Head Movement

In this section, I will consider data that could potentially tease apart the strength-in-the-moving-elements and the Attract-all-F accounts of multiple movement to the same position. To find the relevant data, I will go beyond multiple *wh*-fronting constructions. In particular, I will reexamine V-clustering constructions discussed in Bošković 1997d. The abstract pattern exhibited by these constructions is the same as that found in multiple *wh*-fronting constructions: a number of different elements move to check a feature against one head. As a result, both the account that posits a strong feature in moving elements and the account that posits an Attract-all-F feature in the target can account for the basic V-clustering paradigm. However, we will see that V-clustering constructions provide ways of teasing apart the two accounts that are not available with multiple *wh*-fronting constructions.

In Bošković 1997d, I argued that in several languages (I examined Serbo-Croatian, Standard Dutch, and Polish), in multiple V constructions involving auxiliaries/modals and participles, all verbal elements adjoin in overt syntax to the highest verbal head in the V sequence.[24] Here, I will reexamine some of the relevant data from Standard Dutch, where I argued the adjunction is optional (at least in overt syntax), and Serbo-Croatian, where the adjunction is obligatory. I will first consider Dutch.

7.2.1   V-Clustering in Standard Dutch

Following Zwart (1993, 1994, 1997), I assume that Dutch is a V-initial or, more generally, head-initial language. According to Zwart, direct objects in Dutch are generated following verbs and then undergo movement to the left of the verb. On this analysis, the surface order of the verbal elements in (24) corresponds to their base-generated order.[25]

(24) ik denk dat Jan het boek$_i$ [$_{VP}$ moet [$_{VP}$ hebben [$_{VP}$
     I think that Jan the book   must   have
     gelezen t_i]]] 1-2-3
     read
     'I think that Jan must have read the book'

Under this analysis, constructions such as (25) then must involve participle movement.

(25) dat Jan het boek gelezen moet hebben   3-1-2

As illustrated below, no lexical material is allowed to intervene between the verbal elements in (25). (Compare (26) with (27) and (28)–(29).) This state of affairs can be accounted for if in such constructions, the second and third verbal elements are adjoined to the first.[26]

(26) a. *dat Jan het boek gelezen uit moet hebben   3-1-2
        that Jan the book read   out must have
        'that Jan must have finished reading the book'
     b. *dat Jan het boek gelezen moet uit hebben   3-1-2

(27) dat Jan het boek uit gelezen moet hebben

Significantly, in constructions in which the surface order of verbal elements corresponds to the order in which they are base-generated, non-verbal lexical material can intervene between the verbal elements. This indicates that *gelezen* and *hebben* do not have to move to *moet*.

(28) dat Jan het boek moet uit hebben gelezen   1-2-3

(29) dat Jan het boek moet hebben uit gelezen   1-2-3

The above data thus provide evidence for optional V-adjunction in Dutch. Verbal elements in Dutch V sequences can, but do not have to, adjoin to the highest verbal element in the sequence in overt syntax.

Consider now how this state of affairs would be formally implemented under the two analyses of multiple movement to the same position considered above. I will call the feature that drives V-adjunction *feature X* and leave its precise identity open. Under the analysis that posits a strong feature in the elements undergoing movement, we would have to assume that *hebben* and *gelezen* can be optionally drawn from the lexicon with a strong feature X. Under the Attract-all-F analysis, on the other hand, we would assume that *moet* is optionally specified in the lexicon with the Attract-all-X property.

Although both analyses account for the above facts, they make different predictions in other cases. Since under the multiple strength analysis *hebben* and *gelezen* can be optionally taken from the lexicon with a strong feature X, nothing prevents us from deciding to take only one of these elements—say, *gelezen*—from the lexicon with a strong feature X, and taking the other element without a strong feature X. Only *gelezen* would then move to *moet* overtly. On the other hand, partial V-movement derivations are ruled out under the Attract-all-X analysis. If *moet* has the property Attract-all-X, both *gelezen* and *hebben* must move to it; if it does not, neither will move.[27] Under the strength-in-the-moving-elements account, we would then expect it to be possible to move *gelezen* to *moet*, without moving *hebben*. Under the Attract-all-F account, this would not be possible. The ungrammaticality of (26b), repeated here as (30), indicates that the prediction of the Attract-all-F account is borne out.

(30) *dat Jan het boek gelezen moet uit hebben   3-1-2

If *hebben* could stay in situ when *gelezen* moves to *moet*, we would expect it to be possible for nonverbal lexical material to intervene between *moet* and *hebben* in (30), just as in (28). The fact that this is not possible indicates that when *gelezen* moves to *moet*, *hebben* also must move to *moet*, which can be readily accounted for under the Attract-all-F analysis, but not the strength-in-the-moving-elements analysis.[28]

7.2.2 Double Participle Constructions in Serbo-Croatian

In Bošković 1995, 1997d, I argue that in Serbo-Croatian double participle constructions both participles adjoin to the auxiliary, the direction of adjunction being free. (For ease of exposition, I will refer only to the finite auxiliary as *auxiliary*.) If the auxiliary moves to I to check its inflectional features, it excorporates from the complex head created by the adjunction in accordance with Watanabe's (1993) economy theory of excorporation, which forces excorporation in certain well-defined configurations (see the discussion below). The movement of the auxiliary to I is optional in overt syntax. The constructions in (31)–(32), where the auxiliary remains in situ, illustrate participle adjunction to the auxiliary, which remains in situ overtly. The fact that no phrasal lexical material can intervene between the participles and the auxiliary provides evidence that the verbal elements in the constructions in question are located in the same head position.[29]

(31) čekali$_i$ ste bili t_i Marijinu prijateljicu
    waited are been   Maria's friend
    'you had been waiting for Maria's friend'

(32) bili$_i$ ste t_i čekali Marijinu prijateljicu
    been are   waited Maria's friend
    'you had been waiting for Maria's friend'

(33) a. *čekali ste Marijinu prijateljicu$_i$ bili t_i
        waited are Maria's friend   been
    b. *čekali Marijinu prijateljicu$_i$ ste bili t_i

(34) a. *bili   ste Marijinu prijateljicu$_i$ čekali t_i
        been are Maria's friend   waited
    b. *bili Marijinu prijateljicu$_i$ ste čekali t_i

(35) is an example involving auxiliary movement to I: the auxiliary moves, excorporating from the complex head formed by the adjunction of the participles to check its inflectional features. The fact that no phrasal material can intervene between the participles, as illustrated in (36), is accounted for since the participles are adjoined to the same head position (the base-generated position of the auxiliary), participle movement being obligatory in Serbo-Croatian.

(35) vas dvoje ste Marijinu prijateljicu$_i$ bili   čekali t_i
    you two   are Maria's friend   been waited
    'you two had been waiting for Maria's friend'

(36) *vas dvoje ste bili Marijinu prijateljicu$_i$ čekali t_i

The excorporation takes place under the same circumstances as the excorporation out of verbal clusters in Dutch. Roberts (1991) observes that although the participles in Dutch constructions such as (24) can adjoin to the modal (see section 7.2.1, in particular (25)–(26)), the modal must excorporate from the complex head formed by the adjunction if it undergoes movement to C in verb-second constructions, as illustrated in (37).

(37) a. *[CP gisteren   gelezen moet hebben [IP Jan het boek]]
              yesterday read   must have   Jan the book
           'yesterday, Jan must have read the book'
     b.   [CP gisteren moet [IP Jan het boek gelezen hebben]]

Watanabe's (1993) economy account of excorporation (for additional evidence for this account, see Bošković 1997d) provides a straightforward explanation for excorporation in both (35) and (37). Since the movement to I in (35) and the movement to C in (37) are driven by the features of the auxiliary and the modal, respectively (no feature of the participles is involved in checking), principles of economy ("Carry as little material as possible under movement") force the auxiliary and the modal to excorporate out of the complex heads formed by participle adjunction, moving alone to I and C, respectively.

Serbo-Croatian double participle constructions thus involve multiple movement to the same position. The basic paradigm in (31)–(32) is amenable to both the strength-in-the-moving-elements account and the Attract-all-F account. Call the feature that motivates participle-to-auxiliary movement the +*participle feature*.[30] Under the strength-in-the-moving-elements account, the participles are lexically specified as bearing the strong +participle feature, which is checked against the auxiliary. Under the Attract-all-F account, the auxiliary is lexically specified as having the property Attract-all-+participle, which is satisfied by attraction of +participle-feature-bearing elements. Both analyses thus account for the basic paradigm concerning double participle movement to the auxiliary. However, the analyses make different predictions with respect to double participle constructions involving VP-ellipsis.

Stjepanović (1998b,c) shows that Serbo-Croatian has VP-ellipsis, an example of which is given in (38).

(38) on je čekao Marijinu prijateljicu, a   i   mi smo
       he is waited Maria's friend   and also we are
       'he waited for Maria's friend, and we did too'

Assuming that only constituents can be deleted and given that Serbo-Croatian participles must move to the auxiliary for feature checking, constructions like (38) can be derived by excorporating the auxiliary after participle adjunction to the auxiliary. Ellipsis, which I assume involves PF deletion, can then affect VP_1.[31]

(39) on je čekao Marijinu prijateljicu, a i mi smo$_i$ [$_{VP_+}$ t_i+čekali $_j$
[$_{VP_2}$ t_j Marijinu prijatelicu]]

Let us now turn to more complex examples involving double participle constructions. Significantly, such constructions are acceptable only if both participles are elided.

(40) on je bio čekao Marijinu prijateljicu, a   i   mi smo
      he is been waited Maria's   friend   and also we are

(41) ?*on je bio čekao Marijinu prijateljicu, a   i   mi smo bili
      he is been waited Maria's   friend   and also we are   been

The good example (40) can be derived in the same manner as (38):

1. The participles adjoin to the auxiliary.
2. The auxiliary excorporates to move to I.
3. The highest VP is deleted.

It is easy to verify that this derivation produces a grammatical result under both the strength-in-the-moving-elements approach and the Attract-all-F approach to multiple movement to the same position. (41), however, appears to favor the Attract-all-F approach. Consider how (41) would be derived under this approach. Prior to excorporation, the auxiliary has to attract both participles to satisfy its Attract-all-+participle property. Given the standard assumption that only constituents can be elided, we then cannot derive (41). Regardless of whether or not the auxiliary excorporates to move to I, there is simply no constituent that contains the second but not the first participle. The ungrammaticality of (41) is thus straightforwardly accounted for under the Attract-all-F analysis.

(42) ?*on je bio čekao Marijinu prijateljicu, a i mi smo$_i$
     [$_{VP_1}$ t_i + bili$_j$ + čekali$_k$ [$_{VP_2}$ t_j [$_{VP_3}$ t_k Marijinu prijateljicu]]]

Consider now how the strength-in-the-moving-elements analysis fares with respect to (41). Under this approach, the participles are drawn from the lexicon with a strong +participle feature, which needs to be checked against the auxiliary. The auxiliary itself does not have any strong features that must be checked against the participles. Lasnik (1999) observes that if strong features are defined as illegitimate PF objects, we would expect to be able to prevent the crashing of constructions containing a strong feature X even if X is not checked in overt syntax, by deleting a phrase that contains the strong feature X. X would then not be present in the final PF representation. Lasnik furthermore provides several examples where he suggests this scenario occurs. An element Y with a strong feature X fails to undergo movement that would check the strong feature X in overt syntax. The derivation is saved from crashing in PF by deleting the phrase containing Y, so that the strong feature X is not present in the final PF representation. Lasnik's derivation is available for (41) under the strength-in-the-moving-elements approach. The sentence could be derived as follows:

1. The first participle moves to the auxiliary to check its strong +participle feature.
2. The auxiliary can, but does not have to, excorporate to I.
3. In PF, either VP_2 or VP_3 deletes; both contain the second participle with a strong +participle feature, so that no strong feature is present in the final PF representation.

Since nothing appears to go wrong with the sentence on this derivation, I conclude that the construction is incorrectly predicted to be grammatical under the strength-in-the-moving-elements approach.[32]

(43) ?*on je bio čekao Marijinu prijateljicu, a i mi smo$_i$
    $[_{VP_1}\ t_i +$ bili$_j$ $[_{VP_2}\ t_j\ [_{VP_3}$ čekali Marijinu prijateljicu]]]

I conclude, therefore, that the data discussed in this section favor the Attract-all-F approach to multiple movement to the same position, which places the formal inadequacy driving the movement in the target, over the multiple strength approach, which places the inadequacy driving the movement in the moving elements. Since constructions involving obligatory multiple movement to the same position have previously represented the strongest argument for the possibility that strength (i.e., formal inadequacies driving movement) resides in moving elements, a possibility now opens up that formal inadequacies driving movement always reside in the target. The operation Move could then be handled with a pure Attract system, a conceptually appealing possibility that decreases computational burden, as discussed in section 7.1.2.

It also appears that the approach to multiple checking by the same element argued for here is somewhat more appealing than Chomsky's (1995) approach based on the deletion/erasure distinction, which is dispensable under the current analysis. Chomsky's (1995) system naturally allows +Interpretable features to be involved in multiple feature checking. This not the case with −Interpretable features, which under the most natural interpretation of Chomsky's (1995) system would not be expected to enter into checking relations more than once. Additional assumptions are needed to allow for the possibility of multiple checking of a −Interpretable element. Chomsky argues on empirical grounds that this possibility needs to be allowed. He suggests one way of doing this based on the deletion/erasure distinction, which is relevant only to the checking of −Interpretable features. (According to Chomsky, +Interpretable features cannot be deleted at all owing to the principle of recoverability of deletion.) Chomsky assumes that "a checked feature is deleted when possible" and a deleted feature is "erased when possible," where deleted elements are "invisible at LF but accessible to the computation" and erased elements are "inaccessible to any operation, not just to interpretability at LF" (p. 280). On this approach, certain −Interpretable elements are lexically specified as being able to escape erasure when deleted, as a result of which they remain accessible to the computation (i.e., available for checking) even when they have already been checked once.

The deletion/erasure analysis appears to allow in principle even −Interpretable features that are being attracted rather than serving as attractors to undergo multiple checking since there appears to be no principled reason why such features could not be specified as being able to escape erasure after deletion. However, constructions that would instantiate this option do not seem to exist.[33] The current, Attract-based approach, which dispenses with the deletion/erasure loophole for allowing −Interpretable features to undergo multiple checking, readily accounts for this state of affairs, since it allows −Interpretable elements to undergo multiple checking only if they serve as targets of movement.[34]

Notes

Portions of this material were presented in courses at the University of Connecticut and in a colloquium at New York University. I thank the audiences for their thought-provoking questions. For stimulating comments and discussion, I am especially grateful to Cédric Boeckx, Noam Chomsky, Sam Epstein, Richard Kayne, and Howard Lasnik.

1. However, see Ausín, in preparation, for some exceptions.

2. The Japanese data were brought to my attention by Mamoru Saito (personal communication).

3. I ignore here the possibility of null operator movement in Japanese questions (see Watanabe 1992) and concentrate on what happens to *wh*-phrases themselves.

4. I will confine my discussion of French to nonsubject questions, where it is clear whether the *wh*-movement or the in-situ option is employed.

5. As discussed in Bošković 1998a, in press c, French *wh*-in-situ constructions involve LF *wh*-movement. (I show that even argument *wh*-in-situ constructions in French are sensitive to locality restrictions on movement; see also note 23.) If this LF movement affects the whole *wh*-phrase, (5a) and (5b) will have the same structure in LF, which will make it very difficult to account for the fact that they receive different interpretations. In Chomsky's (1995) Move F system, on the other hand, (5a) and (5b) will have different structures in LF. The operation Move will affect only the formal features of the higher *wh*-phrase in (5a). In contrast to what happens in (5b), its semantic features will remain in their base-generated position in (5a). The fact that (5a) and (5b) receive different interpretations may thus provide an argument for Move F.

6. The element that intervenes between the fronted *wh*-phrases, *je*, is a second-position clitic. Serbo-Croatian second-position cliticization is a very murky phenomenon that involves both phonology and syntax (see Bošković, in press b, and references therein). Throughout the chapter, I will ignore second-position clitics. I discuss their relevance for determining the position of *wh*-phrases in work in progress.

7. There are a few exceptions to the obligatoriness of fronting Serbo-Croatian *wh*-phrases that need not concern us here. For relevant discussion, see Bošković 1997c, 1998c.

8. I will continue to use the term *Superiority Condition* for ease of exposition.

9. In Bošković 1997a,c, 1998c, I show that in some constructions Serbo-Croatian does exhibit Superiority effects with multiple *wh*-fronting. However, I also show that the constructions in question actually involve "real" *wh*-movement, that is, movement to [Spec, CP]. I will ignore such constructions here.

10. A somewhat similar proposal is made by Izvorski (1993). Notice that, as in Serbo-Croatian, contrastively focused phrases undergo overt fronting in Bulgarian (see, however, the discussion below). Furthermore, as in Serbo-Croatian, in Bulgarian *wh*-phrases are fronted even on the echo question reading. Thus, (i) is ungrammatical even as an echo question.

(i) *Ivan e popravil kakvo
    Ivan is fixed   what
    'Ivan fixed what'

In Bošković 1997a, I argue that Bulgarian differs minimally from Serbo-Croatian in that in Bulgarian, the interrogative C is the focus licenser for *wh*-phrases, whereas in Serbo-Croatian, either the interrogative C or I (Agr in the split framework) can focus-license *wh*-phrases. (Both options are not always available in Serbo-Croatian. See Bošković 1997a for details of the analysis. One of my Bulgarian informants does not front contrastively focused non-*wh*-phrases. This is not totally unexpected, given that, unlike the focus licenser in Serbo-Croatian, the focus licenser in Bulgarian is a +*wh*-element, namely, [+wh] C. It is possible that for the speaker in question, [+wh] C fails to attract −*wh* focused elements because of a feature conflict. Notice that Serbo-Croatian has a focus licenser unspecified for the *wh*-feature.)

11. Recall that movement to [Spec, CP] obligatorily triggers specifier-head agreement with C, so that the *wh*-phrase that moves first to [Spec, CP] necessarily checks the strong +*wh*-feature of C.

12. In Bošković 1997b, I argue that *kogo* is higher than *kak* prior to *wh*-movement because it moves to [Spec, Agr$_O$P] before undergoing *wh*-movement.

Notice also that the ungrammaticality of (ia,b) indicates that we cannot be dealing here with the same type of phenomenon as in English constructions like (iia,b), noted by Kayne (1984), where addition of a lower *wh*-phrase for some reason saves the derivation from a Superiority violation.

(i) a. *kogo koj kak e tselunal
       whom who how is kissed
   b. *kogo koj kakvo e pital
       whom who what   is asked

(ii) a. *what did who buy
    b. (?)what did who buy where

13. I have in mind here Morphological Merger and Prosodic Inversion.

14. Another syntactic analysis is presented by Richards (1997), based on his Principle of Minimal Compliance. However, I show in Bošković 1998c that, though very interesting, the analysis cannot be maintained since it does not cover the full range of relevant data. The analysis accounts for the relevant data in Bulgarian, but cannot be extended to account for the entire relevant paradigm in Serbo-Croatian.

15. Sam Epstein (personal communication) suggests that the ungrammaticality of (i) can be interpreted as indicating that adjuncts such as *why* and *how* have a strong +*wh*-feature and therefore cannot remain in situ. However, see Bošković, in press c, for an alternative analysis of (i) that does not posit any strong features in *why/how*. The analysis also accounts for the fact that constructions such as (i) are acceptable in German (see, e.g., Haider 1986; Müller and Sternefeld 1996).

(i) *I wonder who left why/how

16. Note that, as observed by Pesetsky (MIT class lectures, 1997) with respect to Bulgarian, (21b), where two *wh*-phrases remain in situ, is actually somewhat worse than (21c,d), where only one of the *wh*-phrases remains in situ. This is expected, given that in (21b) two strong features remain unchecked and in (21c,d) only one strong feature remains unchecked.

Notice also that the focus-licensing head in Serbo-Croatian must be able to focus-check more than one *wh*-phrase, a possibility available in Chomsky's (1995) system, which allows multiple checking of the same feature by one element (see the discussion below).

17. It is important to bear in mind that, as a result, the account holds even if something other than focus serves as the driving force of non-*wh*-fronting (i.e.,

if the relevant strong feature of *wh*-phrases is something other than focus). For example, as pointed out by Steven Franks (personal communication), the analysis to be given in the text can be applied to Bulgarian even if, instead of a strong focus feature, Bulgarian *wh*-phrases have a strong +*wh*-feature (i.e., if both the interrogative C and *wh*-phrases have a strong +*wh*-feature in Bulgarian).

18. Linear order indicates asymmetrical c-command in (22)–(23).

19. Hornstein's (1995) analysis of Superiority, based on Chierchia's (1991) weak crossover account of the pair-list interpretation, faces a different problem. Hornstein proposes two ways of accounting for the contrasts in Bulgarian (11a–d): one based on the inability of *wh*-traces within [+wh] CPs to be interpreted functionally and one based on the semantic inertness of elements to which other elements have adjoined. It appears to me that the first analysis rules out all Bulgarian multiple questions with three or more preposed *wh*-phrases, whereas the second analysis allows even ungrammatical constructions such as (ia,b) in note 12.

20. Note that I assume that once the interrogative C is inserted, it is not possible to zero in on one particular strong feature (e.g., the strong focus feature of *kogo*) and ignore other relevant strong features. All strong features (of both the target and the moving elements) must be considered in determining what to do next. This will become clearer under the alternative account sketched below.

21. This approach to multiple feature checking by the same element is very similar to Chomsky's (1995) unforced-violations-of-Procrastinate analysis.

Given that counting has no natural place in natural language, it would not be surprising if only the Attract-all-F, Attract-1F, and possibly Attract-2F options are utilized.

Checking a feature of X through lexical insertion might also be considered to involve attraction, with X attracting an element from the numeration. (Chomsky (MIT class lectures, 1997) in fact considers this an instance of Attract.)

22. Consider how his analysis applies to Bulgarian. In Bulgarian, the interrogative C has two attracting features: an Attract-1F +*wh*-feature and an Attract-all-F focus feature. It is clear that the most economical way of overcoming the formal inadequacies of C would require moving the highest *wh*-phrase first. After that, it would not matter in which order the *wh*-phrases move to C.

Notice also that again, nothing hinges on focus being the exact driving force of non-*wh*-fronting in Serbo-Croatian and Bulgarian. However, it is now crucial that two different features be involved in Bulgarian, which was not the case under the Move/Attract analysis (see note 17).

23. Under the Attract-all-focused-elements analysis, it appears that we need to assume that phrases that are already located in a focus position are immune from attraction (i.e., cannot be caused to move) by another focus head; otherwise, the possibility of having focused elements in different clauses of the same sentence will be ruled out. (The matrix focus attractor would attract all focused phrases.) A similar assumption is actually needed in Chomsky's (1995) system even for Attract-1F cases; if this assumption were not made, the ungrammaticality of constructions such as (i) would remain unaccounted for. ((i) is syntactically well

formed in Chomsky's system if we do not ban a [+wh] C from attracting (i.e., causing to move) a *wh*-phrase located in a +*wh*-feature-checking position (interrogative [Spec, CP]).)

(i) *what$_i$ do you wonder t_i John bought t_i (when)

Notice also that although a head with an Attract-all-X property obligatorily undergoes multiple checking if more than one X is present in the structure, it does not have to undergo checking at all if no X is present. The Attract-all-X property is then trivially satisfied. This seems desirable. Notice, for example, that although all contrastively focused elements and *wh*-phrases must undergo focus movement in the languages under consideration, constructions in which focus movement does not take place because no candidate (a contrastively focused phrase or a *wh*-phrase) is present in the structure are well formed.

The Attract-all-F/Attract-1F distinction might also be relevant in LF. It is well known that at least in certain contexts, French allows both the *wh*-in-situ (*tu as vu qui* 'you saw who') and the *wh*-movement (*qui as-tu vu* 'who did you see') strategy in questions. In Bošković 1998a I argue that French *wh*-in-situ constructions involve LF *wh*-movement, evidence for which is provided by severe locality restrictions they exhibit. Thus, (ii) shows that long-distance *wh*-in-situ constructions are unacceptable in French. (See Bošković 1998a for an explanation of why, in contrast to overt *wh*-movement, covert *wh*-movement is clause-bounded based on Move F. Notice that I assume that, as argued by Watanabe (1992), Aoun and Li (1993), and Cole and Hermon (1995), languages such as Japanese and Chinese have overt *wh*-movement. The movement, however, does not affect *wh*-phrases themselves.)

(ii) ?*Jean et   Pierre croient que Marie a   vu   qui
     Jean and Pierre believe that Marie has seen whom
     'whom do Jean and Pierre believe that Marie saw'

In Bošković 1998a I interpret the grammaticality of (iii) as indicating that only one *wh*-phrase needs to move to the interrogative [Spec, CP] in French, which in current terms means that French [+wh] C has an Attract-1F property. In (iii), the Attract-1*wh*-feature property of the C is satisfied by attracting the matrix *wh*-phrase, so that, in contrast to what happens with (ii), in (iii) there is no need for the embedded-clause *wh*-phrase to move to C in LF. The clause-boundedness of LF *wh*-movement therefore has no effect on (iii).

(iii) qui croit   que Marie a   vu   qui
      who believes that Marie has seen whom

It is well known that some languages, in particular, Iraqi Arabic and Hindi, do not allow any *wh*-phrases to remain in situ within an embedded finite clause. (I ignore here constructions involving dummy scope markers, which are in many respects similar to German partial *wh*-movement constructions.) The counterparts of both (ii) and (iii) are unacceptable in these languages. In fact, no matter how many *wh*-phrases are located in the same clause as a [+wh] C, as long as one *wh*-phrase is separated from the [+wh] C by a finite clause boundary, no acceptable construction results in these languages. Given that, as demonstrated in Bošković 1998a,

LF *wh*-movement is clause-bounded, this can be interpreted as indicating that in Iraqi Arabic and Hindi *wh*-in-situ constructions, C attracts all *wh*-phrases in LF, whereas in French *wh*-in-situ constructions, C attracts only one *wh*-phrase in LF.

24. I also conjectured that in languages in which the adjunction does not take place overtly, it takes place in covert syntax. Empirical evidence is, however, difficult to find in such cases.

25. All the Dutch data discussed below are due to Zwart (1994 and personal communication). Following Zwart (1994), for ease of exposition, I will indicate the S-Structure order of verbal elements through numbering next to the examples, the numbers corresponding to the order in which the verbal elements are generated. (For discussion and further references concerning V-clustering in Dutch, see, e.g., Broekhuis et al. 1995; Den Besten and Edmondson 1983; Den Dikken and Hoekstra 1997; Evers 1975; Haegeman 1992b, 1994, 1995a; Haegeman and Van Riemsdijk 1986; Hoeksema 1988; Hoekstra 1994; Kaan 1992; Rutten 1991; Zwart 1993, 1994, 1995.)

26. As in Bošković 1997d, where I essentially follow Zwart (1993, 1994), I assume that *uit*, the predicate of the small clause *het boek uit* 'the book out' that functions as the complement of *gelezen*, must move overtly to a [Spec, VP]. (Ignoring verb-second clauses, *uit* is licensed by being in a specifier-head relation with a lexical verb at S-Structure. See Bošković 1997d for details of the analysis.)

27. The property X in this case would probably have to be related to non-finiteness. Note also that under the Attract-all-X account we somehow need to ensure that only clause-mate nonfinite elements can be attracted by the modal.

28. Optional multiple XP-movement, such as movement of negative constituents in West Flemish (see Haegeman 1992a, 1995b), is also potentially relevant here. Focusing on West Flemish, even if we disregard the potentially interfering fact that moved and unmoved negative constituents in West Flemish typically receive different interpretations, it would be dangerous to try to draw any definite conclusions concerning multiple feature attraction based on West Flemish neg movement, owing to the availability of scrambling in West Flemish. Because scrambling is available, it is not clear whether the relevant examples in West Flemish involve optional multiple attraction of the neg feature or simply optional application of scrambling. (Simpson (1995) argues for the second possibility.) In fact, quite generally, for this reason it is difficult to reliably run the test performed here on V-clustering with respect to XP-movement in languages that have scrambling.

29. Notice that Serbo-Croatian is a heavy scrambling language. (In fact, Serbo-Croatian is even more permissive with respect to scrambling than traditionally cited scrambling languages such as Japanese.)

Notice also that the finite auxiliary in (31)–(34) is a second-position clitic. The ungrammaticality of (33b) and (34b) then may be due to a violation of the second-position requirement. (For discussion of the second-position requirement on clitics in Serbo-Croatian, see Bošković, in press b, and references therein. See also Bošković 1995, 1997d, for additional evidence that the participles in (31)–(34) are adjoined to the auxiliary.) Notice that pronominal second-position clitics can intervene between the participles and the auxiliary. However, such clitics also apear to undergo adjunction to the auxiliary in the constructions in question. Notice also that Stjepanović (1998b,c) shows that the internal order within the clitic cluster (which may contain question particle, auxiliary, and pronominal clitics) is at least to some extent determined in PF. This makes it difficult to draw any definite conclusions about syntax based on the relative order of clitics.

30. The precise identity of the feature is not important here. +*Participle* is used simply for ease of exposition. For relevant discussion, see Bošković 1997d and Boeckx 1998.

31. Notice that VP_1 can also be fronted. As argued in Bošković 1995, 1997d, (i) involves auxiliary excorporation to Σ (note that *jesmo* is translated as emphatic *do*), followed by VP_1-preposing.

(i) $[_{VP_1}$ t_i + čekali$_j$ $[_{VP_2}$ t_j Marijinu prijateljicu]] mi je + smo$_i$
        waited   Maria's friend   we ARE
    'wait for Maria's friend, we DID'

32. The conclusion is, of course, somewhat tentative because we cannot with absolute certainty assume that no condition that is unrelated to multiple movement to the same position is violated in the construction under consideration.

33. A relevant example would be a construction in which one NP would check the Case feature of more than one "traditional" Case assigner.

34. This is desirable. Although the situation described in note 33 does not seem to exist, we do find examples of a target Case feature, a −Interpretable element, undergoing multiple checking, as in the multiple nominative construction in Japanese. For another such case, see Boeckx 1998.

References

Aoun, Joseph, and Yen-hui Audrey Li. 1993. *Wh*-elements in situ: Syntax or LF? *Linguistic Inquiry* 24, 199–238.

Ausín, Adolfo. In preparation. Two types of questions in English. Ms., University of Connecticut, Storrs.

Besten, Hans den, and Jerold Edmondson. 1983. The verbal complex in continental West Germanic. In *On the formal syntax of the Westgermania*, ed. Werner Abraham, 155–216. Amsterdam: John Benjamins.

Boeckx, Cédric. 1998. A minimalist view on the passive. (UConn Working Papers Occasional Papers in Linguistics 2.) Department of Linguistics, University of Connecticut, Storrs. [Distributed by MITWPL, Department of Linguistics and Philosophy, MIT, Cambridge, Mass.]

Bošković, Željko. 1995. Participle movement and second position cliticization in Serbo-Croatian. *Lingua* 96, 245–266.

Bošković, Željko. 1997a. Fronting *wh*-phrases in Serbo-Croatian. In *Annual Workshop on Formal Approaches to Slavic Linguistics: The Indiana meeting, 1996*, eds. Martina Lindseth and Steven Franks, 86–107. Ann Arbor, Mich.: Michigan Slavic Publications.

Bošković, Željko. 1997b. On certain violations of the Superiority Condition, AgrO, and economy of derivation. *Journal of Linguistics* 33, 227–254.

Bošković, Željko. 1997c. Superiority effects with multiple *wh*-fronting in Serbo-Croatian. *Lingua* 102, 1–20.

Bošković, Željko. 1997d. *The syntax of nonfinite complementation: An economy approach.* Cambridge, Mass.: MIT Press.

Bošković, Željko. 1998a. LF movement and the Minimalist Program. In *NELS 28*, eds. Pius Tamanji and Kiyomi Kusumoto, 43–57. GLSA, University of Massachusetts, Amherst.

Bošković, Željko. 1998b. On the interpretation of multiple questions. Ms., University of Connecticut, Storrs. [Available at http://mitpress.mit.edu/celebration]

Bošković, Željko. 1998c. *Wh*-movement and *wh*-phrases in Slavic. Paper presented at the Comparative Slavic Morphosyntax Workshop, Spencer, Ind. [Available at http://www.indiana.edu/ ~ slavconf/linguistics/index.html]

Bošković, Željko. In press a. Multiple *wh*-fronting and economy of derivation. In *Proceedings of the Sixteenth West Coast Conference on Formal Linguistics.* Stanford, Calif.: CSLI Publications.

Bošković, Željko. In press b. Second position clitics: Syntax and/or phonology? In *Clitics in Europe*, eds. Frits Beukema and Marcel den Dikken. Dordrecht: Foris.

Bošković, Željko. In press c. Sometimes in SpecCP, sometimes in-situ. In *Step by step: Essays on minimalism in honor of Howard Lasnik*, eds. Roger Martin, David Michaels, and Juan Uriagereka. Cambridge, Mass.: MIT Press.

Broekhuis, Hans, Hans den Besten, Kees Hoekstra, and Jean Rutten. 1995. Infinitival complementation in Dutch: On remnant extraposition. *The Linguistic Review* 12, 93–122.

Cheng, Lisa. 1997. *On the typology of* wh-*questions.* New York: Garland.

Cheng, Lisa, and Hamida Demirdache. 1990. Superiority violations. In *Papers on* wh-*movement*, eds. Lisa Cheng and Hamida Demirdache, 27–46. (MIT Working Papers in Linguistics 13.) MITWPL, Department of Linguistics and Philosophy, MIT, Cambridge, Mass.

Chierchia, Gennaro. 1991. Functional *wh* and weak crossover. In *Proceedings of the Tenth West Coast Conference on Formal Linguistics*, ed. Dawn Bates, 75–90. Stanford, Calif.: CSLI Publications. [Distributed by Cambridge University Press.]

Chomsky, Noam. 1973. Conditions on transformations. In *A festschrift for Morris Halle*, eds. Stephen Anderson and Paul Kiparsky, 232–286. New York: Holt, Rinehart and Winston.

Chomsky, Noam. 1995. Categories and transformations. In *The Minimalist Program*, 219–394. Cambridge, Mass.: MIT Press.

Cole, Peter, and Gabriella Hermon. 1995. Is *wh*-in-situ really in-situ? Evidence from Malay and Chinese. In *Proceedings of the Thirteenth West Coast Conference on Formal Linguistics*, eds. Raul Aranovich, William Byrne, Susanne Preuss, and Martha Senturia, 189–204. Stanford, Calif: CSLI Publications. [Distributed by Cambridge University Press.]

Dikken, Marcel den, and Teun Hoekstra. 1997. Parasitic participles. *Linguistics* 35, 1057–1089.

Evers, Arnold. 1975. The transformational cycle in Dutch and German. Doctoral dissertation, University of Utrecht.

Haegeman, Liliane. 1992a. Negation in West Flemish and the Neg Criterion. In *NELS 22*, ed. K. Broderick, 195–208. GLSA, University of Massachusetts, Amherst.

Haegeman, Liliane. 1992b. *Theory and description in generative grammar: A case study in West Flemish*. Cambridge: Cambridge University Press.

Haegeman, Liliane. 1994. Verb raising as verb projection raising: Some empirical problems. *Linguistic Inquiry* 25, 509–521.

Haegeman, Liliane. 1995a. IPP constructions and V-movement in West-Flemish. Ms., University of Geneva.

Haegeman, Liliane. 1995b. *The syntax of negation*. Cambridge: Cambridge University Press.

Haegeman, Liliane, and Henk van Riemsdijk. 1986. Verb projection raising, scope, and the typology of rules affecting verbs. *Linguistic Inquiry* 17, 417–466.

Haider, Hubert. 1986. Affect α: A reply to Lasnik and Saito, On the nature of proper government. *Linguistic Inquiry* 17, 113–126.

Hoeksema, Jack. 1988. A constraint on governors in the West Germanic verb cluster. In *Morphology and modularity: In honor of Henk Shultink*, eds. Martin Everaert, Arnold Evers, and Mieke Trommelen, 147–161. Dordrecht: Foris.

Hoekstra, Eric. 1994. Analyzing linear asymmetries in the verb clusters of Dutch and Frisian and their dialects. Ms., Meertens Institute, Amsterdam.

Hornstein, Norbert. 1995. *Logical Form: From GB to minimalism*. Cambridge, Mass.: Blackwell.

Horvath, Julia. 1986. *Focus in the theory of grammar and the syntax of Hungarian*. Dordrecht: Foris.

Izvorski, Roumyana. 1993. On *wh*-movement and focus-movement in Bulgarian. Presented at *CONSOLE 2*, University of Tübingen.

Kaan, Edith. 1992. A minimalist approach to extraposition of CP and verb (projection) raising. *Language and Cognition* 2, 169–179.

Kayne, Richard. 1984. *Connectedness and binary branching*. Dordrecht: Foris.

É. Kiss, Katalin. 1995. *Discourse configurational languages*. New York: Oxford University Press.

Kitahara, Hisatsugu. 1993. Deducing Superiority effects from the shortest chain requirement. In *Harvard working papers in linguistic 3*, eds. Höskuldur Thráinsson, Samuel David Epstein, and Susumu Kuno, 109–119. Department of Linguistics, Harvard University, Cambridge, Mass.

Koizumi, Masatoshi. 1994. Layered specifiers. In *NELS 24*, vol. 1, ed. Mercè Gonzàlez, 255–269. GLSA, University of Massachusetts, Amherst.

Lasnik, Howard. 1999. On feature strength: Three minimalist approaches to overt movement. *Linguistic Inquiry* 30, 197–217.

Lasnik, Howard, and Mamoru Saito. 1992. *Move α: Conditions on its application and output*. Cambridge, Mass.: MIT Press.

Müller, Gereon, and Wolfgang Sternefeld. 1996. Ā-chain formation and economy of derivation. *Linguistic Inquiry* 27, 480–511.

Oka, Toshifusa. 1993. Shallowness. In *Papers on Case and agreement II*, ed. Colin Phillips, 255–320. (MIT Working Papers in Linguistics 19.) MITWPL, Department of Linguistics and Philosophy, MIT, Cambridge, Mass.

Pesetsky, David. 1982. Paths and categories. Doctoral dissertation, MIT, Cambridge, Mass.

Richards, Norvin. 1997. What moves where when in which language? Doctoral dissertation, MIT, Cambridge, Mass.

Roberts, Ian. 1991. Excorporation and minimality. *Linguistic Inquiry* 22, 209–218.

Rochemont, Michael. 1986. *Focus in generative grammar*. Philadelphia: John Benjamins.

Rudin, Catherine. 1988. On multiple questions and multiple *wh*-fronting. *Natural Language & Linguistic Theory* 6, 445–501.

Rutten, Jean. 1991. Infinitival complements and auxiliaries. Doctoral dissertation, University of Utrecht.

Simpson, Andrew. 1995. *Wh*-movement, licensing, and the locality of feature-checking. Doctoral dissertation, School of Oriental and African Studies, University of London.

Stjepanović, Sandra. 1998a. Movement of *wh*-phrases in Serbo-Croatian matrix clauses. Paper presented at the Comparative Slavic Morphosyntax Workshop, Spencer, Ind.

Stjepanović, Sandra. 1998b. On the placement of Serbo-Croatian clitics: Evidence from clitic climbing and VP ellipsis. In *Annual Workshop on Formal Approaches to Slavic Linguistics: The Connecticut meeting, 1997*, eds. Željko Bošković, Steven Franks, and William Snyder, 267–286. Ann Arbor, Mich.: Michigan Slavic Publications.

Stjepanović, Sandra. 1998c. On the placement of Serbo-Croatian clitics: Evidence from VP-ellipsis. *Linguistic Inquiry* 29, 527–537.

Watanabe, Akira. 1992. Subjacency and S-Structure movement of *wh*-in-situ. *Journal of East Asian Linguistics* 1, 255–291.

Watanabe, Akira. 1993. Agr-based Case theory and its interaction with the Ā-system. Doctoral dissertation, MIT, Cambridge, Mass.

Zwart, C. Jan-Wouter. 1993. Dutch syntax: A minimalist approach. Doctoral dissertation, University of Groningen.

Zwart, C. Jan-Wouter. 1994. Verb clusters in Continental West Germanic dialects. Paper presented at the 18th Meeting of the Atlantic Provinces Linguistic Association, University of New Brunswick, Saint John.

Zwart, C. Jan-Wouter. 1995. A note on verb clusters in the Stellingwerfs dialect. In *Linguistics in the Netherlands 1995*, eds. Marcel den Dikken and Kees Hengeveld, 215–226. Philadelphia: John Benjamins.

Zwart, C. Jan-Wouter. 1997. *Morphosyntax of verb movement: A minimalist approach to the syntax of Dutch.* Dordrecht: Kluwer.

Chapter 8

Chains of Arguments   Howard Lasnik

In this chapter, I will be concerned with some of the properties of configurations resulting from A-movement and of the chains—A-chains—created by such movement. I will concentrate particularly on several arguments about A-chains presented by Chomsky (1995), and the consequences, sometimes surprising, of those arguments.

As my point of departure, I take Chomsky's (1995, 326) claim about a contrast between Ā-movement and A-movement: "That reconstruction should be barred in A-chains is ... plausible on conceptual grounds." I begin by examining those conceptual grounds. Chomsky's immediate concern at this point of his exposition is trace deletion, particularly intermediate trace deletion. He suggests that certain analyses proposed in Chomsky 1991 and Chomsky and Lasnik 1993 based on intermediate trace deletion are incorrect and that there is, in fact, no process of trace deletion. Rather, the effects of trace deletion follow from reconstruction "understood in minimalist terms."[1]

First, a very brief reminder of those earlier analyses and the role of trace deletion in them. Chomsky, and Chomsky and Lasnik, were concerned with the fact that a range of "island" violations do not have the severely degraded status of Empty Category Principle (ECP) violations, even though the derivations of the examples seem to produce intermediate traces that are not properly governed. One such example is (1), first discussed in roughly these terms by Lasnik and Saito (1984).

(1) ??who do you wonder [$_{CP}$ whether [$_{IP}$ John said [$_{CP}$ t' e [$_{IP}$ t solved the problem]]]]

The intermediate trace t' is marked * since it is too distant from its nearest antecedent (by any standard measure) to be properly governed, but the example is merely marginal. The accounts of this fact at issue incorporated a process of deletion, constrained (like all transformational operations) by economy. Deletion is possible only to turn an illegitimate LF object into a legitimate one, where the legitimate LF objects are uniform chains (whose members are all in A-positions, all in Ā-positions, or all in X^0-positions) and operator-variable pairs.

Deletion in the chain (*who*, t', t) is permissible since the chain is neither uniform (*who* and t' are in Ā-positions; t is in an A-position) nor an operator-variable *pair*. More generally, in the case of successive-cyclic Ā-movement of an argument, an intermediate trace (starred or otherwise) can (in fact must) be deleted in LF, voiding an ECP violation when the trace to be deleted is starred. On the other hand, long movement as in (2) will violate the ECP, since the movement chain in this instance is uniformly an Ā-chain and economy therefore prevents the deletion of t'.

(2) *how do you wonder [CP whether [IP John said [CP t' e [IP Mary solved the problem t]]]]

Similarly, ultralong A-movement will also be properly excluded, even when the first step is "short," as in (3).

(3) *John seems [that [it is likely [t' to be arrested t]]]

With this much background, I return to the main point. Chomsky (1995) is concerned with long A-movement, but via an intermediate *Ā*-position.

(4) *John seems [that [t_2 [it was told t_1 [that ...]]]]

Notice that the chain of *John* in (4) is nonuniform, so the deletion process outlined above should be applicable—incorrectly, it appears. Chomsky (1995, 326) concludes,

We do not want to permit the intermediate (offending) trace t_2 to delete, unlike what happens in [long *wh*-movement of an argument]. The distinction suggests a different approach to intermediate trace deletion: perhaps it is a reflex of the process of reconstruction, understood in minimalist terms.... The basic assumption here is that there is no process of reconstruction; rather, the phenomenon is a consequence of the formation of operator-variable constructions driven by F[ull] I[nterpretation], a process that may (or sometimes must) leave part of the trace—a copy of the moved element—intact at LF, deleting only its operator part.

In fact, it does seem that the only successful uses of economy-constrained deletion in chains involve long *wh*-movement of arguments, where a nonuniform chain is turned into an operator-variable pair. I know of no comparable instances where an ECP violation is voided by deletion of an offending intermediate trace turning a nonuniform chain into a uniform chain. Since this new approach predicts this fact, there is some justification for the approach. On the other hand, it raises questions of its own. First, it is not clear that t_2 in (4) is an offending trace in the relevant sense (i.e., in the sense of the earlier theory). Is movement from that intermediate position to the surface position of *John* too long? Maybe, or maybe not. And even if it is, that could presumably be remedied by further adjunction steps. There is, however, a way to retain the essence of the new analysis. Suppose we were to continue to assume that there is no trace deletion. But suppose we retained from the earlier approach the idea that only operator-variable pairs and uniform chains are legitimate LF objects. Then (4) would be correctly excluded, but not because of an offending trace per se. Rather, the whole *chain* would be the offender.

The account of (3) remains unchanged. Though the chain is legitimate, it does contain an offending trace, one that now cannot be eliminated under any circumstances, since (3) does not involve an operator chain. Ironically, though, the major phenomenon originally motivating the uniform chain approach now loses its account. Recall that the offending intermediate trace in the case of argument movement (1) was deletable by virtue of being part of a nonuniform chain, whereas the corresponding offending trace in the case of adjunct movement (2), as part of a uniform chain, was not deletable. But in the new approach, deletability has nothing to do with uniformity. Rather, the intermediate trace in (1) deletes as a direct consequence of operator-variable formation. Similarly, the intermediate trace in (2) should be able to delete. As a consequence, the difference in status of the two examples is no longer explained. I put this question aside and return to aspects of the analysis more directly related to properties of A-chains.

As Chomsky observes, his (1995) approach to intermediate trace deletion makes it a subcase of "reconstruction." Further, "[t]he reconstruction process would then be restricted to the special case of Ā-movement that involves operators. That reconstruction should be barred in A-chains is thus plausible on conceptual grounds" (p. 326). In passing, I note that the argument actually seems more empirical than conceptual, based, as it is, on an acceptability contrast between long A-movement and long (argument) *wh*-movement. Momentarily, I will discuss some of Chomsky's several arguments that there is, in fact, no reconstruction with A-movement. Before that, though, I want to briefly examine the somewhat

curious account that Chomsky has offered for the claimed fact. Chomsky
assumes that movement invariably leaves behind a "trace" in the form of
a copy of the moved item. Further, as just discussed, he argues that there
is no process of trace deletion per se. Rather, traces are (sometimes)
eliminated as part of the process of operator-variable creation. Thus,
traces in other types of constructions are never eliminated. That they are
not eliminated in A-constructions provided part of Chomsky's account of
the extreme ungrammaticality of "improper" movement, as in (4). Reconstruction phenomena are simply situations where a (portion of a)
moved item behaves, for some purposes, as if it were in some position it
occupied earlier in the derivation. Yet, almost paradoxically, Chomsky
concludes that the impossibility of *eliminating* an A-trace makes it plausible that reconstruction should be *barred* in A-chains. If anything, one
might expect, on the contrary, that on this theory reconstruction is always
necessary in A-chains. Thus, although the intuition that reconstruction
should be specifically a property of operator-variable constructions is
fairly clear, Chomsky's mechanism for instantiating the intuition is far
from straightforward.

Alongside the above argument, which Chomsky regards as conceptual,
he gives some empirical arguments. The first is a binding-theoretic argument based on (5).

(5) *John expected [him to seem to me [$_\alpha$ t to be intelligent]]

Chomsky observes that "[u]nder the relevant interpretation, [(5)] can only
be understood as a Condition B violation, though under reconstruction
the violation should be obviated, with *him* interpreted in the position of
t..." (p. 326). Notice that this argument tacitly assumes a formulation of
governing category (GC), the domain in which a pronoun must be free,
such that the "reconstructed" (6) would not also violate Condition B.

(6) John expected [to seem to me [$_\alpha$ him to be intelligent]]

The formulation in Chomsky 1981, 209–211, is not obviously consistent
with the argument.

(7) β is a governing category for α if and only if β is the minimal category
    containing α, a governor of α, and a SUBJECT accessible to α.

(8) SUBJECT = AGR in a finite clause; NP of S in an infinitival; NP of
    NP in an NP.

(9) γ is accessible to α iff α is in the c-command domain of γ and ...

α in (6) is not the GC for *him*, since there is no SUBJECT accessible to *him* in that domain. Further, by hypothesis, there is no SUBJECT at all in the intermediate clause, after reconstruction. Thus, the GC for *him* would actually be the matrix, and the required Condition B effect is obtained after all. On the other hand, under the formulation in Chomsky 1986, or the related one in Chomsky and Lasnik 1993, 552, Chomsky's argument does go through. Consider the latter formulation:

(10) The GC for α is the minimal complete functional complex (CFC) that contains α and in which α's binding condition could, in principle, be satisfied.

The requirement on *him*, that it be A-free in a local domain, could, in principle, be satisfied in α in (6). And since *him* is, in fact, A-free in that domain (which is a CFC), Condition B is satisfied, incorrectly so, as Chomsky implies. Chomsky's argument thus seems valid. It should be pointed out, though, that the type of formulation of GC that makes it valid might have difficulty with another construction.

(11) *John$_i$ believes him$_i$ to be intelligent

If *him*, the "exceptional-Case-marking" (ECM) subject, is in the lower clause, then, by the above line of reasoning, (11) is incorrectly not a Condition B violation. Below, I will present an analysis of ECM in which the ECM subject raises into the matrix clause. The analysis has as a by-product the elimination of the problem just noted.

Chomsky's argument against A-movement reconstruction based on (5) is abstractly reminiscent of a problem that Belletti and Rizzi (1988) deal with in their theory of anaphora. To account for certain instances of apparently "backward" binding, Belletti and Rizzi propose that Condition A can be satisfied anywhere in the course of a derivation.[2] Given this theory, something needs to be said about examples like the following:

(12) *himself seems to him [*t* to be clever]

Prior to movement, Condition A is presumably satisfied, since as (13) (from Chomsky 1995, 304) shows, the (NP in the) *to* phrase c-commands into the complement infinitival.

(13) *they seem to him$_i$ [*t* to like John$_i$]

For Belletti and Rizzi, (12) satisfies Condition A, but it violates Condition B, which, according to Belletti and Rizzi, must be satisfied specifically at S-Structure, unlike Condition A. Observe that Chomsky's (5) could also be ruled out in the same way, if, as is plausible (though not logically necessary), its S-Structure configuration violates Condition B. However, one of Chomsky's major minimalist tenets is that there is no S-Structure as a significant level of representation: all binding conditions are assumed to apply at the LF level. In particular, Condition B must be satisfied at LF. So far, then, Chomsky's Condition B argument against A-movement reconstruction stands.

Chomsky's next major argument is based on a curious scope interaction in English between clausal negation and a universal quantifier in subject position. Chomsky presents the following paradigm:[3]

(14) a. (it seems that) everyone isn't there yet
     b. I expected [everyone not to be there yet]
     c. everyone seems [*t* not to be there yet]

He then argues as follows: "Negation can have wide scope over the quantifier in [(14a)], and it seems in [(14b)] but not in [(14c)]," concluding that "reconstruction in the A-chain does not take place, so it appears" (p. 327).

Hornstein (1995, 239) challenges the empirical basis for this argument.[4] He acknowledges that there is a contrast of the kind seen in (14). He gives the following examples, parallel to (14a,c):[5]

(15) a. everyone didn't leave
     b. everyone seems not to have left

However, he claims that there is an empirical flaw in the argument. He gives the following examples, claiming that they do not allow negation to take scope over *everyone* either:

(16) a. John would prefer for everyone not to leave
     b. John wanted very much for everyone not to leave

Thus, we would not expect such a reading in (15b) regardless. Hornstein (personal communication) suggests that the crucial property is contraction: the wide scope for negation is possible only when negation has contracted, as in (14a) and (15a). My informants do find wide scope for negation in (16a,b) somewhat less accessible than in (14a) and (15a). However, they do not find it as inaccessible as in (14c) and (15b). Their judgment on (14b) is similar: wide scope for negation is possible, at least to a significant extent. Some other examples with uncontracted negation seem to allow wide scope negation rather readily. Consider the following examples, in a situation where a teacher is being reprimanded for giving all the students As:

(17) school policy requires that everyone not get an A

(18) it is important for everyone not to get an A

Both examples seem reasonably appropriate to the situation, indicating that the reading in question is available. Thus, there is reason to think that Chomsky is correct in suggesting that there is something special about raising constructions in their inability to allow the reading. It is not implausible to take this, as Chomsky does, as evidence that there is no A-movement reconstruction.

It will be of interest to examine ECM constructions in this connection. I suspect that Chomsky intended his (14b) to instantiate ECM. It well might; however, the situation is somewhat equivocal, since, as shown by Bresnan (1972), *expect* has multiple subcategorization frames. "True" ECM constructions will be particularly interesting since there is substantial evidence that they exhibit raising—in fact, overt raising. I will briefly summarize the arguments, which fall into two basic classes. First, there are the several paradigms discussed by Lasnik and Saito (1991), some of them following Postal (1974), indicating that an ECM subject can bind into a matrix-clause adverbial. When combined with Lasnik and Saito's arguments that covert raising does not create new binding configurations (and the modern minimalist versions of those arguments in Lasnik 1995a,b, 1997), those paradigms strongly argue for overt raising in ECM constructions. Second, there is the combination of Chomsky and Lasnik's (1993) argument that (at least some) ellipsis is a PF deletion phenomenon and the argument from Lasnik 1995c that an ECM subject can "escape" an ellipsis site via raising.

Representative examples showing "high" binding behavior for ECM subjects are as follows, displaying, respectively, Condition A satisfaction, weak crossover mitigation, and negative polarity item licensing:

(19) the DA proved [two men to have been at the scene of the crime] during each other's trials

(20) the DA proved [no suspect$_i$ to have been at the scene of the crime] during his$_i$ trial

(21) the DA proved [no one to have been at the scene of the crime] during any of the trials

For most speakers I have interviewed, (19)–(21) contrast significantly with corresponding examples with finite complements.

(22) ?*the DA proved [that two men were at the scene of the crime] during each other's trials

(23) ?*the DA proved [that no suspect$_i$ was at the scene of the crime] during his$_i$ trial

(24) ?*the DA proved [that no one was guilty] during any of the trials

This contrast strongly suggests that the ECM subject is in the higher clause at some relevant level of representation, the conclusion reached by Lasnik and Saito, and by Postal much earlier. Working within the Government-Binding framework of assumptions, Lasnik and Saito argue that the relevant level of representation is S-Structure, hence, that raising is overt. In Lasnik 1995a,b, 1997, I present arguments that that conclusion is still valid under minimalist assumptions. The movement is presumably feature driven, the relevant feature being Case, or, more likely, an Extended Projection Principle (EPP) feature in Agr$_O$.[6] Given Chomsky's (1995) powerful conceptual argument that covert (formal) feature-driven movement should affect (formal) features alone, the question arises whether raising of mere features creates new binding-type relations. There is very good reason to believe that it does not.

Beginning with Chomsky 1986, a series of arguments have been made that in existential constructions such as (25), a movement relation connects the expletive and the "associate."

(25) there is a man here

The standard argument for movement is a compelling one: that movement provides the basis for an account of the familiar superficially bizarre agreement paradigms displayed by these constructions, where the verb agrees with something that is not its formal subject.

(26) a. there is/*are a man here
     b. there are/*is men here

The several approaches under which the associate raises in toto have all had a major empirical defect: they have failed to capture the fact that the associate is always interpreted in situ with respect to scope, as in (27) from Chomsky 1991.

(27) there aren't many linguistics students here

Chomsky (1995) argues that this scope fact can be captured if the movement affects only the formal features (including the agreement features) of the associate, a consequence in line with a general economy condition mandating that a movement operation move as little as possible. For covert movement, nothing would require that more than the formal features move.

Given this analysis, it is straightforward to show that covert movement (at least of the feature-driven variety) does not create new binding-type relations. (19)–(21), repeated here as the (a) cases of (28)–(30), sharply contrast with corresponding examples with *there*, the (b) cases of (28)–(30).[7]

(28) a. the DA proved [two men to have been at the scene of the crime] during each other's trials
     b. *the DA proved [there to have been two men at the scene of the crime] during each other's trials

(29) a. the DA proved [no suspect$_i$ to have been at the scene of the crime] during his$_i$ trial
     b. *the DA proved [there to have been no suspect$_i$ at the scene of the crime] during his$_i$ trial

(30) a. the DA proved [no one to have been at the scene of the crime] during any of the trials
     b. *the DA proved [there to have been no one at the scene of the crime] during any of the trials

We are led to the conclusion that the high behavior of the ECM subject in the (a) cases is the result of overt raising. Koizumi (1993, 1995), developing ideas of Johnson (1991), outlines a theory that makes this possible, whereby the ECM subject raises to [Spec, Agr$_O$] of the matrix clause and the matrix verb raises to a still higher "shell" V position.

The second argument for overt raising of an ECM subject has to do with the pseudogapping ellipsis construction. This construction is exemplified in (31).

(31) Mary hired John, and Susan will ~~hire~~ Bill

Following Jayaseelan (1990), in Lasnik 1995c I argue that the construction involves VP-ellipsis, the remnant having escaped from the ellipsis site via a movement operation. Departing from Jayaseelan, I argue that the movement operation is not heavy NP shift (HNPS) but raising to [Spec,

Agr$_O$]. In part, the argument is based on a divergence between pseudo-gapping and HNPS possibilities in double object constructions (for discussion, see Lasnik 1995c, 1999). In particular, the first object is a good pseudogapping remnant yet resists HNPS.

(32) ?John gave Bill a lot of money, and Mary will ~~give~~ Susan ~~a lot of money~~

(33) *John gave t a lot of money [the fund for the preservation of VOS languages]

Conversely, the *second* object is a poor pseudogapping remnant but freely undergoes HNPS.

(34) *John gave Bill a lot of money, and Mary will ~~give Bill~~ a lot of advice

(35) John gave Bill t yesterday [more money than he had ever seen]

Note that there *is* a correlation with typical A-movement. The first object, but not the second, can undergo passive.

(36) Bill was given t a lot of money

(37) ?*a lot of money was given Bill t

Now notice that an ECM subject makes a good pseudogapping remnant.

(38) the DA proved Jones (to be) guilty and the Assistant DA will ~~prove~~ Smith ~~(to be) guilty~~

Thus, we have additional reason for thinking that an ECM subject (like an object, as a matter of fact) undergoes overt raising.[8]

I now return to the main question of this part of the discussion: how do universal ECM subjects interact with clausal negation? The prediction is now that negation cannot take wide scope, just as it cannot in raising-to-subject constructions (Chomsky's observation), since both constructions involve overt A-movement into the higher clause, and Chomsky's account of his observation should carry over: there is no A-movement reconstruction. The prediction is clearly correct for certain ECM constructions. For example, in the rather unusual ECM particle construction (based on *make . . . out*) discussed by Kayne (1985), a universal ECM subject is clearly outside the scope of negation, as seen in (39).

(39) the mathematician made every even number out not to be the sum of two primes

Note that the only reading is the implausible one where the mathematician was engaged in the futile activity of trying to convince someone that no even number is the sum of two primes (and not the far more plausible one of merely trying to convince someone that Goldbach's conjecture is false). Thus, even with strong pragmatic bias toward wide scope for the negation, it still is not available, consistent with the raising analysis combined with Chomsky's claim.

It is perhaps unsurprising that (39) should pattern with Chomsky's (14c), repeated here.

(40) everyone seems [*t* not to be there yet]

(40) clearly displays overt raising; indeed, it is a paradigmatic instance of the phenomenon. But the interest of the construction exemplified in (39) is that it, too, clearly displays overt raising. *Every even number* is the thematic subject of the lower clause, yet it appears to the left of the particle *out*, which is part of the higher predicate.

Since I have argued that even more conventional ECM constructions involve overt raising, they too would be expected to require wide scope for the thematic subject over lower clausal negation. Curiously, most of my informants find narrow scope possible, even if somewhat disfavored, unlike the situation with raising to subject or with the *make*-NP-*out* construction. Some representative examples are as follows:[9]

(41) I believe everyone not to have arrived yet

(42) I proved every Mersenne number not to be prime

Those same informants (along with every other native English speaker, I believe) disallow narrow scope for the universal when it undergoes passive/raising to subject position.

(43) everyone is believed not to have arrived yet

(44) every Mersenne number was proved not to be prime

In (44), there is strong bias toward narrow scope, but it is still not available. Only the wildly false wide scope reading exists.

The task immediately at hand is to reconcile the substantial evidence that ECM subjects undergo overt raising with the scope fact in (41)–(42). Narrow scope for the universal subject should not be possible if it has raised, just as narrow scope is not possible in Chomsky's (14c) or in (39) and (43)–(44).[10] Descriptively, the situation so far is that when it is completely clear from the word order that raising has taken place, narrow scope for a universal ECM subject is impossible. But when the word order is equivocal, narrow scope is possible. This suggests that in the latter circumstance, overt raising has not necessarily taken place. The question now is whether this is a flat contradiction or merely a problem. The former will be true if *in the very same sentence* there is evidence both for and against raising. Some of the tests *for* raising are difficult to carry out with a universal quantifier as ECM subject. But pseudogapping does seem to be possible in that circumstance.

(45) Mary proved every Mersenne number not to be prime, and John will
      every Fibonacci number

The fact that *every Fibonacci number* is a pseudogapping remnant indicates that it has overtly raised. If, simultaneously, it could take scope under the (elided) negation as it can in (46), we would have a contradiction.

(46) John proved every Fibonacci number not to be prime

However, it seems that unlike the situation in (46), narrow scope is not possible for *every Fibonacci number* in (45).[11] Thus, there is no direct contradiction. Rather, we are led to the conclusion that raising must be *optional*. Note that that conclusion is consistent with all the binding and ellipsis evidence for raising summarized above. All of these phenomena simply indicate that raising is *possible*, available when necessary but not necessarily obligatory.

There is actually one phenomenon discussed by Postal (1974) and Lasnik and Saito (1991), but not yet discussed here, that argues that raising *is* obligatory. Postal's statement of the argument is based on "a fundamental pronominalization constraint" due to Langacker (1969) that states that a pronoun cannot both precede and command its antecedent. There are a number of more recent formulations of this constraint, including my (1976) noncoreference rule and Chomsky's (1981) Condition C. Any of these formulations can correctly distinguish (47) from (48), but only if the embedded subject in (47) has (necessarily) raised into the higher clause.

(47) *John believes him$_i$ to be a genius even more fervently than Bob$_i$
      does

(48)   Joan believes he$_i$ is a genius even more fervently than Bob$_i$ does

This phenomenon is, perhaps, not as problematic as it might first appear. After all, it is not uncommon for "object shift" to be obligatory with pronouns even when it is optional with lexical NPs (for discussion, see Johnson 1991 and Diesing 1996). In fact, even in English, there is a bit of independent evidence for this state of affairs. In the *make out* construction discussed above, many speakers allow the ECM subject to the right of *out* as well as to the left.

(49) Mary made John out to be a fool

(50) Mary made out John to be a fool

If, as assumed above, an example like (49) exhibits overt raising, it is reasonable to conjecture that there has been no overt raising in (50). Significantly, the analogue of (49) with a pronoun as ECM subject is still good, but the analogue of (50) is bad, even for speakers who find (50) itself fully acceptable.

(51) Mary made him out to be a fool

(52) *Mary made out him to be a fool

This is abstractly quite parallel to the situation seen above, which also argued that raising is optional, yet obligatory with pronouns. In fact, the parallel is still deeper. Recall that a universal to the left of *out* cannot have narrow scope under clausal negation in the infinitival, as seen in (39), repeated here.

(53) the mathematician made every even number out not to be the sum
      of two primes

Those speakers I have interviewed who accept the alternative word order for the construction, as in (54), do allow narrow scope for the universal in that instance.

(54) the mathematician made out every even number not to be the sum
      of two primes

I believe that other "height" tests summarized above also conform to the pattern just outlined, though more data collection is clearly in order. For example, a negative ECM subject to the left of *out* seems much more comfortable with a negative polarity item in the matrix clause than does one to the right of *out*.

(55) a.   the lawyer made no witnesses out to be idiots during any of
          the trials

     b.   ?*the lawyer made out no witnesses to be idiots during any of
          the trials

And, though judgments are subtle, I find similar effects with the two other
height tests considered earlier, anaphor binding and weak crossover.

(56) a.   the DA made the defendants out to be guilty during each
          other's trials

     b.   ?*the DA made out the defendants to be guilty during each
          other's trials

(57) a.   the DA made no suspect$_i$ out to have been at the scene of the
          crime during his$_i$ trial

     b.   ?*the DA made out no suspect$_i$ to have been at the scene of the
          crime during his$_i$ trial

Thus, it is still reasonable to think that (overt) raising of an ECM subject is optional, obligatory only with pronouns. When raising of a universal does take place, as evidenced by position to the left of *out* or high
binding or survival as a pseudogapping remnant, that universal cannot
"reconstruct" so as to take scope under lower clausal negation. That is,
"raising to object" parallels "raising to subject" and provides further
evidence for Chomsky's claim that "reconstruction in [an] A-chain does
not take place..."

The next question is how the optionality of "raising to object" is to be
instantiated. I continue to assume that when the ECM subject raises, it
raises to [Spec, Agr$_O$].[12] This is essentially as in Chomsky 1991, except
that I take the movement to be overt rather than covert, for all the
reasons outlined above. As briefly mentioned earlier, given the word order
of English, the fact that the raising is overt further entails that the verb
normally raises to a still higher position, as in Koizumi's (1993, 1995)
"split-VP" hypothesis, which I adopt in its essentials. The relevant portion of an ECM structure with raising, (58), is as shown in (59).

(58) she will prove Bob to be guilty

(59)

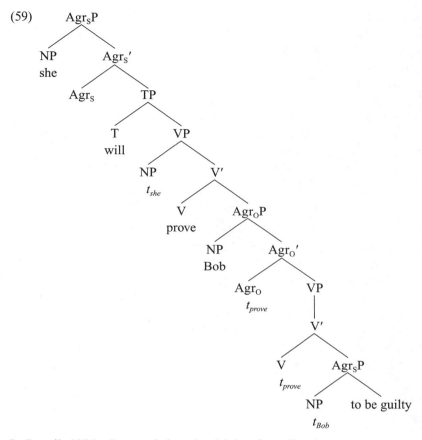

In Lasnik 1995c, I argued that the driving force for the overt movement of the NP is a strong EPP feature in Agr$_O$. Following Chomsky (1991), I took Agr$_O$ to be the same item as Agr$_S$, the labels being merely mnemonic. Overt "object shift" is then analyzable as the same phenomenon as the standard EPP. I assume that Case checking is just a side effect of EPP satisfaction;[13] there is no requirement that Case per se be checked overtly. One way to make the raising optional might be to abandon the idea that Agr$_O$ is the same item as Agr$_S$, assuming, instead, that only the latter obligatorily has an EPP feature. Agr$_O$ would only optionally have the feature. Some of the discussion in Chomsky 1995 hints at another possibility. Chomsky reasons that "[i]f Agr has no strong feature, then PF considerations, at least, give no reason for it to be present at all, and LF considerations do not seem relevant" (p. 350). He thus suggests that "Agr exists only when it has strong features" (p. 351). Along these lines, suppose that the optionality of raising is the optionality of Agr_O.[14] If Agr_O is present, overt raising will be forced by its strong EPP feature. If Agr_O is absent, there will be no overt raising; the nominal's Case will be checked by covert raising of its formal features to the V.[15] Under that circumstance, the nominal will not participate in high binding, nor will it survive as a pseudogapping remnant. On the other hand, it will be able to take low scope, as in the instances of ambiguous interaction between universal and negation discussed earlier.

I return now to another scope "reconstruction" phenomenon briefly alluded to above: so-called Quantifier Lowering (QL). (60) is a classic example, from the groundbreaking discussion in May 1977.

(60) some politician is likely to address John's constituency

The intuition about (60) is that it is ambiguous. To quote May, "[(60)] may be taken as asserting either (i) that there is a politician, e.g., Rockefeller, who is likely to address John's constituency, or (ii) that it is likely that there is some politician (or other) who will address John's constituency" (p. 189). Since May 1977, that ambiguity has been taken to stem from whether the surface subject "lowers" or not. Chomsky distinguishes this phenomenon from the one found in low scope under negation for a universal quantifier subject. Recall that Chomsky observes that a raised NP cannot reconstruct to take narrow scope in that way, as in (14c), repeated here.

(61) everyone seems [t not to be there yet]

On the other hand, Chomsky accepts the standard claim that (60) is ambiguous and that the ambiguity is a structural property. As mentioned in note 3, to reconcile his conclusion based on (61) with standard QL as in (60), Chomsky suggests that the "lowered" reading in the latter instance

could result from adjunction of the matrix quantifier to the lower IP (c-commanding the trace of raising and yielding a well-formed structure if the trace of quantifier lowering is deleted, along the lines of May's original proposal). But reconstruction in the A-chain does not take place, so it appears. (p. 327)

However, as also mentioned in note 3, Zubizarreta (1982) takes the two phenomena to be related, indicating that the lack of low scope in an example like (61) is a potential argument against QL. Hornstein (1995) also takes the two phenomena to be related and regards (61) as potentially arguing against QL (which he treats as A-movement reconstruction). Although this is clearly not Chomsky's position, it does, in fact, seem to be the null hypothesis.

Under the null hypothesis, some other way of resolving the apparent contradiction must be found. In this connection, it must first be noted that it is not entirely clear precisely what the phenomenon of QL is. It is often taken as paraphrasability by a sentence with an expletive subject, as perhaps intended in the quotation from May 1977 given above. Thus, the QL version of (62) is taken to be synonymous with (63).

(62) some politician is likely to address John's constituency

(63) it is likely that some politician will address John's constituency

Given this characterization, QL turns out to be far more limited than it is generally taken to be. Consider first the following two subject-raising examples with negative subjects:

(64) no large Mersenne number was proven to be prime

(65) no one is certain to solve the problem

Neither of these has a "lowered" reading, at least on the paraphrase characterization. (64) is not accurately paraphrasable as (66), nor is (65) as (67).

(66) it was proven that no large Mersenne number is prime

(67) it is certain that no one will solve the problem

This paraphrase failure is not limited to negative contexts. Consider (68) in a situation where there are five fair coins, flipped in a fair way.

(68) every coin is 3% likely to land heads

This situation strongly biases the sentence toward the lowered reading, but that reading still is not possible. (68) cannot be accurately paraphrased as (69).

(69) it is 3% likely that every coin will land heads

Thus, at least on this characterization, there is reason to believe that Zubizarreta and Hornstein are correct in taking absence of a low reading in an example like (70) to potentially argue for failure of QL, and that Chomsky is correct that that absence indicates impossibility of reconstruction with A-movement.

(70) everyone seems [t not to be there yet]

What of the successful instances of QL, such as (71)?

(71) some politician is likely to address John's constituency

As far as I can tell, these obtain exclusively with indefinite subjects. If QL is an instance of A-movement reconstruction, it is not obvious how this restriction is to be captured. For that matter, the same is true under Chomsky's suggested characterization of the phenomenon, following May. I therefore offer the tentative speculation that there is no QL at all,[16] and that the reason, following Chomsky in essence (though not in specific detail), is that there is no A-movement reconstruction. The apparent paraphrasability with indefinites might then be a consequence of the meaning of indefinites, rather than the result of a syntactic operation, though I readily concede that much further investigation is needed.

May (1985) presents an important, and often cited, argument that actual syntactic lowering must be involved in the second reading of examples like (71): namely, that such a "lowered" reading for the quantifier is incompatible with the binding of a pronoun in the upper clause. He gives the following example:

(72) no agent$_i$ was believed by his$_i$ superior to be a spy for the other side

It does seem correct that there is no lowered reading for the subject in (72). However, the same is apparently true even with no bound pronoun, as in examples (64)–(65). A more relevant test would involve an indefinite subject, as in (73).

(73) some professor$_i$ is believed by his$_i$ students to be a tyrant

It is certainly true that (73) cannot be paraphrased as (74).

(74) *it is believed by his$_i$ students that some professor$_i$, is a tyrant

But it is not clear what we can conclude from the fact that a sentence cannot be paraphrased by an ungrammatical sentence (in this case, one that violates the Weak Crossover Constraint). I will thus continue to tentatively assume that it is not a syntactic operation that is responsible for the "lowered" reading of raised indefinites.

The more fundamental question remains: if, indeed, there is no A-movement reconstruction, why should that be? Recall that for Chomsky, there is simply the stipulation that reconstruction is a property solely of operator-variable constructions. Further, the mechanism for instantiating the property—no deletion of traces in A-chains—does not seem to capture it at all. As an alternative, I would like to suggest that A-movement, unlike Ā-movement, does not leave a trace, where a trace is, following Chomsky, a copy of the item that moves, and LF reconstruction effects result from failure to delete (a portion of) a lower copy. This distinction is conceptually plausible: Ā-movement typically creates an operator-variable relation, so at least an "initial" trace is necessary. For A-movement, on the other hand, the trace is seemingly a theoretical excrescence. There are not two separate interpretive roles for a moved NP and its trace to fulfill. It might therefore be conceptually desirable for A-movement not to leave a trace. However, Chomsky (1995) offers an indirect argument against that possibility, to which I now turn.

Chomsky's argument specifically concerns trace deletion, but it straight-forwardly extends to not leaving a trace in the first place. The argument is that at least the initial trace of A-movement is needed for θ-theoretic reasons.

In the phonological component, traces delete. We have found no reason to extend that convention to the N → λ computation, and indeed cannot; were we to do so, θ-positions would be invisible at LF . . . (p. 301)

In effect, Chomsky seems to take θ-role assignment as an A-movement reconstruction effect (so his stipulation barring reconstruction becomes more specific). An alternative approach is imaginable. Suppose that instead of being determined specifically at the LF level, θ-roles are "checked" in the course of a derivation.[17] The moved argument is then itself a record of the crucial part of the history of its derivation. This view of θ-roles as features is argued for on independent grounds in Bošković and Takahashi 1998 and Lasnik 1995c. To the extent that such an analysis can be maintained, we can circumvent Chomsky's conclusion that the trace of A-movement must persist to the interface level (hence, a fortiori, must exist in the first place). The absence of scope reconstruction[18] would then follow from the fact that, plausibly, determination of scope is not satisfaction of a formal feature, but a matter of interpretation at the interface.[19]

Chomsky himself, in a different (but not unrelated) context, presents an argument that would appear to have the consequence for θ-role assign-ment that I just arrived at (and paradoxically so, since it ostensibly argues just the opposite). Section 4.6 of Chomsky 1995 is devoted to arguing that "there should be no interaction between θ-theory and the theory of movement" (p. 312). In particular, according to Chomsky, movement can never create a θ-configuration. In a theory with D-Structure, this is virtually automatic. But within a minimalist approach where LF is assumed to be the sole interface with semantics, the consequence that "θ-relatedness is a 'base property' " would be considerably more surprising and interesting. Chomsky suggests that this follows from the "configurational" view of θ-roles: "A θ-role is assigned in a certain structural configuration. . ." (p. 313). The reasoning is as follows:

If α raises to a θ-position Th, forming the chain CH $= (α, t)$, the argument that must bear a θ-role is CH, not α. But CH is not in any configuration, and α is not an argument that can receive a θ-role. (p. 313)

If this argument is valid, it appears to have an obviously unintended consequence. A-movement of an argument should *never* be permitted. This is so since such movement will always create a chain; at LF, by the reasoning in the quoted passage, the moved argument would not be able to receive a θ-role. That is, whether the movement is *to* a θ-position or *from* a θ-position, the result is a chain, and chains are not in "configurations." If the constraint Chomsky suggests is valid, the only obvious way it can be satisfied is for θ-roles to be assigned prior to movement. But then, as discussed above, whether A-movement leaves a trace or not is irrelevant to θ-assignment. Ironically, this conclusion undermines the argument against movement into a θ-position. If an A-trace is not only not helpful in the assignment of a θ-role, but would actually make such assignment impossible, then, obviously, the argument that such a trace must exist for θ-theoretic reasons fails. But if A-traces do not exist, then an argument will invariably be a single-membered chain no matter how many times it moves. Thus, even if it were to move into a θ-position, it would still be in a "configuration" in the relevant sense, so the θ-role should be assignable. And, indeed, there are a number of recent arguments that movement into a θ-position does occur (see, e.g., Bošković 1994; Bošković and Takahashi 1998; Lasnik 1995c; Hornstein 1999).

This discussion is, admittedly, very far from conclusive. To the extent that it is on the right track, it partly resurrects older ideas, but within a more modern framework of assumptions. For example, the idea that θ-assignment is a "base property," whereas scope belongs to late derived structure, is familiar from the Extended Standard Theory, and even from the Standard Theory (Chomsky 1965). In the theory sketched here, as in Chomsky 1995, this is captured without a level of D-Structure, but rather with what might be regarded as a "D-Structure component," to use a phrase suggested to me by Juan Uriagereka and Roger Martin. If, as claimed by Chomsky (1995), and further supported above, there is no A-movement scope reconstruction, this receives a principled account if A-movement leaves no trace (i.e., copy). I will conclude with a problem: how can movement without a trace possibly be reconciled with a "bare phrase structure" theory of structure building? A-movement not leaving a trace means that a "term" in the sense of Chomsky (1994) is eliminated. Whether this is a serious problem only further research can reveal.

Notes

I am indebted to Željko Bošković and to all the participants in my 1998 syntax seminar at the University of Connecticut for very helpful comments, questions, and suggestions; to Arthur Stepanov for invaluable assistance in the preparation of the manuscript; and to Norbert Hornstein and Juan Uriagereka for spirited encouragement.

1. Chomsky (1993, 34–35) discusses another apparent difference between Ā-movement and A-movement with respect to reconstruction. He contrasts (i) with (ii), indicating that (i) shows a Condition C effect between *John* and *he* whereas (ii) does not.

(i) which claim that John was asleep was he willing to discuss

(ii) the claim that John was asleep seems to him to be correct

Lebeaux (1988, 1991) also grapples with a contrast like this. Although the contrast could be accommodated by Chomsky's approach, or by the one I will develop below, I am not certain how significant that fact is, since I am not certain how clear the facts are. (i) does seem peculiar to me, but other examples that are syntactically parallel, like (iii), seem fine.

(iii) which piece of evidence that John was asleep was he willing to discuss

In Lasnik 1998, I discuss this issue further.

2. Below, I will consider implications of the factual basis of Belletti and Rizzi's proposal for Chomsky's claim that there is no A-movement reconstruction.

3. To my knowledge, the contrast between examples like (14a) and ones like (14c) was first discussed by Zubizarreta (1982), who attributes the observation to Chomsky. Zubizarreta presents the phenomenon as a possible argument against Quantifier Lowering (QL) in the sense of May (1977). Interestingly, Chomsky (1995) suggests that these facts might be compatible with QL. Chomsky hints that " 'lowering effects' of the kind first discussed by Robert May ... could result from adjunction of the matrix quantifier to the lower IP (c-commanding the trace of raising and yielding a well-formed structure if the trace of quantifier lowering is deleted, along the lines of May's original proposal)" (p. 327). I will return to further consideration of QL.

4. Hornstein actually attributes the argument to Chomsky and Lasnik (1993; cited by Hornstein as 1991). But Chomsky and Lasnik do not discuss the phenomenon at all. Perhaps what Hornstein has in mind is Chomsky's (1995) argument that I summarized above. On the other hand, he reports it as an attempted argument against QL, but, as noted above, Chomsky's (1995) argument explicitly allows QL.

5. Hornstein attributes these two examples to Chomsky and Lasnik.

6. See Lasnik 1995c for discussion.

7. Den Dikken (1995) points out a parallel contrast with raising to subject position.

(i) some applicants$_i$ seem to each other$_i$ to be eligible for the job

(ii) *there seem to each other$_i$ to be some applicants$_i$ eligible for the job

Under the general assumptions adopted here, this is particularly revealing, since subject raising to subject of *there* shows the same agreement effects seen in (26).

(iii) there seems/*seem to be a man here

(iv) there seem/*seems to be men here

I take this to indicate covert raising of the formal features of the associate to matrix Agr$_S$. Symmetrically, I take it that the formal features of the associate raise to Agr$_O$ in the (b) cases of (28)–(30).

8. Bošković (1997) provides another argument, showing that under very plausible assumptions, sentences like (i) must involve Agr$_O$P coordination and overt raising, with the matrix subject and verb undergoing across-the-board extraction from matrix Agr$_O$P.

(i) John believes Peter to be crazy and Mary to be smart

9. I am not sure how the coordination structures mentioned in note 8 fare in this regard. Given Bošković's argument, the prediction is that in an example like (i), narrow scope under negation should not be possible for the ECM subjects.

(i) Mary proved every Mersenne number not to be prime and every Fibonacci
    number not to be even

Unfortunately, judgments fail at this point.

10. It should be kept in mind that so far there is no clear *explanation* for Chomsky's fact, but there is a strong descriptive generalization. I return to the question of how the generalization is to be explained.

11. The ECM subject in the first conjunct in (45), *every Mersenne number*, also cannot take narrow scope under the negation in its clause. I assume this is a parallelism effect of the sort investigated in Lasnik 1972 and, more recently and more interestingly, in Fox 1995.

12. I also assume that that is the position an object in a simple transitive construction raises to, given Lasnik and Saito's (1991) binding arguments showing that objects (like ECM subjects) can bind into adverbials, and given that an object can be a pseudogapping remnant.

13. That is, Agr has no Case feature of its own. When T or V along with its Case feature merges with Agr, then a nominal expression that has raised to [Spec, Agr] will be in a Case-checking configuration, even though the raising was driven by the EPP.

14. See Kim 1997 for arguments that the position of a pseudogapping remnant has a focus feature. Given the optionality of (the target of) raising that I have suggested, a fruitful line of inquiry would center on focus effects with raised ECM subjects in general.

15. There is now the question of why Agr$_S$ is obligatory. This is exactly the question of why the standard EPP holds. At this time, I have no more to contribute to this than anyone else.

16. Interestingly, Postal (1974) claims that a quantifier that has undergone subject raising to subject position invariably takes high scope, that is, that there is no QL. He suggests that the same is true for subject raising to object position (i.e., ECM constructions), but that seems much less clear. First, there are the universal-negative interactions discussed earlier. Second, quantificational subjects do seem to allow scope beneath ECM verbs, as in (i), which, in contrast to (ii), has a pragmatically sensible reading.

(i) the defense attorney proved none of the defendants to be guilty

(ii) none of the defendants were proved to be guilty by the defense attorney

17. A-movement Condition A reconstruction of the sort discussed by, among others, Barss (1986), Belletti and Rizzi (1988), and Lebeaux (1988, 1991) might be treated in a similar on-line fashion, as proposed by Belletti and Rizzi. This makes sense if satisfaction of Condition A involves a formal feature, a not implausible assumption. Such a possibility is hinted at by Chomsky (1995, 381) (though not for A-movement). I must offer a slight disclaimer, though, as I am no longer entirely confident that psych and raising constructions, as in (i)–(ii), sharply contrast with ones with simple transitive or control predicates, as in (iii)–(iv). The standard judgments are in parentheses.

(i)   (√) each other's supporters frightened the candidates

(ii) (√) each other's supporters seem to the candidates to be unscrupulous

(iii) (*) each other's supporters attacked the candidates

(iv) (*) each other's supporters asked the candidates to be more honest

18. Here and throughout, I abstract away from scope interactions between subject and object in sentences such as (i).

(i) someone loves everyone

The classic treatment, developed by May (1977), captures the ambiguity via an LF Ā-movement operation, QR: both quantifiers move and either can move to a position above the other. However, Kitahara (1992) and Hornstein (1995) argue that we are instead dealing with an A-movement scope reconstruction effect, with the subject possibly reconstructing to its base position inside the VP and lower than the LF position of the object. Note that on the phrase structure I adopt, of the type proposed by Koizumi, subject is higher than object throughout the derivation, so Kitahara's and Hornstein's account is unavailable.

19. Another tempting alternative is provided by the strictly derivational approaches of Epstein (this volume) and Uriagereka (this volume). Of necessity, θ-roles would be determined on-line in such an approach, so no trace would be necessary at some late derived representation. At the moment, however, I see no way under these approaches to draw the desired distinction between θ-role assignment and scope determination.

References

Barss, Andrew. 1986. Chains and anaphoric dependence: On reconstruction and its implications. Doctoral dissertation, MIT, Cambridge, Mass.

Belletti, Adriana, and Luigi Rizzi. 1988. Psych-verbs and θ-theory. *Natural Language & Linguistic Theory* 6, 291–352.

Bošković, Željko. 1994. D-Structure, θ-Criterion, and movement into θ-positions. *Linguistic Analysis* 24, 247–286.

Bošković, Željko. 1997. Coordination, object shift, and V-movement. *Linguistic Inquiry* 28, 357–365.

Bošković, Željko, and Daiko Takahashi. 1998. Scrambling and Last Resort. *Linguistic Inquiry* 29, 347–366.

Bresnan, Joan W. 1972. Theory of complementation in English syntax. Doctoral dissertation, MIT, Cambridge, Mass.

Chomsky, Noam. 1965. *Aspects of the theory of syntax*. Cambridge, Mass.: MIT Press.

Chomsky, Noam. 1981. *Lectures on government and binding*. Dordrecht: Foris.

Chomsky, Noam. 1986. *Knowledge of language: Its nature, origin, and use*. New York: Praeger.

Chomsky, Noam. 1991. Some notes on economy of derivation and representation. In *Principles and parameters in comparative grammar*, ed. Robert Freidin, 417–454. Cambridge, Mass.: MIT Press. [Reprinted in *The Minimalist Program*, Noam Chomsky, 129–166. Cambridge, Mass.: MIT Press, 1995.]

Chomsky, Noam. 1993. A minimalist program for linguistic theory. In *The view from Building 20: Essays in linguistics in honor of Sylvain Bromberger*, eds. Kenneth Hale and Samuel Jay Keyser, 1–52. Cambridge, Mass.: MIT Press. [Reprinted in *The Minimalist Program*, Noam Chomsky, 167–217. Cambridge, Mass.: MIT Press, 1995.]

Chomsky, Noam. 1994. Bare phrase structure. (MIT Occasional Papers in Linguistics 5.) MITWPL, Department of Linguistics and Philosophy, MIT, Cambridge, Mass. [Also in *Government and Binding Theory and the Minimalist*

Program, ed. Gert Webelhuth, 383–439. Oxford: Blackwell, 1995, and *Evolution and revolution in linguistic theory: Essays in honor of Carlos Otero*, eds. Héctor Campos and Paula Kempchinsky, 51–109. Washington, D.C.: Georgetown University Press, 1995.]

Chomsky, Noam, 1995. Categories and transformations. In *The Minimalist Program*, 219–394. Cambridge, Mass.: MIT Press.

Chomsky, Noam, and Howard Lasnik. 1993. The theory of principles and parameters. In *Syntax: An international handbook of contemporary research*, vol. 1, eds. Joachim Jacobs, Arnim von Stechow, Wolfgang Sternefeld, and Theo Vennemann, 506–569. Berlin: Walter de Gruyter. [Reprinted in *The Minimalist Program*, Noam Chomsky, 13–127. Cambridge, Mass.: MIT Press, 1995.]

Diesing, Molly. 1996. Semantic variables and object shift. In *Studies in comparative Germanic syntax*, vol. II, eds. Höskuldur Thráinsson, Samuel David Epstein, and Steve Peter, 66–84. Dordrecht: Kluwer.

Dikken, Marcel den. 1995. Binding, expletives, and levels. *Linguistic Inquiry* 26, 347–354.

Fox, Danny. 1995. Economy and scope. *Natural Language Semantics* 3, 283–341.

Hornstein, Norbert. 1995. *Logical Form: From GB to minimalism*. Oxford: Blackwell.

Hornstein, Norbert. 1999. Movement and control. *Linguistic Inquiry* 30, 69–96.

Jayaseelan, Karattuparambil A. 1990. Incomplete VP deletion and gapping. *Linguistic Analysis* 20, 64–81.

Johnson, Kyle. 1991. Object positions. *Natural Language & Linguistic Theory* 9, 577–636.

Kayne, Richard. 1985. Principles of particle constructions. In *Grammatical representation*, eds. Jacqueline Guéron, Hans-Georg Obenauer, and Jean-Yves Pollock, 101–140. Dordrecht: Foris.

Kim, Jeong-Seok. 1997. Syntactic focus movement and ellipsis: A minimalist approach. Doctoral dissertation, University of Connecticut, Storrs.

Kitahara, Hisatsugu. 1992. Checking theory and scope interpretation without Quantifier Raising. In *Harvard working papers in linguistics 1*, eds. Susumu Kuno and Höskuldur Thráinsson, 51–71. Department of Linguistics, Harvard University, Cambridge, Mass.

Koizumi, Masatoshi. 1993. Object agreement phrases and the split VP hypothesis. In *Papers on Case and agreement I*, eds. Jonathan D. Bobaljik and Colin Phillips, 99–148. (MIT Working Papers in Linguistics 18.) MITWPL, Department of Linguistics and Philosophy, MIT, Cambridge, Mass.

Koizumi, Masatoshi. 1995. Phrase structure in minimalist syntax. Doctoral dissertation, MIT, Cambridge, Mass.

Langacker, Ronald W. 1969. On pronominalization and the chain of command. In *Modern studies in English*, eds. David A. Reibel and Sanford A. Schane, 160–186. Englewood Cliffs, N.J.: Prentice-Hall.

Lasnik, Howard. 1972. Analyses of negation in English. Doctoral dissertation, MIT, Cambridge, Mass.

Lasnik, Howard. 1976. Remarks on coreference. *Linguistic Analysis* 2, 1–22. [Reprinted in *Essays on anaphora*, Howard Lasnik, 90–109. Dordrecht: Kluwer, 1989.]

Lasnik, Howard. 1995a. Last Resort. In *Minimalism and linguistic theory*, eds. Shosuke Haraguchi and Michio Funaki, 1–32. Tokyo: Hituzi Syobo. [Reprinted in *Minimalist Analysis*, Howard Lasnik, 120–150. Oxford: Blackwell, 1999.]

Lasnik, Howard. 1995b. Last Resort and Attract F. In *Proceedings of the Sixth Annual Meeting of the Formal Linguistics Society of Mid-America*, eds. Leslie Gabriele, Debra Hardison, and Robert Westmoreland, 62–81. Indiana University Linguistics Club, Bloomington.

Lasnik, Howard. 1995c. A note on pseudogapping. In *Papers on minimalist syntax*, eds. Rob Pensalfini and Hiroyuki Ura, 143–163. (MIT Working Papers in Linguistics 27.) MITWPL, Department of Linguistics and Philosophy, MIT, Cambridge, Mass. [Reprinted in *Minimalist analysis*, Howard Lasnik, 151–174. Oxford: Blackwell, 1999.]

Lasnik, Howard. 1997. Levels of representation and the elements of anaphora. In *Atomism and binding*, eds. Hans Bennis, Johan Rooryck, and Pierre Pica, 251–268. Dordrecht: Foris.

Lasnik, Howard. 1998. Some reconstruction riddles. In *University of Pennsylvania working papers in linguistics 5.1*, eds. Alexis Dimitriadis, Hikyoung Lee, Christine Moisset, and Alexander Williams, 83–98. Penn Linguistics Club, Department of Linguistics, University of Pennsylvania, Philadelphia.

Lasnik, Howard. 1999. Pseudogapping puzzles. In *Fragments: Studies in ellipsis*, eds. Elabbas Benmamoun, and Shalom Lappin, 141–174. Oxford: Oxford University Press.

Lasnik, Howard, and Mamoru Saito. 1984. On the nature of proper government. *Linguistic Inquiry* 15, 235–289.

Lasnik, Howard, and Mamoru Saito. 1991. On the subject of infinitives. In *CLS 27. Part I, The General Session*, eds. Lise M. Dobrin, Lynn Nichols, and Rosa M. Rodriguez, 324–343. Chicago Linguistic Society, University of Chicago, Chicago, Ill. [Reprinted in *Minimalist analysis*, Howard Lasnik, 7–24. Oxford: Blackwell, 1999.]

Lebeaux, David. 1988. Language acquisition and the form of the grammar. Doctoral dissertation, University of Massachusetts, Amherst.

Lebeaux, David. 1991. Relative clauses, licensing, and the nature of the derivation. In *Perspectives on phrase structure: Heads and licensing*, ed. Susan Rothstein, 209–239. San Diego, Calif.: Academic Press.

May, Robert. 1977. The grammar of quantification. Doctoral dissertation, MIT, Cambridge, Mass.

May, Robert. 1985. *Logical Form: Its structure and derivation*. Cambridge, Mass.: MIT Press.

Postal, Paul M. 1974. *On raising: One rule of English grammar and its theoretical implications*. Cambridge, Mass.: MIT Press.

Zubizarreta, Maria Luisa. 1982. On the relationship of the lexicon to syntax. Doctoral dissertation, MIT, Cambridge, Mass.

Chapter 9

Linearization of Chains and Phonetic Realization of Chain Links   Jairo Nunes

Within the principles-and-parameters framework (see Chomsky 1981, 1986; Chomsky and Lasnik 1993), the notion of *trace* encompasses several types of objects that have in common the properties of being produced by a movement operation and being phonetically null. Regardless of whether traces have intrinsic features or acquire some feature specification in the course of the derivation (see, e.g., Chomsky 1982), they end up being different entities. A trace of an NP occupying an A-position, for instance, is subject to Principle A of binding theory, a trace of an NP occupying an operator position is a variable subject to Principle C, and a trace of a verb is subject to neither. The distinct nature of different types of traces is standardly captured by means of a procedure coindexing the moved element and its trace(s).[1]

Chomsky (1993) revives the "copy theory of movement," according to which a moved element leaves behind a copy that is deleted in the phonological component, but remains available for interpretation at LF. As discussed by Chomsky (1993), the copy theory accords well with the general conceptual concerns of the Minimalist Program in that it allows binding theory to be stated without reference to noninterface levels, it provides the basis for the interpretation of displaced idiom chunks at LF, and it paves the way for eliminating reconstruction as an additional operation of the computational system.

From a minimalist perspective, another conceptual advantage of the copy theory is that is satisfies Chomsky's (1995, 228–229) Inclusiveness Condition, according to which an LF object must be built from the features of the lexical items of the corresponding initial numeration. If traces are grammatical primitives, their introduction in the course of the derivation violates this condition because they are not present in the initial numeration. Under the copy theory, on the other hand, a trace is either a copy of a lexical item of the numeration or a copy of an X-bar-theoretic object built from lexical items of the numeration.

Pursuing the simplest—and therefore most desirable—version of the copy theory of movement, one should take heads of chains and traces to be subject to the same constraints and the notion of trace should be treated as epiphenomenal, akin to the taxonomic notions of passive and *wh*-movement. The properties of different traces should thus be derived either from the content of the copies themselves or from the movement operation. For instance, the locality restriction on the distribution of traces may follow from the Minimal Link Condition (see Chomsky 1995, 311), whereas the interpretation of a *wh*-trace as a variable may be due to its intrinsic features (see, e.g., Chierchia 1991; Hornstein 1995, chap. 6).

Such a minimalist approach to the copy theory of movement appears to be unfeasible, however, because one of the fundamental properties of traces is that they (usually) cannot be phonetically realized. In addition to this unexplained difference between heads of chains and traces, it has been proposed that traces are not subject to Kayne's (1994) Linear Correspondence Axiom (LCA; see Kayne 1994, chap. 2, n. 3; Chomsky 1995, 337).[2] Assuming the general framework proposed in Chomsky 1995, I take some steps in this chapter toward eliminating traces as grammatical primitives by providing an account of the fact that traces usually lack phonetic realization, while crucially assuming that heads of chains and traces are both subject to the LCA.

The discussion is organized as follows. In section 9.1, I outline the main issues that any version of the copy theory of movement has to address as far as phonetic realization of chain links is concerned. In section 9.2, I discuss some attempts to derive deletion of traces within the Minimalist Program, and in section 9.3, I discuss the claim that traces are not subject to the LCA. Section 9.4 is the core of the chapter. In section 9.4.1, I show that the phonological component distinguishes real copies from constituents that happen to have the same set of features; in section 9.4.2, I argue that deletion of chain links is triggered for linearization purposes; and in section 9.4.3, I show that the choice of the links to be deleted is determined by economy considerations. In section 9.5, I pay closer attention to some technical details of the proposed analysis. Finally, in section 9.6, I present a brief conclusion.

9.1   The Issues

Any analysis that adopts some version of the copy theory of movement has to address the following questions: (a) why is it the case that a non-trivial chain cannot have all of its links phonetically realized? and (b) why is it the case that traces and not heads of chains are the links that are deleted? That is, given the derivation sketched in (1), for instance, why is it not possible for the structure in (1c) to yield the PF output associated with (2a) or (2b)?[3]

(1) a. K = [$_{TP}$ T [$_{VP}$ was [$_{VP}$ kissed John]]]
    b. Copy: K = [$_{TP}$ T [$_{VP}$ was [$_{VP}$ kissed John]]]
                L = John
    c. Merge: [$_{TP}$ John [$_{T'}$ T [$_{VP}$ was [$_{VP}$ kissed John]]]]

(2) a. *John was kissed John
    b. *was kissed John
    c.   John was kissed

The unacceptability of (2a) resulting from the derivation in (1) raises an additional puzzle within the minimalist framework. The derivations of (2b) and (2c) from (1c) involve an operation eliminating one of the copies of *John*, whereas no such operation is invoked in (2a). Thus, were the derivations of (2b) and (2c), on the one hand, and the derivation of (2a), on the other, to be compared for economy purposes, the derivation of (2a) should be preferred over the other two because it involves fewer operations, thus being more economical. Since (2a) is unacceptable, its derivation from (1c) must either crash or be canceled (see Chomsky 1995, 219–220, 225–226), thereby being irrelevant for economy computations.

Finally, there are languages that apparently allow some traces to be phonetically realized, as illustrated in (3).

(3) *German* (from McDaniel 1986)
    mit wem glaubst du *mit wem* Hans spricht
    with whom think   you *with whom* Hans talks
    'with whom do you think Hans is talking'

Assuming that appearances are not misleading in these cases, whatever is the explanation for the deletion of the trace in (1c), for instance, it should be flexible enough to permit some phonetically realized traces in some languages, but restricted enough not to allow every trace to be phonetically realized. Even languages that admit constructions such as (3) do not allow traces of full *wh*-phrases to be phonetically realized in intermediate positions, as illustrated in (4).

(4) *German* (from McDaniel 1986)
  **wessen Buch* glaubst du   *wessen Buch* Hans liest
  whose book think   you *whose book* Hans reads
  'whose book do you think Hans is reading'

9.2 Approaches to Deletion of Traces within the Minimalist Program

Chomsky (1993, 35) suggests that deletion of traces in the phonological component is an obligatory variant of a more general process that converts the structure in (5a), for instance, into the sentence in (5b), by deleting E in the phonological component.

(5) a. John said that he was looking for a cat, and so did Bill [E say that he was looking for a cat]
  b. John said that he was looking for a cat, and so did Bill

Regardless of whether this derivational approach to the pair of sentences in (5) is correct, it is arguably the case that deletion of traces is unrelated to ellipsis. First, the bracketed material in (5a), for instance, is supposed to be either deleted or realized with a distinctive low-flat intonation (see Chomsky and Lasnik 1993, 564), whereas traces are obligatorily deleted in the general case; a low-flat intonation on the trace of the subject in (6b), for instance, does not make the pronunciation of the trace acceptable.

(6) a. [that John said he was looking for a cat] is believed [that John said he was looking for a cat] by everyone
  b. *that John said he was looking for a cat is believed that John said he was looking for a cat by everyone
  c. that John said he was looking for a cat is believed by everyone

It should also be noted that deletion of traces operates with elements that are not distinguished in the initial numeration; by contrast, the alleged deletion in the mapping from (5a) to (5b) operates with elements that are morphologically identical, but distinctively specified in the numeration (e.g., *he*) or even lexical items that are not identical at all (e.g., *say* is allegedly deleted in (5a) on the basis of its relation to *said*). This is therefore another reason not to take deletion of traces to be a subcase of ellipsis.

Chomsky (1995, 252–253) takes the opposite view on the relation between ellipsis and deletion of traces, suggesting that it is ellipsis that is a subcase of deletion of traces. Under this view, the numeration markings of the bracketed element in (5a), for instance, are changed to those of the first conjunct before Spell-Out, rendering the bracketed element subject to parallelism constraints at LF; assuming that the antecedent and its "copy" constitute a chain, the copy should then delete "by whatever mechanism deletes traces in the phonological component" (Chomsky 1995, 253).

This suggestion sketches a technical unification of ellipsis and deletion of traces, but provides no independent account of the fact that "ellipsis chains" are not subject to Last Resort or the C-Command Condition, which do apply to regular chains. More importantly, deletion of traces remains unexplained under this approach.

Other minimalist implementations of the copy theory have also been unable to provide a successful account of the issues raised in section 9.1, because they incorporate a variant of Chomsky's (1993) stipulation that traces must be deleted in the phonological component. Brody (1995), for instance, proposes the principle of Transparency, according to which "if all chain members c-commanded by the contentive element are copies of the contentive, then it must be the case that only the highest member of such a set of copies (i.e., the contentive itself) is visible for SPELLOUT" (Brody 1995, 106).[4] The principle of Transparency is conceptually justified on the grounds that "the grammar is designed in such a way that where possible PF makes the (L)LF chain relations explicit" (Brody 1995, 107). It is not obvious, however, how this line of argumentation explains the unacceptability of (2a) with the structure represented in (1c); the chain relation between the two copies of (1c) seems to be more explicit in (2a) than in (2c). It is also unclear how contrasts such as the one between (3) and (4) can be accounted for under this approach.

Before I present my proposal that the phonetic realization of chain links is tied to the issue of linearization of chains, I review in the next section the positions taken by Kayne (1994) and Chomsky (1995) with respect to the question of whether traces are subject to the LCA.

9.3   Traces and the LCA (Kayne 1994 and Chomsky 1995)

Kayne (1994) makes the influential proposal that the mapping from a phrase marker into a linear order of terminal symbols is governed by the Linear Correspondence Axiom (LCA) defined in (7) (from Kayne 1994, 33).

(7) *Linear Correspondence Axiom* (LCA)

Let X, Y be nonterminals and x, y terminals such that X dominates x and Y dominates y. Then if X asymmetrically c-commands Y, x precedes y.

Assuming that the LCA is correct in its essentials, an interesting question arises: are traces computed for the purposes of linearization? The question is even more intriguing if one assumes that a trace is a copy of the moved element.

Consider (8).

(8)

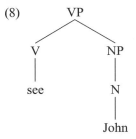

Discussing the structure resulting from moving *John* in (8), Kayne (1994, chap. 2, n. 3) points out that no issue of linearization should arise if the movement leaves a copy behind; in other words, traces do not differ from unmoved elements with respect to the well-formedness conditions on phrase markers imposed by the LCA. However, it is worth noting that if the links of a chain are in a sense the same element (they form a discontinuous object), it is not clear that the LCA is observed in structures formed by movement, because any material intervening between two links asymmetrically c-commands and is asymmetrically c-commanded by the same element. I return to a fuller discussion of this point in section 9.4.

In case movement of *John* in (8) leaves a trace, the internal structure of the NP is lost, rendering it impossible for *see* and the trace to be ordered with respect to one another. Kayne (1994, chap. 2, n. 3) suggests that "[t]his might conceivably be a tolerable consequence, since traces are in any event not visible." This suggestion is nevertheless at odds with his conceptual argument that given the role of the LCA as the source of the major properties of standard X-bar theory, it should apply to all syntactic representations (see Kayne 1994, 49); according to this reasoning, LF should not allow a structure containing a head and the trace of its complement because such a structure would violate the LCA.

Addressing similar issues within the bare phrase structure system, Chomsky (1995, 337) also suggests that "there is no reason for the LCA to order an element that will disappear at PF, for example, a trace."[5] Although this hypothesis makes the plausible assumption that the (still to be explained) deletion of traces takes place after Linearize, it tacitly assumes that the output of Linearize may be a partially linearized object. It is however very likely that the phonological rules that apply after Linearize operate with a sequence of X^0 elements rather than a phrase structure; hence, if Linearize failed to yield a sequence of X^0 items, no PF object would be formed and the derivation should be canceled. Furthermore, the logic of Chomsky's suggestion confers too much power on global computations. The linearization of a given element at a given derivational step is taken to be contingent on different operations' targeting that element later in the derivation.[6]

Another suggestion by Chomsky (1995, 337) is that the LCA may delete traces. This is intended to provide the bare phrase structure system with means to circumvent the problem of linearizing the trace of a complement lacking internal structure with respect to its sister. Notice, however, that there would be a redundancy under this approach: both Linearize and the phonological rules that apply to the output of Linearize can delete traces. In addition, although a motivation for the deletion of traces is provided when it is executed by Linearize, the motivation for the deletion after Linearize is still missing. The minimalist assumption that the language faculty is a nonredundant system, however, leads us to expect a unique motivation for deletion of traces and a unique operation to execute it.

In the next section, I argue that copies are subject to the LCA and that deletion of chain links is actually triggered by linearization considerations.

9.4   Linearization of Chains and Phonetic Realization

9.4.1   Nondistinctiveness of Copies

Once the copy theory of movement is assumed, the system needs to determine whether two terms with the same set of features are to be interpreted as distinct elements or copies. Consider the structure in (9), for example.

(9) [John [was [kissed John]]]

If the pair (*John*, *John*) of (9) were to from a chain, it would satisfy both the Minimal Link condition and Last Resort; actual chain formation thus depends on whether or not the two instances of *John* are to be taken as copies or elements distinctively specified in the numeration (see section 9.5.2 for further discussion). Addressing this issue, Chomsky (1995, 227) proposes that two lexical items l and l' should be marked as distinct for the computational system if they are formed by distinct applications of Select accessing the same lexical item of a numeration (see Nunes 1995, 1998b for further discussion).

The observations above have focused on the relevance of nondistinctiveness for chain formation and, consequently, for convergence at LF and interpretation at the conceptual-intentional (C-I) interface. Clearly, the notion of nondistinctiveness of constituents plays no role at the PF level and at the articulatory-perceptual (A-P) interface; however, it is relevant for the computations of the phonological component having to do with deletion of traces. Consider for instance the structure in (10), with cosuperscripting used to annotate copies. Assuming that PF should reflect the number of occurrences of each lexical item specified in the initial numeration of a given derivation (see section 9.4.3.3 for some refinements), (10) could in principle surface as any of the sentences in (11).

(10) $[_{TP}$ John^i T $[_{vP}$ John^i $[_{v'}$ said $[_{CP}$ that $[_{TP}$ John^k was $[_{vP}$ kissed John$^k]]]]]]$

(11) a.   John said that John was kissed
     b. *John John said that was kissed
     c. *John said that was kissed John
     d. *said that John was kissed John

The fact that the only possible PF output for (10) is the one in which the trace of each chain is deleted (i.e., (11a)) shows that the phonological component applies the deletion operation (for reasons yet to be determined) to members of a chain and not simply to constituents with identical sets of features. This in turn suggests that, when performing deletion, the phonological component does take nondistinctiveness of constituents into consideration.

Let us examine the consequences of this conclusion for linearization.

9.4.2 Nontrivial Chains and the LCA

Assuming that computations in the phonological component differentiate nondistinct constituents (copies) from distinct constituents that happen to have the same set of features, let us consider the asymmetric c-command relations in (12) to determine how this structure should be linearized according to the LCA.[7]

(12) [$_{TP}$ John^i [$_{T'}$ was + T [$_{VP}$ kissed John^i]]]

According to the cosuperscripting notation adopted above, the initial numeration corresponding to (12) contains a single instance of *John* (the two occurrences of *John* are nondistinct). Consider the relation between these copies and the copula *was*, for instance. Since the upper copy of *John* asymmetrically c-commands *was*, we should obtain the order ⟨*John*, *was*⟩, according to the LCA; likewise, since the copula asymmetrically c-commands the lower copy of *John*, the order ⟨*was*, *John*⟩ should be derived. Combining these two results, we should obtain the partial sequence σ = ⟨*John*, *was*, *John*⟩. Were the two instances of *John* distinct, σ would be a well-formed linear order, with the copula following one occurrence of *John* and preceding a different occurrence of *John*, as in (11a), for example, where *said* precedes and is preceded by a distinct occurrence of *John*. However, since the two instances of *John* in (12) are nondistinct, *was* should precede and be preceded by the same element, *John*. σ is therefore not a linear order because it lacks asymmetry (if α precedes β, then it must be the case that β does not precede α), which is a defining property of a (strict) linear order.

The structure in (12) also violates the irreflexivity condition on (strict) linear order (if α precedes β, then it must be the case that α ≠ β). Since the upper copy of *John* asymmetrically c-commands the lower one, the former should precede the latter in accordance with the LCA. Given that the two copies of *John* in (12) are nondistinct, that would amount to saying that *John* should precede itself.

Failure to yield a linear order thus provides a straightforward account of the fact that the structure in (12) cannot surface as the sentence in (13a). To put it more generally, if the links of a chain count as nondistinct for linearization purposes in virtue of their being nondistinct in the initial numeration, we have an explanation for why a chain cannot surface at PF with more than one link overtly realized: the syntactic object containing such a chain cannot be linearized.

(13) a. *John was kissed John
      b.   John was kissed

Under the assumption that the rules of the phonological component that apply after Linearize operate on a sequence of X^0 elements, the attempted derivation of (13a) from (12) is canceled, because Linearize yields no output and, therefore, no PF object is formed. This is a welcome result. Recall that the derivation of (13a) should be prevented from being compared for purposes of economy with the derivation of (13b) from (12); otherwise, it would incorrectly outrank the derivation of (13b) because it is more economical in not employing one application of deletion (see section 9.1). If the derivation of (13a) from (12) is canceled because it cannot be linearized, no questions of convergence or economy arise.

I therefore propose that deletion of chain links is required for a structure containing nontrivial chains to be linearized in accordance with the LCA. This proposal has the welcome conceptual advantage that it takes both heads of chains and traces to be subject to linearization. What is required at this point is an independent motivation for why deletion targets traces and not heads of chains. This is the topic of section 9.4.3.2. Before beginning this discussion, let us examine the more general case regarding the optimality of deletion for purposes of linearization.

9.4.3 Optimality of Deletion

9.4.3.1 Full versus Scattered Deletion Consider the simplified structure in (14), in which the embedded object DP raises to the matrix subject position, leaving two copies behind.

(14) $[_{TP} [_{DP}$ the $[_{NP}$ tall man$]]^i$ appears $[_{TP} [_{DP}$ the $[_{NP}$ tall man$]]^i$ to have been kissed $[_{DP}$ the $[_{NP}$ tall man$]]^i]]$

As discussed in section 9.4.2, a structure such as (14) cannot be linearized as is. The highest instance of *the tall man* asymmetrically c-commands the verb *appears*, for instance, which in turn asymmetrically c-commands the other two instances of *the tall man*. Given that these three copies are nondistinct, no linear order between *the tall man* and *appears* can be established in accordance with the LCA. Thus, if Linearize applies to (14), the derivation will be canceled, because Linearize will yield no output for further computations in the phonological component and no PF object will be formed.

I proposed in section 9.4.2 that deletion may allow a structure containing nontrivial chains to be linearized by eliminating "repeated" material that induces lack of asymmetry and irreflexivity in the intended linear order. Nothing that has been said so far, however, prevents deletion from applying within different links of a chain, in what may be called *scattered deletion*; deletion could target different constituents in each of the links of the DP chain in (14), for instance, yielding a structure such as

(15). Despite the fact that the coindexed DPs in (14) are nondistinct, the terms that survive deletion in (15) are distinct. (15) should then be linearized in accordance with the LCA, yielding the sentence in (16), which is however unacceptable.

(15) [$_{TP}$ [$_{DP}$ the [$_{NP}$ ~~tall man~~]]^i appears [$_{TP}$ [$_{DP}$ ~~the~~ [$_{NP}$ tall ~~man~~]]^i to have been kissed [$_{DP}$ ~~the~~ [$_{NP}$ ~~tall~~ man]]^i]]

(16) *the appears tall to have been kissed man

I propose that although the derivation of (16) converges at PF, it is not the most economical derivation starting from (14). To put it more generally, scattered deletion does not yield an optimal derivation. Take (14), for example. Under the assumption that deletion for purposes of linearization only targets constituents (one constituent per application), the derivation of (15) from (14) requires that the deletion operation apply (at least) five times, targeting the following constituents: the NP of the chain link in the matrix subject position, the constituents *the* and *man* of the link in the embedded subject position, and the constituents *the* and *tall* of the link in the object position. However, three other derivations starting from (14) that employ *full deletion* of chain links are more economical; if deletion targets the whole DP of two links of the DP chain in (14), the structures in (17) will be derived.

(17) a. [$_{TP}$ [$_{DP}$ the [$_{NP}$ tall man]]^i appears [$_{TP}$ ~~[$_{DP}$ the [$_{NP}$ tall man]]~~^{i} to have been kissed ~~[$_{DP}$ the [$_{NP}$ tall man]]~~^{i}]]

   b. [$_{TP}$ ~~[$_{DP}$ the [$_{NP}$ tall man]]~~^{i} appears [$_{TP}$ [$_{DP}$ the [$_{NP}$ tall man]]^i to have been kissed ~~[$_{DP}$ the [$_{NP}$ tall man]]~~^{i}]]

   c. [$_{TP}$ ~~[$_{DP}$ the [$_{NP}$ tall man]]~~^{i} appears [$_{TP}$ ~~[$_{DP}$ the [$_{NP}$ tall man]]~~^{i} to have been kissed [$_{DP}$ the [$_{NP}$ tall man]]^i]]

Each structure of (17) can be linearized in accordance with the LCA, yielding the sentences in (18a–c), respectively. Given that the derivation of any of the sentences in (18) may employ only two applications of deletion, the derivation of (16), which requires (at least) five applications of this operation, is blocked.

(18) a.   the tall man appears to have been kissed
   b.   *appears the tall man to have been kissed
   c.   *appears to have been kissed the tall man

Under the assumption that deletion targets one constituent per application, economy considerations concerning the number of applications of deletion thus block scattered deletion within chains in favor of full deletion of chain links. I refer to the operation of the phonological component that converts (14), for instance, into structures such as (15) or (17) as *Chain Reduction*.

(19) *Chain Reduction*

Delete the minimal number of constituents of a nontrivial chain CH that suffices for CH to be mapped into a linear order in accordance with the LCA.

Although I will assume the formulation in (19) for expository purposes, it is actually unnecessary to specify that Chain Reduction must delete the *minimal number* of constituents; that is, Chain Reduction need not count. Economy considerations regarding the length of a derivation may indirectly determine the number of elements to be deleted by enforcing the minimal number of applications of deletion. All things being equal, a short derivation should block a longer derivation (see Chomsky 1995, 314, 357); hence, a derivation in which constituents are unnecessarily deleted is longer, therefore less economical, than a competing derivation where no such deletion occurs.

For instance, if Chain Reduction had deleted each of the three links of the DP chain in (14), forming the object in (20a), the problem of lack of asymmetry and irreflexivity would be circumvented and (20a) could be linearized in accordance with the LCA, eventually yielding the sentence in (20b).

(20) a. $[_{TP}$ [$_{DP}$ ~~the~~ [$_{NP}$ ~~tall man~~]]^i appears [$_{TP}$ [$_{DP}$ ~~the~~ [$_{NP}$ ~~tall man~~]]^i to have been kissed [$_{DP}$ ~~the~~ [$_{NP}$ ~~tall man~~]]^i]]

b. *appears to have been kissed

The derivation of (20a) from (14), where the deleted material is nonrecoverable, is not optimal, however. Chain Reduction in this derivation employs (at least) three applications of deletion, when only two applications would suffice for the DP chain to be mapped into a linear order, as shown in (17). Therefore, recoverability of deletion in the analysis explored here follows straightforwardly from economy considerations regarding the length of derivations, and nothing additional need be stated in the theory to ensure that it obtains.[8]

9.4.3.2 Deletion of Traces versus Deletion of Heads of Chains We are still left with a problem from section 9.4.3.1: the derivations that convert a structure such as (14) into the PF output associated with the sentences in (18) were taken to be equally economical, but the only derivation that yields an acceptable sentence is the one in which the traces—but not the head of the DP chain—are deleted.

I propose that optimality of deletion of chain links is contingent on the elimination of formal features in the phonological component. Although formal features are relevant for morphological computations, they are not interpretable at PF (only phonological features are); thus, as noted by Chomsky (1995, 230–231), an operation of the phonological component applying after Morphology must eliminate formal features that are visible at PF. Let us assume that this operation proceeds as described in (21), where deletion targets a single feature per application.[9]

(21) *Formal Feature Elimination* (FF-Elimination)
Given the sequence of pairs $\sigma = \langle (F, P)_1, (F, P)_2, \ldots, (F, P)_n \rangle$ such that σ is the output of Linearize, F is a set of formal features, and P is a set of phonological features, delete the minimal number of features of each set of formal features in order for σ to satisfy Full Interpretation at PF.

The difference between the head of a chain and its traces regarding phonetic realization now follows from the number of checking relations a given copy is associated with. In Chomsky's (1995) system, checking operations render −Interpretable features invisible at LF, eventually allowing the derivation to meet Full Interpretation and converge at this level. A natural extension of this approach is to take checking operations to render −Interpretable features invisible at PF as well; after all, no formal feature is interpreted at the A-P interface.[10] Assuming this extension of checking theory, let us reconsider the derivation of (14), repeated in (22) with the relevant Case features represented (unchecked features are in boldface and checked/deleted features are subscripted).[11]

(22) [TP [DP the tall man]^i-CASE$_1$ appears [TP [DP the tall man]^i-**CASE** to have been kissed [DP the tall man]^i-**CASE**]]

After being assembled and merged with the verb *kissed*, the DP *the tall man* raises to the specifier of each T head in order to check their strong features; in addition, the Case feature of the topmost copy of *the tall man* enters into a checking relation with the Case feature of the matrix T. Since Case is a −Interpretable feature, this checking relation renders the Case feature of the highest copy of *the tall man* invisible at LF and, according to the extension of the checking theory proposed above, invisible at PF as well. The Case features of the lower copies of *the tall man*, on the other hand, are unaffected by the Case-checking relation involving the highest copy.

Let us then see how the DP chain of (22) is to be reduced. As discussed in section 9.4.3.1, the optimal reduction of this chain involves only two applications of deletion targeting any two of its links, as shown in (23).

(23) a. $[_{TP} [_{DP}$ the tall man$]^i$-$_{CASE}$ appears $[_{TP} [_{DP}$ ~~the tall man~~$]^i$-**CASE** to have been kissed $[_{DP}$ ~~the tall man~~$]^i$-**CASE**$]]$

   b. $[_{TP} [_{DP}$ ~~the tall man~~$]^i$-$_{CASE}$ appears $[_{TP} [_{DP}$ the tall man$]^i$-**CASE** to have been kissed $[_{DP}$ ~~the tall man~~$]^i$-**CASE**$]]$

   c. $[_{TP} [_{DP}$ ~~the tall man~~$]^i$-$_{CASE}$ appears $[_{TP} [_{DP}$ ~~the tall man~~$]^i$-**CASE** to have been kissed $[_{DP}$ the tall man$]^i$-**CASE**$]]$

If the DP chain of (22) is reduced as in (23a), no further application of FF-Elimination is required to delete the Case feature of *the tall man* in order for Full Interpretation to be satisfied; this feature has been deleted and is therefore invisible at PF. The PF output in (18a) is then derived after further applications of phonological rules. By contrast, if the DP chain is reduced as in (23b) or (23c), the convergent PF outputs in (18b) and (18c) are obtained only if FF-Elimination deletes the unchecked Case feature of the copy that survives. The derivation in which the head of the chain survives Chain Reduction, such as (23a), therefore ends up being more economical than derivations in which other links survive Chain Reduction, as in (23b) and (23c), because it requires fewer additional applications of deletion by FF-Elimination; hence the pattern of acceptability in (18).

Consider now the structures of the sentences in (24), provided in (25). In (25a), *John* moves from the specifier of the embedded light verb to check the strong feature of the infinitival T head, whereas in (25b), *what* moves from the object position to the specifier of the null interrogative complementizer to check its strong *wh*-feature.

(24) a. I expected John to call me
   b. what did you buy

(25) a. $[_{TP}$ I expected $[_{TP}$ John^i-**N** to $[_{vP}$ John^i-**N** $[_{v'}$ call me$]]]]$
   b. $[_{CP}$ what^i-**WH** did + Q $[_{TP}$ you buy what^i-**WH**$]]$

In both chains of (25), it is the categorical feature (a +Interpretable feature) of the moved element that enters into a checking relation with a feature of the target. If +Interpretable features remain unaffected by checking operations, as proposed by Chomsky (1995, 280), the chain links of (25a) and (25b) will be identical with respect to the only checking relation that takes place overtly. Thus, the structures in (25) provide no basis to account for why Chain Reduction deletes the lower copies.

I proposed above that if a −Interpretable feature is checked, it is made invisible at both interface levels. Given that no formal feature is assigned an interpretation by the A-P system, this view of checking relations can be generalized by assuming that a checking operation may render F invisible at PF, regardless of the interpretability of F at the C-I interface. A checked −Interpretable feature will then be invisible at both PF and LF, whereas a checked +Interpretable feature will be invisible at PF, but visible at LF (see section 9.5.1 for further discussion).

Under this revised extension of checking theory, the appropriate representation of the sentences in (24) in the phonological component is as in (26) rather than (25), where the subscript convention is now generalized to mean 'invisible at the relevant interface'.

(26) a. [$_{TP}$ I expected [$_{TP}$ John^i-$_N$ to [$_{vP}$ John^i-**N** [$_{v'}$ call me]]]]

   b. [$_{CP}$ what^i-$_{WH}$ did + Q [$_{TP}$ you buy what^i-**WH**]]

When applied to the chains of (26), Chain Reduction can in principle delete either link of the chains CH$_1$ = (*John^i*-$_N$, *John^i*-**N**) and CH$_2$ = (*what^i*-$_{WH}$, *what^i*-**WH**). If it deletes the upper link of either chain, FF-Elimination will be required to delete the unchecked N-feature and *wh*-feature of the surviving link; if it deletes the lower links, no such application of FF-Elimination is required because the N-feature and the *wh*-feature of the upper links are deleted and therefore invisible at PF. Again, the optimal derivation is the one in which Chain Reduction deletes every chain link except the head of the chain.

To sum up, lack of phonetic realization is not an intrinsic property that would characterize traces as grammatical primitives; as will be discussed in section 9.4.3.3, traces may actually be phonetically realized under circumstances that would make them invisible to the LCA. The fact that traces (in the general case) are not phonetically realized follows from the interaction of independent factors. Since nontrivial chains induce violations of the LCA, they must undergo Chain Reduction. The choice of the link to survive Chain Reduction and be phonetically realized is then determined by economy considerations regarding the number of applications of FF-Elimination: given that the head of a chain participates in more checking relations than its trace(s), it will require fewer (if any) applications of FF-Elimination and will be the optimal option.

9.4.3.3 Traces Phonetically Realized As mentioned in section 9.1, some languages appear to allow traces of *wh*-phrases to be phonetically realized. The sentences in (27)–(31) exemplify this phenomenon.[12]

(27) *Afrikaans* (from Du Plessis 1977)
    met wie het jy   nou weer gesê *met wie* het Sarie gedog   *met*
    with who did you now again said *with who* did Sarie thought *with*
    wie gaan Jan trou
    who go   Jan marry
    'whom did you say (again) that Sarie though Jan is going to marry'

(28) *German* (from McDaniel 1986)
    mit wem glaubst du *mit wem* Hans spricht
    with whom think   you *with whom* Hans talks
    'with whom do you think Hans is talking'

(29) *Romani* (from McDaniel 1986)
    kas   misline   *kas*   o Demìri dikhlâ
    whom you-think *whom* Demir   saw
    'who do you think Demir saw'

(30) *Frisian* (from Hiemstra 1986)
    wêr   tinke jo *wêr*'t   Jan wennet
    where think you *where*-that Jan lives
    'where do you think that Jan lives'

(31) *English child grammar* (from Thornton 1990)
    who do you think really *who*'s in the can

At first sight, these sentences constitute counterevidence to my proposal that deletion of chain links is triggered by linearization considerations: if the *wh*-phrases of each of these sentences are nondistinct copies, they should prevent their structures from being linearized and cause the derivation to be canceled. I show below that when closely inspected, these sentences actually provide additional evidence in favor of the linearization approach pursued here. Before getting into the analysis proper, let us consider two other kinds of data that show that the phenomenon illustrated in (27)–(31) is very restricted in these languages.

    The first thing to note is that in languages that allow multiple *wh*-copies, phonetic realization of traces is restricted to intermediate traces; if the tail of the *wh*-chain in (28), for instance, is phonetically realized, the result is unacceptable.

(32) *German*
  **mit wem* glaubst du *mit wem* Hans *mit wem* spricht
  with whom think you *with whom* Hans *with whom* talks
  'with whom do you think Hans is talking'

Second, as mentioned in section 9.1, the intermediate trace cannot contain a full *wh*-phrase, as illustrated by the Romani sentence in (33), which should be contrasted with (29).

(33) *Romani* (from McDaniel 1986)
  **save čhave* mislinea *save čhave* o Demìri dikhlâ
  which boy you-think *which boy* Demir saw
  'which boy do you think Demir saw'

In order to account for the whole paradigm described above, I will rely on Chomsky's (1995, 337) proposal regarding the linearization of two heads in a mutual c-command relation, as illustrated in (34).

(34)

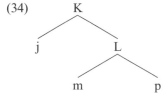

Since the bare phrase structure system does not allow for vacuous projections, neither *m* nor *p* in (34) asymmetrically c-commands the other; therefore, a derivation containing a substructure such as L in (34) should be canceled "unless the structure N = [$_L$ *m p*] has changed by the time the LCA applies so that its internal structure is irrelevant; perhaps N is converted by Morphology to a 'phonological word' not subject internally to the LCA, assuming that the LCA is an operation that applies after Morphology" (Chomsky 1995, 337).

Assuming Chomsky's (1995, 337) proposal that the LCA does not apply word-internally, the data in (27)–(31) can be accounted for if successive-cyclic *wh*-movement in these languages may proceed by adjunction to an intermediate C^0, as schematically represented in (35), and if Morphology in these languages may convert the adjunction structure [$_{C^0}$ X [$_{C^0}$ C^0]] into a phonological word, along the lines suggested by

Chomsky with respect to $[_L m p]$ in (34).[13] Such morphological restructuring is clearly seen in Frisian, where the intermediate complementizer surfaces cliticized to the *wh*-trace, as illustrated in (30).

(35)

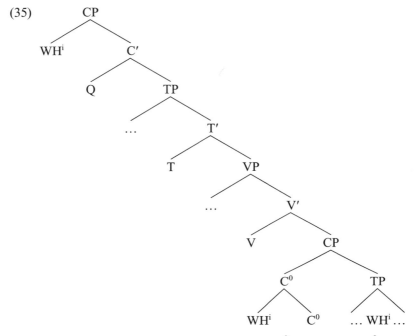

After Morphology restructures $[_{C^0}$ WH $[_{C^0} C^0]]$ in (35) as C^0, the intermediate *wh*-copy becomes invisible to the LCA and need not (therefore must not) be deleted by Chain Reduction; hence, the only copies that are subject to deletion for purposes of linearization are the head and the tail of the *wh*-chain. As in instances of standard movement, deleting the tail of the chain for purposes of the linearization ends up being more economical in that it entails fewer applications of FF-Elimination (see section 9.4.3.2). The unacceptability of (32) is therefore due to a violation of the LCA induced by the head and the tail of the *wh*-chain.

In turn, the contrast between (29) and (33), for instance, follows under the assumption that Morphology cannot deal with nonminimal maximal projections adjoined to heads (see Chomsky 1995, 319). If a full *wh*-phrase adjoined to C^0 cannot be converted into a phonological word by Morphology, *wh*-movement involving full *wh*-phrases must land in the intermediate [Spec, CP] rather than adjoining to C. Once all copies of a full *wh*-phrase are visible to the LCA, Chain Reduction must delete all but one link; hence the unacceptability of (33), for instance.[14]

Another instance of morphological restructuring exempting copies from being deleted is illustrated by clitic reduplication in some dialects of Argentinean Spanish.[15] The data in (36) illustrate the general pattern of clitic placement in Spanish, with the object clitic preceding a finite form or following a nonfinite form. What is relevant for our discussion is that in Argentinean Spanish, a clitic may appear enclitic to a finite verb only if the structure involves clitic reduplication ((37a) vs. (37b)) and reduplication is licensed only if the higher copy is enclitic ((37a) vs. (37c)).

(36) *Spanish*
    a. nos   vamos a divorciar
      us/CL go-1PL to divorce-INF
    b. vamos a divorciarnos
      go-1PL to divorce-INF-us/CL
      'we are going to divorce'

(37) *Argentinean Spanish*
    a. vámo*nos*   a divorciar*nos*
      go-1PL-*us/CL* to divorce-INF-*us/CL*
    b. *vámo*nos*   a divorciar
      go-1PL-*us/CL* to divorce-INF
    c. **nos* vamos a divorciar*nos*
      us/CL go-1PL to divorce-INF-*us/CL*
      'we are going to divorce'

Under the approach developed in this section, the correlation between exceptional enclisis and clitic reduplication receives a straightforward account. Let us assume that when the clitic climbs, it adjoins to the left of a functional category F with the verb adjoined to it, as represented in (38) (see, e.g., Kayne 1991; Uriagereka 1995).

(38)

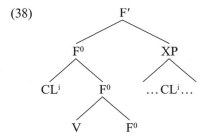

As is, the structure in (38) cannot be linearized because the two copies of the clitic induce violations of the asymmetry and irreflexivity conditions on linear order; hence the unacceptability of sentences such as (37c). Applied to the clitic chain in (38), Chain Reduction then deletes the lower copy (as in any other instance of standard movement), yielding a sentence like (36a). I propose that what distinguishes the dialects under consideration from other Spanish dialects is that Morphology can reanalyze the structure $[_{F^0} \text{ CL } [_{F^0} \text{ V } [_{F^0} \text{ F}^0]]]$ as a phonological word, rendering the adjoined clitic invisible to the LCA. Assuming that enclisis is the reflex of such restructuring, we would expect exceptional enclisis to always cooccur with clitic reduplication. After the three-segment F^0 in (38) is restructured, only the lower copy of the clitic is visible to the LCA and therefore it need not (therefore must not) be deleted by the LCA; hence the contrast between (37a) and (37b).[16]

In other dialects, the proposed morphological restructuring does not have a phonological reflex such as the enclisis seen in Argentinean Spanish. In Chilean Spanish, for instance, clitic reduplication keeps the general pattern of proclisis to finite forms, as shown in (39) (see Oroz 1966; Silva-Corvalán 1989).

(39) *Chilean Spanish* (from Silva-Corvalán 1989)
    yo *lo*   iba   a   matar*lo*
    I *it*/CL went to kill-*it*/CL
    'I was going to kill it'

Interestingly, contexts where clitic climbing is not possible may allow clitic reduplication, as illustrated in (40).[17] The contrast in (40) suggests that the morphological restructuring involving the higher copy of the clitic in (40b) exempts it from being computed not only with respect to the LCA, but also with respect to whatever is responsible for preventing clitic climbing in (40a).[18]

(40) *Chilean Spanish*
    a. *lo   odio   hacer
        it/CL hate-1SG do-INF
    b. *lo*   odio   hacer*lo*
        it/CL hate-1SG do-INF-*it*/CL
        'I hate to do it'

To summarize, the data in (27)–(31), (37a), (39a), and (40b) (see also note 18), rather than being counterexamples, count as further evidence for my proposal that phonetic realization of chain links is (in part) determined by linearization considerations (i.e., heads of chains and traces are subject to the LCA). As the analysis proposed in this chapter predicts, only when chain links become invisible to the LCA can a nontrivial chain surface with more than one link phonetically realized.

9.5 Some Technical Issues Reconsidered

9.5.1 Successive-Cyclic Movement and Deletion of Traces

In section 9.4.3.2, I proposed an extension of checking theory according to which a checked feature becomes invisible at PF, regardless of its interpretability at LF. In light of this extension, let us examine the derivation of instances of successive raising such as (41).

(41) I believe John to be likely to be kissed

When the object of *kissed* moves to check the EPP feature of the most embedded T head, its categorical feature should become invisible at PF, yielding (42a). Assuming that a deleted feature cannot participate in a checking relation (see Nunes 1995, sec. II.14.2), further movement of *John* after the structure in (42b) is assembled should not be able to check the EPP feature of the higher T head and the derivation is incorrectly predicted to crash.

(42) a. $[_{TP}$ John^i-$_N$ to $[_{vP'}$ be kissed John^i-N]]
     b. $[_{TP}$ to be likely $[_{TP}$ John^i-$_N$ to $[_{vP'}$ be kissed John^i-N]]]

Chomsky's (1995, 280) proposal that a +Interpretable feature is able to participate in multiple checking relations can be reinterpreted in the system I am arguing for in the following way. When participating in an overt checking relation, a +Interpretable feature can optionally be deleted with respect to PF, becoming invisible at this level. If it is deleted, it patterns with deleted −Interpretable features in not being able to enter into any further checking relations; if it is not deleted with respect to PF, it is allowed to enter into another checking relation. Since undeleted formal features (regardless of their interpretability at the C-I interface) must be eliminated in the phonological component in order for the derivation to converge at PF, economy considerations dictate that two elements in an overt checking relation should have the greatest number of features deleted with respect to PF, up to convergence. In other words, checking with respect to PF allows the number of applications of FF-Elimination targeting undeleted features to be minimized.

Thus, movement of the object to [Spec, TP] to check the EPP feature in (43) also allows the moved element to have its N-feature checked with respect to PF. However, if (43) is embedded in a structure that requires that another copy of *John* be created such as the one in (44a), a convergent derivation results only if the categorial feature of the higher copy is not deleted with respect to PF, as illustrated in (44b).

(43) [$_{TP}$ John^i-N to [$_{vP}$ be kissed John^i-N]]

(44) a. [$_{TP}$ to be likely [$_{TP}$ John^i-N to [$_{vP}$ be kissed John^i-N]]]
    b. [$_{TP}$ John^i-N to be likely [$_{TP}$ John^i-N to [$_{vP}$ be kissed John^i-N]]]

Again, whether or not the N-feature of the highest copy of *John* in (44b) can be deleted for PF purposes depends on the type of structure (44b) merges with. For instance, if (44b) is embedded in a structure that does not require additional copies of *John*, such as the one in (45), deletion of this feature with respect to PF is forced by economy considerations.

(45) [$_{TP}$ I believe [$_{TP}$ John^i-$_N$ to be likely [$_{TP}$ John^i-N to [$_{vP}$ be kissed John^i-N]]]]

Following Chomsky and Lasnik (1993, 563), I assume that successive movement creates a *linked chain*, which is a chain formed by linking two chains CH$_1$ and CH$_2$ such that the head of CH$_1$ is the tail of CH$_2$. In the case of (45), by linking the chains CH$_1$ = (*John*^{i}-N, *John*^{i}-N) and CH$_2$ = (*John*^{i}-$_N$, *John*^{i}-N), we obtain the linked chain CH$_3$ = (*John*^{i}-$_N$, *John*^{i}-N, *John*^{i}-N). The optimal reduction of CH$_3$ in the phonological component then deletes the lower links, yielding the sentence in (41).

To sum up, in a convergent derivation of successive-cyclic movement, the +Interpretable feature that enters into multiple checking relations must not be deleted with respect to PF in intermediate positions.

9.5.2 Traces with −Interpretable Features and Full Interpretation at LF
Once the copy theory of movement is assumed, it must be ensured that in a convergent derivation, no "traces" have −Interpretable features; otherwise, Full Interpretation will not be met at LF. The structure given in (46b), which I assumed to underlie the sentence in (46a), appears to be problematic under this perspective.

(46) a. John was kissed
    b. [$_{TP}$ John^i-$_{CASE}$ [$_{T'}$ T [$_{vP}$ was [$_{vP}$ kissed John^i-**CASE**]]]]

At first sight, the potential problem posed by the unchecked Case feature of the lower copy of *John* in (46b) does not arise in Chomsky's (1995) system; in this system, if a feature of a chain link is affected by an operation, the corresponding feature of the other links of the same chain is also affected (see Chomsky 1995, 381, n. 12). However, the analysis of complex examples shows that Chomsky's (1995) account also faces problems similar to the one posed by (46b) (see Nunes 1998b, chap. 3, for detailed discussion). Consider for instance the derivation of a sentence such as (47a), illustrated in (47b).

(47) a. what did John see
    b. [$_{CP}$ what-**CASE** did + Q [$_{TP}$ John see what-**CASE**]]

Overt movement of *what* in (47b) only checks the strong *wh*-feature of the interrogative complementizer and does not allow the Case feature of either link of CH$_1$ = (*what*-**CASE**, *what*-**CASE**) to be checked; in the covert component, the formal features of the lower copy of *what* raise to check Case, yielding the chain CH$_2$ = (FF(*what*), FF(*what*)). Deletion of the Case feature of both links of CH$_2$ through this checking operation eliminates the Case feature of the lower link of CH$_1$ (the lower link of CH$_2$ is included in the lower link of CH$_1$), but not the Case feature of the upper link of CH$_1$. This feature should then induce a violation of Full Interpretation at LF, incorrectly ruling (47a) out.

Noting the problem posed by sentences such as (47a), Chomsky (1995, 303) further adds that "a convention is then needed requiring erasure of F throughout the array of chains containing F, so that no −Interpretable feature remains in the operator position." Given that the problems posed by (46b) and (47b) are essentially the same, it is plausible to expect that an adequate implementation for the convention suggested by Chomsky should be able to handle both (46b) and (47b). This is the approach I pursue below.

Let us assume that at LF, all links of a chain must be uniform in terms of feature composition, as stated in (48). We can now formalize Chomsky's convention along the lines of (49), where deletion targets a single feature per application.

(48) *Feature Uniformity Condition*
    Given a chain CH = ($\alpha_1, \ldots, \alpha_n$), every α_i ($1 \leq i \leq n$) must have the same set of features visible at LF.

(49) *Chain Uniformization*
     Delete the minimal number of features of a nontrivial chain CH in
     order for CH to satisfy the Feature Uniformity Condition.

As it stands, the chain CH = (*John*-$_{CASE}$, *John*-**CASE**) in (46b) violates
the Feature Uniformity Condition: the Case feature of the lower link
is visible at LF, whereas that of the upper link is not. Chain Uniformization then deletes the Case feature of the lower link, allowing CH to
comply with the Feature Uniformity Condition. Furthermore, since no
−Interpretable feature survives at LF, Full Interpretation is satisfied and
the derivation converges. Notice that if Chain Uniformization had deleted
all the semantic features of CH in addition to the unchecked Case feature,
CH would also satisfy the Feature Uniformity Condition. However, this
undesirable result does not arise; as stated in (49), Chain Uniformization
resorts to the fewest possible applications of deletion. If a single application of deletion allows CH to comply with the Feature Uniformity Condition, economy considerations block further applications.[19]

The *wh*-movement in (47b) receives a similar account. In the covert
component, the formal features of the lower copy of *what* raise to check
its Case feature, yielding the nonuniform chain CH$_2$ = (FF(*what*-$_{CASE}$),
FF(*what*-**CASE**)). Chain Uniformization deletes the Case feature of the
lower link of CH$_2$ and, as a consequence, the chain CH$_1$ = (*what*, *what*)
becomes nonuniform. Chain Uniformization then applies to CH$_1$, deleting the Case feature of the upper link. Every Case feature of (47) is eliminated and the derivation converges at LF.

Let us finally consider the chain CH = (*Bill*, *Bill*) in (50b).

(50) a. *it was believed Bill to be often kissed
     b. [it was believed [Bill-**CASE** to [be often kissed Bill-**CASE**]]

The categorial feature of the upper copy of *Bill* is deleted with respect to
PF, but not with respect to LF (see section 9.4.3.2); hence, the two copies
remain identical at LF. Although satisfying the Feature Uniformity
Condition, this derivation does not satisfy Full Interpretation and crashes
at LF, because both copies in (50b) have an unchecked Case feature and
there is no available Case checker (the two main verbs are passive and the
matrix T checks the Case feature of the expletive).

If Chain Uniformization had deleted the unchecked Case features of
CH, the Feature Uniformity Condition would also be satisfied and the
derivation in (50b) would be incorrectly allowed to converge. This incorrect result does not arise because Chain Uniformization does not apply to

chains that are already uniform with respect to feature composition. The important thing to keep in mind is that, as stated in (49), deletion of features by Chain Uniformization is triggered by the Feature Uniformity Condition, not by Full Interpretation at LF. This is a natural assumption to make: if Full Interpretation at LF could lead Chain Uniformization to delete −Interpretable features, no movement operation would ever be necessary.

9.5.3 FF-Elimination, Chain Uniformization, and Economy Considerations

I have been tacitly assuming that Chain Uniformization applies in the covert component. However, given that the uniformity condition on the mapping from a given numeration to LF makes the same set of operations available in overt syntax and in the covert component (see Chomsky 1995, 229), one wonders whether Chain Uniformization could apply to the chain of (51), for instance, before Spell-Out.

(51) [John-$_{CASE}$ [was [kissed John-**CASE**]]]

If that were possible, it would enable the NP chain to satisfy Full Interpretation at both LF and PF without any other operation eliminating the unchecked Case features, and there would be no basis for the trace to be deleted in the phonological component instead of the head of the chain.

A similar problem arises with respect to the computations of the phonological component. I have assumed that FF-Elimination applies after Chain Reduction. If this were not the case, FF-Elimination would delete the Case feature of the lower link of CH = (*John*-$_{CASE}$, *John*-**CASE**) in (51) and, again, there would be no asymmetry between the head and the tail of the chain on the basis of which Chain Reduction could delete the latter instead of the former.

In order to address these issues, I will rely on a suggestion by Chomsky (1995, 226) according to which the computation of derivational cost hinges on whether an operation is a defining property of derivations or whether it is associated with a convergence condition on derivations. For Chomsky (1995, 225–226), a derivation is a sequence of symbolic elements S mapped from a numeration N such that the last member of S is a pair (PF object, LF object) and N has been exhausted. If the applications of Select, for instance, are insufficient to exhaust the numeration, no derivation is obtained and no questions of convergence or economy arise.

Similar considerations hold of the operation Merge, under the assumption that it is a defining property of a derivation that an LF object must be a unique single-rooted syntactic object. The operation Move, on the other hand, is associated with convergence conditions; if it does not apply, a derivation may be formed, but at least one object of the pair (PF object, LF object) violates Full Interpretation. Therefore, the operations Select and Merge, which define what is a possible derivation, have no cost, whereas the operation Move, which is required for the pair (PF object, LF object) to be legitimate, is derivationally costly.

Returning to the problems raised above, I propose that although available throughout the mapping from a given numeration to LF, Chain Uniformization is prevented from applying overtly by economy considerations. Consider a derivational step after all strong features have been checked and the numeration has been exhausted. The computational system may then apply Chain Uniformization to the chains formed overtly before, or it may submit the structure to Spell-Out. Since Spell-Out is required for a derivation to be generated, it is costless, therefore being more economical than Chain Uniformization, which is an operation related to a convergence condition (the Feature Uniformity Condition). Thus, since the structure in (51) is spelled out without the NP chain being uniformized, an asymmetry between the head and the tail is created that will be the basis for the choice of the link to be deleted in the phonological component.

The same reasoning can account for the ordering between Chain Reduction and FF-Elimination. If the chain CH = (*John*-CASE, *John*-**CASE**) in (51), for instance, is not reduced, the structure containing it cannot be linearized and no PF object can be formed (see section 9.4.2); hence, Chain Reduction is costless. If FF-Elimination does not apply to (51), on the other hand, an illegitimate PF object may eventually be formed; applications of FF-Elimination therefore have derivational cost. Thus, at the derivational step where a chain can in principle undergo Chain Reduction or FF-Elimination, economy considerations will ensure its reduction. Optimality considerations concerning the number of applications of FF-Elimination then mandate that the lower link(s) of the chain be deleted.

Chomsky's (1995, 303) suggestion regarding the conceptual basis for economy computation therefore ensures that no chain is uniformized before Spell-Out, and that chains are reduced in the phonological component before applications of FF-Elimination.[20]

9.6   Conclusion

In this chapter, I have argued in favor of the null hypothesis concerning the copy theory of movement in the Minimalist Program, namely, that traces do not have distinct intrinsic properties that would characterize them as grammatical primitives. In particular, I have shown that traces do not intrinsically differ from heads of chains with respect to linearization or phonetic realization. Eventual differences between traces and heads of chains arise in the course of the derivation owing to independently motivated conditions.

The reason why traces usually are not phonetically realized, for instance, follows from the interaction between the fact that traces are subject to the LCA and economy considerations concerning the number of applications of deletion to eliminate unchecked formal features in the phonological component (the FF-Elimination operation). A syntactic object containing a nontrivial chain CH cannot be linearized in accordance with the LCA; since the links of CH are nondistinct, they induce a violation of the asymmetry condition on linear order, canceling the derivation because no PF object is formed. In order to prevent this state of affairs, the phonological component can resort to the operation Chain Reduction, which in the general case deletes all but one link of a nontrivial chain.

Assuming that a given head only checks the relevant features of the chain link that is in its checking domain, the head of a chain CH will always have fewer unchecked formal features (if any) to be deleted by FF-Elimination than the lower links of CH. Thus, a derivation in which Chain Reduction deletes all the links except the head of the chain is in principle more economical than a derivation in which Chain Reduction deletes all of the links of the chain except one trace. Since FF-Elimination must delete the unchecked formal features (if any) of the link that survives in order for Full Interpretation to be satisfied at PF, the derivation in which the head of the chain is the link that survives Chain Reduction requires fewer additional applications (if any) of FF-Elimination than a derivation in which a trace survives.

This analysis also accounts for the restricted instances of phonetically realized *wh*-traces and clitic reduplication found in some languages. The additional possibilities in these languages are tied to the possibility of morphological restructuring. Assuming that the LCA does not apply word-internally (see Chomsky 1995, 337), if a chain link is reanalyzed by

Morphology as part of a word, it becomes invisible to the LCA and need not (therefore must not) be deleted by Chain Reduction.

If this picture is essentially correct, the "syntactic" computations of the phonological component after Morphology proceed as follows. If the phonological component has received from Spell-Out a syntactic object Σ containing discontinuous objects (nontrivial chains), Chain Reduction must delete constituents of each nontrivial chain in such a way that Σ could in principle be mapped into a linear order. If possible, Linearize converts the structure resulting from applications of Chain Reduction into a sequence of pairs of sets of phonological features and sets of formal features; otherwise, the derivation is canceled. If linearization is successful, FF-Elimination deletes unchecked formal features, yielding a PF object π, which can be legitimate or not.

Notes

The preparation of this chapter was partly supported by an Andrew W. Mellon Postdoctoral Fellowship while I was at the University of Southern California. The chapter is based on chapter III of my dissertation (see Nunes 1995). Early versions of the ideas presented here appeared in Nunes 1994, 1996. I would like to thank Mark Arnold, Norbert Hornstein, Richard Kayne, Ellen Thompson, and Juan Uriagereka for valuable comments and suggestions.

1. For relevant discussion, see Chomsky 1973, 1981, 1982, 1986, Fiengo 1977, Aoun et al. 1987, Rizzi 1990, and Epstein 1991, among others.

2. For a discussion of other apparent differences between heads of chains and traces, see Nunes 1995, chap. III, and Nunes 1998b, chap. 3.

3. At first sight, the unacceptability of (2b) has an obvious explanation within Chomsky's (1995) system: the strong feature of T has not been checked. Although this is a straightforward account of one potential derivation of (2b), it does not extend to the derivation outlined in (1). In (1c), a copy of *John* merges with the structure in (1a), becoming the specifier of T and being able to check the strong feature of T.

4. Analogous principles are Bobaljik's (1995, 350) Speak Up ("Pronounce the topmost/leftmost copy of each element"), Groat and O'Neil's (1996, 135) Form-chain ("Forming a chain results in copying all syntactic features of the category moved, but does not copy the category's phonological matrix: it either moves it to the new position or fails to move it"), and Pesetsky's (1997, 153) Silent Trace ("Don't pronounce the traces of a moved constituent").

5. In Chomsky 1995, the term *LCA* is used to refer both to the Linear Correspondence Axiom and to the mapping operation that conforms to this axiom, as becomes clear when it is suggested that the LCA may delete traces (see Chomsky 1995, 337). I will avoid this ambiguity and use the term *Linearize* for the operation

that maps a phrase structure into a linear order of X^0 elements in accordance with the LCA.

6. If this logic were to extend to morphological operations, which are taken to precede Linearize (see Chomsky 1995, 337), we could ask why Morphology should not ignore traces, allowing contraction to proceed over them, given that they will be deleted later in the derivation. Clearly, this would yield wrong results with respect to *wanna* contraction over *wh*-traces.

7. In section 9.4.3.3, I address the issue of how two heads in a mutual c-command relation, such as *kissed* and *John* in (12), can be linearized.

8. It may also be possible that owing to constraints of the phonological component, full deletion of chain links does not yield a convergent derivation and scattered deletion is not blocked. This may well be the case of extraposition. The sentence in (ia), for instance, is analyzed by Wilder (1995, 292) as involving movement of the PP *about the claim that Mary will hire Peter* to the left of the temporal adverb (see (ib)), followed by a process of "Chain-Internal Selective Deletion," according to which phonological deletion can remove part of the antecedent and the complementary part of the trace (see (ic)). From the perspective of the proposal made in section 9.4.2, the complementary deletion operations of Wilder's Chain-Internal Selective Deletion are imposed by linearization considerations: if some constituent of the PP chain in (ib) appears in both links, the structure cannot be linearized in accordance with the LCA and the derivation is canceled.

(i) a. we talked about the claim yesterday that Mary will hire Peter
   b. [we talked [PP about [DP the [NP claim [CP that Mary will hire Peter]]]]]^i
      yesterday [PP about [DP the [NP claim [NP claim [CP that Mary will hire Peter]]]]]^i]
   c. [we talked [PP about [DP the [NP claim [CP that Mary will hire Peter]]]]]^i
      yesterday [PP about [DP the [NP claim [CP that Mary will hire Peter]]]]]^i]

Other potential instances of scattered deletion motivated (in part) by phonological considerations are split constituents in Germanic and Slavic languages. Ćavar and Fanselow (1997) argue that in the Croatian sentence in (iia), for instance, the PP *na kakav krov* 'on what-kind-of roof' moves first to a Focus position and then to a Topic position (see (iib)). Assuming that elements bearing topic and focus features must be realized in the checking domain of the relevant heads, the authors show that full deletion of the lower copies cannot license the realization of both topic and focus features; scattered deletion is then employed and both requirements are met.

(i) a. na kakav   je Ivan krov bacio loptu
      on what-kind-of be Ivan roof ball   throw
      'on what kind of roof did Ivan throw the ball'
   b. [[PP na kakav krov]^i je Ivan [PP na kakav krov]^i bacio loptu [PP na kakav krov]^i]
   c. [[PP na [kakav krov]]^i je [van [PP na [kakav krov]]^i bacio loptu [PP na [kakav krov]]^i]

9. Like the case of Chain Reduction, the specification of the number of features to be deleted by FF-Elimination is taken to follow from economy considerations concerning derivational length. As before, I will keep the description of FF-Elimination in (21) for expository purposes.

10. Notice that this extension does not prevent Morphology from accessing deleted features. According to Chomsky's (1995, 280) definition of deletion, which is adopted here, a feature that is deleted through a checking operation becomes invisible at the interface, but is accessible to the computational system. The proposal in the text only extends invisibility at LF to invisibility at PF. For reasons discussed in Nunes 1995, 1998b, I will not adopt Chomsky's (1995) extra operation of erasure.

11. The issue of how the unchecked −Interpretable features of traces are eliminated in the covert component will be addressed in section 9.5.2.

12. The analysis of the data in this section differs substantially from the one offered in Nunes 1995.

13. Elements adjoined to a head H are in the checking domain of H; hence, *wh*-movement via adjunction to C^0 in (35) is able to license any feature checking that takes place in intermediate C positions. On the optimality of adjunction to heads versus movement to specifiers, see Nunes 1998a.

14. Fanselow and Mahajan (1995) propose that in German, intermediate traces may cliticize to C^0 in the phonological component, thereby being invisible to deletion. Although this proposal can explain why full *wh*-traces cannot be phonetically realized in intermediate trace positions, it does not have a principled explanation for the fact that in the general case, traces cannot be phonetically realized.

15 Clitic reduplication is also found in other varieties of South American Spanish, with very interesting dialectal variation. I am thankful to Monica Zoppi-Fontana for discussion of the data in (37).

16. Given that cases of clitic reduplication such as (37a) do not allow concomitant verb reduplication (phonetic realization of both the moved verb and its trace), it must be the case that the moved verb is still visible to the LCA after restructuring. Two possibilities come to mind that would derive the correct results: either the clitic adjoins to V and the two-segment V category is the one that is restructured, or the category resulting from restructuring the three-segment F^0 structure is actually V, rather than F. Since I do not have evidence one way or the other, I will leave this issue open, pending further research, and assume the analysis outlined in the text, for concreteness.

17. The contrast in (40) was pointed out to me by Héctor Campos (personal communication), to whom I am also thankful for general discussion of clitic reduplication in Chilean Spanish.

18. Another potential instance of morphological restructuring involves auxiliary doubling in English child grammar, as illustrated in (i). If children allow the complex formed by negation and the tail of the auxiliary chain to be morpholog-

ically restructured, only the copy of the auxiliary in C will be visible to the LCA and Chain Reduction will not be necessary.

(i) *English child grammar* (from Guasti, Thornton, and Wexler 1995)
    a. what *did* he *did*n't wanna bring to school (Darrell 4;1)
    b. what kind of bread *do* you *do*n't like (Rosy 3;10)
    c. why *could* Snoopy *could*n't fit in the boat (Kathy 4;0)

19. Similar to the case of Chain Reduction and FF-Elimination, it is unnecessary to specify that Chain Uniformization deletes as few features as possible; the exact number of features to be deleted is indirectly determined by economy considerations regarding derivational length. For expository purposes, I will assume the formulation of Chain Uniformization in (49).

20. Further evidence for Chomsky's (1995, 303) suggestion is found in Nunes, forthcoming, where the effects of Procrastinate are derived through a comparison between Move and Spell-Out in terms of derivational cost.

References

Aoun, Joseph, Norbert Hornstein, David Lightfoot, and Amy Weinberg. 1987. Two types of locality. *Linguistic Inquiry* 18, 537–577.

Bobaljik, Jonathan David. 1995. Morphosyntax: The syntax of verbal inflection. Doctoral dissertation, MIT, Cambridge, Mass.

Brody, Michael. 1995. *Lexico-Logical Form: A radically minimalist theory*. Cambridge, Mass.: MIT Press.

Ćavar, Damir, and Gisbert Fanselow. 1997. Split constituents in Germanic and Slavic. Paper presented at International Conference on Pied-Piping, Friedrich-Schiller-Universität Jena, June.

Chierchia, Gennaro. 1991. Functional *wh* and weak crossover. In *Proceedings of the Tenth West Coast Conference on Formal Linguistics*, ed. Dawn Bates, 75–90. Stanford, Calif.: CSLI Publications. [Distributed by Cambridge University Press.]

Chomsky, Noam. 1973. Conditions on transformations. In *A festschrift for Morris Halle*, eds. Stephen Anderson and Paul Kiparsky, 232–286. New York: Holt, Rinehart and Winston.

Chomsky, Noam. 1981. *Lectures on government and binding*. Dordrecht: Foris.

Chomsky, Noam. 1982. *Some concepts and consequences of the theory of government and binding*. Cambridge, Mass.: MIT Press.

Chomsky, Noam. 1986. *Knowledge of language: Its nature, origin, and use*. New York: Praeger.

Chomsky, Noam. 1993. A minimalist program for linguistic theory. In *The view from Building 20: Essays in linguistics in honor of Sylvain Bromberger*, eds. Kenneth Hale and Samuel Jay Keyser, 1–52. Cambridge, Mass.: MIT Press. [Reprinted in *The Minimalist Program*, Noam Chomsky, 167–217. Cambridge, Mass.: MIT Press, 1995.]

Chomsky, Noam. 1995. Categories and transformations. In *The Minimalist Program*, 219–394. Cambridge, Mass.: MIT Press.

Chomsky, Noam, and Howard Lasnik. 1993. The theory of principles and parameters. In *Syntax: An international handbook of contemporary research*, eds. Joachim Jacobs, Arnim von Stechow, Wolfgang Sternefeld, and Theo Vennemann, 506–569. Berlin: Walter de Gruyter. [Reprinted in *The Minimalist Program*, Noam Chomsky, 13–127. Cambridge, Mass.: MIT Press, 1995.]

Du Plessis, Hans. 1977. *Wh* movement in Afrikaans. *Linguistic Inquiry* 8, 723–726.

Epstein, Samuel David. 1991. *Traces and their antecedents*. Oxford: Oxford University Press.

Fanselow, Gisbert, and Anoop Mahajan. 1995. Partial movement and successive cyclicity. In *Papers on* wh-*scope marking*, eds. Uli Lutz and Gereon Müller, 131–161. Bericht Nr. 76, Arbeitspapiere des Sonderforschungsbereichs 340, Sprachtheoretische Grundlagen für die Computer Linguistik.

Fiengo, Robert. 1977. On trace theory. *Linguistic Inquiry* 8, 35–61.

Groat, Erich, and John O'Neil. 1996. Spell-Out at the interface: Achieving a unified syntactic computational system in the minimalist framework. In *Minimal ideas: Syntactic studies in the minimalist framework*, eds. Werner Abraham, Samuel David Epstein, Höskuldur Thráinsson, and C. Jan-Wouter Zwart, 113–139. Amsterdam: John Benjamins.

Guasti, Maria Teresa, Rosalind Thornton, and Kenneth Wexler. 1995. Negation in children's questions: The case of English. In *Proceedings of the 19th Boston University Conference on Language Development*, eds. Dawn MacLaughlin and Susan McEwen, 228–239. Somerville, Mass.: Cascadilla Press.

Hiemstra, Inge. 1986. Some aspects of *wh*-questions is Frisian. *NOWELE* 8, 97–110.

Hornstein, Norbert. 1995. *Logical Form: From GB to minimalism*. Oxford: Blackwell.

Kayne, Richard. 1991. Romance clitics, verb movement, and PRO. *Linguistic Inquiry* 22, 589–646.

Kayne, Richard. 1994. *The antisymmetry of syntax*. Cambridge, Mass.: MIT Press.

McDaniel, Dana. 1986. Conditions on *wh*-chains. Doctoral dissertation, City University of New York.

Nunes, Jairo. 1994. Linearization of non-trivial chains at PF. In *University of Maryland working papers in linguistics 2*, eds. Jairo Nunes, Ellen Thompson, and Spyridoula Varlokosta, 159–177. Department of Linguistics, University of Maryland, College Park.

Nunes, Jairo. 1995. The copy theory of movement and linearization of chains in the Minimalist Program. Doctoral dissertation, University of Maryland, College Park.

Nunes, Jairo. 1996. On why traces are not phonetically realized. In *NELS 26*, ed. Kiyomi Kusumoto, 211–225. GLSA, University of Massachusetts, Amherst.

Nunes, Jairo. 1998a. Bare X-bar theory and structures formed by movement. *Lingusitic Inquiry* 29, 160–168.

Nunes, Jairo. 1998b. Linearization of chains and sideward movement. Ms., Universidade Estadual de Campinas.

Nunes, Jairo. Forthcoming. Some notes on Procrastinate and other economy matters. *D.E.L.T.A.*

Oroz, Rodolfo. 1966. *La lengua castellana en Chile*. Facultad de Filosofia y Educacion, Universidad de Chile, Santiago.

Pesetsky, David. 1997. Optimality Theory and syntax: Movement and pronunciation. In *Optimality Theory: An overview*, eds. Diana Archangeli and D. Terence Langendoen, 134–170. Malden, Mass.: Blackwell.

Rizzi, Luigi. 1990. *Relativized Minimality*. Cambridge, Mass.: MIT Press.

Silva-Corvalán, Carmen. 1989. *Sociolingüística: Teoría e análysis*. Madrid: Alhambra.

Thornton, Rosalind. 1990. Adventures in long-distance moving: The acquisition of complex *wh*-questions. Doctoral dissertation, University of Connecticut, Storrs.

Uriagereka, Juan. 1995. Aspects of clitic placement in Western Romance. *Linguistic Inquiry* 26, 79–123.

Wilder, Chris. 1995. Rightward movement as leftward deletion. In *On extraction and extraposition in German*, eds. Uli Lutz and Jürgen Pafel, 273–309. Amsterdam: John Benjamins.

Chapter 10

Multiple Spell-Out
Juan Uriagereka

10.1 Deducing the Base Step of the LCA

A main desideratum of the Minimalist Program is reducing substantive principles to interface (or bare output) conditions, and formal principles to economy conditions. Much energy has been devoted to rethinking constraints and phenomena that appear to challenge this idea, in the process sharpening observations and descriptions. In this chapter, I attempt to reduce a version of Kayne's (1994) Linear Correspondence Axiom (LCA).

Chomsky (1995) already limits the LCA's place in the grammar. Kayne's version of the axiom is a formal condition on the shape of phrase markers. Chomsky's (for reasons that go back to Higginbotham 1983) is a condition that operates at Spell-Out, because of PF demands. Kayne's intuition is that a nonlinearized phrase marker is ill formed, in itself, whereas for Chomsky such an object is ill formed only at PF—hence the need to linearize it upon branching to this component. Chomsky's version is arguably "more minimalist" in that linearization is taken to follow from bare output conditions.

The axiom has a formal and a substantive character. The formal part demands the linearization of a complex object (assembled by the Merge operation, which produces mere associations among terms). A visual image to keep in mind is a mobile by Calder. The hanging pieces relate in a fixed way, but are not *linearly ordered* with respect to one another; one way to linearize the mobile (e.g., so as to measure it) is to lay it on the ground. The substantive part of Kayne's axiom does for the complex linguistic object what the ground does for the mobile: it tells us how to map the unordered set of terms into a sequence of PF slots. But even if

Chomsky's reasoning helps us deduce the formal part of the axiom (assuming that PF demands linearization), the question remains of exactly *how* the mapping works.

Kayne is explicit about that. Unfairly, I will adapt his ideas to Chomsky's minimalist "bare phrase structure" (Chomsky avoids committing to a definition in either 1994 or 1995).

(1) *Linear Correspondence Axiom*
   a. Base step: If α commands β, then α precedes β.
   b. Induction step: If γ precedes β and γ dominates α, then α precedes β.

I will discuss each of the steps in (1) in turn, with an eye toward deducing their substantive character from either bare output or economy considerations. Consider why command should be a sufficient condition for precedence. It is best to ask this question with a formal object in mind. I will call this object a *command unit* (CU), for the simple reason that it emerges in a derivation through the continuous application of Merge. That is, if we merge elements to an already merged phrase marker, then we obtain a CU, as in (2a). In contrast, (2b) is not a CU, since it implies the application of Merge to different objects.

(2) a. *Command unit: formed by continuous application of Merge to the same object*

$$\{\alpha, \{\gamma, \{\alpha, \{\alpha, \{\beta \ldots\}\}\}\}\}$$

$$\gamma \leftarrow \overset{\uparrow}{|} \rightarrow \{\alpha, \{\alpha, \{\beta \ldots\}\}\}$$

$$\alpha \leftarrow \overset{\uparrow}{|} \rightarrow \{\beta \ldots\}$$

   b. *Not a command unit: formed by discontinuous application of Merge to two separately assembled objects*

$$\{\alpha, \{\{\gamma, \{\gamma, \{\delta \ldots\}\}\}, \{\alpha, \{\alpha, \{\beta \ldots\}\}\}\}\}$$

$$\{\gamma, \{\gamma, \{\delta \ldots\}\}\} \leftarrow \overset{\uparrow}{|} \rightarrow \{\alpha, \{\alpha, \{\beta \ldots\}\}\}$$

$$\gamma \leftarrow \overset{\uparrow}{|} \rightarrow \{\delta \ldots\} \qquad \alpha \leftarrow \overset{\uparrow}{|} \rightarrow \{\beta \ldots\}$$

Regarding CUs, the ultimate question is why, among the possible linearizations in (3), (3d) is chosen.

(3) a.

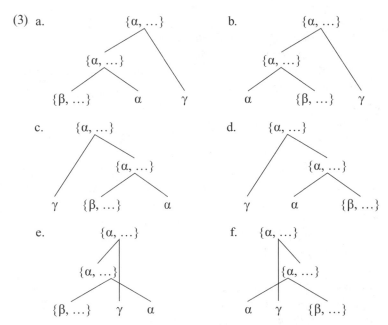

To continue with the mobile image, there are *n!* ways in which we can lay it on the ground, for *n* the number of hanging elements. Why is it that, among all the apparently reasonable permutations, the linguistic mobile collapses into a linearized sequence specifically in the order $\langle \gamma, \alpha, \{\beta \ldots\} \rangle$?

We may ask the question from the point of view of what syntactic relations are relevant to the terminals of the structures in (3). Concentrating on the terminals, we see that the only relation that exists between them in a CU is "I have merged with your ancestors." We can produce an order within CUs in terms of this relation, which essentially keeps track of what has merged with what when. This is, essentially, the insight behind Epstein's (this volume) interpretation of command, which has the effect of ordering the terminal objects in (3) as follows: $\langle \gamma, \alpha, \{\beta \ldots\} \rangle$. If PF requirements demand that the Merge mobile collapse into a flat object, it is not unreasonable to expect that the collapse piggybacks on a previously existing relation. Indeed, minimalist assumptions lead us to expect precisely this sort of parsimony.

However, we have not yet achieved the desired results. To see this, imagine a group of people trapped inside a building, with access to a window that allows them to exit just one at a time. These people may order themselves according to some previously existing relation (e.g., age). But having found an order does not mean having decided how to leave the building. Does the youngest exit first or last—or in the middle? Likewise, a decision has to be made with regard to the $\langle \gamma, \alpha, \{\beta \ldots\}\rangle$ order. Exactly how do we map it to the PF order?

In minimalist terms, the question is not just how to map the collapsed $\langle \gamma, \alpha, \{\beta \ldots\}\rangle$ sequence to a PF order, but actually how to do it *optimally*. The hope is that mapping the collapsed $\langle \gamma, \alpha, \{\beta \ldots\}\rangle$ command order to the $\langle \gamma, \alpha, \{\beta \ldots\}\rangle$ PF order in (3d) is (one among) the best solution(s).

Another analogy might help clarify the intuition. Visualize a house of cards, and imagine how pulling out one crucial card makes it collapse. To a reasonable extent, the order in which the cards fall maps homomorphically to the order in which they were assembled, with higher cards landing on top, and cards placed on the left or right falling more or less in those directions (assuming no forces other than gravity). If Merge operations could be conceived as producing what amounts to a merge-wave of terminals, it is not unreasonable to expect such a wave to collapse into a linearized terminal sequence in a way that harmonizes (in the same local direction) the various wave states, thus essentially mapping the merge order into the PF linear order in a homomorphic way. This, of course, is hand-waving until one establishes what such a merge-wave is, but I will not go into that here (see Martin and Uriagereka, in progress, on the concept of collapsed waves in syntax).

Even if we managed to collapse the merge order into the PF sequence that most directly reflects it, why have we chosen (3d) over the equally plausible (3a)? In short, why does the command relation collapse into *precedence*, and not the opposite? The harmonized collapse problem seems to have not one optimal solution, but two.

Three different answers are possible. First, one can attribute the choice of (3d) over (3a) to something deep; it would have to be as deep as whatever explains the forward movement of time ... (I'm not entirely joking here; physical properties are taken by many biologists to affect core aspects of the morphology of organisms, and Kayne (1994) speculates in this direction.)

Second, one can say (assuming that (3a) and (3d) are equally optimal solutions) that (3d) gave humans an adaptive edge of some sort, in terms of parsing or perhaps learnability. One could also imagine that a species that had chosen (3a) over (3d) as a collapsing technique might equally well have evolved a parser and an acquisition device for the relevant structures (but see Weinberg, this volume).

Third, one can shrug one's shoulders. So what if (3a) and (3d) are equally harmonic? Two equally valid solutions exist, so pick the one that does the work. (This view of the world would be very consistent with Stephen Jay Gould's punctuated equilibrium perspective in biology; see Uriagereka 1998.) This situation is acceptable within the Minimalist Program, or for that matter within any program that seeks to understand how optimality works in nature, which cannot reasonably seek *the* best solution to optimality problems, but instead expects *an* optimal solution; often, even mathematically optimal solutions are various.

If I am ultimately on the right track, (3d) can correctly be chosen as the actual PF ordering that the system employs; that is, we should not need to state (1a) as an axiom. In a nutshell, command maps to a PF linearization convention in simple CUs (those (1a) is designed to target) because this state of affairs is optimal. I will not claim I have proven this, for I have only indicated the direction in which a demonstration could proceed, raising some obvious questions. I have little more to say about this here and will proceed on the assumption that the base step of the LCA can be turned into a theorem.

10.2   Deducing the Induction Step of the LCA

Having met the demands of the Minimalist Program by showing how part of the LCA can reduce to more justifiable conditions, we should naturally ask whether the whole LCA can be deduced this way. I know of no deduction of the sort sketched above, given standard assumptions about the model.

Nonetheless, an older model provides an intriguing way of deducing the LCA.[1] For reasons that become apparent shortly, I refer to it as a *dynamically split model*. The origins of this outlook are discussions about successive cyclicity and whether this condition affects interpretation: are the interpretive components accessed in successive derivational cascades? Much of this debate was abandoned the moment a single level, S-Structure, was postulated as the interface to the interpretive components. Now that S-Structure has itself been abandoned, the question is alive again: what would it mean for the system to access the interpretation split in a dynamic way?

I want to demonstrate that the simplest assumption (i.e., nothing prevents a dynamically split access to interpretation) allows the LCA's induction step to be satisfied trivially. In effect, this would permit the deduction of (1b), albeit in a drastically changed model that neither Chomsky (1995) nor Kayne (1994) was assuming.

One way of framing the issue is to ask how many times the rule of Spell-Out should apply. If we stipulate that it applies only once, then PF and LF are accessed only once, at that point. On the other hand, liberally accessing PF and LF in successive derivational cascades entails multiple applications of Spell-Out. Surely, assuming that computational steps are costly, economy considerations favor a single application of Spell-Out. But are there circumstances in which a derivation is forced to spell out different chunks of structure in different steps?

One such instance might arise when a derivation involves more than one CU. As noted, CUs emerge as the derivational process unfolds, and they are trivially collapsible by means of the base step of the LCA. Now, what if only those trivially linearizable chunks of structure (e.g., (2a)) are in fact linearized? That is, what if, instead of complicating the LCA by including (1b), when we encounter a complex structure of the sort in (2b) we simply do not collapse it (thus linearizing it), causing a derivational crash? Only two results are then logically possible: either structures like (2b) do not exist, or they are linearized in various steps, each of which involves only CUs. The first possibility is factually wrong, so we conclude that multiple Spell-Out (MSO) is an alternative.

Before we explore whether MSO is empirically desirable, consider its possible mechanics. Bear in mind that CUs are singly spelled out—the most economical alternative. The issue, then, is what happens beyond CUs. By assumption, we have no way of collapsing them into given linearizations, so we must do the job prior to their merger, when they are still individual CUs. What we need, then, is a procedure to relate a structure that has already been spelled out to the still "active" phrase marker. Otherwise, we cannot assemble a final unified *and linearized* object.

The procedure for relating CUs can be conceived in conservative or radical terms, either solution being consistent with the program in this chapter. The conservative proposal is based on the fact that the collapsed Merge structure is no longer phrasal, after Spell-Out; in essence, the phrase marker that has undergone Spell-Out is like a giant lexical compound, whose syntactic terms are obviously interpretable but are not accessible to movement, ellipsis, and so forth.[2] The radical proposal assumes that each spelled-out CU does not even merge with the rest of the structure, the final process of interphrasal association being accomplished in the performative components.[3] I will briefly detail each of these versions.

In the conservative version, the spelled-out phrase marker behaves like a word, so that it can associate with the rest of the structure; this means it must keep its label after Spell-Out. Technically, if a phrase marker $\{\alpha, \{L, K\}\}$ collapses through Spell-Out, the result is $\{\alpha, \langle L, K \rangle\}$, which is mathematically equivalent to $\{\alpha, \{\{L\}, \{L, K\}\}\}$.[4] Since this object is not a syntactic object, it clearly can behave like a "frozen" compound. As a consequence, we need not add any further stipulations: the collapsing procedure of Spell-Out itself results in something akin to a word.

To see how we reach this conclusion, we need to take seriously Chomsky's (1995) notion of *syntactic object*. Syntactic objects can take two forms.

(4) a. Base: A word is a syntactic object.
   b. Induction: $\{\alpha, \{L, K\}\}$ is a syntactic object, for L and K syntactic objects and α a label.

(4a) speaks for itself, although it is not innocent. The general instance is not too complicated: a word is an item from the lexicon. However, the Minimalist Program permits the formation of complex words, whose internal structure and structural properties are not determined by the syntax. (Indeed, the object resulting from Spell-Out also qualifies as a word, in the technical sense of having a label and a structure that is inaccessible to the syntax.) (4b) is obtained through Merge and involves a labeling function that Chomsky argues is necessarily *projection*. What is relevant here is how a label is structurally expressed.

(5) Within a syntactic object, a label α is not a term.

(6) K is a term if and only if (a) or (b):
   a. Base: K is a phrase marker.
   b. Induction: K is a member of a member of a term.

(6a) hides no secrets. (6b) is based on the sort of object that is obtained by merging K and L: one set containing K and L, and another containing $\{L, K\}$ and label α—namely, $\{\alpha, \{L, K\}$. This whole object (a phrase marker) is a term, by (6a). Members of members of this term (L and K) are also terms, by (6b). Label α is a member of the first term, hence not a term. All of these results are as desired.

Consider next the collapse of $\{\alpha, \{L, K\}\}$ as $\{\alpha, \langle L, K \rangle\}$, equivalent to $\{\alpha, \{\{L\}, \{L, K\}\}\}$. By (6b), $\{L\}$ and $\{L, K\}$ are terms. However, $\{L, K\}$ is not a syntactic object, by either (4a) or (4b). Therefore, $\{\alpha, \{\{L\}, \{L, K\}\}\}$ cannot be a syntactic object by (4b); if it is to be merged higher up, it can be a syntactic object only by (4a)—as a word. This is good; we want the collapsed object to be like a compound, that is, essentially a word: it has a label, and it has terms, but they are not objects accessible to the syntax.

Note that set-theoretic notions have been taken very seriously here; for example, such notions as linearity have been expressed without any coding tricks (angled brackets, as opposed to particular sets). In essence, the discussion has revealed that generally merged structures (those that go beyond the head-complement relation) are fundamentally nonlinear, to the point that linearizing them literally destroys their phrasal base. This conclusion lends some credibility to Chomsky's conjectures that (a) Merge produces a completely basic and merely associative set-theoretic object, with no internal ordering, and (b) only if collapsed into a flat structure can this unordered object be interpreted at PF.

Though the current notation does the job, the appropriate results can be achieved regardless of the notation. Various positions can be taken, the most radical having been mentioned already. In the version that ships spelled-out phrase markers to performance, one must assume a procedure by which already processed (henceforth, "cashed out") phrase markers find their way "back" to their interpretation site. Plausibly, this is the role agreement plays in the grammar.

It is interesting to note that, according to present assumptions, MSO applies to noncomplements (which are not part of CUs). Similarly, agreement does not manifest itself in complements, which makes it reasonable to suppose that what agreement does is "glue together" separate derivational cascades that are split at Spell-Out, the way an address links two separate computers.

In either version of MSO, we have now deduced (1b), which stipulates that the elements dominated by γ in a CU precede whatever γ precedes. That γ should precede or be preceded by the other elements in its CU was shown in section 10.1. The fact that the elements dominated by γ act as γ does within its CU is a direct consequence of the fact that γ has been spelled out separately from the CU it is attached to, in a different derivational cascade. The elements dominated by γ cannot interact with those that γ interacts with, in the "mother" CU. Thus, their place in the structure is as frozen under γ's dominance as would be the place of the members of a compound γ, the syllables of a word γ, or worse still, elements that have already "gone to performance."[5]

I should point out one final, important assumption I am making. The situation we have been considering can be schematized as in (7). But what prevents a projection like the one in (8)?

(7)

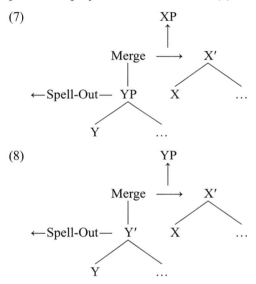

(8)

In (8), it is the spelled-out category Y′ that projects a YP. This results in forcing the linearization of X's projection prior to that of Y's, contrary to fact.

The problem is somewhat familiar. In systems with a single Spell-Out, both Kayne and Chomsky must resort to ad hoc solutions to avoid this sort of undesired result involving specifiers. Kayne eliminates the distinction between adjuncts and specifiers,[6] and Chomsky defines command in a peculiar way: only for heads and maximal projections, although intermediate projections must be "taken into account" as well.[7]

Within the conservative implementation of MSO, (8) can be prevented if *only lexical items project*. Again, MSO is designed to collapse a phrase marker into a compound of sorts. Yet this "word" cannot be seen as an item that projects any further; it can merge with something else, but it can never be the item that supports further lexical dependencies. This might relate to some of Chomsky's (to appear) conjectures regarding a fundamental asymmetry indirectly involved in the labeling of the Merge function; in particular, it may be that Merge (like Move) implies a form of Attract, where certain properties of one of the merging items are met by the other. It is conceivable that properties relevant to Attract are "active" only in lexical items within the lexical array, or numeration, that leads to a derivation, and not in words formed in the course of the derivation. This would include collapsed units of the sort discussed here, but it may extend as well to complex predicate formation, which is typically capped off after it takes place (there is no complex complex-predicate formation, and so on).[8] At any rate, the price to pay for unequivocal attachment of spelled-out noncomplements is to have two (perhaps not unreasonable) notions of terminals: lexicon-born ones and derived ones.

Under the radically performative interpretation of MSO, there is a trivial reason why a spelled-out chunk of structure should not project: it is gone from the syntax. The price to pay for equivocal attachment of spelled-out noncomplements is, as noted earlier, the agreement of these elements with corresponding heads.

10.3   Some Predictions for Derivations

I have essentially shown how the base step of the LCA may follow from economy, and how the induction step may follow from a minimalist architecture that makes central use of MSO, thus yielding dynamically bifurcated access to interpretive components. Given the central position it accords CUs, this architecture makes certain predictions. In a nutshell, command is important because it is only within CUs that syntactic terms "communicate" with each other, in a derivational cascade.

To get a taste of this sort of prediction, consider Chomsky's (1995) notion of *distance*, which is sensitive to command. The reason for involving command in the characterization of distance is empirical and concerns Superiority effects of the following sort:

(9) a.   who *t* saw what
     b.   *what did who see *t*
     c.   which professor *t* saw which student
     d.   which student did which professor see *t*

Chomsky's account capitalizes on the simple fact that the competing *wh*-elements (*who, what, which*) stand in a command relation in (9a,b), but clearly not in (9c,d), as (10a) and (10b) show, respectively.[9]

(10) a. [C [who ... [saw what]]]

    b. [C [[which professor] ... [saw [which student]]]]

Thus, he defines distance in terms of the following proviso:

(11) Only if α commands β can α be closer to a higher γ than β is.

This is the case in (10a): the target C is closer to *who* than to *what*. Crucially, though, in (10b) the target C is as close to the *which* in *which professor* as it is to the *which* in *which student*; these positions being equidistant from C, both movements in (9c) and (9d) are allowed, as desired. Needless to say, this solution works. But why should this be? Why is command relevant?

In MSO terms, the explanation is direct. The two *wh*-elements in (10a) belong to the same derivational cascade, since they are assembled through Merge into the same CU. This is not true of the two *wh*-phrases in (10b); in particular, *which professor* and *which student* are assembled in different CUs and hence do not compete within the same derivational space (I return below to how the *wh*-features in each instance are even accessible). The fact that the phrases are equally close to the target C is thus expected, being architecturally true, and need not be stated in a definition of distance.

It might seem that this idea does not carry through to the radically performative interpretation of MSO; but in fact it does. Even if *which professor* in (10b) is in some sense gone from the syntactic computation, the relevant (here, *wh*-) feature that is attracted to the periphery of the clause stays accessible, again for reasons that I return to shortly.

The general architectural reasoning that determines what information is and is not gone from the computation extends to classical restrictions on extraction domains, which must be complements.[10] The contrast in (12) is extremely problematic for the Minimalist Program.

(12) a. [... X [... *t* ...]]

    e.g., *who did you see [a critic of* t*]*

    b. [[... *t* ...] X ...]

    e.g., **who did [a critic of* t*] see you*

The problem is that whatever licenses (12a) in terms of the Minimal Link Condition or Last Resort should also license (12b); so what is wrong with the latter? A minimalist should not simply translate the observation in (12) into a new principle; such a principle must again fall within the general desiderata of the program—and thus reduce to economy or bare output conditions. I know of no minimalist way of explaining the contrast in (12).[11]

But now consider the problem from the MSO perspective. A complement is very different from any other dependent of a head in that the elements a complement dominates are within the same CU of the "governing" head, whereas this is not true for the elements a noncomplement dominates. As a result, extraction from a complement can occur within the same derivational cascade, whereas extraction from a noncomplement cannot, given my assumptions. Basically, the following paradox arises. If a noncomplement is spelled out independently from its head, any extraction from the noncomplement will involve material from something that is not even a syntactic object (or, more radically, not even there); thus, it should be as hard as extracting part of a compound (or worse). On the other hand, if the noncomplement is not spelled out in order to allow extraction from it, then it will not be possible to collapse its elements, always assuming that the only procedure for linearization is the command-precedence correspondence that economy considerations sanction.

Of course, one might now wonder how such simple structures as (13) can ever be generated, with movement of a complex *wh*-phrase.

(13) [[which professor] [did you say [*t* left]]]

If, for the collapse of a complex noncomplement's elements to be sanctioned, they must be spelled out before they merge with the rest of the phrase marker, how can movement of noncomplements exist? Shouldn't such elements be pronounced where they are spelled out?

(14) *[did you say [[which professor] left]]

The answer to this puzzle relates to the pending question of *wh*-feature accessibility in spelled-out phrases. I address both matters in the following section.

10.4   General Predictions for the Interpretive Components

The dynamically split model that MSO involves produces derivational cascades, each of which reaches the interpretive components in its own derivational life. If this model is correct, we should see some evidence of the relevant dynamics.

Let us start with PF matters. The first sort of prediction that comes to mind relates to work by Cinque (1993), which goes back to Chomsky's

(1972) observations on focus "projections." Generally speaking, the focus that manifests itself on a (complement) "right branch" may project higher up in the phrase marker, whereas this is not the case for the focus that manifests itself on a (noncomplement) "left branch." For instance, consider (15).

(15) a. Michaelangelo painted THOSE FRESCOES
     b. MICHAELANGELO painted those frescoes

(15a) can answer several questions: "What did Michaelangelo paint?", "What did Michaelangelo do?", and even "What happened?" In contrast, (15b) can only answer the question "Who painted those frescoes?" Why?

The architecture discussed here is very consistent with the asymmetry, regardless of the ultimate nature of focal "projection" or spreading (about which I will say nothing). The main contribution that MSO can make to the matter is evident: for this model, focus can only spread within a CU— that is, through a "right branch." Spreading up a "left branch" would involve moving across two different CUs and hence would be an instance of a "cross-dimensional" communication between different elements.[12]

There are other phonological domains that conform to this picture, predicting that a pause or a parenthetical phrase will sound natural between subject and predicate, for instance, or between any phrase and its adjuncts.

(16) a. Natural: Michaelangelo ... painted those frescoes
        Unnatural or emphatic: Michaelangelo painted ... those frescoes
     b. Natural: Michaelangelo painted those frescoes ... in Florence
        Unnatural or emphatic, or different in interpretation:
        Michaelangelo painted ... those frescoes in Florence

The same results are obtained by replacing the dots in (16) with standard fillers like *you know*, *I'm told*, or *I've heard* (see Selkirk 1984).

There are interesting complications, too. For example, Kaisse (1985) and Nespor and Vogel (1986) suggest that functional items phonologically associate to the lexical head they govern. Consider the examples in (17), from Lebeaux 1996, where underlined items are phonologically phrased together.

(17) a. <u>John</u> <u>may have seen</u> <u>Mary</u>
     b. <u>the picture</u> <u>of Mary</u>

These sorts of paradigms are compatible with the MSO proposal, although something else must be responsible for the cliticization (note, within a given CU).

One can think of harder cases. A particularly difficult one from Galician is mentioned in Uriagereka 1988.

(18) vimo-los   pallasos chegar
     saw.we-the clowns   arrive
     'we saw the clowns arrive'

In this language, determiners surprisingly cliticize to previous, often thematically nonrelated heads; in (18), for instance, the determiner introducing the embedded subject attaches to the verb that takes as internal argument the reduced clause that this subject is part of. The sort of analysis I have given elsewhere (Uriagereka 1988, 1996a), whereby the determiner syntactically moves to the position shown in (18), is contrary to expectations, given my present account of the paradigm in (12). Otero (1996) gives reasons to believe that the determiner cliticization cannot be syntactic, but is instead a late morphophonological process; if my present analysis is correct, then Otero's general conclusion must also be correct.

Otero's suggestion is in fact compatible with the general MSO architecture, so long as prosodic phrasing is allowed to take place after Spell-Out, naturally enough in terms of the edges of "adjacent" (or successively spelled out) cascades of structure (see Otero 1996, 316; Lasnik 1995; and more generally Bobaljik 1995 and references cited there). This is straightforward for the conservative version of MSO, but is possible as well in the radical version, so long as prosody is a unifying mechanism in performance (in the same league as agreement, in the sense above).

In fact, the radical version of MSO can rather naturally account for the variant of (18) given in (19).

(19) *vimo-los   pallasos chegaren (but OK: *vimos os pallasos chegaren*)
     saw.we-the clowns   arrive.they
     'we saw the clowns arrive'

A minor change in the form of (18)—introducing agreement in the infinitival, the *-en* morpheme after *chegar* 'arrive'—makes the determiner cliticization impossible. This can be explained if the cliticization is a form of agreement, in which case the subject of the embedded clause in (19) is forced to agree with two elements at once: the inflected infinitival and the matrix verb. If agreement is indeed an address, as is expected in the radical version of MSO, the kind of duplicity in (19) is unwanted; see the Agreement Criterion below.[13]

Needless to say, this bird's-eye view of the problem does little justice to
the complex issues involved in prosodic phrasing, not to mention liaison,
phrasal stress, pausing, and other related topics. My only intention has
been to point out what is perhaps already obvious: within the MSO system, "left branches" should be natural bifurcation points for PF processes, if the present architecture is correct. At the same time, if we find
"communication" across the outputs of derivational cascades, the natural
thing to do is attribute it to performative (at any rate, post-Spell-Out)
representations, plausibly under cascade adjacency.

Similar issues arise for the LF component, where immediate predictions
can be made and rather interesting problems again arise. The general
prediction should by now be rather obvious: CUs are natural domains for
LF phenomena. This is true for a variety of processes (binding of different
sorts, obviation, scopal interactions, negative polarity licensing); it is indeed much harder to find instances of LF processes that do not involve
command than otherwise. (Though there are such instances, to which I
return.) More importantly, we must observe that CUs are just a subcase
of the situations where command emerges.

A problematic instance is patent in a now familiar structure, (20).

(20)

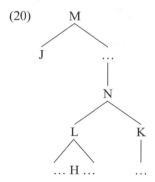

Although J and H are not part of the same CU (the latter is part of a CU
dominated by L), J commands H. Empirically, we want the relation in
(20) to hold in cases of antecedence, where J tries to be H's antecedent
(*every boy thinks that* [*his father*] *hates him*). The question is, if J and H
are in different "syntactic dimensions"—after L is spelled out—how can J
ever relate to H?

The logic of the system forces an answer that is worth pursuing: there
are aspects of the notion of antecedence that are irreducibly nonderiva-
tional. This might mean that antecedence is a semantic or pragmatic

notion; either way, we are pushing it out of the architecture seen thus far—at least in part. The hedge is needed because we still want antecedence to be sensitive to command, even if it does not hold within the CUs that determine derivational cascades. As it turns out, the dynamically split system has a bearing on this as well.

Essentially, we want to be able to say that J in (20) can be the antecedent of H, but H cannot antecede anything within K. The radical and the conservative versions of the proposal deal with this matter differently, as follows.

For the conservative view, recall that although L in (20) is not a syntactic object after Spell-Out, it does have internal structure, and its information is not lost. To see this in detail, suppose that before Spell-Out, L had the internal structure of *his father*, that is, {*his*, {*his*, *father*}}. After Spell-Out, the structure becomes {*his*, ⟨*his*, *father*⟩}, equivalent to {*his*, {{*his*}, {*his*, *father*}}}. By (6b), we can identify {*his*} and {*his*, *father*} as terms (and see note 4). This is an important fact because, although the linearized object is not a syntactic object, it contains terms, which the system can identify even if not operate with: they do not constitute a licit structure.[14] The point is, if the relation of antecedence is based on the identification of a term like {*his*}, even the linearized structure does the job, inaccessible as it is to any further syntactic operation. (This highlights, I believe, the fact that *accessibility* is not the same as *interpretability*.)

But consider the converse situation, where in spite of H's being a term in (21), it cannot be the antecedent of L or K.[15]

(21)

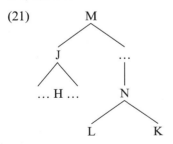

This suggests that α's *antecedent* be characterized as in (22).

(22) Where α is a term in a derivational cascade D, a term β is α's antecedent only if β has accessed interpretation in D.

This determination of *α's antecedent* is derivational, unlike the notion *term* in (6), which is neutral with respect to whether it is characterized derivationally or not. It is worth noting that (22) is suggested as part of a definition, not of *antecedence*, but of *antecedent of* α.[16] The formal aspects of the notion in (22) are compatible with the system presented thus far, but its substantive character—that only a term that accesses LF in D can be an antecedent of the terms in D—does not follow from the architecture, at least in its conservative shape.

Under the radical version of the MSO architecture, the internal structure of the spelled-out phrase isn't relevant, since in this instance the phrasal architecture of the syntactic object needn't be destroyed (what guarantees inaccessibility is the fact that the phrase has been sent to performance). In turn, this version has an intriguing way of justifying (22).

As noted earlier, a problem for the performative approach is how to associate cashed-out structures to the positions where they make the intended sense. Antecedence as a process may be intricately related to this association problem. Simply put, the system ships structure X to the interpretive components; later, it comes up with structure Y, within which X must meaningfully find its place. This presupposes an addressing technique, so that X "knows" where in Y it belongs; by hypothesis, agreement is the relevant technique. It is natural, then, that X *as a whole* should seek a place *within a part* of Y. Now consider (22), and let α be a term within an active structure Y, and β an already cashed-out term (either X itself or part of it). Why should β be the antecedent of α only if β accesses interpretation in Y's derivational cascade?

To answer this question, observe, first of all, that the performative version of MSO makes slightly more sense if the system works "top down" than if it works "bottom up." Chomsky (to appear) discusses this type of system and correctly points out that it is perfectly reasonable within present assumptions; Drury (1998) develops one such alternative. The only point that is relevant here is whether a series of noncomplements are sent to performance starting from the root of the phrase marker or from its foot. The logic of the system always forces a given noncomplement to access performance prior to the CU it associates with. Suppose this "top-down" behavior is generalized, so that the first noncomplement after the root of the phrase marker is shipped to performance first, the second noncomplement next, and so on, until finally the root CU is cashed out—as in Drury's (1998) system.

With regard to antecedence, then, (22) amounts to this: for β to be α's antecedent, β must have been sent to performance before α—in fact, in a derivational cascade that is "live" through the address mechanism of agreement. In other words, antecedence presupposes agreement, which is very consistent with the well-known diachronic fact that agreement systems are grammaticalizations of antecedence/pronoun relations (see Barlow and Fergusson 1988).

The intuition is that agreement is merely a pointer between two phrase markers, one that is gone from the system, and one that is still active in syntactic terms. Material within the cashed-out phrase marker is "out of sight"; the system only sees the unit as a whole for conceptual-intentional reasons (as the label that hooks up the agreement mechanism), and perhaps the phonological edges (under adjacency among cascades) for articulatory-perceptual reasons. Consequently, just as prosodic adjustments can take place only in the visible edges of the cashed-out material, so antecedence can be established only via the visible top of the phrase that establishes agreement with the syntactically active phrase (cf. (21)).

The fact that the variable bound by the antecedent *can* be inside a cashed-out noncomplement (as in (20)) is perfectly reasonable if this variable serves no syntactic purpose vis-à-vis the antecedent. Differently put, whereas the syntactically active part of the structure needs to know where the antecedent is, it does not need to know precisely where the variable is, so long as it is interpretable within the cashed-out structure. This makes sense. The antecedent is a unique element that determines the referential or quantificational properties of an expression; in contrast, the variable (a) is not unique (many semantic variables can be associated with a given antecedent) and (b) serves no purpose beyond its own direct association to some particular predicate—it determines nothing for other parts of the structure.

In sum, if the radical MSO view is correct, antecedence is a semantic process that is paratactically instantiated through the transderivational phenomenon of agreement: the antecedent must syntactically agree (abstractly, of course; the agreement may or may not be realized morphologically with the structure that contains its associated variable). There is no structural restriction on the variable,[17] although semantically it will be a successful variable only if it happens to match up with the agreement features of its antecedent.

10.5   How Noncomplements Can Move

Consider next a question we left pending: why (13), repeated here, is perfect.

(23) [[which professor] [did you say [*t* left]]]

Let us first evaluate this example from the perspective of the radical version of MSO. Strictly speaking, the phrase *which professor* is never directly connected to the structure above it—not even to the predicate *left*. Rather, it agrees with the relevant connecting points, which are presumably occupied by some categorial placeholder [D] (much in the spirit of ideas that go back to Lebeaux 1988). It is [D] that receives a θ-role, moves to a Case-checking position, and eventually ends up in the *wh*-site—which must mean that [D] hosts thematic, Case, and *wh*-information, at least. It is thus not that surprising, from this perspective, that the *wh*-feature should be accessible to the system even after the spelling out of *which professor* (wherever it takes place), since what stays accessible is not an element within *which professor*, but an element the [D] category carries all along, which eventually matches up with the appropriate features of *which professor*, as in (24).

(24) [which professor]$_i$ ... [[D]$_i$ [you say [[D]$_i$ left]]]

An immediate question is why the "minitext" in (24) is not pronounced as follows:

(25) [[D]$_i$ [you say [[D]$_i$ left]]] ... [which professor]$_i$

Reasonably, though, this relates again to the phenomenon of antecedence, and in particular the familiarity/novelty condition; in speech, information that sets up a discourse comes before old or anaphoric information (see Hoffman 1996 for essentially this idea).

A second question relates to the Condition on Extraction Domain (CED) effect account: why can't (12b) now be salvaged as in (26a)? Strictly, (26a) cannot be linearized, since the subject of *see you* is too complex. But suppose we proceed in two steps, as in (26b).

(26) a. [who]$_i$ ... [[a critic of [D]$_i$] see you]
    b. [who]$_j$ ... [a critic of [D]$_j$]$_i$ ... [[D]$_i$ see you]

There is a minimal, yet important, difference between (26b) and (20), where we do want J to relate to H as its antecedent. Whereas there is a relation of grammar that tries to connect *who* and [D] (the equivalent of its trace) in (26b), no relation of grammar connects an antecedent J to a bound variable H in (20). In other words, we want the long-distance relation in (26b) to be akin to movement, but clearly not in (20). But how is long-distance movement captured in the radical version of MSO, if we allow associations like the one in (24), where *which professor* has never been inside the skeletal phrase?

The key is the [D] element, which moves to the relevant sites and associates via agreement to whatever phrase has been cashed out. In (26b), the [D] inside *a critic of* must associate to *who* (alternatively, if *of who* is a complement of *critic*, this element moves out directly—but see note 14). Now, how does *who* associate to the matrix C position? If *who* associates inside *a critic of*, then it does not associate in the matrix C; conversely, if *who* associates in the matrix C, as a question operator, then it cannot associate inside *a critic of*. The only way an element like *who* can grammatically relate to two or more positions at once—that is, to θ-, Case, or *wh*-positions—is if all these positions are syntactically connected, in which case it is the [D] element that moves through them and eventually associates to *who*. This, of course, is what happens in the perfect (12a), repeated here.

(27) [who]$_i$ ... [[D]$_i$ [you see [a critic of [D]$_i$]]]

Here again, agreement uniqueness is at play, as I speculatively suggested regarding the ungrammaticality of (19). This important point can be stated explicitly as follows:

(28) *Agreement Criterion*
A phrase α that determines agreement in a phrase β cannot at the same time determine agreement in a phrase γ.

This criterion is tantamount to saying that agreement is a rigidly unique address. It may well be that (28) follows from deeper information-theoretic matters, but I will not pursue that possibility here.[18]

The conservative version of MSO can also account successfully for (23), although (naturally) with assumptions that do not bear on agreement considerations and instead introduce very different operational mechanics. As before, the issue is to somehow have access to *which professor*, even though this phrase must also be sent to Spell-Out if it attaches as a noncomplement. This statement looks contradictory; but whether it is or not depends on exactly how the details of movement are assumed to work.

Consider whether the two steps involved in movement—copying some material and then merging it—must immediately feed one another, within a given derivation. Suppose we assume that Move is a collection of operations, as several researchers have recently argued (see, e.g., Kitahara

1994; Nunes 1995). Thus, movement of a complex phrase marker may proceed in several steps—for example, as in (29).

(29) a. Copy one of two independently merged phrases

b. Spell out the lower copy as trace

c. Merge the trace

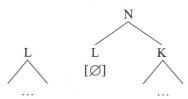

d. Merge the higher copy (possibly in a separate derivation)

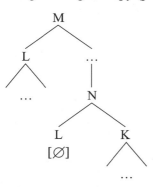

The key is the "in parallel" strategy implicit in (29a,b); the rest of the steps are straightforward. So let us see whether those initial steps can be justified.

Technically, what takes place in (29a,b) is, at least at first sight, the same as what takes place in the formation of a phrase marker as in (30).

(30) a. Numeration: {the, a, man, saw, woman, ...}

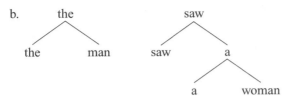

Prior to merging [*the man*] and [*saw* [*a woman*]], the system must assemble them in separate, completely parallel derivational spaces; there is no way of avoiding this, assuming Merge and standard phrasal properties of DPs and VPs. (29a) capitalizes on this possibility; instead of copying lexical items from the numeration, as in (30), in (29a) the system copies the items from the assembled phrase marker.

In turn, (29b) employs the option of deleting phonetic material, thus making it unavailable for PF interpretation. It is reasonable to ask why this step is involved, but the question is no different from that posed by Nunes (this volume), concerning why the copy of K in (31) is not pronounced when K is moved.

(31) a. [K ... [... K ...] ...]

 b. [K ... [... [∅] ...] ...]

Why is *who did you see* not pronounced *who did you see who*? After all, if movement is copying plus deletion, why is deletion necessary, particularly at PF?

Nunes's answer capitalizes on the LCA, by assuming that identical copies are indeed identical. Hence, Kayne's linearization question has no solution; for instance, in the above example does *who* command, or is it commanded by, *you*? It depends on which *who* we're talking about. One is tempted to treat each of these as a token of a lexical type, but they are not; each *who* (other than the lexically inserted occurrence) emerges as a result of mere derivational dynamics. Then there is no solution unless, Nunes reasons, the system deletes one of the copies on its way to PF (the place where linearization is required in Chomsky's system). If only one copy of *who* is left, the linearization answer is trivial: in standard terms, the remaining copy precedes whatever it commands.[19]

(29b) has the same justification as Nunes's copy deletion. Note that if the system does not spell out the lower copy of L as a trace, when it reaches the stage represented in (29d), it will not be able to determine whether L commands or is commanded by all other elements in the phrase marker, and thus this object will not collapse into a valid PF realization.

In effect, then, there is a way to keep something like *which professor* accessible even if it starts its derivational life as a subject, by making a copy of it in advance and having that copy be the one that merges in the ultimate spell-out site, the other(s) being spelled out as trace(s). A question remains, however: why can't this procedure provide a gambit for escaping the ungrammaticality of CED effects? For example, what prevents the following grammatical derivation of (26)?

1. Assemble *see you* and *a critic of who*.
2. Copy *who* in parallel.
3. Realize the first copy of *who* as a trace.
4. Merge *a critic of t* to *see you* and all the way up to the C projection.
5. Attach the stored copy of *who* as the specifier of C.

A way to prevent this unwanted derivation capitalizes on the desire to limit the globality of computational operations, as argued for in Chomsky, to appear, and references cited there. Step 2 in the derivation is clearly very global: at the point of merging *who*, the system must know that this element will be attracted further up in the phrase marker—in a completely different derivational cascade. Crucially, the system cannot wait until the matrix C appears in order to make a copy (in a parallel derivational space) of *who*, thereby making the already attached copy of *who* silent (i.e., a trace); in particular, it cannot simply go back to the site of *who* and add the instruction to delete after it has abandoned the "cycle" *a critic of who*, since that operation would be countercyclic. It is literally when the "lower" *who* attaches that the system must know to take it as a trace (cf. (29)), which entails that the system must have access to the C that attracts *who*, even when it has not yet left the numeration.

Let us again consider all the relevant examples side by side (CUs are boxed, trace copies are parenthesized).

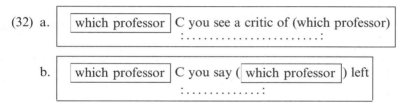

(32) a. | which professor | C you see a critic of (which professor)

b. | which professor | C you say (| which professor |) left c.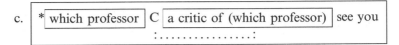

(32a) is straightforward. Before the movement of *which professor*, the sentence involves a single CU, within which C trivially attracts the necessary *wh*-feature; after *which professor* pied-pipes along with this *wh*-feature, a new CU emerges, which is of no particular interest. (32b) and (32c) are more complicated, since they involve two CUs *prior* to *wh*-movement. The issue is how they differ.

We saw earlier that the derivation in (32c) cannot proceed cyclically if it is allowed to go all the way up to the CP level, then to return to the lower *which professor* and delete it. Rather, at the point when *which professor* attaches, the system must know that it is being (overtly) attracted by C and hence must copy it in parallel and attach the initial copy as a trace. The same is true of *which professor* in (32b), but there C and (the entire phrase) *which professor* are at least part of the same CU, whereas in (32c) (the entire phrase) *which professor* is part of the CU of *a critic of which professor*, and C is not. This must be the key: as expected, only elements within the same CU can relate.

But then, isn't (33) still a problem?

(33) a critic of which professor saw you

(34) | a critic of which professor | C (| a critic of which professor |) see you

The difference between (32c) and (33)/(34) is this. In the former, the system must decide to copy *which professor* as a trace while in the CU of *a critic of which professor*. In the latter, it is not *which professor* but *a critic of which professor* that is copied as a trace; hence, the system can reach the copying decision while in the CU where C is merged—that is, locally. At the same time, deletion of *a critic of which professor* is a cyclic process if we define the "cycle" within the confines of a CU that hasn't been abandoned.

To make matters explicit, I state the following principle:

(35) *Principle of Strict Cyclicity*
All syntactic operations take place within the derivational cycles of CUs.

In other words, the cascades of derivational activity that we have seen all along are responsible for limiting the class of activities the system engages in, in purely operational terms. Cross-cascade relations of any sort—Attract, Move, backtracking for deletion purposes, or presumably any others—are strictly forbidden by (35); a derivation that violates (35) is immediately canceled.

10.6 Beyond Derivations

In both versions of MSO, CUs are crucial. This is explicitly encoded in (35), for the conservative view, and is trivially true in the radical view, where only CUs exist in competence grammar—unification of CUs being left for performance. If the present model is anywhere near right, this fact can be used as a wedge to separate various sorts of phenomena; essentially, cyclic ones are syntactic, whereas noncyclic ones are paratactic, or perhaps not syntactic at all. We looked at two of the former: cliticization across CUs in the PF component, and the establishment of antecedent relations in the LF component. Even though these phenomena were suggested not to be strictly derivational, the derivational results were taken to importantly limit the class of possible relations involved in each instance —adjacency of cascades for PF, "top" of CUs for LF—as if syntax carved the path interpretation must blindly follow. But are there situations in which syntax leaves no significant imprint on representational shapes?

Presumably that would happen, within present assumptions, whenever a systematic phenomenon simply does not care about command, or even exhibits anticommand behavior. Weak crossover may well be one such instance. I want to suggest the possibility of analyzing a typical weak crossover effect, as in (36b), as a violation of the condition on novelty/ familiarity, which I take to be pragmatic.

(36) a. his friend knocked on the door / a man came in
      b. his friend killed a man

The familiar *his* cannot antecede the novel *a man* in (36b) any more than it can in (36a). This is so, of course, only if we adopt the null hypothesis that the novelty or familiarity of a given file is assumed not just across separate sentences (36a), but also intrasententially (36b). (This must be the case, virtually by definition, for the radical version of MSO, for which each separate CU is a text.)

In order to extend this sort of analysis to the examples in (37), we must postulate that the operators that trigger weak crossover involve an existence predicate of the sort postulated by Klima and Kuroda in the 1960s (see Chomsky 1964), which gives them a characteristic indefinite or existential character.[20]

(37) a. his friend killed everyone
     b. who did his friend kill

That is, the logical form of *everyone* must be as coded in its morphology: *every x*, *one (x)*. Something similar must be said about *who*; this would be consistent with the morphological shape of such elements in East Asian languages (see, e.g., Kim 1991; Watanabe 1992; and references cited there). Then the existence element will induce a novelty effect with regard to the familiar pronoun, as desired.

The point I am trying to establish is simple. Postsyntactic machinery may be needed to account for some familiar phenomena. The fact that they involve LF representations in the Government-Binding model doesn't necessarily force us to treat them as LF phenomena in the present system —so long as we treat them somehow. I strongly suspect that Condition C of the binding theory is another such phenomenon—as are, more generally, matters pertaining to long-distance processes that are extremely difficult to capture in purely syntactic terms (e.g., some kinds of anaphora, unbounded ellipsis under parallelism).

10.7 Conclusions

The system I have programmatically sketched in this chapter is much more dynamically derivational than its alternative in Chomsky 1995 (although it approximates the one in Chomsky, to appear, to the point of being conceptually indistinguishable). That the system is derivational, and that it is dynamically (or cyclically) so, are both interesting ideas in their own right, with a variety of consequences for locality and the class of representations the architecture allows. Curiously, one consequence (best illustrated in Weinberg, this volume) is that the gap between competence and performance is partly bridged, radically so in one version of the program. This has a repercussion for competence: it provides a rationale for the existence of agreement.

Notes

The contents of this chapter have been presented in several lectures, at the Universities of Connecticut, Delaware, Maryland, Pennsylvania, Stuttgart, Portoalegre (Catholic), Potsdam, and Rio de Janeiro (Federal); the City University of

New York; the National University of Comahue; Oxford and Yale Universities; the Max Planck (Berlin), San Raffaelle (Milan), and Ortega y Gasset (Madrid) Institutes; and the School of African Studies in London. Warm thanks to the generous hosts of these institutions, as well as the various audiences, for comments, questions, and criticisms. I am indebted to Juan Carlos Castillo, Stephen Crain, John Drury, Jim Higginbotham, Howard Lasnik, Roger Martin, Javi Ormazabal, and especially Norbert Hornstein and Jairo Nunes for very useful commentary, and both Maggie Browning (initially) and Norbert Hornstein (eventually) for their interest, as editors, in these ideas. This research was partially funded by NSF grant SBR 9601559.

1. For instance, in Bresnan 1971, Jackendoff 1972, or Lasnik 1972. Tree-adjoining grammars explored in, for example, Kroch 1989 also have the desired feature.

2. The reasons why compounds and spelled-out phrase markers are "frozen" are completely different (a real compound does not collapse), but the formal effect is the same.

3. This would be very much in the spirit of Hoffman's (1996) idea that syntactic unification is not given by the derivation itself.

4. I assume the standard definition of a sequence $\langle a, b \rangle$ as a set $\{\{a\}, \{a, b\}\}$ (see, for instance, Quine 1970, 65). Jim Higginbotham (personal communication) observes that the notation $\{a, \{a, b\}\}$ would also have the desired effects, although touching on a deep issue concerning whether one assumes the Foundation Axiom (or whether the individual a is allowed to be identified with the set $\{a\}$). For the most part, I would like to put these issues aside, although I cannot fail to mention two things. One, if one assumes Quine's notation, as we will see shortly, syntactic terminals will ultimately turn out to be defined as objects of the form $\{terminal\}$, rather than objects of the form $terminal$. Two, this might not be a bad result, given that in general we want to distinguish labels from terms, which could be done by way of the definition of term in (6), stating that labels are members of (set) phrase markers that are not terms. Then the problem is terminal items, which clearly are terms but need to be labeled as well. One possibility is to consider a given terminal term as labeled only after it has been linearized, hence having been turned by the system to a $\{terminal\}$ (the whole object is a term; thus, $terminal$ is its label).

5. Note that the most natural interpretation of the radical version of MSO ships noncomplements to performance prior to the rest of the structure, thus proceeds top-down. This matter becomes even more significant below, when we discuss antecedence.

6. If specifiers are adjuncts, one can then attribute their being linearized prior to corresponding heads to the (poorly understood) concept of adjunction.

7. If command is not defined for an intermediate projection, this category will never command (hence precede) its specifier. The converse is true by fiat, given that a specifier is by definition a maximal projection. At the same time, intermediate projections must be relevant in computing command; if they were not, a head and its specifier would command, hence precede, each other.

8. The most difficult case does not arise when a specifier projects (the system prevents this on grounds of chain uniformity and similar considerations pertaining to checking domains). Rather, it arises when the system sees an intermediate projection as a branch to Spell-Out and later, after spelling it out, continues projecting it by merging it with a specifier. That should be perfectly fine, and it leads to an object that is linearized "backward," with the specifier coming last.

9. See Kitahara 1993 and 1994 for the source of these ideas.

10. The presentation that follows owes much to useful discussions with Jairo Nunes and to Nunes 1995.

11. Ormazabal, Uriagereka, and Uribe-Etxebarria (1994) and (independently) Takahashi (1994) do make proposals about the matter, which prevent extractions from inside subjects in terms of the Uniformity Condition. However, unlike the present proposal, neither of these naturally extends to extractions from inside adjuncts (assuming adjuncts are noncomplements). This view is generally contrary to the spirit of Larson 1988—in particular, the idea that direct objects are structurally high in the phrase marker.

12. Note that the facts are no different if the subject is a pronoun. That is, (i) allows no more of a focus projection than (15b).

(i) HE painted those frescoes

This must mean that, despite appearances, pronouns (at least focused ones) are complex enough, in phrasal terms, to trigger a separate Spell-Out.

13. Certainly, instances of a phrase simultaneously agreeing with two heads are not attested (setting aside chains, which are not phrases). The intuition is that multiple agreement as in (19) creates a "Necker cube" effect, which the Agreement Criterion explicitly prevents (see section 10.6).

14. Interestingly, *father* does not turn out to be a term. In fact, no "last" element in a right branch ever turns out to be a term after a phrase marker is linearized. (Of course, prior to that, these elements are normal terms.) Technically, this entails that such elements cannot have an antecedent, which if pushed to a logical extreme might well mean that they cannot have reference. This would lend itself nicely to the idea, expressed in Uriagereka 1996b, that the "last" element in a right branch is always the predicate of a small clause; and it bears on the analysis of examples like (i).

(i) every politician thinks that [some picture of him] should be destroyed

Castillo (1998) argues that the correct structure for *picture of him* involves, in the lexical base, the small clause [*him* [*picture*]]; if that analysis is correct, *him* is actually not a complement, but a subject of sorts (of which *picture* is "integrally" predicated, in the sense developed in Hornstein, Rosen, and Uriagereka 1996). If so, *him* turns out to be a term and can be bound by *every*.

15. At least, it is not obvious that an antecedent buried inside a "left branch" can hook up with a variable in a different command path. There are well-known (apparent?) exceptions, such as (i), or similar instances involving "inverse linking" or what look like bound anaphors in East Asian languages.

(i) ?everyone's mother likes him

To the extent that these examples are acceptable, they may well involve a process akin to, but formally unlike, variable binding. If pronouns like *him* in (i) can be analyzed as incomplete definite descriptions, then (i) may have the meaning of something like (ii):

(ii) everyone's mother likes "the one that is relevant"

By cooperatively confining the range of the context variable of *him*, we may end up with a semantics that is truth-conditionally equivalent to that implicit in (i). (See Uriagereka 1997 for a similar treatment of certain anaphors, which may extend to the East Asian instances.) Then the question is what conditions govern context confinement, something that need not be sensitive to the strict command restrictions that are presently being explored for the syntax.

16. I mention this to address a reasonable objection that Jim Higginbotham raises in personal communication: semantically, it makes sense to say that "an anaphor seeks an antecedent"; but what does it mean to say that "an antecedent seeks an anaphor"? The issue is turned on its head immediately below, where I show how the radical version of the MSO proposal can deal with general issues of antecedence.

17. Evidently, I am speaking of bound-variable pronouns, not of anaphors subject to local principles—which presumably involve some sort of movement to the antecedent. Those, of course, are impossible unless antecedent and anaphor share the same CU, as expected given the MSO architecture.

18. The Agreement Criterion does not preclude an antecedent from binding two different pronouns, since the definition of antecedence requires only that the would-be antecedent agree with the phrase containing the bindee(s).

19. Why is it the lower and not the upper copy that deletes (although to solve the linearization riddle either one would do)? Here, Nunes relies on the mechanics of feature checking. Basically, feature checking takes place in the checking domain of the attracting phrase marker, and thus it is the copy in that domain that remains within the system. For present purposes, this is immaterial.

20. In the past few years, this sort of idea has been revamped by various researchers (see, e.g., Pica and Snyder 1995).

References

Barlow, Michael, and Charles Fergusson. 1988. *Agreement in natural language.* Chicago: University of Chicago Press.

Bobaljik, Jonathan David. 1995. Morphosyntax: The syntax of verbal inflection. Doctoral dissertation, MIT, Cambridge, Mass.

Bresnan, Joan. 1971. Sentence stress and syntactic transformations. *Language* 47, 257–281.

Castillo, Juan Carlos. 1998. The syntax of container/content relations. In *University of Maryland working papers in linguistics 6*, eds. Elixabete Murgia,

Acrisio Pires, and Lucia Quintana. Department of Linguistics, University of Maryland, College Park.

Chomsky, Noam. 1964. *Current issues in linguistic theory*. The Hague: Mouton.

Chomsky, Noam. 1972. *Studies in semantics in generative grammar*. The Hague: Mouton.

Chomsky, Noam. 1994. Bare phrase structure. (MIT Occasional Papers in Linguistics 5.) MITWPL, Department of Linguistics and Philosophy, MIT, Cambridge, Mass. [Also in *Government and Binding Theory and the Minimalist Program*, ed. Gert Webelhuth. Oxford: Blackwell, 1995, and *Evolution and revolution in linguistic theory: Essays in honor of Carlos Otero*, eds. Héctor Campos and Paula Kempchinsky. Washington, D.C.: Georgetown University Press, 1995.]

Chomsky, Noam. 1995. Categories and transformations. In *The Minimalist Program*. Cambridge, Mass.: MIT Press.

Chomsky, Noam. To appear. Minimalist inquires: The framework. In *Step by step: Essays on minimalism in honor of Howard Lasnik*, eds. Roger Martin, David Michaels, and Juan Uriagereka. Cambridge, Mass.: MIT Press.

Cinque, Guglielmo. 1993. A null theory of phrase and compound stress. *Linguistic Inquiry* 24, 239–298.

Drury, John. 1998. Root-first command-path derivations and multiple Spellout. In *University of Maryland working papers in linguistics 6*, eds. Elixabete Murgia, Acrisio Pires, and Lucia Quintana. Department of Linguistics, University of Maryland, College Park.

Higginbotham, James. 1983. A note on phrase markers. *Revue québécoise de linguistique* 13, 147–166.

Hoffman, Joel. 1996. Syntactic and paratactic word-order effects. Doctoral dissertation, University of Maryland, College Park.

Hornstein, Norbert, Sara Rosen, and Juan Uriagereka. 1996. Integral existentials. In *Proceedings of the Fourteenth West Coast Conference on Formal Linguistics*, eds. José Camacho, Lina Choueiri, and Maki Watanabe. Stanford, Calif.: CSLI Publications. [Distributed by Cambridge University Press.]

Jackendoff, Ray. 1972. Semantic interpretation in generative grammar. Cambridge, Mass.: MIT Press.

Kaisse, Ellen. 1985. *Connected speech: The interaction of syntax and phonology*. New York: Academic Press.

Kayne, Richard. 1994. *The antisymmetry of syntax*. Cambridge, Mass.: MIT Press.

Kim, Soo Won. 1991. Scope and multiple quantification. Doctoral dissertation, Brandeis University, Waltham, Mass.

Kitahara, Hisatsugu. 1993. Deducing Superiority effects from the shortest chain requirement. In *Harvard working papers in linguistics 3*, eds. Höskuldur Thráinsson, Samuel David Epstein, and Susumu Kuno. Department of Linguistics, Harvard University, Cambridge, Mass.

Kitahara, Hisatsugu. 1994. Target α: A unified theory of movement and structure. Doctoral dissertation, Harvard University, Cambridge, Mass.

Kroch, Anthony. 1989. Asymmetries in long-distance extraction in Tree-Adjoining Grammar. In *Alternative conceptions of phrase structure*, eds. Mark Baltin and Anthony Kroch. Chicago: University of Chicago Press.

Larson, Richard. 1988. On the double object construction. *Linguistic Inquiry* 19, 335–391.

Lasnik, Howard. 1972. Analyses of negation in English. Doctoral dissertation, MIT, Cambridge, Mass.

Lasnik, Howard. 1995. Verbal morphology: *Syntactic Structures* meets the Minimalist Program. In *Evolution and revolution in linguistic theory: Essays in honor of Carlos Otero*, eds. Héctor Campos and Paula Kempchinsky. Washington, D.C.: Georgetown University Press.

Lebeaux, David. 1988. Language acquisition and the form of the grammar. Doctoral dissertation, University of Massachusetts, Amherst.

Lebeaux, David. 1996. Determining the kernel. In *Phrase structure and the lexicon*, eds. Johan Rooryck and Lauri Zaring. Dordrecht: Kluwer.

Martin, Roger, and Juan Uriagereka. In progress. Collapsed waves in syntax. Ms., Tsukuba University and University of Maryland, College Park.

Nespor, Marina, and Irene Vogel. 1986. *Prosodic phonology*. Dordrecht: Foris.

Nunes, Jairo. 1995. The copy theory of movement and linearization of chains in the Minimalist Program. Doctoral dissertation, University of Maryland, College Park.

Ormazabal, Javier, Juan Uriagereka, and Myriam Uribe-Etxebarria. 1994. Word order and *wh*-movement: Towards a parametric account. Talk presented at the 17th GLOW Colloquium, Vienna.

Otero, Carlos. 1996. Head movement, cliticization, precompilation, and word insertion. In *Current issues in comparative grammar*, ed. Robert Freidin. Dordrecht: Kluwer.

Pica, Pierre, and William Snyder. 1995. Weak crossover, scope, and agreement in a minimalist framework. In *Proceedings of the Thirteenth West Coast Conference on Formal Linguistics*, eds. Raul Aranovich, William Byrne, Susanne Preuss, and Martha Senturia. Stanford, Calif.: CSLI Publications. [Distributed by Cambridge University Press.]

Quine, W. V. O. 1970. *Philosophy of logic*. Englewood Cliffs, N.J.: Prentice-Hall.

Selkirk, Elisabeth. 1984. *Phonology and syntax*. Cambridge, Mass.: MIT Press.

Takahashi, Daiko. 1994. Minimality of movement. Doctoral dissertation, University of Connecticut, Storrs.

Uriagereka, Juan. 1988. On government. Doctoral dissertation, University of Connecticut, Storrs.

Uriagereka, Juan. 1996a. Determiner clitic placement. In *Current issues in comparative grammar*, ed. Robert Freidin. Dordrecht: Kluwer.

Uriagereka, Juan. 1996b. Warps: Some remarks on categorization. In *University of Maryland working papers in linguistics 4*, eds. Viola Miglio and Rikardo Etxepare. Department of Linguistics, University of Maryland, College Park.

Uriagereka, Juan. 1997. Formal and substantive elegance in the Minimalist Program. In *The role of economy principles in linguistic theory*, eds. Chris Wilder, Hans-Martin Gärtner, and Manfred Bierwisch. Berlin: Akademie-Verlag.

Uriagereka, Juan. 1998. *Rhyme and reason: An introduction to minimalist syntax.* Cambridge, Mass.: MIT Press.

Watanabe, Akira. 1992. Subjacency and S-Structure movement of *wh*-in-situ. *Journal of East Asian Linguistics* 1, 255–291.

Chapter 11

A Minimalist Theory of Human Sentence Processing

Amy Weinberg

Research in the theory of human sentence processing can be characterized by three styles of explanation. Researchers taking the first track have tried to motivate principles of structural preference from extralinguistic considerations like storage capacity in working memory or bounds on complexity of incremental analysis. Frazier and Rayner's (1982) Minimal Attachment and Right Association Principles, and Gorrell's (1995) simplicity metric, are examples of this type of theory.

The second track eschews "parsing strategies," replacing them with a fairly complex tuning by speaker/hearers to frequency in the hearer's linguistic environment. The difficulty of recovering an analysis of a construction in a particular case is a function of how often similar structures or thematic role arrays appear in the language as a whole. The work of Trueswell and Tanenhaus (1994), Jurafsky (1996), and MacDonald, Pearlmutter, and Seidenberg (1994) exemplifies frequency- or probability-based constraint satisfaction theories.

The third track takes a more representational view and ties processing principles to independently needed restrictions derived from competence and language learning. This approach claims that the natural language faculty is extremely well designed in the sense that the same principles that govern language learning also contribute to a theory of sentence processing. This track is represented by the work of Gibson (1991), Gorrell (1995), Pritchett (1992), Phillips (1995, 1996), and myself (Weinberg 1992), who argue that processing can be seen as the rapid incremental satisfaction of grammatical constraints such as the θ-Criterion, which are needed independently to explain language learning or language variation. A variant of this approach, developed by Crain and Steedman (1985) among others, retains the grammatical source for parsing principles but locates these principles within a discourse or semantic, rather than syntactic, component.

In this chapter, I propose a model of the last type. I argue that a particular version of the Minimalist Program (Chomsky 1993; Uriagereka, this volume) both provides principles needed to explain initial human preferences for ambiguous structures and provides a theory of reanalysis, explaining when initial preferences can be revised given subsequent disconfirming data and when they lead to unrevisable garden paths. I then argue that this type of theory is to be preferred to theories motivated on extralinguistic principles.

In sections 11.1 and 11.2, I discuss the Minimalist Program for syntax upon which my parsing proposals are based. The following features distinguish this theory from its precursors:

(1) The theory is derivational, providing principles that determine how an analysis is constructed rather than filtering conditions that constrain output representations. The main derivational constraints are the so-called economy conditions (Chomsky 1993).

(2) The theory applies constraints strictly locally. Derivations are evaluated at each point in the analysis. They are optimized with respect to how well they satisfy constraints of a given item that is a candidate for integration into the structure at each point. How a proposed structure satisfies constraints imposed by the derivation as a whole is irrelevant.

(3) The theory incorporates a claim about a one-to-one mapping between precedence order and structural hierarchy or dominance that is embodied in the Linear Correspondence Axiom (Kayne 1994; Uriagereka, this volume).

In sections 11.3 and 11.4, I show how to interpret minimalist principles as a parsing algorithm. Specifically, I show that the economy conditions define a crosslinguistically attested theory of preference judgments. (2) and (3) combined distinguish cases where an initial preference can be reanalyzed from those cases where reanalysis into the appropriate structure is impossible, resulting in a garden path.

In section 11.5, I compare my model of sentence processing with Colin Phillips's. Phillips shares my view that the theory of sentence processing should be based on principles of grammatical theory. The processing principles that he invokes are based on a slightly different grammatical theory, one that he claims is identical to the theory of linguistic competence. I first discuss what I see as strengths of his theory and then look at three types of problems with his approach.

In section 11.6, I argue that this type of theory has advantages over theories relying on extralinguistic frequency or parsing strategy principles, and in section 11.7, I present conclusions.

11.1 Some Minimalist Assumptions

Readers of this volume are already familiar with many of the features of the minimalist system. Here, I briefly review the features that are important for the construction of my parsing algorithm.

The two most salient features of this system are its derivational character and the role that economy conditions play in regulating possible derived structures. At least at the level of competence, the model has moved away from the overgeneration-and-filtering character of its Government-Binding precursor. Structures that do not satisfy the economy conditions are simply not generated. The two major grammatical operations (Merge and Move) used to generate structure are seen as feature checking. Categories are input from the lexicon with features such as Case and θ-role that must be checked. Checking is satisfied when a category needing a feature is in construction with some other element in the sentence that can supply that feature. Movement or merger operations are licensed only if they allow feature checking to occur. Movement or merger serves to allow an element to transfer a feature necessary to satisfy some constraint. The relevant conditions that rule out overgeneration are the following:

(4) *Last Resort*
    Operations do not apply unless required to satisfy a constraint. The minimal number of operations is applied to satisfy the constraint.

(5) *Greed*
    "The operation cannot apply to α to enable some different element β to satisfy its properties.... Benefiting other elements is not allowed." (Chomsky 1995, 201)

11.2 Multiple Spell-Out

A corollary assumption that has been incorporated into the Minimalist Program is the derivation of a correlation originally due to Kayne (1994). Previous grammatical formalisms had argued that restrictions on linear precedence and immediate dominance were the product of two separate subsystems. Kayne (1994) suggested that these two systems are linked, and that one can derive precedence information from information about dominance. This conjecture is known as the Linear Correspondence Axiom (LCA). The initial definition derived precedence from dominance. I invert the claim to make the definition relevant for parsing.

(6) *Linear Correspondence Axiom*
    a. Base step: If α precedes β, then α c-commands β.
    b. Induction step: If γ precedes β, and γ dominates α, then α precedes β.

C-command is defined as in Epstein, this volume.

(7) α c-commands all and only the terms of the category β with which α was paired by Merge or by Move in the course of the derivation.

(8) illustrates the relationships licensed by these definitions.

(8)

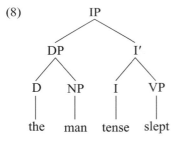

The precedence relations among elements in the subject are licensed because the determiner c-commands and precedes the NP (*man*). The second part of the definition is needed since the terminal elements in the subject position did not directly combine with the elements in the VP by either Merge or Move. Therefore, they do not c-command these VP elements even though the terminals in the subject precede those in the VP as required by the base step of the LCA. Their presence is allowed, however, by the second clause in the definition because the DP dominating both these terminals precedes the VP and dominates both the determiner and the NP, which inherit precedence by a kind of transitivity. Uriagereka (this volume) argues that the base step of the definition follows from the kind of "virtual conceptual necessity" inherent in the Minimalist Program. The simplest kind of mapping between precedence and dominance is one to one, and therefore we might expect a grammar that specifies linear and dominance order to have this simplifying restriction (see Uria-gereka, this volume, for details). The induction step forces trees to obey a "no tangling" condition as proposed by Partee, Wall, and Ter Meulen (1990) and Chametzky (1996).[1] General goals of the Minimalist Program, which try to derive features of the grammatical system from "virtual conceptual necessity," force us to either derive the induction step from other considerations or eliminate it from the system. Uriagereka adopts the latter course.

Uriagereka claims that we can maintain the simple relationship between command and precedence given by the base step in (6) if we allow Spell-Out to apply many times during the course of the derivation. Spell-Out is the operation that removes material from the syntactic component and feeds it to the interpretive components of Logical Form (LF) and Phonetic Form (PF) when it is ready for interpretation. Uriagereka points out that since the minimalist system dispenses with a global level of S-Structure as the conduit to the interpretive components, there is nothing to stop material from being passed for interpretation multiple times.

I assume that Spell-Out applies whenever two categories cannot be joined together by the Merge operation. If Merge does not apply, then the category currently being built is spelled out or reduced. I retain the notion from earlier theories of grammar (see Jackendoff 1972) that Spell-Out is a conduit between the syntax and the phonology. It is well known that the constituency established by the syntax is not relevant for phonological processes.[2] Spell-Out turns a syntactic structure with relevant constituent relationships into a string ready for phonological interpretation. Uriagereka uses Spell-Out as a repair mechanism to retain one-to-one correspondence between dominance and precedence. He assumes that both precedence and dominance must be established between terminal elements at all points of the derivation. Precedence implies merger, and merger is possible only when a chain of dominance can be established. When merger is not possible, the string is linearized (turned into an unstructured string where only previously established precedence relations are preserved). Since the elements that have been linearized are invisible in the syntax, precedence does not have to be established between them and other items in the structure. Thus, when two categories cannot be combined through merger or movement (the only syntactic operations) to form a dominating category, the material that has been given structure so far is "spelled out" or linearized.

(9) "L is an operation L(c) = p mapping command units [units that can be formed through merger] c to intermediate PF sequences p and removing phrasal boundaries from c representations." (Uriagereka 1998)

This idea preserves the one-to-one mapping between precedence and dominance but at the cost of never building single phrase markers. Instead, the system builds blocks (Uriagereka calls them "command units") where all elements stand in a c-command relation to each other. When this c-command relation is interrupted, the unit is spelled out, an unstructured unit being shipped to the phonology for phonological interpretation and a structured unit being shipped to LF for semantic interpretation. The result of Spell-Out is an unstructured string (a syntactic word) with no further internal phrase structure. Within the context of the Minimalist Program, Spell-Out is a grammatical operation, on a par with movement transformations. As such, it is governed by conditions on transformations, in particular by the economy conditions discussed above. These conditions establish a preference for derivations that utilize the fewest operations possible. An operation is applied only to satisfy some independent grammatical condition. In this case, this means that the system spells out or linearizes only when it cannot otherwise establish a chain of precedence.

11.3 Minimalist Principles as a Parsing Algorithm

I will now apply a theory incorporating economy conditions and multiple Spell-Out to parsing. I assume that the algorithm applies left to right and evaluates ambiguities with respect to the economy conditions. As in minimalist theory, items are inserted into the derivation (or moved) with the goal of checking features. The feature-checking aspect of the theory will impose an argument-over-adjunct-attachment preference along lines suggested by Pritchett (1992) and Gibson (1991) on the assumption that θ-roles are relevant features for checking.[3] Attachment as an adjunct will never lead to receipt or transfer of θ-, Case, or other features, whereas insertion into an argument position will allow this transfer to occur. I will show that this preference is well attested. Unlike Pritchett (1992) and Gibson (1991), I assume that feature transfer is optimized locally. Pritchett and Gibson allow the parser to scan the entire derivation up to the position of an item's attachment and to compare whether the attachment of a category optimizes the assignment of features over all elements of the tree built so far. By contrast, since feature checking is subject to Greed in the minimalist system, this theory allows optimal feature checking only on the particular category that is being attached, irrespective of whether this optimizes feature checking across the derivation as a whole. This will be crucial for some of the examples below.

Insertion or movement is governed by the economy conditions discussed above. The preference to attach a category using minimal structure follows immediately from this notion of economy. At each point, a category is inserted using the fewest operations necessary for feature transfer or merger. This ban on unnecessary operations subsumes Frazier and Rayner's (1982) Minimal Attachment Principle and Gorrell's (1995) simplicity metric and has the advantage of following from independently motivated grammatical principles. Minimal Attachment or simplicity follows because the fewest mergers will be performed that are needed to incorporate an incoming category.

Following Uriagereka, I assume that Spell-Out occurs whenever a derivation would otherwise violate the LCA (now containing only the base step). The spell-out conditions thus also provide an independently motivated theory of reanalysis. If a preferred reading induces a precedence/dominance mismatch, the category that precedes but does not dominate will be spelled out. Again following Uriagereka, this means that the material inside the spelled-out category is linearized and all internal syntactic structure is removed, creating a nondecomposable syntactic word. Given this, reanalysis from the preferred to the dispreferred reading that requires either extraction of material from, or insertion of material into, this syntactic word will be impossible. As a lexical item, the spelled-out material is an atomic unit, which can no longer be decomposed into its component pieces. However, if reanalysis occurs within a domain where Spell-Out has not applied, then material can be accessed and the preferred reading can be transformed into the dispreferred reading. Incorporating Spell-Out and economy conditions into the grammar also explains the preference for right-branching derivations without the need for extra explicit principles that favor this type of derivation.[4]

As a grammatical operation, Spell-Out is governed by economy. Since it does not allow the checking of any features, it is a last resort operation. As such, it is invoked only when no other feature-checking operation can apply, and the minimal number of spell-outs to guarantee satisfaction of the LCA operate at each time step in the derivation. A right-branching structure ensures that an element that precedes also dominates a category, thus minimizing the need for Spell-Out. Therefore, right-branching structures are preferred because they economize on the need for Spell-Out.

The algorithm in (10) embodies these principles.

(10) A derivation proceeds left to right. At each point in the derivation, merge using the fewest operations needed to check a feature on the category about to be attached. If merger is not possible, try to insert a trace bound to some element within the current command path. If neither merger nor movement is licensed, spell out the command path. Repeat until all terminals are incorporated into the derivation.

11.4   Some Cases

11.4.1   Argument/Adjunct Attachment Ambiguities
Cases of argument/adjunct attachment ambiguity illustrate the role of optimizing feature checking relative to economy conditions. In all cases, attachment as an argument is preferred because it allows assignment of features.

11.4.1.1   Direct Object/Complement Subject Ambiguity   The sentences and the relevant structures that illustrate direct object/complement subject ambiguity are given in (11).

(11) a. the man believed his sister to be a genius
      b. the man believed his sister

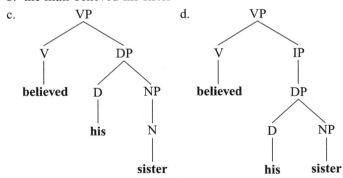

The DP *his sister* will be assigned both Case and θ-features by the preceding verb if it is attached as the direct object. Appropriate θ-features can only be assigned by the θ-assigner, the head of the complement clause. Since this category has not yet been processed, no features will be assigned if *his sister* is attached as the subject of the complement clause. Therefore, (11c) is the preferred structure. It is also the more economical structure, involving fewer operations, although this is not a crucial determinant of attachment for this case. In neither case is Spell-Out necessary at the site where *his sister* is attached.

Since there has been no spell-out within the VP, both the verb and the object are available when the embedded verb is encountered in a case like (11a). Therefore, the object NP is available for reinsertion as the embedded subject in (11d) even though the initial structure chosen for this case is (11c). All elements remain on the command path.

11.4.1.2 Preposed Object/Matrix Subject Ambiguity Next consider (12a), where there is a preference to treat the word following the first verb as an object in the preposed adverbial (see (12b)), rather than as the subject of the matrix sentence.

(12) a. after Mary mended the socks fell off the table
      b. after Mary mended the socks they fell off the table

Again, incorporation as an object allows Case and θ-features to be checked off from the phrase *the socks*. Incorporation as the matrix subject does not allow any Case or θ-feature checking, again because the Case- and θ-assigning head of the IP has not yet been incorporated into the structure. The relevant structures are given in (13).

(13) a.

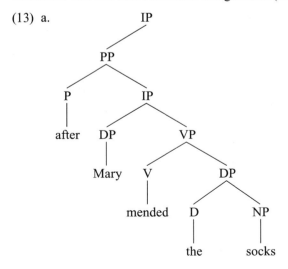

b.

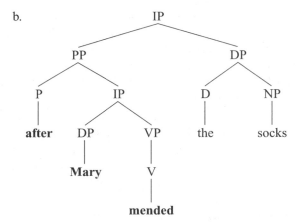

We do not expect reanalysis to be possible given the algorithm (10). After the optimal structure in (13) is built, the phrase *fell* cannot be incorporated into the preposed adverbial clause. A globally optimizing algorithm might look to see what series of transformations could be applied to incorporate this category. However, algorithm (10) is a dumb one that acts only to incorporate local material. Since the second VP cannot incorporate into any node within the preposed adverbial, the adverbial is spelled out in a phrase-by-phrase manner, leaving the structure in (14). This structure respects the LCA.

(14)

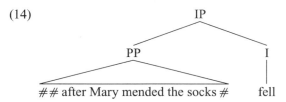

However, there is no way to incorporate the structure into this remnant either. Since the preceding material has been spelled out, there is no way to retrieve anything from this phrase to be inserted as the necessary matrix subject. Since no further operations apply, and there is remaining unincorporated terminal material, the parse fails and a garden path is detected.

11.4.1.3 Ditransitive/Complex Transitive Object Ambiguity   Next consider (15).

(15) a. John gave the man the dog for Christmas
     b. John gave the man the dog bit a bandage

The preferred reading for (15b) is to treat *the dog* as a ditransitive object, as in (16), rather than as the subject of a relative clause modifying *the man*, as in (17).

(16)

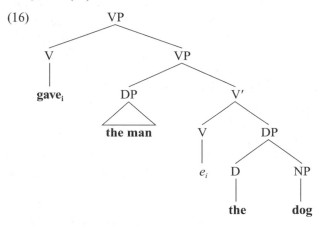

(17)

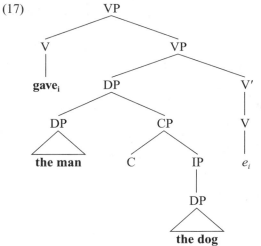

Clearly, (17) is more complicated and requires more mergers than (16), violating economy. This is again not crucial because the analysis as an indirect object allows features to be checked on the DP *the dog* whereas attachment as material in the embedded subject does not allow feature transfer.

Reanalysis is not possible in this structure. To explain why, I crucially assume the Larsonian shell structure in (16). Reanalysis would involve incorporation of the category in the indirect object position originally part of the relative clause on the direct object. However, this cannot be accomplished while the trace of the moved V remains in the structure because a relative clause inside the direct object would not command the verb trace. Therefore, maintaining the terminals of the preceding relative and the verb trace in the same tree would violate the LCA. Therefore, the V' in (17) must be spelled out. If this category is spelled out, however, there is no host site for subsequent attachment of the true indirect object because all structure under the V' node is no longer accessible.

11.4.1.4 Subcategorized PP/NP Modifier Ambiguities Consideration of (18a,b) shows that there is a preference to treat the PP *on the table* as an argument of the verb *put* rather than as a modifier of the NP *the book*. I will assume (noncrucially) the Larsonian analysis of PP complements as well. Whatever the structure is, attachment as an argument allows the PP to receive and the V to discharge features. The structures are given in (18c,d).

(18) a. I put the book on the table
       b. I put the book on the table into my bag
       c.

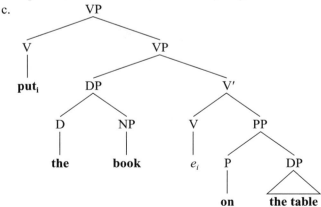

d.

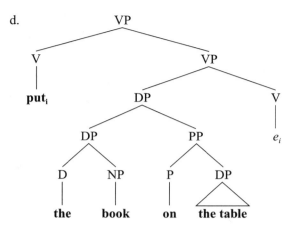

Reanalysis is not possible for the same reason as in the ditransitive case above. To reanalyze the PP as part of the direct object as the adjunct to *the book* requires spell-out of the V′, since material inside the relative would not command this category. If this category is spelled out, though, there is no site for the true locative PP *into my bag* to merge to.

The final case of an argument/adjunct ambiguity is the famous main clause/relative clause ambiguity exhibited in cases like (19).

(19) the horse raced past the barn fell

These are strict garden paths, for which native speakers prefer a main-clause reading (*the horse raced past the barn*), being unable to reanalyze them as reduced relative clauses.

Interestingly, Pritchett (1992) and Stevenson and Merlo (1997) have suggested that these types of ambiguities do not always yield garden paths. When transitive and unaccusative verbs replace unergatives like those in (19), the sentences become quite easy to process.[5]

(20) a. the student found in the classroom was asleep
     b. the butter melted in the pan was burnt

Within the context of the minimalist framework, these subtle facts are accounted for because both transitives and unaccusatives must have traces inserted in the postverbal position, whether or not these structures are analyzed as main clauses or relative clauses. This is because the θ-grid of both transitives and unaccusatives signals to the parser that these verbs both require NP objects. Since there is no overt object in the postverbal position, a trace must be inserted here. So, even if the preferred analysis for these cases is as main clauses, the structure needed to appropriately interpret them as open sentences, with traces in postverbal position, is built as part of the main-clause analysis, *before* the spell-out required by the disambiguating main verb for cases that are truly reduced relatives. The initial analyses are given in (21a,b).

(21) a. [$_{IP}$ the student$_i$ [$_{VP}$ found e_i [in the classroom]]]]
      b. [$_{IP}$ the butter$_i$ [$_{VP}$ melted e_i [in the pan]]]]

The reanalysis proceeds along the lines discussed above. The material preceding the main verb is initially analyzed as a main clause. When the true matrix verb is encountered, everything preceding the verb is spelled out in accordance with the LCA. Now, however, the spelled-out material can be appropriately interpreted as a relative clause, and so no garden path results.

In all of the above cases, economy seemed to redundantly track feature checking in the sense that the most economical structure was also the one that allowed features to be checked. I now turn to cases where local economy is crucial to predicting both preference and reanalysis judgments. Primarily, in these cases the ambiguity is between two different types of adjunct attachment. In neither situation is a feature checked, so economy is the only factor in play.

14.4.2   Adjunct/Adjunct Attachment

14.4.2.1   Adverb or Particle Placement   The grammar presents multiple attachment sites directly after the italicized words in all the cases in (22). The parser always chooses the position after the most recently encountered word as the preferred attachment site.

(22) a. I told Mary that I will *come* yesterday
      b. I called to *pick* the box up
      c. I yelled to *take* the cat out

In (22a), the adverb *yesterday* is construed with the embedded verb even though this reading is semantically anomalous and even though an alternative attachment to the matrix verb would result in an acceptable reading. (22b,c) show that the particle prefers low attachment as well.

These preferences can be explained on the assumption that Spell-Out, as one of the grammatically licensed operations, is also subject to the economy conditions. Therefore, mergers involving fewer spell-outs will be preferred. Consider (23) at the point when the adverb *yesterday* enters the derivation.

(23)

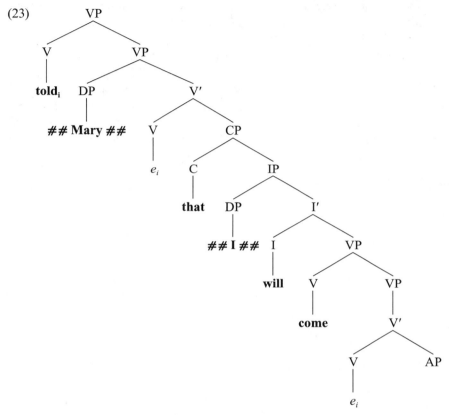

Assuming attachment into a Larsonian shell associated with the lowest verb, where adverbs assume the position of complements, would require no spell-outs at this point. The adverb would simply be merged under the boldfaced phrase. Assuming Uriagereka's version of the LCA, though, attachment as an adjunct to the higher verb would require spell-out of the lower VP, I′, and IP, respectively, given the algorithm in (10). This algorithm requires spell-out only of the material that would not c-command the site of a potential merger. Therefore, if the parser has processed everything up to the lowest clause in the preposed position, it will require multiple spell-outs to return to the highest level of the preposed adverbial. In the competence model, one could think of high or low attachment as requiring an equal number of spell-outs, each with a different number of

phrases in the spelled-out component of the analysis. In a parser, however, one does not keep the whole structure in memory at a given point
and therefore, one must provide an explicit procedure for dealing with
previously processed material. The parser cannot retrieve a site for attachment in this case without successive iterations of Spell-Out, given
(10). Since lower attachment involves fewer iterations of Spell-Out, economy considerations favor this attachment choice. This will also be true for
(22b,c). Attachment of the particle to the higher verb will cause the phrases
remaining on the c-command path of the lower clause (boldfaced in (24))
to be spelled out (only the structure of (22b) is illustrated; the structure of
(22c) is the same). Attachment as the particle of the lower verb requires
no Spell-Out and will again be preferred by economy considerations.

(24)

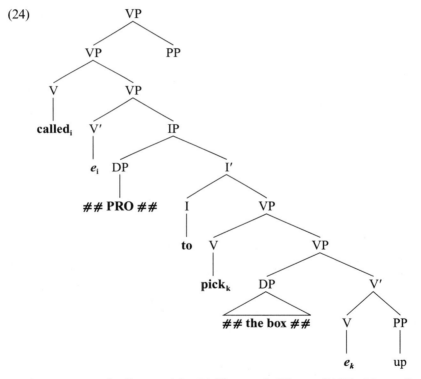

The next case is discussed by Phillips and Gibson (1997). Normally,
relative-clause attachments are dispreferred, but in this case they are favored.

(25) a. although Erica hated the house she had owned it for years
    b. although Erica hated the house she owned her family lived in it
       for years

Phillips and Gibson presented sentences like these to experimental subjects with either temporal or nontemporal adverbial modifiers in a word-by-word self-paced reading task with a moving window display. At the disambiguation point (either *it* or *her family*), subjects showed a clear preference for attaching the preceding clause as a relative clause modifying the noun phrase *the house*. There was a significant increase in reaction time at the disambiguation point if the ambiguous noun phrase was disambiguated as the matrix subject.

This preference can again be explained with reference to economy of Spell-Out. Again at the relevant point, neither attachment will allow the discharge of a feature. However, attachment as a relative clause permits much more of the preceding material to remain in the derivation, as it will still command the incoming merged material. Attachment as the matrix subject requires spell-out of the entire preposed adverbial. The relevant structure is given in (26); nodes that need to be spelled out for the matrix-subject reading are boldfaced, and those that need to be spelled out for the relative-clause reading are underlined.

(26)

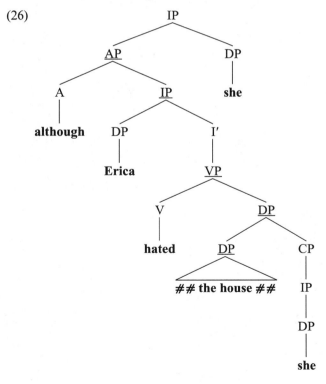

11.5   Right-Branching Structure in the Grammar and in the Parser: A Comparison with Phillips's (1995, 1996) Approach

Phillips (1995, 1996) presents very interesting work that argues for an alternative grammatically based processing theory. In fact, Phillips claims that there is no distinction between the parser and the grammar. Derivations in both the competence and performance systems are built up incrementally, left to right.

Given this grammatical underpinning, Phillips tries to link performance preferences to thé grammar in the following way. First, he defines a condition called *Branch Right*.

(27) *Branch Right*
    "Select the most right branching available attachment of an incoming item Reference Set: all attachments of a new item that are compatible with a given interpretation." (Phillips 1996, 29)

The preference for right-branching structure is in turn derived from a principle that ensures that the base step of the LCA is incrementally satisfied to the greatest extent possible. As Phillips writes: "I assume that a structure is right branching to the extent that there is a match between precedence relations among terminal elements and c-command relations among terminal elements" (1996, 29).

To handle a variety of bracketing paradoxes, Phillips couples this with the idea that grammatical as well as parsing derivations proceed left to right. Consider (28).

(28) a. John showed the men each other's pictures
     b. John showed each other the men's pictures

These examples suggest that double object constructions have right-branching structures in which the indirect object c-commands the direct object as in (29).

(29)

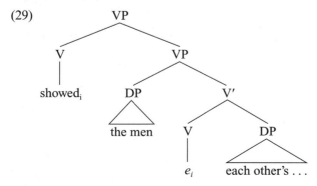

The fact that (30a–c) are grammatical as VP-fronting structures suggests that the structure for the PPs (given in (31)) should be left branching, allowing the right subparts to be constituents.

(30) I said I would show the men the pictures in libraries on weekends, and
   a. show the men the pictures in libraries on weekends, I will
   b. show the men the pictures in libraries, I will on weekends
   c. show the men the pictures, I will in libraries, on weekends

(31)

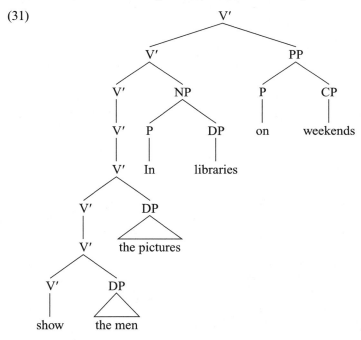

Phillips shows that we can derive the effects of a structure like (31) without the need to assume it, by assuming that Branch Right applies from left to right with the apparently left-branching structures actually being intermediate structures in the derivation. For example, Branch Right would first combine *show* and *the men* to form a constituent. This constituent would then be reconfigured when subsequent material was uncovered.

Phillips presents a variety of advantages for his approach over other treatments of paradoxical constituency. The definition in (27) suffices to handle all of these paradoxes. Phillips claims that Branch Right can be used to resolve various parsing ambiguities. In order to do this, he redefines Branch Right as follows (1996, 111):

(32) *Branch Right*
    a. Metric: Select the attachment that uses the shortest path(s) from the last item in the input to the current input item.
    b. Reference set: all attachments of a new item that are compatible with a given interpretation.

(33), repeated from (11), is a simple illustration of how the principle works.

(33) a. the man believed his sister to be a genius
    b. the man believed his sister

Branch Right predicts the preference for construing *his sister* as a direct object because there are fewer branches in the path between *believed* and *his sister* if one construes the postverbal NP as a direct object than if one construes this phrase as the subject of an embedded clause as shown in (34).

(34) a.

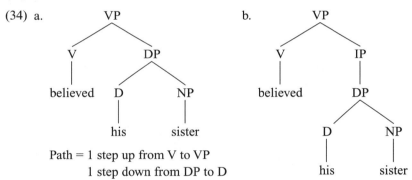

Path = 1 step up from V to VP
1 step down from DP to D

Path = 1 step up from V to VP
3 steps down from VP
to IP, DP, and D

Since the embedded-subject reading requires more steps on the downward path, it is dispreferred.

    Phillips uses this simple principle to handle a wide range of data from English and illustrative cases from German and Japanese. The principle's empirical coverage is impressive. In addition, its use is argued to be independently justified by the LCA or at least by its ability to handle bracketing paradoxes; thus, it appears that we are getting a parsing principle for free from an independently needed competence principle. For these reasons, Phillips's approach is quite interesting. Nonetheless, I will argue against it on several grounds.

The problems I will discuss do not focus on the empirical coverage of Phillips's theory per se. I note in passing, however, that this theory is intended merely to be a theory of initial preference. It is well known that certain initial preferences, such as the one exemplified in (33), can be overridden given subsequent disambiguating material, whereas cases like (35) are not subject to reanalysis and remain garden paths.[6]

(35) the horse raced past the barn fell

(35) is initially interpreted as a main clause, *the horse raced past the barn*. Reanalysis as a reduced relative, *the horse that was raced past the barn*, is impossible. As is well known, the availability of this grammatically licensed interpretation has to be pointed out to naive speakers. Phillips's theory is silent on the issue of when reanalysis is possible. Phillips claims that reanalysis should not be part of the theory of sentence processing:

[i]t is not clear that one should want Branch Right to account for recovery from error. I assume that Branch Right is a property of the system that generates and parses sentences in a single left-to-right pass, and that reanalyses require back-tracking and are handled by other mechanisms. (1996, 161)

I agree with Phillips that the actual mechanisms of reanalysis, particularly in cases where conscious breakdown occurs, may not be the domain of the processor. However, I see no reason not to demand that a full theory of sentence processing distinguish cases where these mechanisms can apply, where the human sentence processor presents the appropriate representations for these mechanisms to operate on, from cases where the sentence processor does not present the appropriate representations for the operation of potentially external general-purpose reanalysis mechanisms. Phillips's theory is mute on this domain of empirical prediction. Moreover, given that both interpretations in (33) are easily processible, it is hard to see why these reanalyses are not the domain of the human sentence processor. Branch Right predicts that (33a) is the preferred interpretation. Therefore, there must be some principle that is part of normal sentence processing that transforms (33a) into (33b).

I turn now from the domain of prediction to that of independent motivation. Part of the main appeal of the Branch Right theory is its independent motivation in terms of the LCA and the bracketing paradoxes. We get a processing principle for nothing. However, I will show that this motivation is partial at best.

Again consider (32). (32) crucially relies on comparing the number of steps needed to derive both possible readings independently of whether either reading causes a precedence/c-command mismatch. Both structures in (33) respect the grammatically relevant version of Branch Right given in (27) where "right-branchingness" is defined in terms of respect for the base step of the LCA. In both structures, the verb both precedes and dominates the following NP whether or not it is construed as the direct object, as in (33b), or the complement subject, as in (33a). Nonetheless, speakers have a clear preference for interpretation (33b) over interpretation (33a). This prediction thus rests on the notion of *shortest* path. This, however, is not independently motivated by any of Phillips's grammatical considerations. In effect, Phillips has sneaked in a branch-counting principle similar to the grammatically unmotivated Minimal Attachment Principle of Frazier and Rayner (1982), yielding a principle that is only half motivated by the grammar. Without the "node-counting" part of this principle, the theory is too weak to predict the preference for (33b) over (33a).

In (36), I present a case where the theory without the minimal attachment addendum is too strong.

(36) a. the man told the doctor that he was having trouble with his feet
     b. the man told the doctor that he was having trouble with to leave

Building either structure at the ambiguous point involves creating a precedence/dominance mismatch. Nonetheless, there is a strong preference for (36a) over (36b). Phillips assumes that the preferred structure is analyzed as a VP shell. As such, it would look like (37) (ambiguous material italicized).

(37)

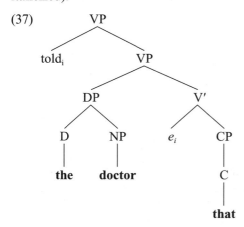

In this structure, the direct object *the doctor* dominates neither the trace of the verb *told* nor the complementizer of the complement clause. This structure induces a precedence/dominance mismatch. As (38) shows, the same is true in the less highly valued relative reading.

(38)

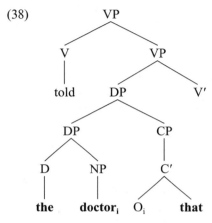

Again, then, the difference in these cases is not attributable to the metric of precedence/dominance correspondence or mismatch, but to the length of the path between *man* and the next terminal node. Again, this reduces to the unprincipled "node-counting" portion of Branch Right.

To sum up: I have identified two problems with Branch Right. First, it fails to provide a theory of reanalysis; more precisely, it does not distinguish representations in such a way as to form a basis even for an independent theory of reanalysis. Second, it incorporates a "minimal path" condition as well as a preference for right-branching structure in such a way that the minimal path condition cannot be derived from the latter part of the condition. As a result, a large portion of the constraint is not grammatically motivated. Without this unmotivated portion, the theory is empirically both too strong and too weak.

11.6 Constraint-Based Theories

In this section, I contrast a grammatically based approach, such as the two previously discussed, with frequency-based or probabilistic constraint-based theories. MacDonald, Pearlmutter, and Seidenberg (1994) present a theory of this type, summarizing it as follows:

Processing involves factors such as the frequencies of occurrence and co-occurrence of different types of information and the weighing of probabilistic and grammatical constraints. Our approach has suggested ... that syntactic parsing, including ambiguity resolution, can be seen as a lexical process. (1994, 700)

Under this view, structural heuristics are replaced with frequency data about use of either a lexical item or, in some theories, a construction type.[7] For example, the "minimal attachment preference" in (33) would not derive from a minimal attachment preference, or from its grammatical derivation through economy. Rather, speakers can tune either to the fact that *believe* is used much more frequently with a simple NP as its direct object than with a sentential complement, or to the fact that simple sentences occur more frequently in the language than sentences with embeddings. Since this theory is "verb sensitive," it can easily account for the verb sensitivity of a variety of preference judgments. For example, verbs like *decide*, which occur much more frequently with sentential complements, are correctly predicted to be immune from the "minimal attachment" effect.[8]

(39) John decided the contest was fair

I would like to argue that, although speakers may very likely track frequency, this variable works in tandem with independent grammatical constraints. If a structure is chosen, based on an amalgam of frequency and grammatical variables, the grammatically driven reanalysis principles decide what will or will not be a garden path.

In (20), repeated as (40), I considered a case where lexical choice is also relevant to preference judgments. Stevenson and Merlo (1997) have suggested that unaccusative and transitive cases are much better as reduced relative clauses than are unergative verbs.

(40) a. the student found in the classroom was asleep
      b. the butter melted in the pan was burnt

Table 11.1 gives grammaticality ratings for unaccusative versus unergative single-argument verbs (all tables are from Merlo and Stevenson 1996). Stevenson and Merlo found that unaccusatives were indistinguishable from transitives with respect to grammaticality judgments, yielding a two-way distinction, with unergatives being terrible as reduced relatives, and transitives and unaccusatives being fine. They surveyed corpora with the goal of determining whether grammatical preferences could be derived from frequency of occurrence in a corpus. Using the *Wall Street Journal*

Table 11.1
Grammaticality ratings (1 = perfect; 5 = terrible)

	Ambiguous		Unambiguous	
	Verb	Score	Verb	Score
Unaccusative	melt	2	begin	2
	mutate	1.66	break	1
	pour	1.66	freeze	1.5
	reach	1	grow	1
Unergative	advance	5	sink	3.25
	glide	5	fly	4.25
	march	5	ring	3.75
	rotate	5	run	5
	sail	5	withdraw	3.40
	walk	3.75		

corpus as the reference, they counted how many times a structure appeared as a reduced relative versus how many times it appeared as a main clause. They looked at the relative frequencies of three lexical classes of verbs: unergative, unaccusative, and "ordinary." "Ordinary" verbs are distinguished from unergative and unaccusative verbs in that adding the second argument does not invoke a "causative interpretation on the predicate." A paradigm is given in (41).

(41) a. *Unergative*
      I raced the horse (caused the horse to race) *vs.* the horse raced
    b. *Unaccusative*
      I broke the vase (caused the vase to break) *vs.* the vase broke
    c. *"Ordinary"*
      John played soccer *vs.* John played
    d. *"Ordinary"*
      John kicked the soccer ball *vs.* John kicked

The results are given in table 11.2. Notice that both unergatives and unaccusatives appear less frequently in relative clauses than do "ordinary" verbs.

In a frequency-based approach, it is reasonable to correlate other factors that are presupposed by a reduced-relative-clause analysis with preference for this analysis to be interpreted as a relative clause. Reduced relative clauses can only be formed from passivized transitive verbs.

Table 11.2
Number of reduced relatives versus main clauses in 1.5-million-word *Wall Street Journal* corpus

	Reduced relatives	Main clauses	Total
Unergatives	1	327	328
Unaccusatives	6	358	364
Ordinary	16	361	377

Table 11.3
Number of transitive versus intransitive frames from Penn treebanked subsection of *Wall Street Journal*

	Transitives	Intransitives	Total
Unergatives	86	242	328
Unaccusatives	176	228	404
Ordinary	268	114	382

Therefore, the ability of a lexical class of verbs to appear in transitive or passive constructions irrespective of whether these constructions are reduced relatives could be used to predict the compatibility of this class with the main-clause or relative-clause interpretation. Stevenson and Merlo (1997) looked at these factors for the three classes of verbs.

First, they looked at the number of times a verb appeared as a transitive or an intransitive verb. Interestingly, as table 11.3 indicates, these data seem to show a three-way distinction: unergatives are normally used with one argument, unaccusatives show a more even distribution, and "ordinary" verbs show a distinct tendency to be transitive. Merlo and Stevenson report that all of these differences are significant.

When Merlo and Stevenson tested frequency of occurrence in the passive voice, they found no significant difference between unergative and unaccusative verbs: both types occur relatively infrequently as passives. However, they observed a significant difference between unaccusative and "ordinary" verbs: the latter occur significantly more frequently as passives. They observed a similar pattern for frequency of occurrence as a past participle. The relative frequencies are summarized in table 11.4. In all cases, the "ordinary" verbs show up significantly more frequently in constructions supporting the reduced-relative-clause interpretation. This would predict that speaker preference for a reduced-relative-clause anal-

Table 11.4
Relative frequencies for several values of voice in the three verb classes

	Transitive	Passive	Past participle
Unergative verbs	.26	.02	.12
Unaccusative verbs	.44	.05	.18
"Ordinary" verbs	.70	.26	.40

ysis should be most strongly correlated with ordinary verbs, less strongly with unaccusative verbs, and least strongly with unergative verbs. Merlo and Stevenson (1998) did not test ordinary verbs in their grammaticality study. Nevertheless, they claim that ordinary verbs "are readily interpretable as an RR [a reduced relative]" (p. 136), citing MacDonald 1994 as support. However, a closer look at MacDonald's experiments yields the opposite conclusion. MacDonald contrasted the sentences in (42) with respect to self-paced reading times at the underlined position.

(42) a. the dictator *fought* in the violent coup <u>was hated</u> throughout the country
   b. the dictator *chased* in the violent coup <u>was hated</u> throughout the country
   c. the dictator *overthrown* in the violent coup <u>was hated</u> throughout the country

Fought is an "ordinary" verb, as is *chased Chased*, however, occurs overwhelmingly as a transitive verb, whereas *overthrown* is an unambiguous passive participle that is obligatorily transitive. MacDonald (1994) reports that verbs from the first class led to significantly greater reading times at the disambiguating region than did the second and third types. This means that verbs like *fought* were originally treated as main verbs in these constructions, yielding garden paths and increased reading times at the disambiguating main verb. Such verbs must be strongly disambiguated within the relative clause; otherwise, they will lead to a garden path. (43) is much easier to interpret as a relative clause because the *by* phrase disambiguates the structure as passive before the relative VP is closed.

(43) the dictator fought by the opposition was hated throughout the country

Interestingly, five of the eight "ordinary" verbs from table 11.3 were part of the *fought* class tested by MacDonald.[9] This means that even though the *fought* class appears more frequently in the transitive construction than either the unergative or the unaccusative class in Merlo and Stevenson's frequency counts, it is difficult for speakers to interpret occurrences of these verbs as a reduced relatives. If this is correct, it poses a problem for frequency-based approaches, which would predict that this class should be the least difficult to intrepret as it most frequently appears in constructions that relative-clause interpretations presuppose.[10]

These remarks are also relevant to evaluating work by Filip et al. (to appear). This work claims that Merlo and Stevenson's results can be accounted for by a constraint-based theory. The first part of the paper essentially replicates Stevenson and Merlo's finding that a frequency-based approach can predict an unergative/unaccusative split for reduced-relative-clause interpretations since unaccusatives occur significantly more often than unergatives in constructions supporting the reduced-relative-clause interpretation. Since Filip et al. do not contrast these constructions with constructions containing "ordinary" verbs, however, they do not refute the claim that the difficulty of interpreting these constructions is unrelated to their frequency distribution. Nor does their hypothesis (19), shown here in (44), account for the relative difficulty of these cases.

(44) "The acceptability of sentences with reduced relative clauses, headed by passive participles derived from unergative and unaccusative verbs, increases when the passive participle and the main verb of a matrix clause assign their subject-NPs more Proto-Patient and fewer Proto-Agent properties." (p. 17)

Proto-patient and *proto-agent* are terms taken from Dowty 1991. Perfect proto-agents are volitional, sentient causers of the event described, and they move and exist independently of the verb descirbed. Perfect proto-patients undergo a change of state, serve as incremental themes, are causally affected by another event participant, are stationary relative to another event participant, and do not exist independently of the event described. Dowty allows a category to serve in either of these roles if it is the argument bearing the greatest number of the role's defining properties, even if it is not perfectly correlated with them. Given (44), this analysis distinguishes (45) from (46). (45) is predicted to be unparsable because both the main verb and the embedded verb assign proto-agent properties to the head of the relative clause (italicized), even though it must be the proto-patient in the reduced-relative-clause interpretation.

(46) is parsable because the embedded verb assigns only proto-patient properties to its subject.

(45) *the horse* raced past the barn fell
(*Horse* is sentient, causes the movement, and exists independently both as the object of *race* and as the subject of *fell*.)

(46) *the fish* fried in the pan made me sick
(*Fish* undergoes a change of state, is the incremental theme, and is affected by *fry* in the reduced-relative-clause reading. It is a proto-agent of the predicate *make sick* because it is causal, does not undergo a change of state, and so on.)

Notice, however, that even though the head of the relative is a proto-patient in the reduced-relative reading, (47) (from MacDonald 1994) is still a garden path sentence.

(47) the cattle moved into the crowded room were afraid of the cowboys

Both *move* and *be afraid* assign *the cattle* proto-patient properties, because both imply that this argument undergoes a change of state, is the incremental theme, and is causally affected by another participant. Despite being assigned a relatively high number of proto-patient properties, this sentence is a clear garden path.

Results like these suggest that frequency has a role to play, but is filtered through grammatically justified constraints. Given the minimalist theory discussed above, "ordinary" verbs pattern like unergatives because when they are given their preferred interpretation as main-clause verbs, they are pure intransitives with no trace in the object position. The main-clause verb *were* in a case like (48) triggers reanalysis of *moved . . . room* as a relative clause. However, by the time that happens, the material preceding *were* is already spelled out, and the trace neccessary for interpreting *moved . . . room* as a reduced relative cannot be inserted. The structure is given in (48).

(48)

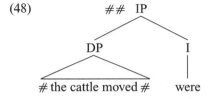

Frequency, coupled with economy-driven conditions, may drive the initial preference for a given verb to be part of either a main clause or a reduced relative, but if the former, incorrect interpretation is chosen, reanalysis as a reduced relative will be impossible. This contrasts with the unaccusative cases, as discussed above. In these cases, a trace must be inserted in post-verbal position whether or not the structure is interpreted as a main clause or as a reduced relative. Therefore, whether or not the main-clause or relative-clause reading is initially chosen (perhaps based on frequency), reanalysis is possible. If this account is correct, we are driven to a theory where frequency information interacts with grammatically based principles, but frequency does not replace these principles.

11.7 Conclusions

In this chapter, I have argued for a theory of processing preference and reanalysis that is heavily based on independently needed conditions within Chomsky's grammatical theory. There are no independent "parsing principles." In this case, the theory of preference is grounded in the economy conditions of Chomsky's (1993) Minimalist Program.

I contrasted my approach with one proposed by Phillips (1995, 1996). The two theories are similar in that principles are all independently motivated by grammatical consideration. I argued, however, that the economy conditions allow us to derive the unmotivated "shortest path" portion of Phillips's Branch Right. The Last Resort principle discussed above favors feature passing that involves the minimal number of steps.

I followed Uriagereka (this volume) in eliminating the induction step of the LCA in favor of a theory involving multiple instances of Spell-Out. I showed that multiple Spell-Out, when combined with the independently motivated economy conditions, also accounts for the preference for right-branching structures and an independently motivated theory of reanalysis.

Finally, I argued that these principles interact with frequency-derived parsing constraints in interesting ways and can explain subtle differences between the garden path status of reduced relatives derived from unergatives, unaccusatives, and transitives that are otherwise mysterious. This argues in turn for a theory where grammatical principles are supplemented but not replaced by considerations of frequency or probability.

Notes

I gratefully acknowledge support from the following agencies: the Army Research Laboratory under contract DAAL0197K0135, the National Security Agency under contract MDA90496C1250, and MicroAnalysis and Design under SBIR contract 7030. Thanks to audiences at the CUNY Sentence Processing and Computational Psycholinguistics Conferences, to audiences at Yale University and the Basque Country Summer Courses, and to Robert Berwick, Stephen Crain, Samuel Epstein, Norbert Hornstein, Colin Phillips, and Juan Uriagereka for helpful discussion. Errors remain my own.

1. Thanks to Colin Phillips for pointing this out to me.

2. But see Steedman 1996 for a different view within the framework of Combinatory Categorial Grammar.

3. Colin Phillips (personal communication) points out that feature checking could also capitalize on the fact that VP adjuncts express a restricted set of relations (time, location, instrument). NP adjuncts form a looser modifying relationship to the NP head that they adjoin to. Assuming this, we could construe VP adjunction as potentially checking a feature that NP adjunction would not. This would allow us to predict a preference for VP adjuncts over NP adjuncts.

4. This point will become important in the discussion of Phillips's proposals in section 11.5.

5. Stevenson and Merlo explain this contrast using a lexical theory devised by Hale and Keyser (1993). This theory is embedded in the processing model proposed by Stevenson (1993). Stevenson and Merlo's central claim is that the lexical representations needed to process unergative reduced-relative clauses cannot be computed by a model like Stevenson's, given lexical representations of the type Hale and Keyser propose. The account is extremely interesting; however, as shown in (i), it is too strong in that even unegatives can be improved in the appropriate discourse context.

(i) a. only horses raced at good tracks are eligible for the Triple Crown
   b. I saw a horse raced with a good jockey, and a horse raced with a bad one
   c. a horse raced with a good jockey will learn to go for the inside

This type of improvement due to different types of quantification was first pointed out by Crain and Steedman (1985) and has been elaborated on in much subsequent work by these authors. I will have more to say about these cases in section 11.6.

6. This is not to say that the initial preference as either a main or a relative clause cannot be shifted. It is merely to say that the initial preference is difficult to change once it is set.

7. Jurafsky (1996) explores the use of construction type frequency.

8. Space considerations preclude fully contrasting a grammatically based account with the constraint-based theory. Important topics that I will not review or contrast here involve the importance of pragmatic and semantic factors. Do pragmatic factors interact with frequency or syntactically derived constraints in a modular or nonmodular way? My goal in this section is simply to discuss the role of grammatical principles in a theory where it is assumed that frequency plays some role.

9. The verbs *fought, studied, lectured, watched*, and *surrendered* were tested as biased intransitive verbs in MacDonald's set. She also tested the verbs *raced, moved*, and *marched*, which Stevenson and Merlo treat as unergative.

10. Clearly, these results are only suggestive since the class of verbs that yielded difficulty in MacDonald's experiments was primarily but not completely composed of Merlo and Stevenson's "ordinary" verbs. I am planning to retest MacDonald's stimuli with a class of nonmixed purely "ordinary" verbs. My intuitions suggest, however, that the "ordinary" verbs pattern with the unergative verbs.

References

Chametzky, Robert. 1996. *A theory of phrase structure and the extended base.* Albany, NY: SUNY Press.

Chomsky, Noam. 1993. A minimalist program for linguistic theory. In *The view from Building 20: Essays in linguistics in honor of Sylvain Bromberger*, eds. Kenneth Hale and Samuel Jay Keyser. Cambridge, Mass.: MIT Press. [Reprinted in *The Minimalist Program*, Noam Chomsky. Cambridge, Mass.: MIT Press, 1995.]

Chomsky, Noam. 1995. *Categories and transformations.* In *The Minimalist Program*. Cambridge, Mass.: MIT Press.

Crain, Stephen, and Mark Steedman. 1985. On not being led up the garden path. In *Natural language parsing*, eds. David R. Dowty, Lauri Karttunen, and Arnold Zwicky. New York: Cambridge University Press.

Dowty, David R. 1991. Thematic proto-roles and argument selection. *Language* 67, 547–619.

Filip, Hana, Michael K. Tanenhaus, Gregory Carlson, Paul D. Allopena, and Joshua Blatt. To appear. Reduced relatives judged hard require constraint-based analyses. In *Proceedings of the Rutgers 1998 CUNY Conference*, eds. Suzanne Stevenson and Paola Merlo. Amsteram: John Benjamins.

Frazier, Lyn, and Keith Rayner. 1982. Making and correcting errors during sentence comprehension: Eye movements in the analysis of structurally ambiguous sentences. *Cognitive Psychology* 14, 178–210.

Gibson, Edward. 1991. A computational theory of human language processing: Memory limitations and processing breakdown. Doctoral dissertation, Carnegie Mellon University, Pittsburgh, Pa.

Gorrell, Paul. 1995 *Syntax and parsing.* Cambridge: Cambridge University Press.

Hale, Kenneth, and Samuel Jay Keyser. 1993. On argument structure and the lexical expression of syntactic relations. In *The view from Building 20: Essays in linguistics in honor of Sylvain Bromberger*, eds. Kenneth Hale and Samuel Jay Keyser. Cambridge, Mass.: MIT Press.

Jackendoff, Ray. 1972. *Semantic interpretation in generative grammar.* Cambridge, Mass.: MIT Press.

Jurafsky, Daniel. 1996. A probabilistic model of lexical and syntactic access and disambiguation. *Cognitive Science* 20, 137–194.

Kayne, Richard. 1994. *The antisymmetry of syntax*. Cambridge, Mass.: MIT Press.

MacDonald, Mary Ellen. 1994. Probabilistic constraints and syntactic ambiguity resolution. *Language and Cognitive Processes* 9, 157–201.

MacDonald, Mary Ellen, Neil Pearlmutter, and Mark Seidenberg. 1994. The lexical nature of syntactic ambiguity resolution. *Psychological Review* 101, 678–703.

Merlo, Paola, and Suzanne Stevenson. 1996. Integrating statistical and structural information in a distributed architecture for syntactic disambiguation. Technical report TR-25. Center for Cognitive Science, Rutgers University, New Brunswick, N.J.

Merlo, Paola, and Suzanne Stevenson. 1998. What grammars tell us about corpora: The case of reduced relative clauses. In *Proceedings of the Sixth Workshop in Very Large Corpora*, ed. Eugene Charniak. Hillsdale, NJ: Lawrence Erlbaum.

Partee, Barbara H., Alice ter Meulen, and Robert Wall. 1990. *Mathematical methods in linguistics*. Dordrecht: Kluwer.

Phillips, Colin. 1995. Right association in parsing and grammar. In *Papers in language processing and acquisition*, eds. Carson Schütze, Jennifer Ganger, and Kevin Broihier. (MIT Working Papers in Linguistics 26.) MITWPL, Department of Linguistics and Philosophy, MIT, Cambridge, Mass.

Phillips, Colin. 1996. Order and structure. Doctoral dissertation, MIT, Cambridge, Mass.

Phillips, Colin, and Edward Gibson. 1997. On the strength of the local attachment preference. *Journal of Psycholinguistic Research* 23, 323–346.

Pritchett, Bradley. 1992. *Grammatical competence and parsing preference*. Chicago: University of Chicago Press.

Steedman, Mark. 1996. *Surface structure and interpretation*. Cambridge, Mass.: MIT Press.

Stevenson, Suzanne. 1993. A competition-based explanation of syntactic attachment preferences and garden path phenomena. In *Proceedings of the 31st Annual Meeting of the Association for Computational Linguistics*. San Francisco, CA: Morgan Kaufmann.

Stevenson, Suzanne, and Paola Merlo. 1997. Lexical structure and processing complexity. *Language and Cognitive Processes* 12, 349–399.

Trueswell, John C., and Michael K. Tanenhaus. 1994. Towards a lexicalist framework for constraint based syntactic ambiguity resolution. In *Perspectives on sentence processing*, eds. Charles Clifton, Lyn Frazier, and Keith Rayner. Hillsdale, N.J.: Lawrence Erlbaum.

Uriagereka, Juan. 1998. Multiple Spell-Out. MS., University of Maryland, College Park.

Weinberg, Amy. 1992. Parameters in the theory of sentence processing: Minimal commitment theory goes east. *Journal of Psycholinguistic Research* 22, 339–364.

Chapter 12

Un-Principled Syntax: The Derivation of Syntactic Relations

Samuel David Epstein

Nash (1963, 173–174) writes,

[H]aving learned to reject, as delusive, the hope that theoretical premises are, or can be made, self-evident—we cannot but recognize that always our explanations are *incomplete*. Hall [(1956, 177)] attributes to Galileo and Newton the opinion that:

The explanation of phenomena at one level is the description of phenomena at a more fundamental level, ...

Complete understanding then fails by the margin of those theoretical premises which are *stipulated*, perhaps "described," but certainly not themselves explained or explicable for so long as they remain our ultimate premises.

... Resolved to maximize our understanding, we find ourselves committed to a highly characteristic effort to minimize the *number* of theoretical premises required for explanation. Einstein [(1954, 282)] speaks of:

... the grand aim of all science, which is to cover the greatest possible number of empirical facts by logical deductions from the smallest number of hypotheses or axioms.

Some centuries earlier Newton had expressed the same "grand aim" in the first of his Rules of Reasoning:

We are to admit no more causes of natural things than such as are both true and sufficient to explain their appearances.

... Each "quality" imputed to a premised entity figures as an additional postulate. Our desire for parsimony of postulates thus evokes a search for theoretical posits having the slenderest possible qualitative endowment.

12.1 Introduction: Syntactic Relations

Alongside "syntactic feature" and "permissible syntactic feature bundle" (i.e., a possible syntactic category), perhaps the most fundamental construct postulated within syntactic theory is "syntactic relation." In fact, broadly conceived, syntactic theory is precisely a theory of relations and the elements that enter into them. For example, each of the following is considered to be a core syntactic relation:

(1) a. (Subject-verb) agreement   The dog kick<u>s</u> walls.
    b. (Object-verb) θ-relation   The dog <u>kicks</u> <u>walls</u>.
    c. (Accusative) Case relation   The dog <u>kicks</u> <u>them</u>.
    d. (Reflexive) binding relation   The dog <u>kicks</u> <u>herself</u>.
    e. (Passive) movement relation   (Sadly) <u>the dog</u> was kicked <u>t</u>.
    f. The "is a" relation   The dog [_{VP}[_V kicks] [_{DP} walls]].
                                        (*kicks*, a V, and *walls*, a DP,
                                        together constitute—i.e.,
                                        are—a VP)

Such relations are apparently very heavily constrained. That is, we do not find empirical evidence for all of the logically possible syntactic relations; instead, at least from the perspective of unified theories (to be discussed momentarily), we find only one, or perhaps "a few," to be distinguished on a principled basis.

Given that syntactic relations are heavily constrained, the questions we confront include "What are they?" "How are they to be formally expressed?" and, more deeply, "Why do we find *these* and not any of the infinite number of other logically possible relations?" Within the framework of Chomsky 1981, 1982, there were, by hypothesis, at least two fundamental syntactic relations. The first, *government* (see also Chomsky 1986), was a unified construct, a binary relation, intended to subsume all the seemingly disparate phenomena illustrated in the English examples (1a–e) (but not (1f)). The second, "*is a*" (1f), was a relation created by the base component, upon which government relations were defined. For example, the trinary relation in (1f)—"V and DP *are a* VP"—is not a government relation.

This type of theory of syntactic relations arguably faces several conceptual (and empirical) problems:

1. *Unification.* Unification is, in a sense, precluded in that the "is a" relation is divorced from the government relation. Government relations are defined on base-generated representations already exhibiting "is a" relations. Why isn't there just one relation? And if there is indeed more than one, why are (1a–e) the cases that are unified, under government, and why is (1f), the "is a" relation, the one that is left out?

2. *Explanation.* Explanation at a certain level is lacking to the extent that the (or one of the) fundamental relations, government (Chomsky 1981,

1986)—or more recently minimal domain (Chomsky 1993), a binary relation defined on representations—is merely a definition. That is, the following question is unanswered: "Why is government as defined in (3) or minimal domain (see (38)) the fundamental syntactic relation and not any of the infinite number of other logically possible syntactically definable relations?"

3. *Primitive constructs*. Government and minimal domain are not in fact primitives; instead, each incorporates a more fundamental binary relational construct, *command*. Thus, contrary to standard assumptions, government or minimal domain is not the fundamental unexplained definition; rather, the relation *command* is. Of course, if command is to express a fundamental syntactic relation, and it remains an (unexplained) *definition*, then, in the same sense as in point 2, explanation is lacking: "Why is *this* relation, so defined, syntactically significant?"

4. *Complexity*. Government and minimal domain definitions are complex. Of course, this claim has no substance in the absence of an explicit, principled complexity metric. Hence, I will leave it to the reader's intuition that the alternative theory of syntactic relations proposed here achieves significant simplification and (I hope) does not lose (perhaps even gains) in empirical adequacy.

In this chapter, I will address each of these (closely related) problems confronting the fundamental construct "syntactic relation" as it is expressed in contemporary syntactic theories. The analysis will be couched within the Minimalist Program (Chomsky 1993, 1994), which makes the following important innovations:

• D-Structure is eliminated and, along with it, the bifurcation of the D-Structure-generating base component and the transformational component.

• The concept of generalized transformation (= Merge), arguably unifiable with the concept of singulary transformation (= Move α), as proposed by Kitahara (1994, 1995, 1997), is reinstated.

The central hypothesis I will propose here can be expressed in an informal and preliminary fashion as follows:

(2) *Preliminary hypothesis*
   a. The fundamental concept "syntactic relation" (e.g., "government" or "minimal domain") is not an unexplained definition defined on representations (i.e., already built-up phrase structure representations). Rather, syntactic relations are properties of

independently motivated, simple, and minimal transformations. That is, syntactic relations are established between a syntactic category X and a syntactic category Y when (and only when) X and Y are transformationally concatenated (thereby entering into sister relations with each other) by either Merge or Move during the tree-building, iterative, universal rule application that constitutes the derivation.

b. The fundamental structure-building operation is neither Move α (Chomsky 1981, 1982) nor Affect α (Lasnik and Saito 1992) but "Concatenate X and Y, thereby forming Z."

The analysis I will propose is entirely natural in that concatenation and only concatenation establishes syntactic relations between categories. Given this hypothesis, and given that any syntactic system, by definition, requires concatenation, the fundamental construct "syntactic relation" should be deducible from (hence explained by appeal to) the independently and strongly motivated postulate "Concatenate," as simply expressed by Merge and Move in the Minimalist Program. To the extent that "syntactic relation" is indeed (contra contemporary theories of syntax) an explicable derivational construct, not a definitional (unexplained) representational notion, the four central obstacles 1–4 that confront all current syntactic explanations will be overcome.

Before proceeding, I would like to briefly place this hypothesis—that fundamental, representational, unexplained definitions can be replaced by derivational explanations—in a broader historical context. As is well known, the "rule-less," representation-based principles-and-parameters theory evolved from earlier rule-based systems. The construction specificity and language specificity of the postulated phrase structure and transformational rules represented a serious obstacle to explanatory adequacy: "How does the learner select *this* grammar with *these* rules, on the basis of exposure to degenerate data?" An entirely natural development was the gradual abandonment of rule-based grammars and the concomitant postulation of universal constraints on representations or principles (expressing the properties common to rules), which were consequently neither construction- nor language-particular entities. The residue—the language-specific properties of rules, to be fixed by experience—was ascribed the status of parameters with the hope that construction specificity would be altogether eliminated from core grammar.

Although the abandonment of rule systems and the adoption of principles (i.e., filters or well-formedness conditions on rule-generated representations, such as binding theory, Case theory, X-bar theory, and θ-theory) was an entirely natural development, there is an alternative, which I believe is reflected (perhaps only implicitly) in Chomsky 1991, 1993, 1994. Given that it was the language specificity and construction specificity of rules and not the fact that they were rules per se that apparently threatened explanatory adequacy, the alternative approach is to retain a rule-based framework, but eliminate from the rules their language-particular and construction-particular formal properties. That is, instead of universal principles, such an approach postulates universal iteratively applied rules, thereby maintaining a strongly derivational theory of syntax. The approach is like Standard Theory in that it incorporates iterative application of rules but unlike Standard Theory in that the rules are "universalized" as generalized transformation (Merge) and Move; that is, they are purged of language-specific and construction-specific properties, their apparent crosslinguistic differences being attributed, by hypothesis, to irreducible morphological variation.

In this chapter, I will argue that this strongly derivational universal-rule approach, in which iterative rule application characterizes syntactic derivations while constraints on output representations and on levels of representation (hence levels themselves) are altogether eliminated (see Chomsky 1994, 1995), exhibits vast explanatory advantages over the existing representational, rule-free, principle-based (hence representation-based) theories—at least in the domain of accounting for the central construct "syntactic relation."

12.2 Syntactic Relations in a Principle-Based Theory

In the pre-minimalist, principle-based framework of Chomsky 1981, 1986, representations (phrase structure trees) are built freely by an unconstrained (implicit) base. The output is constrained by the X-bar schema, a filter on output representations. The unifying construct "government" is a binary, unidirectional (asymmetric) syntactic relation holding between two syntactic categories in a derived representation. It is defined as follows:

(3) *Government*
  a. X *governs* Y iff
    i. X m-commands Y *and*
    ii. There is no Z, Z a barrier for Y, such that Z excludes X.
  b. X *m-commands* Y iff the minimal maximal projection dominating X dominates Y (see Aoun and Sportiche 1983).

c. X *excludes* Y iff no segment of X dominates Y.

d. X *dominates* Y only if every segment of X dominates Y (see Chomsky 1986, n. 10).

e. Z is a *barrier* for Y iff
   i.   Z immediately dominates W, W a blocking category for Y, *or*
   ii. Z is a blocking category for Y and Z ≠ IP.

f. A maximal projection X *immediately dominates* a maximal projection Y iff there is no maximal projection Z such that X dominates Z and Z dominates Y.

g. Z is a *blocking category* for Y iff
   i.   Z is not L-marked *and*
   ii. Z dominates Y.

h. X *L-marks* Y iff X is a lexical category that θ-governs Y.

i. X θ-*governs* Y iff
   i.   X is a zero-level category *and*
   ii. X θ-marks Y *and*
   iii. X and Y are sisters.

Although such an approach offers an impressive, highly explicit, and unified analysis of a number of seemingly disparate syntactic phenomena, it arguably suffers from the four problems noted above:

1. It is not wholly unified since the "is a" relation is not a government relation.
2. "Government" is a definition; hence, it is entirely unexplained why syntactic phenomena, by hypothesis, conform to this particular relation and not to any of the infinite number of alternative syntactically definable relations.
3. "Government" is not really a primitive relation since it incorporates the more primitive relation "m-command."
4. The definition of "government" is arguably complex (but see section 12.1 regarding the unclarity of such inexplicit claims).

Following Chomsky (1993, n. 9), I will assume that m-command is not a primitive. I will however assume that c-command is. In the next section, I will show that contrary to syntactic analyses from Reinhart 1979 to Kayne 1994, c-command need not be expressed as an unexplained representational definition but can instead be expressed as a natural, explicable, derivational construct, assuming Chomsky's (1993, 1994) elimination of a distinct base component (and, along with it, the elimination of a base-generated D-Structure level of representation) and the postulation of a syntactic component in which derivations are characterized by iterative, bottom-up application of universalized, simple, and perhaps unifiable rules, Merge and Move.

12.3   C-Command

12.3.1   Representational C-Command
Consider the following representational definition of c-command (Reinhart 1979):

(4) *The representational definition of c-command*
   A c-commands B iff
   a. The first branching node dominating A dominates B, *and*
   b. A does not dominate B, *and*
   c. A ≠ B.

Four important properties of c-command should be noted here. First, (4) constitutes a *definition*, hence explanation is lacking. That is, we have no answer to the question, "Why is this particular binary relation syntactically significant?" As an illustration, consider (5).

(5) *A schematic illustration of c-command*
   (certain irrelevant categories—e.g., AgrP and TP—are omitted)

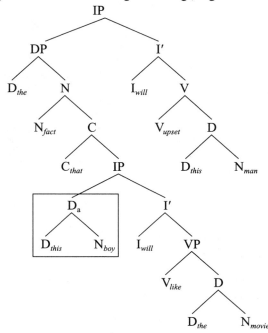

In (5), [Spec, IP] = D_a c-commands I', I_{will}, VP, V_{like}, D, D_{the}, N_{movie}, and no other categories. It is as if the other categories in (5) are inexplicably invisible with respect to D_a; hence, D_a enters into no relations with them. Why? Second, c-command is pervasive and fundamental, apparently playing a unifying role throughout the different subcomponents of the syntax. Third, it is persistent; that is, despite substantive changes in the theory of syntax, Reinhart's definition, proposed two decades ago, remains, by hypothesis, linguistically significant. Fourth, it is representational; that is, it is a relation defined on representation.

Thus, c-command faces at least these unanswered questions:

(6) a. Why does it exist at all? Why doesn't A enter into relations with all constituents in the tree?

   b. Why is the *first* branching node relevant? Why not "The first or second or third (*n*th?) node dominating A must dominate B?"

   c. Why is *branching* relevant?

   d. Why doesn't A c-command the first branching node dominating A, instead c-commanding only categories dominated by the first branching node?

   e. Why must A not dominate B?

   f. Why must A not equal B?

I will advance the hypothesis that these properties of c-command are not accidental, but are intimately related. First, I believe c-command is fundamental, pervasive, and persistent because it is, by hypothesis, indeed a syntactically significant relation. Second, I propose that it is definitional (nonexplanatory) precisely because it has been formulated or construed as a representational relation. Third, I propose that it is in fact derivational—that is, a relation between two categories X and Y established in the course of a derivation (iterative universal-rule application) when and only when X and Y are paired (concatenated) by transformational rule (i.e., Merge or Move). When c-command is construed derivationally, the unanswered questions confronting the representational definition receive natural answers.

12.3.2 The Derivation of C-Command

To begin with, I will assume that

(7) a. Merge and Move (Chomsky 1993, 1994) are at least partly unifiable (as proposed in Kitahara 1993, 1994, 1995, 1997) in that each pairs (concatenates) exactly two categories, A and B,

rendering them sisters immediately dominated by the same (projected) mother, C (where C = the head of A or of B (Chomsky 1994)).

b. Given (7a), there is a fundamental operation, common to or shared by Merge and Move: "Concatenate A and B, forming C (C = the head of A or of B)."

Crucially, then, each universalized transformational rule, Merge and Move, establishes a syntactic relation between two concatenated syntactic categories A and B by virtue of placing them in the "is a" relation with C, the projected category. I will also assume, with Chomsky (1994), that Merge operates bottom-up—that is, applies cyclically (cyclic application being an independently motivated universal constraint on universal-rule application)—and that Move does so as well. Consider, for example, the derivation in (8).

(8) Merging V_{likes} and D_{it} yields, informally:

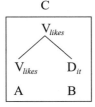

The lower V_{likes} (= A) and D_{it} (= B) are, by virtue of undergoing Merge, in a relation: they are the sister constituents of a V-phrase/projection C, labeled V_{likes}.

Thus, what Merge does is create *sisters*. Crucially, A and B cannot be or become sisters without having a common mother. Conversely, if non-branching projection is disallowed, and only binary branching is permitted, then there cannot be a mother C without exactly two daughters (the sisters A and B). In a nutshell, both the sisterhood relation and the motherhood ("is a") relation are created simultaneously, by a single application of Merge.

Viewed in terms of Standard Theory transformations, A and B (in (8), V_{likes} and D_{it}) constitute the structural description of Merge. The structural change (perhaps deducible, given the structural description; see Chomsky 1995) specifies the categorial status of the mother or output tree/set. Since the two entities in the structural description are rendered sisters (i.e., are placed in the "is a" relation to the projected (perhaps predictable) mother C, all in one application of Merge), there is no need for a representational definition of "sister" or "mother" ("is a"); these two relations are clearly expressed (and unified) within the independently motivated, universal structure-building rules themselves. Representational definitions would therefore be redundant and (being definitions) nonexplanatory.

The tree in (8) is formally represented as $\{V_{likes}, \{V_{likes}, D_{it}\}\}$. This object (set) consists of three terms:

(9) a. The entire tree/set $(= C)$
   b. V_{likes} $(= A)$
   c. D_{it} $(= B)$

That is, following Chomsky (1994, 12; 1995), I assume:

(10) a. Definition of *term* ("constituent")
       i. K is a term of K (i.e., the entire set or tree is a term).
       ii. If L is a term of K, then the members of the members of L are terms of K.
   b. The terms in (8) are as follows:
       i. $K = \{V_{likes}, \{V_{likes}, D_{it}\}\}$ = one term
       ii. K has two members:
          member 1 = V_{likes} = "the label"
          member 2 = a two-membered set = $\{V_{likes}, D_{it}\}$
       iii. The V_{likes} and D_{it} that are each members of member 2 are thus members of a member. Therefore, each is a term.

Thus, "[t]erms correspond to nodes of the informal representations, where each node is understood to stand for the subtree of which it is the root" (Chomsky 1994, 12).

Continuing with the derivation, suppose that concurrent with the construction of (8), we construct the separate phrase marker (11) (recall that separate phrase markers may be constructed in parallel, as long as a single phrase marker results by the end of the derivation (see Collins 1997)).

(11) Merge D_{the} and N_{dog}, yielding informally:

The tree is formally represented as $\{D_{the}, \{D_{the}, N_{dog}\}\}$, similarly consisting of three terms: the entire two-membered set and each of the two categories that are members of a member of the two-membered set (D_{the} and N_{dog}). Now, having constructed the two three-membered trees in (8) and (11), suppose we merge them, yielding (12) (a, b, and c are purely heuristic: $D_a = D_{the}$; V_b and V_c each $= V_{likes}$).

(12)

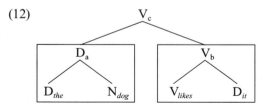

Now notice that there exists a massive redundancy. The representational definition of c-command (4) stipulates c-command relations between sisters in the derived representation (12). But sisters are precisely the objects A and B that invariably undergo Merge in building the representation. Thus:

(13) In (12):
- a. i. D_{the} representationally c-commands N_{dog}; they were merged.
  - ii. N_{dog} representationally c-commands D_{the}; they were merged.
- b. i. V_{likes} representationally c-commands D_{it}; they were merged.
  - ii. D_{it} representationally c-commands V_{likes}; they were merged.
- c. i. D_a representationally c-commands V_b; they were merged.
  - ii. V_b representationally c-commands D_a; they were merged.
- d. V_c representationally c-commands nothing; it has not been merged with any category.
- e. In (12), the 10 binary dominance relations ("X dominates Y") are, by pure stipulation in (4b), not c-command relations; they were not merged.
- f. By pure stipulation in (4c), no category representationally c-commands itself; no category is merged with itself.

Thus, Merge—an entirely simple, natural, minimal, and independently motivated structure-building operation (i.e., transformational rule)—seems to capture representational c-command relations. In other words, if X and Y are concatenated, they enter into (what have been called) c-command relations. Consequently, it would seem that we can eliminate the stipulated, unexplained representational definition of c-command (4).

There is a problem with this suggestion, however. When Merge pairs two categories, the pairing establishes only *symmetrical* (reciprocal) c-command relations. Consider, for example, (14).

(14)

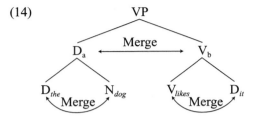

Correctly, each arrow in (14) indicates a c-command relation. But Merge does not totally subsume the representational definition of c-command, precisely because there exist c-command relations between categories that have not been merged. Thus, (15a) is true, but (15b) is false.

(15) a. If A and B were merged, then A c-commands B and B
            c-commands A.
       b. If A c-commands B, then A and B were merged.

To see the falsity of (15b), consider (16).

(16) D_a and V_b are merged:

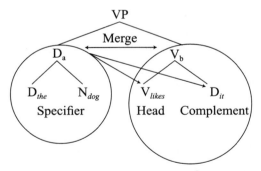

The specifier of V_{likes}, D_a, c-commands the head V_{likes} and the complement D_{it}, but D_a was not merged with either of them.

To solve this problem confronting the attempt to entirely deduce representational, definitional c-command from Merge, notice that although D_a was not merged with V_{likes} or with D_{it}, it was merged with V_b. But now recall that $V_b = \{V_b, \{V_{likes}, D_{it}\}\}$ ("each node is understood to stand for the subtree of which it is the root"). That is, V_b consists of three terms: $\{V_b, \{V_{likes}, D_{it}\}\}$ (the whole V_b subtree in (16)), V_{likes}, and D_{it}. Given that a syntactic category is a set of terms (in dominance/precedence relations), we can propose the following, natural derivational definition of c-command:

(17) *Derivational c-command (preliminary version)*
     X c-commands all and only the terms of the category Y with which
     X was merged in the course of the derivation.

Thus, D_a ([Spec, VP]) c-commands V_b (X′) and all terms of V_b.

Now recall that Move, the other structure-building operation, also pairs/concatenates exactly two categories, projecting the head of one, and in this respect is identical to Merge. Since "is a" relations are created by Move in the same manner as they are created by Merge, we can now propose the final version of the derivational definition.

(18) *Derivational c-command (final version)*
     X c-commands all and only the terms of the category Y with which
     X was paired *by Merge or by Move* in the course of the derivation.

Given (18), consider the case of Move in (19).

(19)

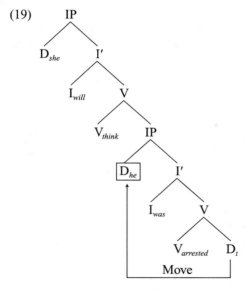

By definition (4), in (19) D_{he} representationally c-commands the five categories (subtrees) I′, I_{was}, V, $V_{arrested}$, D_t, and nothing else. This state of affairs, unexplained representationally, can be explained derivationally.

D_{he} was paired/concatenated (in this case by Move) with I', and I' is a five-term category/tree/set consisting precisely of I', I_{was}, V, $V_{arrested}$, and D_t. It is entirely natural then that, since D_{he} was paired with a five-term object, and since pairing/concatenation is precisely the establishment of syntactic relations, D_{he} enters into a relation (what has hitherto been called c-command) with each of these five terms, and with nothing else.

This analysis also captures a certain (correct) asymmetry. Although D_{he} c-commands each of the five terms of I', the converse is not true. For example, I_{was} is a term of I', but I_{was} does not c-command D_{he}; rather, since in the course of the derivation I was paired (this time by Merge) with V, the derivational analysis rightly predicts that I_{was} c-commands each of the three terms of V (V itself, $V_{arrested}$, D_t) and nothing else.

The derivational definition of c-command (18) enables us to answer questions that the representational definition (4) did not.

Q: (Really an infinite number of questions) Why is it that X c-commands Y if and only if the *first* branching node dominating X dominates Y?
A: The first (not, e.g., the fifth, sixth, or *n*th, for *n* any positive integer) node is relevant because it is the projected node created by pairing of X and Y by Merge and Move.

Q: Why doesn't X c-command the first branching node dominating X, instead of c-commanding only the categories dominated by the first branching node?
A: Merge or Move did not pair X with the first branching node dominating X.

Q: Why is branching relevant?
A: Assuming bare phrase structure (Chomsky 1994), no category is dominated by a nonbranching node. In other words, free projection (as in Chomsky 1993) is eliminated: structure building (Merge and Move) consists of pairing, hence invariably generates binary branching.

Q: Why must X not equal Y; that is, why doesn't X c-command itself?
A: X is never paired with itself by Merge or Move.

Q: Why is it that in order for X to c-command Y, X must not dominate Y?
A: If X dominates Y, X and Y were not paired by Merge or Move.

Thus, as is entirely natural, pairing/concatenating of X and Y, by application of the universal transformational rules Move and Merge, expresses syntactic relations such as c-command.

Thus far, I have provided what I believe to be strong explanatory arguments for derivational construal of c-command. However, I have provided no arguments that representational c-command is empirically inadequate. I will now present one such argument, showing that representational c-command is inconsistent with an independently motivated hypothesis (and that derivational c-command is not). (For more extensive discussion, see Epstein et al. 1998.)

Consider again a tree such as (20).

(20) V_b and V_c each $= V_{likes}$; $D_a = D_{the}$

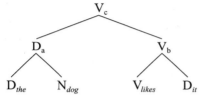

Recall that in the input to (i.e., the structural description of) Merge, there were two categories:

(21) a. D_a = three terms:
          i. D_a itself (K is a term of K; see (10))
          ii. D_{the}
          iii. N_{dog}
      b. V_b = three terms:
          i. V_b itself
          ii. V_{likes}
          iii. D_{it}

Given that D_a and V_b were merged, derivational c-command (18) entails that

(22) a. D_a c-commands V_b, V_{likes}, and D_{it}.
      b. V_b c-commands D_a, D_{the}, and N_{dog}.

But assuming a relational analysis of a syntactic category's phrase structure status (Muysken 1982; Freidin 1992), in the representation (20) V_b, being neither a minimal nor a maximal projection of V, is not a term (or is an "invisible term") of (20) (Chomsky 1994). Therefore, algorithmically speaking, V_b is "stricken from the record" in (22); that is, it is not a c-commander at all. Consequently, Kayne's (1994) reanalysis of the specifier as an X′ adjunct is not required for Linear Correspondence

Axiom compatibility, exactly as Chomsky (1994) proposed. Nor is V' (more generally, X') c-commanded by any category. Thus, the informal representation (20) includes only the following relations, a proper subset of those in (22):

(23) a. D_a asymmetrically c-commands V_{likes} and D_{it}.
    b. D_{the} symmetrically c-commands N_{dog}.
    c. V_{likes} symmetrically c-commands D_{it}.

These are, by hypothesis, the desired results. Importantly, V_b (V'), although representationally invisible (i.e., not a term in the resulting representation (20)), nonetheless blocks c-command of D_a ([Spec, VP]) by V_{likes}, the head, and by D_{it}, the complement (see (23a)). But given that V' is representationally invisible, the representational definition of c-command fails to even stipulate the apparent *fact* stated in (23a). That is, neither V_{likes} nor D_{it} is a term of some other visible term that excludes D_a ([Spec, VP]) in the resulting representation (20). By contrast, since V_{likes} and D_{it} were merged with each other, derivational c-command (18) entails that they c-command each other and nothing else. Notice that at one derivational point, V_{likes} and D_{it} were members of a term, V_b, which was a maximal term (V_{max}) that excluded [Spec, VP] immediately after merging V_{likes} and D_{it}. However, given the invisibility of X', in the resulting representation neither V_{likes} nor D_{it} is a member of a term (other than itself) that excludes D_a ([Spec, VP]); that is, there is no (visible) node (term) that dominates V_{likes} and D_{it} and also excludes D_a ([Spec, VP]). This suggests that the derivational construal of c-command proposed here is not only natural and explanatory but also empirically preferable to the extent that the representational definition wrongly predicts that categories immediately dominated by a representationally invisible single-bar projection (e.g., the complement) c-command the specifier and (worse yet) all members of the specifier.

12.3.3 Discussion

The derivational definition of c-command (18) eliminates massive redundancy (see (13)), provides principled answers to an infinite number of unanswered questions confronting the definition of representational c-command, and overcomes empirical inadequacies resulting from the interaction of the X'-invisibility hypothesis (Chomsky 1993) and representational c-command (Reinhart 1979).

Moreover, the derivational definition is an entirely natural subcase of a more general hypothesis (explored below): all syntactic relations are formally expressed by the operation "Concatenate A and B (the structural description), forming C (the structural change)" common to both structure-building operations (transformational rules), Merge and Move. Thus, Merge and Move establish relations, including "is a" and c-command, by virtue of concatenating categories. Nonetheless, despite its significant advantages over representational c-command and despite its being so natural, the derivational definition is just that: a definition. It (albeit naturally) asserts that X enters into c-command relations with all and only the terms of the category with which X is transformationally concatenated. But it still does not answer at least one very deep question: "Why does c-command exist at all? That is, why doesn't a category X simply enter into relations with *all* constituents in the tree?" I now turn to this question.

12.3.4   Toward Deducing the Derivational Definition of C-Command

First, consider the case of two categories neither of which c-commands the other, illustrated in (24).

(24) V_b and VP each $= V_{likes}$

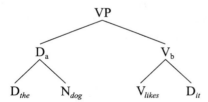

Here, neither D_{the} nor D_{it} c-commands the other, illustrating the generalization that members of the specifier do not c-command members of X′ and members of X′ do not c-command members of the specifier. The first conjunct of this generalization is illustrated by, for example, the binding violation in (25).

(25) *[$_{Spec}$ this picture of *John*] [X′ upsets *himself*]

The derivational definition (18) correctly entails that *John* fails to c-command *himself* in (25). But the nonexistence of such c-command relations is, I think, deducible. Consider what I will call the *First Law*: The largest syntactic object is the single phrase structure tree. Interestingly, this hypothesis is so fundamental that it is usually left entirely implicit. The standard (i.e., representational) construal can be stated as follows:

(26) *The First Law* (representationally *construed*)
A term (tree/category/constituent) T_1 can enter into a syntactic relation with a term T_2 only if there is at least one term T_3 of which both T_1 and T_2 are member terms.

Informally, by the most fundamental definition of "syntax," there are no syntactic relations that hold between trees. In other words, the laws of syntax are intratree laws; X and Y can enter into syntactic relations only if they are both in the same tree. In (24), the Merge-derived representation, there is indeed a tree (the entire tree in (24)) such that D_{the} (a member of the specifier) and D_{it} (the complement) are both in it. But as shown in (12), derivationally prior to cyclic Merge, D_a (the specifier tree) and V_b (the X′ tree) were two unconnected trees; hence, no syntactic relation, including c-command, can hold between their members (the trees themselves can enter into a relation later, if they are merged together). Generally, there can be no relations between members of two unconnected trees.

To capture this, I reformulate the implicit First Law as a derivational law, not a representational one.

(27) *The First Law* (derivationally *construed*)
T_1 can enter into c-command (perhaps, more generally, syntactic) relations with T_2 only if there exists no derivational point at which
a. T_1 is a term of K_1 ($K_1 \neq T_1$), *and*
b. T_2 is a term of K_2 ($K_2 \neq T_2$), *and*
c. There is no K_3 such that K_1 and K_2 are both terms of K_3.

Informally stated: No relations hold between members of two trees that were unconnected at any point in the derivation. (For a formal explication of the First Law, making the intuition presented here explicit, see Groat 1997; Epstein et al. 1998, chap. 6.) Assuming Cyclicity (a universal constraint on universal-rule application), deducible for Move as hypothesized by Kitahara (1993, 1994, 1995), in the derivation of (24) there was necessarily a point at which D_{the} was a member of D_a ([Spec, VP]) and D_{it} was a member of V_b (X′) but there did not yet exist a tree containing both the branching D_a tree and the V_b tree. It follows from the derivational construal of the First Law that there is no relation between D_{the} and D_{it}. More generally, there are no relations between members of the specifier and members of X′. We thus at this point partially derive fundamental syntactic relations like c-command and entirely derive the nonexistence of an infinite number of logically possible but apparently nonexistent syntactic relations, each of which is representationally definable (e.g., the relation *from* X *to* X's great-great-great(...)aunt). We do so with no stipulations, no technicalia, nothing ad hoc—only by appeal to the First Law, derivationally construed.

Notice, incidentally, that in (28) the two merged trees, D_a and V_b themselves, *can* enter into syntactic relations even though at one derivational point they were unconnected. That is, (27) entails that since neither is a member of a term/tree other than itself (i.e., each equals a root node), neither has undergone Merge or Move. Hence, like a lexical entry, each is not yet a participant in syntactic relations.

(28)

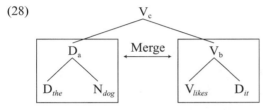

To summarize, for two nodes (trees/terms/categories) X and Y, neither of which c-commands the other, we do not need to stipulate representational c-command (4) to account for the fact that this relation does not hold. In fact, we do not even need to appeal to the far more natural (redundancy-eliminating, X'-invisibility-consistent) derivational definition of c-command (18). The derivational construal of the First Law is sufficient: no syntactic relations hold between X and Y if they were, at any derivational point, members of two unconnected trees.

As a simple illustration, again consider (25), repeated here as (29).

(29) *$[_{\text{Spec}(=D_a)}$ this picture of *John*] $[_{X'(=V_b)}$ upsets *himself*]

This type of binding phenomenon is now easily accounted for. A reflexive requires an antecedent of a particular morphosyntactic type (by hypothesis, an irreducible lexical property). "To have an antecedent" is "to enter into a syntactic relation." However, the First Law, derivationally construed, precludes the reflexive from entering into any syntactic relation with the only morphosyntactically possible candidate, *John*, since, given cyclic Merge, there existed a point in the derivation at which *John* was a member of D_a ([Spec, VP]), *himself* was a member of V_b (X'), and D_a and V_b were unconnected trees.

This completes the discussion of deducing those aspects of the derivational definition of c-command that pertain to two categories X and Y, neither of which c-commands the other.

Next, consider the case of asymmetric c-command, illustrated by (30)—by contrast to (29), a grammatical sentence.

(30) [$_{\text{Spec}}$ *John*], [$_{\text{X}'}$ upsets *himself*]

Here, X c-commands Y, but Y does not c-command X, as shown in the tree representation (31), where the specifier representationally c-commands the complement but not conversely.

(31)

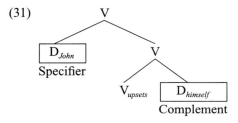

The generalization to be accounted for is that the specifier asymmetrically c-commands the complement. Given cyclic Merge, the derivation of (31) is as shown in (32).

(32) a. *First application of Merge*

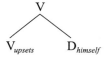

b. *Second application of Merge*

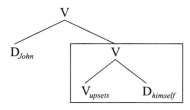

Notice that D$_{John}$ ([Spec, V]) was never a member of a tree that did not contain D$_{himself}$; in other words, there never were two unconnected trees, one containing *John* and the other *himself*. Rather, the second application of Merge pairs/concatenates D$_{John}$ itself (a member of the numeration)

with a tree containing $D_{himself}$. Thus, correctly, the First Law allows (i.e., does not block) a c-command relation from *John* (T_1 of (27)) to *himself* (T_2 of (27)).

In fact, since there never were two unconnected trees in this derivation, the First Law, a relationship blocker, is altogether inapplicable here. Rather, the first application of Merge merges two members of the numeration (V_{likes} and $D_{himself}$), forming $\{V_{likes}, \{V_{likes}, D_{himself}\}\}$, after which the second application of Merge merges yet another element of the numeration, D_{John} (not a set/tree) with this object, yielding (33).

(33) $\{V_{likes}, \{D_{John}, \{V_{likes}, \{V_{likes}, D_{himself}\}\}\}\}$

Since the First Law is inapplicable, a problem arises: *all* relations are now allowed—not only the empirically supported (c-command) relation from the specifier to the complement, but also, incorrectly, a c-command relation from the complement to the specifier. That is, in the absence of any supplementary constraints (relationship blockers), the inapplicability of the First Law allows the complement to c-command the specifier.

As a possible solution, recall that in the Minimalist Program all concatenation/pairing is performed by either Merge or Move. As claimed above, Merge and Move express syntactic relations, including the "is a" relation. Now, if the universal rules Merge and Move are the sole relationship establishers, and in addition apply cyclically, it is altogether natural, if not necessary, that a relation between X and Y is established exactly at the derivational point at which X and Y are concatenated. As a result, complements (and members of complements) never bear any relation to (e.g., never c-command) specifiers, because (a) when a complement (e.g., $D_{himself}$ in (32a)) is transformationally introduced, the specifier does not yet exist, and (b) an entity X can never bear a relation to a non-existent entity (derivational preexistence).

Crucially, then, the matter of "timing" is the issue at hand; when a category X undergoes Merge/Move, it comes into a relation with everything *in the tree with which it is concatenated*. If a category Y isn't yet in the tree, the relation from X to Y does not arise. Hence, the asymmetry of the relation parallels the asymmetry of the iterative derivational procedure.

Thus, derivational c-command—and perhaps more generally the fundamental concept "syntactic relation"—appears to be deducible by appeal only to

- the independently motivated, quite simple, formal properties of two (perhaps unifiable) universalized transformational rules,
- these rules' universalized, similarly simple, and perhaps explicable mode of cyclic application, and
- the fundamental, perhaps irreducible First Law, derivationally construed.

In sections 12.4 and 12.5, I propose a derivational approach to two other apparently fundamental relations, the head-complement and specifier-head relations.

12.4   The Head-Complement Relation

To begin exploring a derivational approach to the head-complement relation, consider (34).

(34)

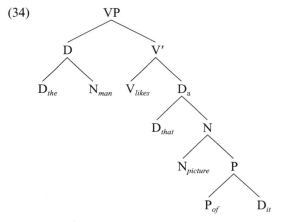

D_a is a category consisting of the following seven terms:

(35) a. The D_a tree/set itself
   b. The branching N tree/set
   c. The branching P tree/set
   d. D_{that}
   e. $N_{picture}$
   f. P_{of}
   g. D_{it}

In the derivation of (34), D_a was paired with V_{likes}. V_{likes} therefore c-commands all seven terms of D_a; it enters into relations with (c-commands) nothing else, since nothing else existed when the merger took place.

In fact, if a syntactic category/tree/term is in part defined as a set of terms (in dominance/precedence relations), then the theory predicts that there should exist two types of relations (using (34) as an illustration):

(36) a. A relation between V_{likes} and each of the seven terms of D_a, including D_a itself (c-command), *and*

   b. A relation between V_{likes} and D_a, the seven-term tree itself (the head-complement relation).

D_a itself is special among the seven terms that constitute D_a, since V_{likes} was paired with D_a itself (i.e., V_{likes} and D_a constituted the structural description of Merge). This completely natural analysis, couched in derivational/transformational terms, captures part of the representational definition of minimal domain proposed in Chomsky 1993. Consider the "enriched" representation of (34) in (37).

(37)

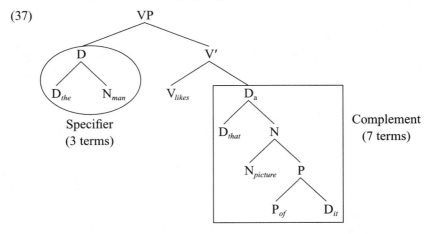

In order to account for (among other things) the head-complement relation, Chomsky (1993) offers the following definitions:

(38) *A representational definition of (specifier-head and) head-complement relations*

   a. The *domain* of a head α = the set of nodes contained in Max(α) that are distinct from and do not contain α.

   b. *Max(α)* = the least full category maximal projection dominating α. (In (37), for α = V_{likes}, Max(α) = the 10-member set consisting of all categories in the circle and all categories in the square.)

   c. The *complement domain* of a head α = the subset of the domain
      reflexively dominated by the complement of the construction. (In
      (37), the complement domain = the 7 terms in the square that
      constitute D_a.)
   d. The *minimal complement domain* of a head α = all members of
      the complement domain that are not dominated by a member of
      the complement domain. (In (37), the minimal complement
      domain = D_a itself.)

Like its predecessor, the representational definition of government in
(3), this representational definition is just that, a definition. Hence, it is not
explanatory, and we still lack answers for the questions "Why is
the complement domain of a head α as defined in (38c) significant?" "Why is
the minimal complement domain of a head α as defined in (38d) significant?" and "Why are these and not any of the infinite number of other logically possible, syntactically definable relations linguistically significant?"

By contrast, the derivational approach reveals the fundamental nature
of the head-complement relation. The syntax—more specifically, Merge
and Move—establishes syntactic relations by pairing (two) categories.
Derivationally, V_{likes} in (37) was paired with D_a, a seven-term category.
Thus, it is entirely natural, if not an inherent property of the concatenative system, that

(39) a. V_{likes} bears a relation to D_a itself, namely, the head-complement
      relation. Thus, the representational (nonexplanatory) definition
      (38d) is unnecessary.
   b. V_{likes} bears a relation to each member of D_a (= the complement
      domain "unminimized" as defined in (38c)) since these members
      constitute D_a. This is the relation that has been called
      c-command.
   c. The converse of (b) does not hold. That is, correctly, it is not the
      case that each member of D_a bears a relation to V_{likes}; certain
      members of D_a underwent pairing prior to the syntactic
      introduction of V_{likes}, thereby permanently fixing their
      derivationally established relations.

12.5   The Specifier-Head Relation

To begin exploring a derivational approach to the specifier-head relation,
consider (40).

(40) a.

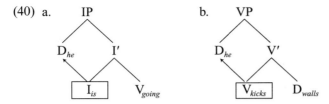

In (40a), I (the head) is assumed to check agreement and nominative Case on [Spec, IP].[1] In (40b), V assigns the agent θ-role to [Spec, VP]. The hypothesized generalization is thus that Case and agreement (and external θ-role) can be (perhaps "can only be") assigned from the head to the specifier. However, a problem has long confronted the expression of this relation: the head does not c-command the specifier, given the "first branching node" definition (4). To solve this problem, the notion of m-command was developed (Aoun and Sportiche 1983). Under the derivational analysis proposed here, the specifier c-commands the head, but the head, having been cyclically merged with the complement, is created prior to and in the absence of the specifier. Therefore, the head bears a relation only to the complement and members of the complement; that is, there is no relation from the head to the specifier.

There is at least one possible solution to this apparent problem. As illustrated in (41), when two categories A and B are merged, they form a new category whose label is identical to the head of either A or B ("... Merge ... is asymmetric, projecting one of the objects to which it applies, its head becoming the label of the complex formed"; Chomsky 1994, 11).

(41)

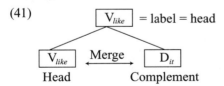

This reflects a more general and heavily restricted hypothesis concerning the inventory of syntactic entities: "There are ... only lexical elements and sets constructed from them" (Chomsky 1994, 27). Therefore, when [Spec, VP] is paired with the entire tree/set in (41), as shown in (42), it is paired with (thus, the structural description contains) a category "head-labeled" V_{likes}.

(42)

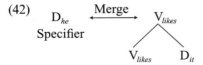

Thus, the specifier is indeed merged with a (complex) category bearing the morphological features (label) of the head V_{likes}. If this analysis is maintainable, the specifier-head relation can also be captured as a relation established by Merge/Move—a result that would represent a clear advance over nonunified, nonexplanatory theories invoking not only a representational definition of c-command but also a representational definition of m-command (postulated precisely to capture the relation from head to specifier, inexpressible as a representationally defined c-command relation).[2]

12.6 Summary and Discussion

In this chapter, I have proposed a syntactic theory in which arguably (at least some of) the most fundamental syntactic relations posited— including c-command, "is a," specifier-head, and head-complement—are not formally expressed as unexplained representational definitions. I have proposed instead that such syntactic relations are derivational constructs expressed by the formally simple ("virtually conceptually necessary"; Chomsky 1994) and unified (Kitahara 1993, 1994, 1995, 1997) universalized transformational rules Merge and Move (each motivated on entirely independent grounds in Chomsky 1993).

This theory of syntactic relations, seeking to eliminate central representational definitions such as "government," "minimal domain," and "c-command," is entirely natural and, I think, explanatory. Concatenation operations are by (minimal) hypothesis a necessary part of the syntax; that is, a concatenative procedure (the application of which, by hypothesis, yields representations of sentences) must exist. By contrast, it is not the case that, in the same sense, principles (i.e., filters or well-formedness conditions on representation) must exist.

The question I have investigated here is thus, "Are the simple, independently motivated, virtually conceptually necessary, structure-building operations themselves—specifically, the universalized transformational rules Merge and Move, iteratively applied in conformity with the cycle— sufficient to capture fundamental syntactic relations?" The tentative answer is that they seem to be. If they are, a theory of syntax that expresses this will attain a much more unified, nonredundant, conceptually simple, and correspondingly explanatory account of the most fundamental syntactic construct, "syntactic relation," known in advance of experience by virtue of the human biological endowment for grammar formation.

Notes

This is a revised version of a draft originally written in the summer of 1994. Portions of this material were presented at the Harvard University Linguistics Department Forum in Synchronic Linguistic Theory in December 1994. I thank the members of that audience for very helpful discussion, in particular Naoki Fukui, Masatoshi Koizumi, and Ken Wexler. A later version was presented in April 1995 at the Linguistics Department at the University of Maryland. I thank members of that department as well for their hospitality and for very insightful comments, especially Norbert Hornstein, Juan Carlos Castillo, and Jairo Nunes. I am especially grateful to the following people for extensive discussion of the ideas presented here: Robert Berwick, Maggie Browning, Noam Chomsky, Robert Frank, Robert Freidin, Günther Grewendorf, Erich Groat, Sam Gutmann, Hisatsugu Kitahara, David Lieb, Elaine McNulty, Joachim Sabel, Esther Torrego, and Larry Wilson. I am also particularly indebted to Suzanne Flynn and to Höskuldur Thráinsson for their help during this project. Finally, I also thank Matthew Murphy, Elizabeth Pyatt, and Steve Peter for indispensable editorial assistance.

A modified version of this work appears as chapter 1 of Epstein et al. 1998. I gratefully acknowledge Oxford University Press and in particular Peter Ohlin for permission to publish this material here.

1. Here, for the purposes of illustration, I assume a pre–Pollock 1989 unsplit I. In fact, the unsplit I may not be simply illustrative; as Thráinsson (1994) argues, it may be empirically correct for English. By contrast, Icelandic would display a truly split I, Agr_S^0 and T^0 (see Jonas and Bobaljik 1993; Bobaljik and Jonas 1996; Bobaljik and Thráinsson 1998).

2. For a different analysis of specifier-head relations, see Epstein et al. 1998.

References

Aoun, Joseph, and Dominique Sportiche. 1983. On the formal theory of government. *The Linguistic Review* 2, 211–235.

Bobaljik, Jonathan David, and Dianne Jonas. 1996. Subject positions and the roles of TP. *Linguistic Inquiry* 27, 195–236.

Bobaljik, Jonathan David, and Höskuldur Thráinsson. 1998. Two heads aren't always better than one. *Syntax* 1, 37–71.

Chomsky, Noam. 1981. *Lectures on government and binding*. Dordrecht: Foris.

Chomsky, Noam. 1982. *Some concepts and consequences of the theory of government and binding*. Cambridge, Mass.: MIT Press.

Chomsky, Noam. 1986. *Barriers*. Cambridge, Mass.: MIT Press.

Chomsky, Noam. 1991. Some notes on economy of derivation and representation. In *Principles and parameters in comparative grammar*, ed. Robert Freidin. Cambridge, Mass.: MIT Press. [Reprinted in *The Minimalist Program*, Noam Chomsky. Cambridge, Mass.: MIT Press, 1995.]

Chomsky, Noam. 1993. A minimalist program for linguistic theory. In *The view from Building 20: Essays in linguistics in honor of Sylvain Bromberger*, eds. Kenneth Hale and Samuel Jay Keyser. Cambridge, Mass.: MIT Press. [Reprinted in *The Minimalist Program*, Noam Chomsky. Cambridge, Mass.: MIT Press, 1995.]

Chomsky, Noam. 1994. Bare phrase structure. (MIT Occasional Papers in Linguistics 5.) MITWPL, Department of Linguistics and Philosophy, MIT, Cambridge, Mass. [Published in *Evolution and revolution in linguistic theory: Essays in honor of Carlos Otero*, eds. Héctor Campos and Paula Kempchinsky. Washington, D.C.: Georgetown University Press, 1995, and *Government and Binding Theory and the Minimalist Program*, ed. Gert Webelhuth. Oxford: Blackwell, 1995.]

Chomsky, Noam. 1995. Categories and transformations. In *The Minimalist Program*, 219–394. Cambridge, Mass.: MIT Press.

Collins, Chris. 1997. *Local economy*. Cambridge, Mass.: MIT Press.

Einstein, Albert. 1954. *Ideas and opinions*. New York: Crown.

Epstein, Samuel David, Erich Groat, Ruriko Kawashima, and Hisatsugu Kitahara. 1998. *A derivational approach to syntactic relations*. Oxford: Oxford University Press.

Freidin, Robert. 1992. *Foundations of generative syntax*. Cambridge, Mass.: MIT Press.

Groat, Erich. 1997. A derivational program for syntactic theory. Doctoral dissertation, Harvard University, Cambridge, Mass.

Hall, Alfred R. 1956. *The scientific revolution*. London: Longmans, Green.

Jonas, Dianne, and Jonathan David Bobaljik. 1993. Specs for subjects. In *Papers on Case and agreement I*, eds. Jonathan David Bobaljik and Colin Phillips. (MIT Working Papers in Linguistics 18.) MITWPL, Department of Linguistics and Philosophy, MIT, Cambridge, Mass.

Kayne, Richard. 1994. *The antisymmetry of syntax*. Cambridge, Mass.: MIT Press.

Kitahara, Hisatsugu. 1993. Deducing strict cyclicity from principles of derivational economy. Paper presented at the 16th GLOW Colloquium, Lund.

Kitahara, Hisatsugu. 1994. Target α: A unified theory of movement and structure-building. Doctoral dissertation, Harvard University, Cambridge, Mass.

Kitahara, Hisatsugu. 1995. Target α: Deducing strict cyclicity from derivational economy. *Linguistic Inquiry* 26, 47–77.

Kitahara, Hisatsugu. 1997. *Elementary operations and optimal derivations*. Cambridge, Mass.: MIT Press.

Lasnik, Howard, and Mamoru Saito. 1992. *Move α: Conditions on its application and output*. Cambridge, Mass.: MIT Press.

Muysken, Pieter. 1982. Parameterizing the notion "head." *Journal of Linguistic Research* 2, 57–75.

Nash, Leonard K. 1963. *The nature of the natural sciences*. Boston: Little, Brown.

Pollock, Jean-Yves. 1989. Verb movement, Universal Grammar, and the structure of IP. *Linguistic Inquiry* 20, 365–424.

Reinhart, Tanya. 1979. The syntactic domain for semantic rules. In *Formal semantics and pragmatics for natural languages*, eds. F. Guenther and S. J. Schmidt. Dordrecht: Reidel.

Thráinsson, Höskuldur. 1994. On the (non-)universality of functional categories. In *Minimal ideas*, eds. Werner Abraham, Samuel David Epstein, Höskuldur Thráinsson, and C. Jan-Wouter Zwart. Amsterdam: John Benjamins.

Index